D1448812

WITHDRAWN
WRIGHT STATE UNIVERSITY LIBRARIES

BILINGUAL EDUCATION AND ENGLISH AS A SECOND LANGUAGE

GARLAND REFERENCE LIBRARY
OF SOCIAL SCIENCE
(VOL. 634)

BILINGUAL EDUCATION AND ENGLISH AS A SECOND LANGUAGE
A Research Handbook, 1988–1990

Alba N. Ambert

GARLAND PUBLISHING, INC. • NEW YORK & LONDON
1991

© 1991 Alba N. Ambert
All rights reserved

Library of Congress Cataloging-in-Publication Data

Bilingual education and English as a second language : a research
handbook, 1988–1990 / [edited by] Alba N. Ambert.
     p.   cm. — (Garland reference library of social science ; vol.
634)
   Includes bibliographical references and index.
   ISBN 0–8240–5410–5 (alk. paper); ISBN 0–8153–0466–8 (pbk.
alk. paper)
   1. Education, Bilingual—United States. 2. English language—
Study and teaching—United States—Foreign speakers. 3. Second
language acquisition. 4. Educational literature—United States.
I. Ambert, Alba N., 1946– . II. Series: Garland reference library
of social science ; v. 634
LC3731.B5468   1991
371.97'00973—dc20   91–2418
                                             CIP

Printed on acid-free, 250-year-life paper
Manufactured in the United States of America

To language minority students and their families.

CONTENTS

About the Editor   ix

Contributing Authors   xi

Introduction   xv

I.   Social and Cultural Dimensions of the Education of Language Minority Students
Virginia Vogel Zanger   3

II.   The Acculturation of Ethnolinguistic Minorities
Nancy Cloud   55

III.   Bilingualism and Second Language Acquisition in Academic Contexts
Eugene E. García   97

IV.   Early Childhood Education: The Effects of Language on Learning
Evangeline Harris Stefanakis   139

V.   Native and Second Language Literacy: The Promise of a New Decade
Carmen I. Mercado   171

VI.   Literature and the Language Minority Child: A Multicultural Perspective
Milga Morales-Nadal   197

VII.   Bilingual Gifted and Talented Students
Deborah M. Harris and Jeanne Weismantel   215

VIII.   Teacher Training in Bilingual Education and English as a Second Language: Recent Research Developments
Liliana Minaya-Rowe   259

IX.   Psychoeducational Assessment of Language Minority Children: Current Perspectives and Future Trends
María D. Alvarez   299

X.   The Education of Language Minorities: An Overview of Findings and a Research Agenda
Alba N. Ambert   347

Appendices
    I.   Multifunctional Resource Centers   359
   II. Organizations   362
  III. Journals and Newsletters   364

Indexes
    Author Index   367
    Subject Index   377

ABOUT THE EDITOR

ALBA N. AMBERT is Senior Research Scholar at Athens College, Athens, Greece, where she conducts psycholinguistic and educational research and offers inservice teacher training. Previously, she was Visiting Scientist at the Department of Linguistics and Philosophy, Massachusetts Institute of Technology. As a National Research Council Postdoctoral Fellow, Dr. Ambert performed research on the language development and language disorders of Puerto Rican children living in the United States. She was Assistant Professor and Director of the Bilingual Special Education Teacher Training Program at the University of Hartford in Connecticut. Dr. Ambert has written numerous articles and several books on bilingualism, bilingual special education, and language disorders in Spanish-speaking children, including the co-authored book *Bilingual Education: A Sourcebook.* She has recently co-edited the volume *Puerto Rican Children on the Mainland: Interdisciplinary Perspectives.* The *Ambert Reading Test (ART),* developed by Dr. Ambert to diagnose reading problems in Spanish-speaking children, grades K-6, is currently used by school districts in the Northeast. She has presented her research findings at national and international conferences. She received her B.A. from Universidad de Puerto Rico and her M.Ed. and Ed.D. degrees from Harvard University. Dr. Ambert has recently been awarded the Literature Award of the Institute for Puerto Rican Literature for her novel *Porque Hay Silencio.* She has published two volumes of poetry. Her poetry and short stories have been published in literary journals in the United States and Puerto Rico.

CONTRIBUTING AUTHORS

MARIA D. ALVAREZ received her Ph.D. in School Psychology from New York University. She has worked as a school psychologist in the public schools of Boston, New York City, and New Britain (Connecticut), and is currently an Adjunct Associate Professor at the Center for Latin American Studies of the University of Florida in Gainesville, Florida. Fluent in four languages, Dr. Alvarez specializes in the non-biased assessment of language minority groups, in the design of educational planning for bilingual children with special learning needs, and in bilingual schooling. Using anthropological methods, she has conducted ethnographic research in different cultures, especially in Haiti, where she has studied child socialization, health-seeking behaviors among rural families, and child feeding beliefs and practices.

NANCY CLOUD is Assistant Professor in the Department of Curriculum and Teaching at Hofstra University, where she coordinates the Bilingual Education and Masters of Science in Teaching English as a Second Language Programs. Formerly, she served as a coordinator of various federally funded projects for the Institute for Urban and Minority Education, Teachers College, Columbia University. From 1972 to 1979, she worked as a bilingual/ESL classroom teacher and Title VII program coordinator in San Francisco. She has worked as a consultant at the Illinois Resource Center providing training and technical assistance to districts serving limited English proficient students throughout the midwest. She specializes in the area of curriculum and instruction for language minority students and in the area of bilingual special education and frequently writes on these topics. Ms. Cloud received advanced degrees from Syracuse University and the University of San Francisco. She is currently completing her doctoral degree at Teachers College, Columbia University, in the area of mental retardation and bilingualism.

EUGENE E. GARCÍA is Dean of the Division of Social Sciences and Professor of Education and Psychology at the University of California, Santa Cruz. He received his B.A. from the University of

Utah in psychology and his Ph.D. in human development from the University of Kansas. He was a postdoctoral fellow in human development at Harvard University and a National Research Council Fellow. He received a three-year National Kellogg Fellowship and has received numerous academic and public honors. He served as a faculty member at the University of Utah, the University of California, Santa Barbara, and Arizona State University before joining the faculty at the University of California, Santa Cruz. He has served as a research center director and an academic department chair. Dr. García is involved in various community activities and has served as an elected member of a board of education. He has published extensively in the area of language teaching and bilingual development. He holds leadership positions in professional organizations and continues to serve in an editorial capacity for psychological, linguistic, and educational journals. He is presently conducting research in the area of effective schooling for diverse student populations. His work is funded by the California Policy Seminar, the Kellogg Foundation, the California State Department of Education, and the Organization for Education, Collaboration and Development.

DEBORAH M. HARRIS has taught elementary school for twelve years in the United States and abroad. She received her Ph.D. in school psychology at the University of Florida with an emphasis in gifted education. She has developed and directed the K–12 gifted program for the past eight years at P.K. Yonge Laboratory School at the University of Florida. In that capacity she has served as a consultant for gifted education throughout Florida. During that time she has assisted in teaching university courses in gifted education, directed a community-wide summer enrichment program, and has also been on the staff for three consecutive years at Confratute, a summer institute for gifted education at the University of Connecticut, directed by Joseph Renzulli, a national leader in gifted education. Dr. Harris is also on the executive board of the Florida Association for Gifted Education and is president of the North Central Florida Association for the Gifted, a local parent-teacher organization. She has presented at state, national, and international conferences on gifted education. Dr. Harris also works as a school psychologist counseling and assessing gifted children and adolescents. She also works with families of gifted youngsters and consults with educators and parent groups.

EVANGELINE HARRIS STEFANAKIS is Assistant Professor at Lesley College in Cambridge, Massachusetts. Her professional areas of interest include bilingual early childhood and special education. During the past several years, she has worked collaboratively with the Boston and Somerville Public Schools to modify the mandated preschool screening process to better serve linguistic minority children. In this effort, she has been part of a team of educators and parents who have worked together to create integrated preschool programs to mainstream special needs children into regular classes. She has served as an early childhood consultant to the Chelsea Public Schools and has developed a training video to explain preschool screening procedures to parents and day care providers. Ms. Harris Stefanakis has spent nine years overseas as a special educator and school psychologist in Greece and Bahrain. She holds a Masters of Science in special education and art therapy from Lesley College and a Bachelors of Science in psychology and child study from Tufts University. She is currently pursuing advanced studies in Administration, Planning and Social Policy with a concentration in International Education at the Harvard University Graduate School of Education. The overriding theme of her academic and professional work has focused on attempting to understand the difference between a language and learning issue in children and how best to serve children with language or learning difficulties.

CARMEN I. MERCADO is Assistant Professor of Education in the Department of Curriculum and Teaching at Hunter College of the City University of New York. She received her Ph.D. in language and literacy from Fordham University. Formerly, Dr. Mercado served as Program Coordinator of the New York Multifunctional Resource Center (MRC) based at Hunter College. She was also an elementary school teacher for eight years in the second Spanish/English bilingual school in New York City. Her major research interest is in conducting ethnographic research with teachers and students in elementary and intermediate grades.

LILIANA MINAYA-ROWE is an Associate Professor of Bilingual Bicultural Education and Title VII Project Director at the University of Connecticut. She received her Ph.D. from the University of Texas. Her areas of research publications include second language acquisition processes, bilingual bicultural education policies and practices, staff development, discourse analysis, and Spanish dialectology. As a practitioner, she has trained graduate students at the masters, sixth-year professional diploma, and Ph.D. levels. She has also conducted long-term staff development projects at school districts in Connecticut with teachers of potentially English proficient students.

MILGA MORALES-NADAL has a Ph.D. from Yeshiva University in bilingual education and developmental psychology. She is Assistant

Professor of Education and Director of the Bilingual Personnel Training Program (Title VII) in Brooklyn College's School of Education. She has been teaching and counseling limited English proficient and language minority students in New York City for twenty years. Dr. Morales-Nadal formerly contributed to the Puerto Rican-based newspaper *Claridad* on educational and other issues relevant to the Puerto Rican/Latino community and other minority groups in the United States. She has made numerous scholarly presentations on native and second language acquisition, literacy, the politics of language in the Puerto Rican Barrio, and cultural issues and perspectives in the Latino community. She is presently teaching in the undergraduate and graduate bilingual teacher education programs at Brooklyn College and collaborating on the development of a TESOL/Multicultural Studies Masters Degree Program for Brooklyn College.

JEANNE WEISMANTEL has been an English teacher and has worked for grant-funded projects in bilingual special education in the Department of Special Education, University of Florida. She has been a mentor for gifted students and has co-authored a book and articles in the field of bilingual special education. Ms. Weismantel is currently involved in dance therapy and aquatherapy for children with motor disabilities and has recently published articles on the topic.

VIRGINIA VOGEL ZANGER has worked in language minority education in Massachusetts for twenty years, as a bilingual teacher, curriculum developer, textbook author, researcher, college instructor, and a trainer of teachers, parents, and administrators. She attended high school in Argentina, did her undergraduate work at Harvard, and received her doctorate in cross-cultural issues in bilingual education at Boston University. Her dissertation was awarded first prize by the National Association for Bilingual Education. Her ESL textbook, *Face to Face: The Cross-Cultural Workbook*, is used around the world and a revised edition is planned. She recently directed the Intercultural Leadership Training Institute for the Massachusetts Department of Education. During the past several years, she has worked for the Boston University/Boston Public Schools Collaborative. As an independent consultant, she conducts staff development training and produces educational videos.

INTRODUCTION

Alba N. Ambert

The growing linguistic and cultural diversity of students in the United States requires a closer look at the distinctive features these students and their families bring to their schools and communities. Researchers who have studied linguistically and culturally diverse populations in this country and elsewhere are convinced that it is no longer useful to explore linguistic minority populations in the limited—and limiting—realm of language. Even while examining language issues, researchers can no longer avoid the multitude of nonlinguistic factors which affect language and, therefore, need to be incorporated into any discussion on bilingualism and second language acquisition (Hakuta & García, 1989; Trueba, 1989; Zanger, 1989).

Second language development is not an isolated or linear process removed from the cultural, social, economic, and general environment in which it occurs. Nor is it isolated from issues that affect the students' general academic performance. Many factors impact the language development and academic performance of language minority children. Though internal factors, such as cognition, learning styles, motivation, aptitude, and social and psychological adjustment, affect language learning and academic performance, we are now examining external factors that affect learning as well. These include socioeconomic conditions, negative attitudes of the mainstream society toward minority languages and cultures, discrimination, and for those who are racially as well as ethnically distinct, there is the added burden of racism.

An alarming change has occurred in the last decade and affects a substantial proportion of language minority children: the increase of poverty in the United States. The social and economic safety nets available to less privileged members of society have collapsed with a resultant increase in poverty levels. Child poverty is now one-third higher than in the late 1970's. There are 12.6 million children living at or below the poverty line. Nearly one out of every three children under the age of six, lives in poverty (Kozol, 1988) and of children entering elementary school in 1988, one in five was poor, one in six had no health insurance, one in seven would probably dropout of school, and one in five would probably become a teenage parent (Smith, 1989). The environment is becoming increasingly hazardous for children.

In view of the lack of basic necessities, such as adequate housing (in New York City alone one third of the 90,000 homeless are children), proper nutrition, and health care for poor children (Bradley, 1989), it is not surprising that their education is in peril. The educational situation of language minority children, who are likely to be poor, needs to be given serious consideration within this socioeconomic context. A disproportionate number of poor minority children are undereducated in this country (Comer, 1988). Language minority children tend to lag behind language majority children academically and the dropout rate for some linguistic minority groups is as high as 70% (Rodríguez, in press). This situation condemns a large proportion of the nation's population to a cycle of poverty with deleterious effects continuing to affect future generations. The loss of so much human potential is incalculable.

Furthermore, growing hostility toward language minority groups is evident in organized groups such as the English-only movement. As a result of policies implemented in response to an existing climate of extreme conservatism and concerted attacks against language minorities, major setbacks have occurred in programs for minorities, including bilingual education. Bilingual education and the teaching of English as a second language have become hotly contested issues (Crawford, 1989). Times have been very difficult for language minorities indeed.

A better understanding of the complex issues which affect language minority students and their families is essential to remedy this situation. The positive results of a number of research projects reported in this volume argue persuasively that successful programs for language minority students are viable.

In this second volume in the series *Bilingual Education and English as a Second Language*, intended to survey current research on the education of language minority students, a shift from the first volume (Ambert, 1988) in the research emphasis is evident. The shift reflects the changing realities of language minority children in the United States. The research presented in this volume stresses the complex nature of bilingualism and the process of acquiring a second language. But more importantly, the research explores the societal and acculturative factors affecting language minority children. Some of the chapters discuss research conducted with language minority adults in an effort to provide educators and others working with language minority children with an understanding not only of their students, but their families and communities as well. Research on refugees and other recent immigrants are discussed in detail. The effects of discrimination, racism, and negative teacher attitudes toward linguistic minorities on academic performance are also topics discussed in the research. The chapters on social contexts and acculturation respond to this current.

Topics not included in the first volume are represented here. In addition to the topics of social contexts and acculturation mentioned above, chapters on the academic contexts of bilingual education, gifted and talented language minority students, teacher training, and children's literature reflect the current trends in the research. The chapters on literacy development, assessment, and early childhood topics included in the previous volume, offer a fresh perspective on the subjects. Literacy development is examined from an ethnographic perspective, following current research activity. The early childhood chapter focuses on an understanding, not only of the linguistic development of young children, but their overall development. The assessment chapter, at the end of this volume, reflects the monumental amount of research activity that has occurred in the area in the last two years in which the actual production of tests specifically geared for language minority children is surprisingly scant and the needs of some populations such as low incidence groups, have still not been addressed. In addition, the chapter discusses the topics discussed previously within the context of assessment.

This volume describes and analyzes the research of the past two years (1988–1990) in areas affecting the education of language minority students. Each chapter contains a general analysis of the research in a specific topic, recommendations for future research, and an annotated bibliography in the area of discussion. The material is relevant to diverse language groups. Although the intention is to describe the most recent research, we have included past research in those cases where it is necessary to grasp the implications of today's studies, in areas where a scarcity of research is available, and in topics not discussed in the first volume.

We hope this book will be of use to teachers, teacher aides, teacher trainers, educational supervisors and administrators, parents, advocates, and other individuals concerned with the trajectory of bilingual education, ESL, and the situation of language minority children.

Contributing authors come from a wide range of disciplines concerned with the education of linguistic minority students. They have the special insights of practitioners who are aware of the problems in the field and are able to temper research findings with the reality of practical issues. The continued dedication of these contributors, evident in their daily endeavors, is the backbone of present and future efforts to guarantee educational equity for language minority children and, hence, the opportunity for a better life. Many thanks for their efforts.

I would like to thank my editor, Marie Ellen Larcada, who thought of developing this series of reference volumes on bilingual education and English as a second language research. Her commitment to educational excellence for all children has always been evident in her strong support of this and other volumes.

Alba N. Ambert
Athens College
December 1990

References

Ambert, A.N. (Ed.) (1988). *Bilingual education and English as a second language: A research handbook, 1986–1987.* New York: Garland.

Bradley, J. (1989). A long, lonely struggle. *The Wesleyan University Alumnus, LXXI*(5), 10–13.

Comer, J. (1988). Educating poor minority children. *Scientific American, 259*(5), 42–48.

Crawford, J. (1989). *Bilingual education: History, politics, theory and practice.* Trenton, NJ: Crane.

Hakuta, K. & García, E. (1989). Bilingualism and education. *American Psychologist, 44*(2), 374–379.

Kozol, J. (1988). *Rachel and her children: Homeless families in America.* New York: Crown.

Rodríguez, A. (in press). On to college: Dropout prevention is possible. In Ambert, A.N. & Alvarez, M.D. *Puerto Rican children on the mainland: Interdisciplinary perspectives.* New York: Garland.

Smith, N. (1989). Children in pain. *The Wesleyan University Alumnus, LXXI*(5), 1.

Trueba, H. (1989). Empowerment and mainstreaming: Culture change and the integration of home and school values. Paper read at the annual meeting of the American Educational Research Association in San Francisco.

Zanger, V.V. (1989). The impact of racial hostility on linguistic minorities' achievement. Paper presented at the annual meeting of the American Educational Research Association in San Francisco.

Bilingual Education and
English as a Second
Language

CHAPTER I

Social and Cultural Dimensions of the Education of Language Minority Students

Virginia Vogel Zanger

Introduction

Cummins' early research (1981) has been used for a decade to argue that bilingual instruction is the best way to promote language minority students' linguistic and cognitive development and academic achievement. In 1986, however, Cummins suggested that it was possible to interpret the effectiveness of bilingual education programs in an entirely different way: "Is this success due to better promotion of L1 (first language) cognitive/academic skills or to the reinforcement of cultural identity provided by an intensive L1 program?" (p. 23). This question suggests the need to reconsider the role of social, cultural, and psychological factors in the learning process of language minority students. In the recent literature on the academic achievement of these students, researchers have increasingly looked beyond narrow, linguistic considerations to explain the success or failure of language minority students (Genesee, 1987; Trueba, 1989).

This chapter presents the variety of approaches followed by social psychologists, sociolinguists, anthropologists, and education researchers in the last twenty years in their efforts to explore the social and cultural dimensions of language minority education. The first section summarizes research which has addressed the topic from a cultural perspective, in a search for answers to explain the academic underachievement of many language minority students occurring in the context of the cultural mismatch between their home and school environments. The second section deals with research which has explored social factors to explain language minority students' difficulties in school. The third section focuses on research related to the social integration of language majority and minority students. The fourth section summarizes the research on two innovative educational approaches which have been developed to respond to concerns about the isolation of language minority students: the cooperative learning method and the enrichment model of bilingual education. The chapter concludes with a brief discussion and suggestions for future research directions.

Cultural Mismatch Paradigm

Beginning in the early seventies, anthropological research methods have been used with increasing frequency to learn more about the hidden obstacles that face students whose cultural backgrounds differ from the dominant culture's. These ethnographic and microethnographic studies have drawn on a theoretical framework which explains the academic difficulties of many language minority students as a result of the cultural mismatch or the cultural discontinuities between home and school. The central thesis of the cultural mismatch paradigm is that the communication process is disrupted when students and school personnel come from backgrounds which have vastly different conventions governing appropriate behaviors, values, and nonverbal styles (Erickson, 1987). The following review summarizes the major areas of difference that have been explored.

Language Use

One focus of research has been to investigate ways in which language is used, the unspoken rules which govern discourse (Mohatt & Erickson, 1981; Wong Fillmore, 1983). In an early effort, a series of papers explored varieties of communicative strategies in different linguistic communities, contrasting these with the kind of language used in classrooms (Cazden, John, & Hymes, 1972). For example, Philips' (1972) study at the Warm Springs Indian Reservation compared the conditions for speech use in the Native American community and in the government school. She identified basic distinctions in participant structures, which are the rules that govern who speaks when. One example of the way in which this cultural discrepancy was found to cause "sociolinguistic interference" in the classroom was the reluctance of Native American students to speak up when called upon in class. Philips attributed this reluctance to differences in the ways in which authority is exercised in the Indian community and the minimal role of verbalization in the teaching styles practiced within Indian families. She contrasted the students' lack of verbal responsiveness in teacher-directed situations to their participation in peer-learning situations, which are more culturally congruent.

Boggs (1972) addressed a similar reluctance among native Hawaiian children to respond to direct questioning by teachers. His analysis of communication patterns within Hawaiian homes sought to explain why children would feel "picked on" or singled out when called upon in school. He documented the low frequency of adult questioning directed at a specific child in native Hawaiian homes. As evidence to support the cultural discontinuities hypothesis, Boggs found that when students were invited to participate in the classroom in ways which were culturally congruent, they did in fact produce long narratives.

A decade later, Heath's (1983) study of ways of talking in middle class white, working-class white, and working-class African-American families in a Southern community extended this line of research. Although the study did not include language minority participants, the work has been so influential that it deserves to be mentioned here. Heath's analysis of one reason why working-class African American children appeared reluctant to answer teachers' questions pointed to yet another difference in communicative patterns. Working-class African American parents, she found, rarely used the "known-answer" question, which is the predominant form of question-asking within classrooms. Thus, working-class African-American children experienced extreme disorientation in their early contact with teachers, for they could not understand why an adult would ask a question to which she already knew the answer.

Heath (1986) later explored "ways with words" within Asian and Latino communities, searching for similar clues in the discontinuities between how language is used at home and at school. She introduced the construct of the oral genre, the type or kind of organizing unit into which smaller segments of units of language fit.

Genres, such as stories, accounts, and recounts, exist among all linguistic communities. However, their frequency varies among groups, as does the kind of language associated with each. Heath's research posited that discrepancies between sociolinguistic conventions are the source of confusion and misunderstanding between children from language minority families and their mainstream teachers. For example, she cited the case of a Mexican-born child: "In Mexico, he had been a reader; in his community he knew what stories were and he could tell them. In his new school setting, definitions of reader and storyteller do not include his ways of recognizing or telling stories" (p. 174). Heath argued that the discontinuity between home and school languages is not as disconcerting and detrimental as is the discontinuity between ways of using language in the community and at school. According to Heath, this explains Dolson's (1984) finding that children from homes where the first language is used achieve better in school than those whose parents and older siblings try to use English. Children whose limited English proficient parents and siblings insist on using their weaker language for communication at home are exposed to a far more restricted array and type of genres.

Nonverbal Communication

Another source of discontinuity between the home and the school which has been studied extensively is the area of nonverbal communication. Nine Curt (1984) identified areas which can cause particular confusion for Puerto Rican students: proxemics (personal space); occulisics (eye contact); haptics (touching); and kinesics (body movements). Gestures fall into the latter category. Nine Curt reported on a study which found a high rate of retention of Puerto Rican gestures among students born and raised on the mainland, suggesting that students may retain more of the nonverbal than the verbal patterns of their parents' native Spanish. The author also defined as a source of confusion the ways in which Puerto Rican and Anglo cultures organize time. Puerto Ricans, she suggested, like other Mediterranean peoples, tend to be polychronic, preferring to attend to several things, people, or activities at once, while Anglo culture is more linear and monochronic.

Nine Curt's observations about Puerto Rican culture are provocative. With the exception of a study she conducted on gestures, however, her work was not conducted using traditional academic research methods. More rigorous approaches to the nonverbal dimensions have been summarized by Irujo (1988). She cited, for example, the extensive research which has documented the cultural variation in eye contact and gaze behavior, among African Americans and white North Americans, Arabs, Latin Americans, southern Europeans, East Asians, Greeks, and northern Europeans.

Cultural Values

Cultural values have been identified as central to the cultural discontinuity experienced by language minority students. Sindell (1988), for example, painted a searing portrait of the cross-cultural conflicts between the traditional values in which Cree children were raised and the values of the dominant culture, enforced in Canadian governmental residential schools. According to Sindell's ethnography, the Cree children who were raised to be self-reliant in their communities were forced into patterns of submissive, dependent behavior. Sindell also identified the tension arising between the competition demanded by the school and the cooperation encouraged by the home culture, a dilemma described by anthropologists studying other cultural groups as well (Boggs, 1972; Jordan, 1977). Delgado-Gaitan's (1987) ethnographic study of Mexican children at home and at school revealed a similar discontinuity between the cooperative interactions encouraged at home and the competitive behaviors which the school demanded of the children. The study concluded that teachers can be trained to recognize and take advantage of students' "native competencies."

Some research, rather than focusing on cultural conflict, has instead documented how students' cultural values have or might be used to increase their motivation to succeed academically. In a study of Central American refugee students at California high schools (Suárez-Orozco, 1987, 1989), their cooperative, family-oriented values were seen as significant factors in their academic success. Students were motivated to overcome the difficulties posed by inner-city school conditions and learning English because of their desire to help the family which they had left behind. Abi-Nader's (1990) study of successful Latino students identified a similar motivation to succeed rooted in strong family ties. Nguyen (1984) identified values in traditional Vietnamese culture which can be used by sensitive educators to help strengthen the motivation of Vietnamese students. She suggested that teachers and counselors use native language proverbs to draw out cultural values and strengths.

   Teacher-student relationship. Within the research highlighting the cultural conflicts which arise from differences in cultural values and interactional styles, it should be noted that teachers have been found to play a key role. For it is in the classroom, in the interactions between students and their teacher, that the discrepancy in cultural values is either made painfully clear or buffered. Some studies (Sindell, 1988; Ortiz, 1988; Heath, 1983) have pointed to the damaging effects of teachers acting as unwitting enforcers of the dominant culture. However, several recent microethnographies of individual classroom teachers have revealed the ways in which sensitive teachers can serve as cultural brokers, guiding their students across the rocky terrain of adjustment to the values and behaviors expected of them by the dominant culture.

   One such study was conducted by Macías (1987). He described the hidden curriculum of native Papago pre-school teachers, who introduced their students to classroom behaviors which they knew would be expected in white schools, at the same time taking care not to compromise Papago values, such as autonomy. Thus, they tolerated nonparticipation and reticence while presenting activities designed to build up verbal skills and self-assertion so valued in the Anglo culture. The teachers defined their dual roles as buffering their students from the cultural discontinuities which they knew their students were bound to encounter in school and preparing them with the skills necessary to function successfully in the dominant culture.

   Similar approaches have been documented in two studies of individual high school teachers. Montero-Sieburth and Pérez (1987) analyzed the techniques employed by a Puerto Rican bilingual teacher who capitalized on her knowledge of the students' cultures, of their circumstances, and of the common cross-cultural misunderstandings they were likely to encounter. She had redefined her goal as a teacher: to reduce the *enajenación* (alienation) of her students. In the process, she had also redefined her own role as a teacher and her relationship to the dominant culture.

   Abi-Nader's (1987, 1990) ethnography of a bilingual teacher suggests that the role of cultural guide need not be restricted to teachers from the same cultural backgrounds as their students. Her ethnography of an Anglo teacher, who was successful in motivating Hispanic students to prepare for college, described the use of motivational strategies which were rooted in the teacher's knowledge about his students' cultural backgrounds. The study identified the language, classroom organization, instructional techniques, and curriculum which he used to create a vision for the future among his students, and to redefine their image of themselves, from a culturally additive perspective.

Learning Styles

Within the cultural mismatch paradigm, most attention has been focused on various dimensions of communication; however, some cognitive differences have been explored. One area which has been investigated, amid some controversy, is the cultural variation which may exist in cognitive learning styles (Cole & Scribner, 1974). Ramírez and Castañeda (1974) conducted studies which led them to conclude that Mexican American students tended to be field sensitive, rather than field independent, a distinction originated by Witkin (1967). According to this conceptual framework, field-dependent learners tend to see things more globally, interact more cooperatively, and pay more attention to the social context in which tasks are framed. The legitimacy of the distinction has been challenged (Ovando & Collier, 1985) and this line of research has received limited attention recently.

Several studies have explored cultural differences in rhetorical styles, that is, ways in which information is processed and presented. Kaplan (1988) analyzed 600 expository writing samples from college students at American universities to reveal differences in thought patterns. He pointed out how culture bound are the American conventions of what constitutes logical thinking and clear writing. His analysis contrasted the Anglo-European linear exposition with conventions which other cultures have adopted: the indirect approach in Asian cultures, in which the main idea is alluded to but not stated; the discursive paragraph development found in Romance languages; the Semitic tradition of parallel constructions. Similarly, Norton (1987) analyzed essays which were considered exemplary writing in Korea and the United States, respectively, to determine variations in styles of discourse. He identified the major cross-cultural difference in terms of preference for an inductive (Korean) or deductive (American) way of presenting an argument.

Tapia (in press) compared the motivational orientations of Puerto Rican and Anglo American children. She distinguished among children who were cooperatively oriented, competitively oriented, and individualistically oriented. Tapia found that Puerto Rican children are more cooperatively oriented and less competitively oriented than Anglo Americans. She suggests changes in the way school activities are traditionally structured by adding cooperative activities to basic learning experiences. She also suggests offering options to students for participating in cooperative as well as individualistic and competitive activities. According to Tapia, educators must accommodate cultural differences in interpersonal orientations in order to facilitate the learning process of children who are culturally different.

It is clear how cross-cultural differences might impede the academic success of a language minority student whose teachers were not conscious of this dimension of culture. It is also clear how this information might be used to improve language minority education, for making both students and teachers aware of the cultural bases of writing styles might help mitigate the confusion and negative impact of this aspect of cultural mismatch. However, other research within the mismatch paradigm has been criticized precisely because the implications for changing practice are far less clear. One important exception is the well-documented success of a project in Hawaii which has used anthropological research on native Hawaiian culture to make the public schools more responsive to these students.

Implications for Educational Program Development

Project KEEP. The Kamehameha Elementary Education Program, or Project KEEP, began in 1971. The initial phase of this research project sought to identify socialization patterns in native Hawaiian homes, as a starting point for understanding the difficulties native Hawaiians were experiencing in schools. A number of studies explored values, discourse, styles, and communicative patterns in the Hawaiian community (Levin, 1990; Boggs, 1972; Gallimore & Au, 1979; Watson-Gegeo & Boggs, 1977; Gallimore, Boggs, & Jordan 1974). This research also attempted to pinpoint the areas in which native Hawaiian patterns diverged most from the conventions used in American classrooms. The second phase of the work consisted of adjusting instructional practice, classroom organization, and motivation management used in the schools to be more culturally congruent.

Reading. An example of classroom intervention in teaching reading was summarized by Vogt, Jordan, and Tharp (1987). In this study, reading instruction was modified to elicit students' participation using narrative forms familiar to the students, before introducing unfamiliar text. Classrooms were reorganized to allow children to assist each other as they were accustomed to doing at home. Teachers learned to use the more culturally congruent practice of indirect praise as a motivational strategy. The significant gains in reading scores for native Hawaiian students participating in Project KEEP, which have been maintained over the years since its early successes, have been the source of much encouragement. When the Project KEEP methods were replicated in a Navajo school, they proved only partially successful. Vogt, Jordan and Tharp concluded that the replication attempt supplied additional evidence to support the thesis of the cultural mismatch paradigm, that "cultural incompatibility is one credible explanation for school failure" (p. 286).

Psycho-social Paradigms

A major criticism of the cultural mismatch paradigm has been that it fails to explain the variability in academic achievement among different minority groups. Some language minority groups underachieve disproportionately, while others do not, and some language minority groups even seem to achieve at higher rates than the native-born population. A study of student achievement in the Stockton, California public schools, for example, revealed that Chinese, Filippino, and Japanese students achieved higher than black or Mexican American students, and at one school they also did better than the white students (Ogbu, 1977). As a result of his research, Ogbu has called attention to the variability in minority group academic performance in different socio-political contexts around the world, citing data from a variety of international studies (Ogbu, 1978, 1987a, 1987b; Ogbu & Matute-Bianchi, 1986).

In some of the studies cited by Ogbu, language minority groups outperformed native speakers of the dominant language: children of immigrants achieved higher than French-Canadian students in Ontario (Cummins, 1982); Catalan-speaking children in Spain outperformed native Spanish speakers (Woolard, 1981); Chinese and Indian students were found to be more successful in Malaysian schools than Malay students (Mat Nor, 1983). In the United States, Gibson (1987a) cited 1984 census data showing that young Asian Americans and Cuban Americans completed more schooling than their white, native-born counterparts. Gibson's own studies have focused on Punjabi Sikh immigrant students in California, who were found to be educationally more successful than white peers (Gibson, 1987a, 1987b). Hoffman (1988) found Iranian immigrant students also to be academically successful despite linguistic and cultural barriers. Given the considerable cultural discontinuities between these groups and the dominant American culture, their academic success challenges the explanatory power of the cultural mismatch paradigm, according to Ogbu.

Other studies suggest that variability in language minority group academic achievement seems to have something to do with social status (Ogbu & Matute-Bianchi, 1986). Finnish children, for example, whose parents occupied low status positions in Sweden, have not tended to do well in schools there, but in Australia, where they are treated like other European immigrants, they have done very well (Skutunabb-Kangas & Toukomaa, 1976). Similarly, Korean and Buraku (ethnic minorities of low status) students have been found to perform poorly in Japanese schools but as well as other Asian immigrants in U.S. schools (Ito, 1967; DeVos, 1983). Data from these studies have been used to question the plausibility of explaining academic underachievement entirely in terms of cultural discontinuity. Surely a Korean child experiences more cultural discontinuity in the United States than in Japan; thus, it would seem that the cultural mismatch explanation is insufficient to explain Korean underachievement in Japanese schools and their achievement in U.S. schools.

The data have influenced some researchers to conclude that cultural and linguistic differences, in and of themselves, cannot fully account for the problems that some linguistic minority groups experience in schools, and that the cultural mismatch paradigm is too simplistic. More significant, they assert, are the ways in which linguistic minority individuals respond to the discontinuity (Roosens, 1987, cited in Trueba, 1989), their cultural orientation as a result of cross-cultural contact (Hoffman, 1988), and the ways in which cultural differences contribute to stigmatization and low status in the dominant culture (Zanger, 1987; 1989). Another way of conceptualizing the problem is to ask, "What difference do differences make?" These considerations have given rise to several theoretical frameworks formed around social, political, and economic factors.

Secondary cultural discontinuity approach. Ogbu (1987a, 1987b; Ogbu & Matute-Bianchi, 1986) has put forward a theory of minority underachievement known variously as a secondary discontinuity approach, a perceived labor market explanation (Erickson, 1987), and a cultural ecological model (Trueba, 1989). He has argued for a distinction between the impact of primary cultural differences, which are those present prior to cross-cultural contact, and secondary cultural differences, which arise in reaction to the contact between two cultures. The latter, according to Ogbu, provide an explanation for the failures of certain minority groups, because they exert a far more negative impact than primary cultural differences.

Ogbu has further proposed that a distinction be made between types of minority groups, and he has contrasted the experiences and mindsets of immigrant minorities with those of castelike or involuntary minorities. The latter, including African Americans, Mexican Americans, Puerto Ricans, and Native Americans, have experienced colonized or castelike treatment by U.S. society for generations, and, according to Ogbu, they have developed secondary cultural differences as coping strategies in response. These include cultural inversion, by which a cultural frame of reference is developed in opposition to that of the dominant culture; folk theories of "making it" and other survival strategies that contradict the achievement ideology of the dominant culture; deep distrust of the institutions of the dominant culture; and a collective oppositional identity in which cultural differences are seen as markers of individual and group identity that must be maintained.

Immigrants, according to Ogbu, respond differently both to cultural discontinuity and to racist treatment, because their reference group is located in their homeland. Their cultural frame of reference allows them to adopt an alternation model of schooling, whereby various behaviors of the dominant culture are adopted without threat to identity. In contrast, Ogbu has characterized castelike minorities as refusing to betray their identity by assuming the dominant culture behavioral modes which the schools define as necessary for academic success. Ogbu's construct of collective oppositional identity relates closely to the research on the impact of identity issues on second language acquisition by Canadian and British researchers.

Another of Ogbu's contributions to the literature on language minority academic achievement is his insistence on the central importance of economic factors, such as discriminatory job ceilings and socio-political factors, such as racism. However, the secondary cultural discontinuity approach has been criticized for failing to take into account the success of many individuals within castelike minority groups. Furthermore, the categories Ogbu has used have been attacked for being unfounded and stereotypic (Trueba, 1989). Questions have also been raised about its narrowly economic determinist position and about the validity of the causal relationships which Ogbu asserts (Erickson, 1987). Furthermore, there is an aspect of blaming the victim in Ogbu's analysis, somewhat reminiscent of the now discredited cultural deprivationist thinking of the sixties (see Ryan, 1976).

The Empowerment Approach

Cummins' framework for empowering minority students (1986, 1989) fills in many gaps left by the cultural mismatch paradigm, avoiding some of the criticisms Ogbu's approach has received. Like Ogbu, Cummins recognized the significance of economic and political power relations, but instead of focusing on the reactions of minorities, he has examined the ways in which schools function to assure the replication of the social order. According to Cummins' empowerment framework, schools academically disable members of politically and economically dominated groups because the social relations within schools replicate the unequal intergroup relations of society at large. For schools to function in such a way as to empower minority students, it is necessary for educators to redefine those relations. Cummins' analysis provides a framework for doing this by identifying the four structural elements in the organization of schooling and the way in which intergroup relations function within each. These elements are cultural/linguistic incorporation, community incorporation, pedagogy, and assessment.

1. Cultural/linguistic incorporation. According to Cummins' analysis, an additive context, incorporating and legitimizing the home cultures and languages of minority students, is necessary to overcome the bicultural ambivalence which the dominant culture has engendered in dominated groups over the generations. This ambivalence undermines the motivation of many individuals within those groups to succeed. Cummins, a longtime advocate of bilingual education, has maintained that although native language instruction is most desirable, it is possible to create a culturally and linguistically additive context without it if the school communicates a strong message about the value of the first language. A recent study seems to support this thesis.

Malik (1990) gave fifteen Iranian students at an American university two passages to read aloud: one about the Moslem belief system, the other about the Japanese belief system. The students, all of whom had been judged proficient English readers, demonstrated significantly better comprehension and reading strategies when given the culturally familiar text.

2. Community incorporation. The school's willingness to collaborate with the minority community is seen as empowering, while its traditional tendency to exclude it from the school is seen as a factor contributing to the academic disablement of young people from minority communities.

3. Pedagogy. According to Cummins, the traditional, transmission models (Freire, 1973) of teaching academically disable minority students because they mirror and thus perpetuate the unequal power relations in the broader society. To transform the social relations so as to empower students, the framework calls for a reciprocal interaction-oriented approach to teaching. Examples of this are whole language techniques and the interactional teaching style which Wong Fillmore (1983) identified as being more effective for Hispanic students in bilingual programs.

4. Assessment. The final element which Cummins' model identifies is the assessment procedure in the school, which can be either advocacy oriented or legitimization oriented, the latter tendency documented extensively in Cummins' earlier book on bilingualism and special education (1984).

Cummins' framework addresses issues ignored by both the cultural mismatch paradigm, such as social status and intergroup relations, and by Ogbu's social discontinuities approach, such as the role of the school. It is also appealing in that it provides theoretical principles which may be used as a blueprint for school improvement, not just an explanation for failure (Trueba, 1989). Another strength is that it represents a more balanced model, taking into account a variety of sociocultural factors. Genesee (1987) proposed a synthesis of sociocultural perspectives into an educational model which would include societal/intergroup factors, minority group factors, and educational factors. Cummins' framework does this.

Another strength of the empowerment framework is its focus on redefining relationships between educators and students, an area which some of the cultural mismatch studies have identified as so problematic. Cummins' framework places these relationships within a socio-political context, consistent with the findings of other research on teacher-student interactions, which suggest that the low status of certain groups in society is reflected in biased teacher attitudes, lowered expectations for minority students, and prejudiced behaviors by teachers.

Teacher Attitudes and Expectations

Research by the educational anthropologist George Spindler (1974) suggests that teachers display unconscious bias toward students most like themselves. This finding is supported more recently in a disturbing study which explored the quality of educational experience for Hispanic students in bilingual classes and in traditional, suburban mainstream classrooms (Ortiz, 1988). Observations in 97 classrooms over six years revealed a pattern of blatant and subtle bias against Hispanic students on the part of mainstream and bilingual teachers. Ortiz noted that the teachers who revealed negative and biased attitudes to her had been classified as highly tolerant and understanding of ethnic differences, according to their responses on an attitude survey conducted in their school district. However, during Ortiz's observations they expressed negative attitudes toward Hispanic students' abilities. When children proved them wrong, they reacted with resentment and suspicion. This pattern was first identified by Rosenthal and Jacobson (1968) in a famous study of teacher expectations which revealed that students who did better than teachers expected them to were seen in quite negative terms by their teachers. In Ortiz's study, traditional classroom teachers also revealed bias by avoiding interaction and eye contact with Hispanic students. In addition, they tended to leave them out of classroom activities. Such behaviors toward minority pupils have been reported in previous studies of classroom interaction cited by Ortiz (Martin, Anderson, & Veldman, 1980; Tikunoff, Berliner, & Rist, 1975; Good, 1970).

Classroom observations by Sleeter (1989) revealed gender and racial bias reflected in whom teachers tended to call on in class.

Genesee (1987) cited a 1973 report by the U.S. Commission on Civil Rights, based on observations of interactions with Hispanic students in 400 classrooms in the Southwest, which found that Mexican American students were praised 36 percent less often, were 40 percent less likely to have their ideas developed, received positive responses from teachers 40 percent less often, and were asked questions 21 percent less frequently.

Ortiz's study also revealed a number of problems with the attitudes of the "bilingual" teachers in her study, many of whom were not Spanish-speaking. Their lowered expectations for limited English speakers resulted in their relinquishing these students to instruction by Spanish-speaking aides for weeks at a time. A consequence of their lowered expectations was that they conceived of bilingual education as entirely remedial. The remedial philosophy was reflected in observations that revealed that bilingual classroom students were more likely to spend most of their time on worksheets and drill activities. This finding is consistent with studies that show tendencies to reduce the complexity of the curriculum for Spanish-speaking students (Díaz, Moll, & Mehan, 1986) and to reserve high status knowledge for students from higher class backgrounds (Oakes, 1985).

Students' perceptions of teacher attitudes were found to reflect an awareness of the various kinds of bias identified by Ortiz, in a study of Hispanic high school student attitudes conducted by Zanger (in press). This study cited student accounts of teachers using racial epithets, isolating them from other students, and communicating lower expectations for Hispanic students. Zanger's findings were consistent with the data collected by Ortiz, but her analysis also raised the possibility that cultural differences in interactional styles and role definitions exacerbated problems in the student-teacher relationships. Students' reports of the coldness and impersonality of teachers, interpreted as personal rejection or racism, were contrasted with the three central features of the traditional Puerto Rican student-teacher relationship reported by Colón (1989). He characterized that relationship as centering on *respeto* (mutual respect); *relajo* (relaxed kidding around); and *apoyo* (support). Abi-Nader's (1990) study showed that when a sympathetic Anglo teacher adopted this more culturally congruent way of relating to Hispanic students, they responded very positively.

Zones of Proximal Development: Neo-Vygotskian Perspectives

When the relationship between teacher and student breaks down due to primary cultural differences, as in the studies cited in the cultural mismatch section, or due to secondary cultural discontinuities, as Ogbu maintains, the consequences are disastrous for the learner. This observation is the foundation of an approach to understanding language minority achievement which has been developed in recent years by Trueba (1986, 1989) and Erickson (1987), drawing on the theoretical framework of the Russian development psychologist L.S. Vygotsky. This paradigm is known variously as context-specific (Trueba, 1989), and neo-Vygotskian. Vygotsky died in 1934, but recent interest in his research has led to the reissue of some of his work (Vygotsky, 1978). Vygotsky argued that learning is a socially constructed, interactive process, not merely an intrapsychic cognitive event. The process by which learning takes place is explained by Vygotsky's theoretical construct of zones of proximal development. Vygotsky thought of learning as a risk-taking endeavor, in which the learner progresses continuously past the level of competence into what he termed the zone of proximal development. In order to move out into the next level of competence, according to Vygotsky, the learner needs the assistance of a teacher or more competent peer. Neo-Vygotskian researchers have used this theoretical framework to analyze the breakdown in trust experienced by language minority students and their teachers and documented by the studies cited here.

Special education labeling. Vygotsky's zones of proximal development have also been used to explain the disproportionate number of language minority students in special education. Neo-Vygotskians have theorized that cultural, linguistic, and social discontinuities experienced by children may inhibit entry into an appropriate zone of proximal development. Trueba, for example, has suggested that language minority children who have been labeled learning disabled may have been barred from entering the zone of proximal development by "the difficulty in relating previous knowledge and experiences, acquired through the mother language and culture, to the new knowledge and experiences of the school" (1989, p. 20). The result, for the learning disabled children he studied, was a downward spiral involving stress, trauma, withdrawal, and/or acting out behaviors. Trueba has found that excessive stress characterizes the schooling experiences of many language minority students and has devastating effects. Stress makes academic activities traumatic, it disrupts efforts at communication, and it makes learning English a longer process. And when children are expected to perform with an insufficient command of the language, a vicious cycle can result. Stress leads to poor participation, resulting in embarrassment and confusion, which, in turn, inhibits the ability to deal with the learning task at hand.

In a recent ethnographic study confirming the process, Jacobs (1990) described the repeated failures of four Hmong students, classified as learning impaired, to engage meaningfully in learning activities in American classrooms. Their difficulties were due to wide disparities in culture and language underestimated by their teachers. The result was deepening frustration and subsequent withdrawal. Jacobs' research revealed the complexity of cultural and linguistic differences. She argues that withdrawal as a reaction to a difficult adjustment process should not be confused with learning impairments.

Erickson (1987) proposed a Vygotskian approach to synthesize the cultural mismatch paradigm and Ogbu's cultural ecological explanation of the failures of some language minority groups. He maintained that the two paradigms were in fact complementary, insofar as they both provided valuable explanations for possible causes of the breakdown in teacher-student trust. He argued that the prevalent pattern resulting in minority student failure began in the early grades with cultural differences contributing to student-teacher miscommunication, escalating into student distrust and resistance in the upper grades. He maintained that the pattern is compounded by the mistrust felt in many minority communities toward the public schools. Erickson's analysis incorporated two additional concepts to illuminate "the politics of legitimacy, trust, and assent," which he concluded were the most fundamental factors in school success. These are cultural hegemony and resistance theories.

Cultural hegemony. Cultural differences become a source of trouble between students and teachers, according to Erickson, when teachers use them to assert cultural hegemony. He cites data from Piestrup's (1973) ethnographic study of a reading lesson during which the white teacher insisted that black first graders pronounce their final consonants before reading instruction could commence. Erickson described this as "cultural border work," whereby cultural communication style is made a negative phenomenon in the classroom.

Resistance. One outcome of negative cultural communication styles which further hinders the educational process is student resistance. According to Erickson, "consistent patterns of refusal to learn in school can be seen as a form of resistance to a stigmatized ethnic or social class identity that is being assigned by the school" (1987, p. 350).

The relationship between students and teachers can thus degenerate into a "regressive relationship," marked by emotional conflict. This process undermines the legitimacy of teachers in the eyes of the students, thus discouraging them from entering into the zone of proximal development with the teacher. Erickson called for "culturally responsive pedagogy" both to reduce the miscommunication between teachers and students and to foster relationships of trust which can allow for the kind of collaborative relationship within which learning best takes place.

Social Integration

The teacher-student relationship is not the only aspect of intergroup relations which has been found to affect the learning of language minority students. Who their classmates are and the nature of peer relations are dimensions of the social context which have been found to affect academic achievement as well. In this section, we will first review research on issues of the segregation of language minority students and then look at studies of desegregated or ethnically mixed schools.

Desegregation Issues

Segregation. As a result of an overview of the social context of the education of Hispanics, Arias (1986) concluded that "as the number of Hispanics has grown, so has their separation from whites" (p. 51). Citing the increasing residential segregation of Mexican Americans and Puerto Ricans as a major cause, she described a trend of increasing segregation in the schooling of Hispanic students. This is in contrast with the pattern for black students who have become less segregated. Arias noted that the Northeast has the most highly segregated schools for Hispanics. Typically such a school is an inner city school with a 98 percent Hispanic population. She labeled this a modern version of the "Mexican" schools in Texas and California segregated by local and state policies of the 1930s and 1940s. A California state law, finally abolished in 1947, permitted the establishment of separate schools for Chinese, Native Americans, Japanese, and "Mongolian" students (Teitelbaum & Hiller, 1977). Mexican Americans were not excluded by statute. Although segregated schools were justified on the basis of the special language needs of the students, in fact they were inferior institutions. Fifty years later, the Mexican American Legal Defense Fund alleged that school boards in the Los Angeles area spend twice as much in the underutilized white schools than they do in the overcrowded minority schools (cited in Orfield, 1986).

Historically, language minority parents have not been satisfied with inferior, segregated schools for their children, as two recent case studies have shown. In fact, the first successful desegregation suit in the history of the United States was launched by a Spanish-speaking community, according to a historical account of the struggle led by Mexican American parents (Alvarez, 1988). In 1931, school trustees of the Lemon Grove Grammar School, in San Diego County, California, ordered the principal to exclude Mexican American students from the school and send them to a two-room school for Mexican Americans. The parents protested and won a ruling granting their children the right to attend Lemon Grove Grammar School, despite local and state support for the segregationist policy. Similarly, 56 years later, Indochinese and Latino parents organized successfully to challenge the right of the city of Lowell, Massachusetts, to educate their children in separate, unequal facilities. In 1988, after 18 months of struggle, the parents' demands for desegregation, curriculum reform, and more bilingual education were granted in an out-of-court settlement (Kiang, 1990). The largest desegregation case won by Hispanics was in San Jose, California, in 1985 (Orfield, 1986). Despite these successes, the segregation of language minority students, especially those from Spanish-speaking backgrounds, has been found to be on the increase. According to Orfield (1986), an expert on racial desegregation, one reason for this segregation has been that "the only significant federal policy response to the special problems of Hispanic education had been the fostering of bilingual education from the late 1960's to 1980" (p. 13).

Desegregation and bilingual education. The relationship between bilingual education and desegregation is a sensitive and complex one, both legally and practically. In 1977, Teitelbaum and Hiller, two legal advocates for bilingual education, wrote an article on the legal bases of bilingual education. In the article they pointed out that pro-bilingual and anti-segregation forces need not be at odds. They argued that opponents of bilingual education have used the threat of separatism to rally people against the rights of students for native language instruction. For example, a recent book attacking bilingual education used the argument that it is "essentially segregative" (Porter, 1990, p. 35). Teitelbaum and Hiller maintained that school districts opposed to bilingual education have used the constitutional constraints against desegregation as merely an excuse to justify their failure to implement bilingual programs. According to the authors, bilingual education programs are not in legal conflict with anti-segregation mandates, such as the federal Emergency School Aid Act regulations prohibiting the separation of minority group students for a substantial portion of the school day. They argue that a federal ruling exists permitting segregation for ability grouping. Thus, in the *Morgan v. Kerrigan* decision in Boston, it was ruled that bilingual programs qualified for this ability grouping sanction and were therefore not in violation of the federal desegregation ruling ordered in the Boston Public Schools.

One distinction which may help to clarify the apparent contradiction between desegregation and bilingual education was made by Imber (1990). In a recent essay on educational discrimination, he elaborated a typology defining three types of school discrimination: active, passive, and systemic discrimination.

1. *Active discrimination.* According to Imber, active discrimination occurs when students are denied educational equity on the basis of race or other characteristics not intrinsically related to students' educational needs.

2. *Passive discrimination.* The failure to offer a specific educational program mandated by a student's special circumstances is passive discrimination. The 1974 Lau decision, a landmark federal ruling which mandated bilingual education, recognized the legitimacy of claiming passive discrimination when it ruled, "There is no equality of treatment merely by providing students with the same facilities, textbooks, teachers, and curriculum; for students who do not understand English are effectively foreclosed from any meaningful education" (quoted in Hakuta, 1986, p. 200).

3. *Systemic discrimination.* This third category is a by-product of the way a school system is organized. It may or may not be intentional.

Desegregationists have traditionally brought suit against practices which fall into Imber's categories of active and systemic discrimination. However, advocates of language minority students in the past two decades have fought primarily against the harmful effects of passive discrimination, typified by English-only instruction. The remedies that have been won have typically involved the creation of separate bilingual programs which have, to one extent or another, isolated language minority students from their peers.

Arias (1986) defined three forms of isolation experienced by Hispanic students within schools and detailed the harmful effects of each. These forms of isolation are particularly relevant to language minority students. The three forms of isolation are racial isolation, linguistic isolation, and curricular tracking.

1. *Racial isolation.* This form of isolation was described as the assignment of Hispanic students to different schools from those attended by language majority students. This practice increases the likelihood of overcrowding, inexperienced teachers, and dangers from gangs. The clear association between racially segregated schools and inferior education for minorities has provided the historical impetus for desegregation efforts, such as those mentioned above.

2. *Linguistic isolation.* Linguistic isolation results from placing language minority students in classes where limited English proficient students constitute the majority. According to Arias, this practice is damaging insofar as it limits access to English language development.

3. *Curricular tracking.* Arias cited studies which indicate that minorities and the poor are found in disproportionate numbers at the bottom of the tracking system. Lower curriculum tracks deny language minority students access to what has been characterized as "high status" knowledge necessary for educational and economic advancement (Oakes, 1985). Furthermore, tracking may be viewed as one mechanism by which schools function to ensure the reproduction of the social order of the larger society (Oakes). A recent study reported that in 1988–89, only one Hispanic student in all Boston high schools was enrolled in calculus (Massachusetts Advocacy Center, 1990). Teacher expectations, classroom climate, and student attitudes are affected by tracking in ways in that have been found to impede low-track students' chances for academic success (Oakes, 1985). Although bilingual education programs cannot be technically considered a track, to the extent that they are perceived as essentially remedial in nature by students, teachers, and

administrators, they may function in much the same way as do conventional low-track programs.

Although the majority of Hispanic students in the United States attend segregated schools, Arias identified ways in which the isolation of language minority students can occur in desegregated institutions as well. This may help explain the inconclusive findings of the extensive body of research (reviewed in St. John, 1975; Patchen, 1982) on whether or not school desegregation leads to improved intergroup relations. Merely placing students from different backgrounds in the same school has not been found to result in automatic changes in attitude (Serow, 1983). It should be mentioned, however, that the vast bulk of desegregation studies in this area have focused on black and white students only.

Desegregated schools. One exception is a study cited in Genesee (1987) which researched ethnically diverse desegregated schools. As a result of his study Cohen (1980) concluded that ethnically mixed schools tend to recreate the same patterns of social inequity and differential expectations as the society at large. Four ways in which status differentials are manifested in ethnically mixed schools were identified: (1) status differentials among the students; (2) power and authority relationships within the school's formal organization; (3) social structure of the classrooms; and 4) social interaction outside the classroom.

Findings of marked differentials in status between language minority and majority students have been revealed in several recent reports and studies (Ortiz, 1988; Massachusetts Advocacy Center, 1990; National Coalition of Advocates for Students (NCAS), 1988). The Massachusetts Advocacy Report, for example, quoted a student who said, "Saying 'bilingual' puts a stigma, a stereotype on you" (p. 82). A similar finding appeared in the NCAS report, the result of a national two-year study of immigrants in U.S. public schools in which data were collected from hearings in five cities and through 180 structured interviews. It reported that their researchers "found immigrant students in every part of the country facing harassment and intergroup tensions as part of their daily school experience" (p. 60).

A series of qualitative studies by Zanger (1983, 1984, 1987, 1989, in press) among Hispanic and Vietnamese adolescents in U.S. schools examined the relationship of students within bilingual programs to the dominant culture. The researcher found that within the context of a desegregated school, the students experienced significant isolation from native speakers of standard English. Two of the barriers to integration were identified as structural and acculturative. However, the most significant barrier was interpersonal: the stigmatization which these students experienced from English-speaking peers severely limited their ability to integrate. Students in one study attributed their stigmatization by black and white native-born students to be the result of their language skills, their ethnicity, and their membership in a low-status transitional bilingual program (Zanger, 1987).

An analysis of students' experiences suggested that the common perception of stigmatization affected students in different ways. In one study (Zanger, 1987), Puerto Rican students, who had spent more time away from their original homeland than had the Vietnamese, had internalized the negative messages of the school environment to some extent. Although they had achieved quite a high degree of English proficiency, their lowered expectations for themselves had decreased their motivation to succeed academically. This is consistent with Walsh's (1987) study of Puerto Rican elementary students, whose sense of positive cultural identity correlated negatively with the amount of time they had spent away from the island. Zanger concluded that the academic underachievement of the Hispanic students she studied resulted from their internalization of negative messages from language majority peers and staff. The Vietnamese students in the study were found to react in a different way to the racial hostility they also experienced: they withdrew from contact with native English-speakers, severely impairing their English language development. Nonetheless, their academic motivation remained so high that they were able to compensate for their low English literacy skills enough to continue on a college track. Similarly, variations in reactions to prejudice by minority groups and by individuals within groups have been reported by Hoffman (1988), Ogbu and Matute-Bianchi (1986), Gibson (1987a, 1987b), and Suárez-Orozco (1987).

Intergroup relations and cognitive processes. The dynamics of how hostile intergroup relations can negatively impact on cognitive processes was demonstrated in an intriguing experimental study with African American participants conducted by Gougis (1986). Individuals in an experimental group and a control group were all given the same task of memorizing a passage of text. However, individuals in the experimental group were exposed to racial prejudice: they overheard racist comments at the back of the room and viewed photographs of lynchings. Results of the experiment showed that those who were exposed to a racist atmosphere (the experimental group) experienced higher levels of emotional stress, spent less time studying, and were less successful in recalling the assigned material than were those in the control group who were not exposed to racial prejudice. Gougis concluded that a racist climate functioned as an "environmental stressor," reducing motivation and interfering with cognitive processes.

Although the impact of intergroup relations on language minority students' learning has begun to stimulate more research attention in the United States in the past five years, a group of Canadian social psychologists has been systematically researching this relationship for thirty years. The focus of the research has been the relationship of social factors to second language learning. According to Taylor (1977), "The success or failure of second language programs is not limited to instructional and learner characteristics[;] account must also be taken of the intergroup relations context within which a second-language program exists" (p. 70). Unfortunately, editorial constraints do not allow a detailed discussion of the studies conducted or the theoretical models of second language acquisition that have been developed. The following summary presents some of the highlights from this research, which has identified various psychosocial factors which correlate with second language learning.

Social factors and second language learning. Gardner and Lambert (1972) identified ethnocentrism, that is, the negative attitudes toward speakers of the target language, as a significant and independent variable that limited the language learner's success in becoming proficient in a second language. Summarizing 12 years of research with foreign language learners in three countries, they concluded that "If the student's attitude is highly ethnocentric and hostile, we have seen that no progress to speak of will be made in acquiring any aspects of the language" (p. 134). Furthermore, they found that those who study a second language for instrumental reasons, to fulfill a language requirement, for example, are not as likely to become proficient as those who have an integrative motivation to associate with native speakers. Spolsky's (1969) study of foreign students studying at American universities found a similar correlation, but later studies among immigrants did not (Lukmani, 1972; Pérez, 1984; Oller, Baca, & Vigil, 1977).

Lambert (1975) later explained these discrepancies by differentiating between additive and subtractive contexts for language learning. Studies of language shift (Veltman, 1983) have revealed that for most immigrant groups in the United States, English eventually replaces the mother tongue. Lambert has contended that where the target language is that of the dominant culture, students from lower status linguistic minority communities tend to lose their native language as they acquire the dominant language. This subtractive context may engender negative attitudes toward the native language and culture and has ramifications for students' cultural identity, self-esteem, and motivation, contributing to what Cummins has referred to as "bicultural ambivalence" (1984). Findings from studies among French Canadians suggest that motivation to learn English is the result of a delicate balance between two factors: integrativeness and fear of assimilation (Clemant, 1980). Clemant also found that motivation was affected by both frequency and pleasantness of contact with native speakers. A related psychosocial factor was identified by Genesee, Rogers, and Holobow (1983): the perception of support from the target language community. In their study of Anglophone students living in Quebec, French proficiency correlated positively with students' perceptions that members of the Francophone community wanted them to learn French.

Reducing Language Minority Isolation

Gardner and Lambert concluded the summary of their research on the impact of attitudes on second language learning with a call for more research devoted to "the troublesome matter of changing attitudes, stereotypes, values, and motivation" (1972, p. 144). Findings from most of the other research reviewed here also underscore the importance of developing successful approaches to improving relations between majority and minority language groups if we are to provide optimal learning conditions for language minority students.

A pioneer in the field of prejudice reduction was Gordon Allport (1958), who developed a widely respected theory on the conditions necessary for reducing intergroup prejudice. He postulated that prejudice is reduced when members of both groups have face-to-face contact in situations where they enjoy equal status and mutual goals. Given the remedial status of many bilingual programs and the limited opportunities which exist for bilingual program students to cooperate on an equal basis with their peers outside the programs, the findings of negative attitudes toward language minority students, cited above, are hardly surprising. They are consistent with the desegregation literature. However, there has been some encouraging research on innovative educational approaches which have the explicit aim of altering the social context of schooling for language minority students. One approach, cooperative learning, is instructional, while the other, two-way bilingual education, is curricular and programmatic.

Educational Approaches

Cooperative learning. The cooperative learning method has many variations, but three essential components: small groups, common goals (positive interdependence), and individual accountability (Slavin, 1990a). Other common elements are heterogeneous grouping, the teacher's role as consultant, group processing, and explicit focus on interpersonal and small group skills (Johnson, Johnson, & Holubec, 1987). "Cooperative learning is one of the most thoroughly researched of all instructional methods," according to Slavin's (1990a, p. 52) review of the research findings on which there is consensus. A summary of the successes attributed to cooperative learning follows. They generally fall into three areas: academic achievement, ethnic relations, and prosocial development (Kagan, 1986).

A great deal of interest has been generated lately in the application of cooperative learning methods for language minority students (Slavin, 1990b). In fact, several textbooks have adapted cooperative learning techniques specifically to the needs of language minority students (Cohen, 1986; Christison & Bassano, 1987; Coelho, Winer, & Olsen, 1989). The source for much of the following discussion is Kagan's (1986) analysis of the results of cooperative learning research in the education of language minorities.

Cooperative learning research and programs for language minority students have two primary concerns: academic achievement gains and improved intergroup relations. While cooperative learning has been shown to promote higher academic achievement among all pupils (compared to traditional instructional methods), the gains for African American and Mexican American children have been even higher than those of mainstream students. Kagan (1986) reviewed three separate studies using different cooperative learning methods among geographically different minority students which found a dramatic rise in minority student achievement (in only one study were they language minorities). He also cited research in Israel showing similarly disproportionate gains in achievement among children from low-status Middle Eastern backgrounds. Kagan related these findings to a larger group of research studies which have concluded that medium and low achievers seem to benefit the most from cooperative learning methods (although not at the expense of the high achievers). Among the various explanations which have been offered for the particular success of cooperative learning with minority students, Kagan theorized that the structure of cooperative classrooms is more culturally compatible with the home environments of minority students. To support his theory, he cited a number of studies documenting the cooperative tendencies of Mexican Americans, Native Americans, African Americans, Asians, rural Americans, and those from poor backgrounds. For these students, Kagan maintained, cooperative learning serves to remove the "structural bias" of the traditionally competitive American classroom. The success of cooperative learning in promoting minority student achievement has implications not just for the ethnically diverse classroom containing language minority students, but for bilingual and ESL classrooms as well.

The positive gains in interethnic relations that have been found to occur in cooperative classrooms (Kagan, 1986) are particularly encouraging in light of the desegregation literature cited earlier, which revealed that true integration is not an automatic concomitant of school desegregation. Kagan cited Slavin's 1983 review of 14 experiments on cross-ethnic friendships in cooperative learning classrooms, concluding that "overall cross-ethnic friendships improved in the cooperative learning classrooms over control classes" (Kagan, p. 247). The findings of one experiment suggest that interethnic gains from cooperative learning experiences may not be short lived. In a follow-up study conducted by Slavin one year after a cooperative learning project, students in the experimental group listed 37.9 percent of their friendship choices outside their own ethnic group, compared to the 9.8 percent rate of the control group. The gains in interethnic relations reported in these studies are not surprising if Allport's prejudice reduction hypothesis is correct, for the cooperative learning method institutionalizes the conditions which Allport maintained were necessary for improving race relations.

Despite these encouraging findings, Kagan (1986) advocated caution in interpreting the results, asserting that the positive results were based on "weak" measures of cross-race friendship patterns.

The most common measure is a sociometric listing of students' friendship choices. Kagan raised the possibility that students may be hesitant to list friends whose names they cannot spell and that racially mixed teams might merely improve students' familiarity with the spelling of some classmates' names, resulting in skewed results.

There is some evidence that limited English proficient students make substantial gains in second language development using cooperative learning methods, according to a 1981 study by Cohen, DeAvila, and Intiti (cited in Kagan, 1986). The increased opportunities for communicative language practice may explain these gains. In one study language majority students were observed drawing out their limited English proficient peers (Aronson, Blaney, Stephen, Sikes, & Snapp, 1978, cited in Kagan). Cooperative learning is structured to promote this interactive pattern. Some of the techniques, such as Jigsaw, are designed so students need to find out information from each other. This is an area which deserves more research. As Slavin (1990b) has commented, the research on language minority students in cooperative language classrooms has neglected language use as an area of study.

Bilingual education. While cooperative learning may prove to be a valuable instructional method for language minority students both within and outside bilingual education classes, it does not address the isolation of students in those bilingual programs which substantially segregate language minority students from their peers in the mainstream. As Collier (1989) pointed out, "Three of the major models used for bilingual education in the U.S. and Canada have been implemented mostly as segregated models: transitional and maintenance for language-minority students and immersion for language-majority students" (p. 1). Although charges of separatism have long been used by those opposed to the concept of bilingual education, some advocates have become increasingly concerned about the the isolation of bilingual students and the evolution of bilingual programs into tracks which would institutionalize *de facto* segregation (Castellanos, cited in Crawford, 1989; Glenn, 1990; Troike, 1978). Similar concerns have been voiced about the experiences of Turkish children in German bilingual programs. Pommerin (1988, cited in Glenn, in press) criticized the ghettoization of Turkish immigrant children enrolled in separatist bilingual classes in Germany: "Separating measures—especially when they last for an extended period—do not protect the foreign child, but rather isolate her."

More concretely, Collier (1989) summarized two negative consequences of segregated program models. First, she cited Swain's 1984 study of language majority immersion students who developed an interlanguage of grammatical deviations, suggesting that students' second language development may be retarded by insufficient contact with native-speaking peers. Second, she raised the possibility that segregated programs do nothing to reduce the social distance from speakers of the target language, a factor which may influence language learning. Making a similar point, Genesee (1987) cited the results of attitudinal studies of majority language students in immersion programs to suggest that "there may be limits to the extent of attitude change that can be achieved and sustained in second language programs that do not provide real meaningful contact between the learner and members of the target language group" (p. 106).

An integrated model. These criticisms of segregated models of bilingual programs have led to increased interest in an integrated model, known variously as two-way, dual-language, interlocking, and an enrichment model of bilingual education. Hornberger's (1990) paper on enrichment bilingual education called for directing more research and policy attention to what she referred to as the third model of bilingual education. Hornberger differentiated the enrichment model from the remedial nature of other bilingual program models because its structure recognizes the minority language as a resource for all students. In Hornberger's revised conceptual framework of bilingual education typologies, the enrichment model covers (a) immersion programs, in which speakers of the majority language typically learn in the language of a language minority group; and (b) two-way programs, in which both majority and minority language students learn together in both languages.

Immersion programs. French immersion programs in Canada began in 1965, with the St. Lambert experiment launched by Anglophone parents who felt that their children were graduating at a disadvantage from English language schools in Francophone Quebec. They also sought to improve relations with French Quebecers (Genesee, 1987). Acceptance and popularity of immersion programs spread throughout Canada, as social and political events that originated in Quebec made themselves felt across the country. The extensive body of research that Canadian social scientists have conducted around immersion programs has been summarized and discussed at length in Genesee's book on two-way bilingual education. The research has looked at the impact of these programs on second language proficiency, academic achievement, and intergroup attitudes. Most of the research, according to Genesee, has used an experimental program design, comparing immersion students with comparable control groups. Another feature of the research has been its longitudinal nature, sometimes 13 years worth of data, as in studies cited by Genesee (Lambert & Tucker, 1972; Swain & Lapkin, 1982). Genesee reviewed the variety of program types studied, including double immersion (Genesee & Lambert, 1983, studied English-speakers learning in French and Hebrew), late immersion (Stevens, 1976, researched a program which began in grade 7), partial immersion (Edwards, McCarrey, & Fue, 1980), and early total immersion (Morrison, 1981). In addition to evaluating the efficacy of immersion as an educational program and the program types that seemed to be most successful, the Canadian researchers have used the opportunity to test hypotheses about basic questions in sociolinguistics, psycholinguistics, and social psychology, from which they have formulated new theories. Much of the work on psychosocial factors in second language learning, discussed previously, was done in the context of studying immersion programs.

The most consistent findings of immersion program research have indicated that program participants become proficient in French at no cost to their academic achievement, measured in English (Genesee, 1987). Attitudinal studies have indicated that the immersion experience reduces social distance to some degree, creates more positive attitudes about the second language, increases confidence in speaking the second language with native speakers, and does not seem to produce a loss of ethnic identity. One particularly relevant finding was that students showed more favorable attitudes toward French Canadians if their immersion program was located in an otherwise all-French school, attended by native French speakers (Genesee, Morin, & Allister, 1974, cited in Genesee).

While the Canadian investigations of academic and linguistic achievement have relied heavily on standardized testing, intergroup issues have been studied using a variety of measures, including questionnaires and diverse instruments which yielded quantifiable data (Gardner & Lambert, 1972). An innovative method used is the matched guise technique. In this assessment procedure, students are asked to listen to tape-recordings of French and English speakers and then rate them on various personality features. Unbeknownst to participants, the speech samples feature the same person speaking in two different languages, thus affording researchers the opportunity to ferret out stereotypes and language attitudes (Gardner & Lambert). Blake's study (cited in Swain & Lapkin, 1981) reported that Canadian immersion students saw their segregation from native French-speakers as the biggest barrier to improved relations between the two groups. Ethnographic techniques have been used very little. The most frequently cited ethnographic study was one which explored interactions among French and English teachers, not students (Cleghorn & Genesee, 1984, cited in Genesee).

Two-way immersion programs. Almost all of the U.S. immersion experiments have been two-way programs incorporating language majority and minority interaction into the structure of the program. One of Lindholm's (1987) four critical features of a two-way immersion program is the participation (preferably in balanced numbers) of language majority and minority students. Other two-way programs, such as the one profiled by Hornberger (1990), have not been classified as immersion programs as defined by Lindholm, for the minority language is not used 50 percent of the time. Yet another two-way program which has been developed is the integrated bilingual school in which both languages are used for instruction. Classrooms are comprised of language majority and minority students, but only the latter are expected to become proficient in both languages (Glenn, 1990).

Hornberger (1990) alluded to the "nascent but growing literature" on two-way bilingual programs. Much of that research has consisted largely of program profiles (Hornberger, 1990; Equity and Choice, 1987; Massachusetts Department of Education Office of Educational Equity, 1990; Lindholm, 1987). There is a scarcity of the rigorous, academic research which was undertaken in Canada, despite the existence of two-way programs in the United States since 1971 (Collier, 1989). Crawford (1989), for example, referred to the "encouraging anecdotal evidence" in support of the effectiveness of two-way programs in the United States. Due to the dearth of research on two-way programs, program advocates refer extensively to the research on Canadian immersion programs to show the benefits of language minority instruction for language majority students.

An example of the nascent literature on two-way programs is Collier's (1989) study on the impact of participation in a two-way elementary school program on native English and native Spanish speakers after ten years. This descriptive study located 20 graduates of the Oyster School, in Washington, D.C., in their early twenties. She found that "all of the students described extensive socializing with speakers of both languages, in professional, academic, and personal settings" (Collier, p. 5). Collier contrasted this finding to the greater social distance found by Swain and Lapkin (1981) in their study of Canadian immersion students schooled separately from speakers of the target language. Collier's other findings on bilingual proficiency, academic achievement, and attitudes toward bilingual schooling are more consistent with the Canadian research. Collier cautioned that her study's generalizability is limited by the non-random sample. However, her findings indicate that the promise that two-way programs have held for improving the social context for language minority learning bears further investigation.

Discussion and Recommendations

"As long as our conceptualization of the educational problems of minority language students emphasizes linguistic and cognitive factors, our responses to these problems will be cognitive and linguistic in nature," warned Genesee (1987, p. 170). For a long time, a linguistic/cognitive conceptualization has, indeed, dominated both the research agenda and the policy debate around language minority learning. The literature reviewed in this chapter has underscored how limited and narrow a conceptualization it is. An increasing number of studies have uncovered cultural and social factors that may prove to be the missing pieces we need to solve the puzzle of why some language minority groups consistently underachieve academically, while others do not.

The review of the literature identifies the range of areas explored, the variety of research approaches taken, and the dominant paradigms in this research effort. Taken as a whole, the literature could be characterized as "pluralistic" insofar as the disparate studies and approaches seem to identify a panoply of complementary rather than mutually exclusive perspectives on what is involved in the learning process for language minority students. To summarize, the review identified some of the key factors involved in this process. These factors can be divided into cultural and social dimensions. However, the research has revealed how closely intertwined these are in life.

Cultural Dimensions

Ethnographic methodological approaches have revealed some of the cultural elements which cause confusion for language minority students in school. It is clear from the research that significant differences exist in how words are used in different cultures and speech communities. These differences may be as disorienting for students as are the differences in languages. Nonverbal communication has also been found to vary significantly cross-culturally, although exactly how the various dimensions of this process impact on students' experiences in school remains to be shown more definitively. More conclusive work has been done around discontinuities in values. Particularly productive have been studies on the cooperative orientations of many language minority groups compared to the competitive orientations existent in the structure of language majority schooling. Investigations of cognitive differences have been less conclusive, although the cross-cultural variations found in styles of rhetoric have clear implications for educational practice. Some of the most promising recent work has focused on strategies used by effective bilingual teachers to mitigate the negative impact of cultural discontinuities.

Social Dimensions

The research has identified quite a number of variables in the social context of language minority education, although the theoretical nature of much of it has yet to be tested. The most compelling evidence thus far for a psychosocial explanation of academic underachievement of some minority groups has emerged from cross-cultural studies which have found that members of the same ethnolinguistic group achieve very differently in high and low status contexts. The impact of unequal power relations on academic achievement has been examined from several perspectives. Ogbu argues that the way different minority groups respond to discrimination is a key issue. Cummins, on the other hand, identified ways in which schools mirror unequal intergroup relations. Finally, Trueba and Erickson have called attention to the importance of engaging students in culturally meaningful activities for cognitive development. More research is clearly needed to provide evidence to support these theoretical frameworks and constructs. Descriptive studies have identified the pervasiveness of intergroup hostility in the schooling experiences of language minority students.

Other research has revealed the ramifications of prejudice on the educational process: lowered teacher expectations; curricular tracking; stress and anxiety leading to impaired cognitive functioning; the erosion of student-teacher trust; and hostile relations with language minority peers. The latter factor has been found to have negative consequences for second language learning in extensive research studies conducted during the past thirty years by Canadian social scientists. Furthermore, discrimination has been shown to result in the isolation of language minority students in separate schools and classes.

Future Research

It seems crucial that research attention be directed to further investigate the precise ways in which negative social influences damage the educational experiences of so many language minority students. Another important area for further research is the continuation of the search for effective educational solutions. Although the desegregation literature has indicated that merely ending the isolation of language minority students does not necessarily lead to improved intergroup relations or even integration, there have been encouraging findings from the research on two other approaches which have been developed to improve language majority and minority relations: cooperative learning and the enrichment model of bilingual education.

This review suggests a tantalizing array of questions which remain only partially answered and of others which have hardly been asked. The success of Project KEEP in applying anthropological findings to educational practice suggests that we need more research based on this model. The finding that the Project KEEP instructional innovations could not be transplanted with equal results to a different cultural setting underscores the need to develop context-specific analyses and interventions using this model.

The studies reviewed within the psychosocial paradigm suggest that learning more about cultural differences from a sympathetic perspective and developing more culturally congruent instructional techniques is not enough, however. We need research that can tell us more about the ways in which racism functions to erode the academic potential of so many language minority students. Why and how do some groups, and some individuals within groups, respond differently to discrimination? The research thus far has just begun to answer these important questions. We also need to know more about the social contexts in which language minority students go to school: what are their relationships to the dominant culture, particularly to language majority peers? The ways in which these factors influence the learning process demand further investigation. As we discover more about the insidious and damaging effects of bias, we will need to find out what kinds of interventions are most successful in reducing prejudice. For example, what kinds of education and training are most effective in preparing language majority teachers and administrators to respond sensitively to multicultural, multilingual diversity? What kinds of program models and instructional techniques effectively raise the social status of language minority students?

Finally, our research needs to confront the issue of social isolation of bilingual program students. We need to explore the quantity and quality of contact with language majority students which individual bilingual programs afford their students. Furthermore, we need to find out more about how much and what kind of contact is optimal for the academic development of bilingual students. One approach is for U.S. researchers to take advantage of the opportunities provided by the two-way bilingual movement to learn more about these issues just as their Canadian counterparts have done with the experiments in language immersion education. The reluctance of researchers sympathetic to bilingual education to focus on the impact of the segregative aspects of bilingual programs may be based on the fear of providing ammunition to opponents of native language instruction in these "English Only" times. Yet this is ultimately a disservice to students in bilingual programs. For it will be to their benefit if research can help identify ways to successfully integrate language majority and language minority students in bilingual programs without diluting the native language component of their education.

References

Abi-Nader, J. (1987). "A house for my mother": An ethnography of motivational strategies in a successful college preparatory program for Hispanic high school students. Unpublished doctoral dissertation, Georgia State University.

Abi-Nader, J. (1990). Helping minority high school students redefine their self-image through culturally sensitive instruction. Paper presented at the annual conference of the American Education Research Association, Boston, MA.

Allport, G. (1958). *The nature of prejudice.* New York: Anchor Books.

Alvarez, R.R. (1988). National politics and local responses: The nation's first successful school desegregation court case. In Trueba, H. & Delgado-Gaitan, C. (Eds.) *School and society: Learning content through culture.* New York: Praeger.

Arias, B. (1986). The context of education for Hispanic students: An overview. *American Journal of Education, 95*(1), 26–57.

Boggs, S.T. (1972). The meaning of questions and narratives to Hawaiian children. In Cazden, C., John, V., & Hymes, D. (Eds.) *Functions of language in the classroom.* New York: Teachers College Press.

Cazden, C., John, V., & Hymes, D. (Eds.) (1972). *Functions of language in the classroom.* New York: Teachers College Press.

Christison, M.E. & Bassano, S. (1987). *Look who's talking.* Hayward, CA: Allemany Press.

Clemant, R. (1980). Ethnicity, contact, and communicative competence in a second language. In Giles, H., Robinson, W.P., & Smith, P.M. (Eds.) *Language: Social psychological perspectives.* Oxford: Pergamon.

Coelho, E., Winer, L., & Olsen, J.W.-B. (1989). *All sides of the issue.* Hayward, CA: Allemany Press.

Cohen, E. (1986). *Designing groupwork: Strategies for the heterogeneous classroom.* New York: Teachers College Press.

Cole, M. & Scribner, S. (1974). *Culture and thought: A psychological introduction.* New York: Wiley.

Collier, V. (1989). Academic achievement, attitudes, and occupations among graduates of two-way bilingual classes. Paper presented at the annual meeting of the American Education Research Association, San Francisco, CA.

Colón, N. (1989). Understanding why Puerto Ricans drop out. Keynote address delivered at "Abriendo Caminos" conference, Holy Cross College, Worcester, MA.

Crawford, J. (1989). *Bilingual education: History, politics, theory and practice.* Trenton, NJ: Crane.

Cummins, J. (1981). Empirical and theoretical underpinnings of bilingual education. *Journal of Education,* Winter, 16–29.

Cummins, J. (1984). *Bilingualism and special education: Issues in assessment and pedagogy.* Clevedon, England: Multilingual Matters.

Cummins, J. (1986). Empowering minority students: A framework for intervention. *Harvard Education Review, 56,* 18–36.

Cummins, J. (1989). *Empowering minority students.* Sacramento, CA: California Association for Bilingual Education.

Delgado-Gaitan, C. (1987). Traditions and transitions in the learning process of Mexican children: An ethnographic view. In Spindler, G. & Spindler, L. (Eds.) *Interpretive ethnography of education: At home and abroad.* Hillsdale, NJ: Lawrence Erlbaum Associates.

Díaz, S., Moll, L.C., & Mehan, H. (1986). Sociocultural resources in instruction: A context-specific approach. In Bilingual Education Office, California State Department of Education (Ed.) *Beyond language: Social and cultural factors in schooling language minority students.* Los Angeles, CA: Evaluation, Dissemination, and Assessment Center, California State University.

Dolson, D. (1984). The influence of various home bilingual environments on the academic achievement, language development, and psychosocial adjustment of fifth and sixth grade Hispanic students. Unpublished doctoral dissertation, University of San Francisco.

Duran, R. (1987). Factors affecting development of second language literacy. In Goldman, S., & Trueba, H. (Eds.) *Becoming literate in English as a second language.* Norwood, NJ: Ablex.

Equity and Choice (1987), *3*(3).

Erickson, F. (1987). Transformation and school success: The politics and culture of educational achievement. *Anthropology and Education Quarterly, 18*(4), 335–356.

Freire, P. (1973). *Education for critical consciousness.* New York: Seabury.

Gallimore, R. & Au, K.H. (1979). The competence/incompetence paradox in the education of minority culture children. *Quarterly Newsletter of the Laboratory for Comparative Human Cognition, 11,* 32–37.

Gallimore, R., Boggs, J., & Jordan, C. (1974). *Culture, behavior and education: A study of Hawaiian Americans.* Beverly Hills, CA: Sage.

Gardner, R. (1979). Social psychological aspects of second language acquisition. In Giles, H. & St. Clair, R. (Eds.) *Language and social psychology.* Baltimore: University Park Press.

Gardner, R.C. & Lambert, W.E. (1972). *Attitudes and motivation in second language learning.* Rowley, MA: Newbury House.

Genesee, F. (1987). *Learning through two languages.* Cambridge, MA: Newbury House.

Genesee, F., Rogers, P., & Holobow, N. (1983). The social psychology of second language learning: Another point of view. *Language Learning, 33*(2), 209–224.

Gibson, M.A. (1987a). The school performance of immigrant minorities: A comparative view. *Anthropology and Education Quarterly, 18*, 262–275.

Gibson, M.A. (1987b). Punjabi immigrants in an American high school. In Spindler, G. & Spindler, L. (Eds.) *Interpretive ethnography of education at home and abroad.* Hillsdale, NJ: Lawrence Erlbaum Associates.

Giroux, H.A. (1983). *Theory and resistance: A pedagogy for the opposition.* South Hadley, MA: Bergin.

Glenn, C.L. (1990). How to integrate bilingual education without tracking. *The School Administrator*, May, 28–31.

Glenn, C.L. (in press). *Work in progress.*

Gougis, R.A. (1986). The effects of prejudice and stress on the academic performance of Black-Americans. In Neisser, U. (Ed.) *The school achievement of minority children.* Hillsdale, NJ: Lawrence Erlbaum Associates.

Hakuta, K. (1986). *Mirror of language: The debate on bilingualism.* New York: Basic Books.

Heath, S.B. (1983). *Ways with words.* Cambridge, England: Cambridge University Press.

Heath, S.B. (1986). Sociocultural contexts of language development. In Evaluation, Dissemination and Assessment Center, *Beyond language: Social and cultural factors in schooling language minority students.* Los Angeles, CA: California State University.

Hoffman, D.M. (1988). Cross-cultural adaptation of learning: Iranians and Americans at school. In Trueba, H.T. & Delgado-Gaitan, C. (Eds.) *School and society: Learning content through culture.* New York: Praeger.

Hornberger, N. (1990). Extending enrichment bilingual education: Revisiting typologies and redirecting policy. Paper presented at the American Educational Research Association, Boston, MA.

Imber, M. (1990). A typology of discrimination in education. In Goldberg, S. (Ed.) *Readings of equal education: Critical issues for a new administration and congress, Vol. 10.* New York: AMS Press.

Irujo, S. (1988). An introduction to intercultural differences and similarities in nonverbal communication. In Wurzel, J. (Ed.) *Toward multiculturalism.* Yarmouth, ME: Intercultural Press.

Jacobs, L. (1990). An ethnographic study of four Hmong students: Implications for educators and schools. In Goldberg, S. (Ed.) *Readings of equal education: Critical issues for a new administration and Congress, Vol. 10.* New York: AMS Press.

Johnson, D.W., Johnson, R.T., & Holubec, E.J. (1987). *Learning together and alone: Cooperative, competitive and individualistic learning.* Minneapolis: Cooperative Learning Center, University of Minnesota.

Jordan, K. (1977). Maternal teaching, peer teaching, and school adaptation in an urban Hawaiian population. Technical Report No. 67. Honolulu: Kamehameha Schools, Kamehameha Early Education Program.

Kagan, S. (1986). Cooperative learning and sociocultural factors in schooling. In *Beyond language: Social and cultural factors in schooling language minority students*. Los Angeles, CA: Evaluation, Dissemination and Assessment Center, California State University.

Kaplan, R. (1988). Cultural thought patterns in inter-cultural education. In Wurzel, J. (Ed.) *Toward multiculturalism*. Yarmouth, ME: Intercultural Press.

Kiang, P. (1990). Southeast Asian parent empowerment: The challenge of changing demographics in Lowell, Massachusetts. Boston: Massachusetts Association for Bilingual Education (ERIC Document Reproduction Service No. UD 027534).

Lambert, W.E. (1975). Culture and language as factors in learning and education. In Wolfgang, A. (Ed.) *Education of immigrant students*. Toronto: O.I.S.E.

Lambert, W.E. (1989). The development of bilingual literacy skills: Experiences with immersion education. In Sonino, E.Z. (Ed.) *Literacy in school and society: Multidisciplinary perspectives*. New York: Plenum.

Levin, P.F. (1990). Culturally contextualized apprenticeship: Teaching and learning through helping in Hawaiian families. *The Quarterly Newsletter of the Laboratory of Comparative Human Cognition, 12*(2), 80–86.

Lindholm, K.J. (1987). *Directory of bilingual immersion programs: Two-way bilingual education for language minority and majority students*. Los Angeles: Center for Language Education and Research, University of California.

Lukmani, Y. (1972). Motivation to learn and language proficiency. *Language Learning, 22*(2), 261–273.

Macias, J. (1987). The hidden curriculum of Papago teachers: American Indian strategies for mitigating cultural discontinuity in early schooling. In Spindler, G. & Spindler, L. (Eds.) *Interpretive ethnography of education: At home and abroad*. Hillsdale, NJ: Lawrence Erlbaum Associates.

Malik, A.M. (1990). A psycholinguistic analysis of the reading behavior of EFL-proficient readers using culturally familiar and culturally nonfamiliar expository texts. *American Educational Research Journal, 27*(1), 205–223.

Massachusetts Advocacy Center (1990). *Locked in/locked out: Tracking and placement practices in Boston Public Schools*. Boston, MA: Massachusetts Advocacy Center.

Massachusetts Department of Education, Office of Educational Equity, (1988). *Schools for the city: Educating linguistic minority students*. Quincy, MA: Massachusetts Department of Education.

Matute-Bianchi, M.E. (1986). Ethnic identities and patterns of school success and failure among Mexican-descent and Japanese-American students in a California high school: An ethnographic analysis. *American Journal of Education, 95*, 233–255.

Mohatt, G. & Erickson, F. (1981). The microethnographic study of bilingual schooling. In Padilla, R.V. (Ed.) *Ethnoperspectives in bilingual education research, Vol. 3: Bilingual education technology.* Ypsilanti, MI: Eastern Michigan University.

Moll, L.C. & Díaz, S. (1987). Change as the goal of educational research. *Anthropology and Education Quarterly, 18*(4), 300–311.

Montero-Sieburth, M. & Pérez, M. (1987). "Echar pa'lante," moving onward: The dilemmas and strategies of a bilingual teacher. *Anthropology and Education Quarterly, 18,* 180–189.

National Coalition of Advocates for Students (NCAS) (1988). *New voices: Immigrant students in U.S. public schools.* Boston, MA: NCAS.

Nguyen, T. (1984). Positive self-concept in the Vietnamese bilingual child. *Bilingual Journal,* Spring, 9–14.

Nine Curt, C.J. (1984). *Nonverbal communication.* Cambridge, MA: Evaluation, Dissemination and Assessment Center.

Norton, R. (1987). A comparison of thinking and writing patterns in Korea and the United States. *AFS occasional papers in intercultural learning.* New York: AFS International/Intercultural Programs.

Oakes, J. (1985). *Keeping track: How schools structure inequality.* New Haven: Yale University Press.

Ogbu, J. (1977). Racial stratification and education: The case of Stockton, California. *ICRD Bulletin, 12*(3), 1–26.

Ogbu, J. (1987a). *Minority education and caste: The American system in cross-cultural perspective.* New York: Academic Press.

Ogbu, J. (1987b). Variability in minority school performance: A problem in search of an explanation. *Anthropology and Education Quarterly, 18*(4), 312–334.

Ogbu, J. & Matute-Bianchi, M.E. (1986). Understanding sociocultural factors: Knowledge, identity and school adjustment. In Bilingual Education Office, California State Department of Education (Ed.), *Beyond language: Social and cultural factors in schooling language minority students.* Los Angeles, CA: Evaluation, Dissemination, and Assessment Center, California State University.

Oller, J., Baca, L., & Vigil, F. (1977). Attitudes and attained proficiency in ESL: A sociolinguistic study of Mexican Americans in the Southwest. *TESOL Quarterly, 11,* 173–183.

Orfield, G. (1986). Hispanic education: Challenges, research, and policies. *American Journal of Education, 95,* 1–25.

Ortiz, F.I. (1988). Hispanic-American children's experiences in classrooms: A comparison between Hispanic and non-Hispanic children. In Weis, L. (Ed.) *Class, race, and gender in American education.* Albany, NY: SUNY Press.

Ovando, C. & Collier, V. (1985). *Bilingual and ESL classrooms.* New York: McGraw-Hill.

Patchen, M. (1982). *Black-white contact in schools: Its social and academic effects.* West Lafayette, IN: Purdue University Press.

Pérez, M. (1984). The relation of social attitudes and language study motivation with English ability among immigrant high school Spanish speaking students. Unpublished doctoral dissertation, University of Houston-University Park.

Philips, S. (1972). Participant structures and communicative competence: Warm Springs children in community and classroom. In Cazden, C., John, V. & Hymes, D. (Eds.) *Functions of language in the classroom.* New York: Teachers College Press.

Porter, R. (1990). *Forked tongue: The politics of bilingual education.* New York, Basic Books.

Ramírez, M. & Castañeda, A. (1974). *Cultural democracy, bicognitive development, and education.* New York: Academic Press.

Rosenthal, R. & Jacobson, L. (1968). *Pygmalion in the classroom.* New York: Holt, Rinehart & Winston.

Ryan, R. (1976). *Blaming the victim* (rev. ed.). New York: Vintage Books.

St. John, N. (1975). *School desegregation outcomes for children.* New York: Wiley & Sons.

Schumann, J.H. (1978). The Pidinization hypothesis. In Hatch, E. (Ed.) *Second language acquisition.* Rowley, MA: Newbury House.

Serow, R.C. (1983). *Schooling for social diversity: An analysis of policy and practice.* New York: Teachers College Press.

Sindell, P. (1988). Some discontinuities in the enculturation of Mistassini Cree children. In Wurzel, J. (Ed.) *Toward multiculturalism: A reader in multicultural education.* Yarmouth, ME: Intercultural Press.

Slavin, R.E. (1990a). Research on cooperative learning: Consensus and controversy. *Educational Leadership, 1,* 52–54.

Slavin, R.E. (1990b). Success for all: Effects on the achievement of limited English proficient children. Paper presented at the annual conference of the American Education Research Association, Boston, MA.

Sleeter, C.E. (1989). Multicultural education staff development: How much can it change classroom teaching? Paper presented at the Annual Meeting of the American Education Research Association, San Francisco, CA.

Spindler, G.D. (1974). Beth Anne—A case study of culturally defined adjustment and teacher perceptions. In Spindler, G.D. (Ed.) *Education and cultural process: Toward an anthropology of education.* New York: Holt, Rinehart & Winston.

Spolsky, B. (1969). Attitudinal aspects of second language learning. *Language Learning, 9,* 3–4.

Suárez-Orozco, M.M. (1987). "Becoming somebody": Central American immigrants in U.S. inner-city schools. *Anthropology and Education Quarterly, 18,* 287–299.

Suárez-Orozco, M.M. (1989). *Central American refugees in U.S. high schools: A psycho-social study of motivation and achievement.* Stanford: Stanford University Press.

Swain, M. & Lapkin, S. (1982). *Evaluating bilingual education: A Canadian case study.* Clevedon, England: Multilingual Matters.

Tapia, M.R. (in press). Motivational orientations, learning, and the Puerto Rican child. In Ambert, A.N. & Alvarez, M.D. (Eds.) *Puerto Rican children on the mainland: Interdisciplinary Perspectives.* New York: Garland.

Taylor, D. M. (1977). Bilingualism and intergroup relations. In Hornby, P.A. (Ed.) *Bilingualism: Psychological, social, and educational implications.* New York: Academic Press.

Teitelbaum, H. & Hiller, R.J. (1977). Bilingual education: The legal mandate. *Harvard Education Review, 47,* 138–170.

Troike, R.D. (1978). Research evidence for the effectiveness of bilingual education. *NABE Journal, 3*(1), 13–24.

Trueba, H. (1987). *Success or failure? Learning and the language minority student.* Scranton, PA: Harper & Row.

Trueba, H. (1989). Empowerment and mainstreaming: Culture change and the integration of home and school values. Paper read at the annual meeting of the American Educational Research Association, San Francisco, CA.

Veltman, C. (1983). *Language shift in the United States.* New York: Mouton.

Vogt, L., Jordan, C., & Tharp, R. (1987). Explaining school failure, producing school success: Two cases. *Anthropology and Education Quarterly, 18*(4), 276–286.

Vygotsky, L.S. (1978). The development of higher psychological processes. In Cole, M., John-Steiner, V, Scribner, S., & Souberman, E. (Eds.) *Mind in society.* Cambridge: Harvard University Press.

Walsh, C. (1987). Language, meaning, and voice: Puerto Rican students' struggle for a speaking consciousness. *Language Arts, 64*(2), 196–206.

Watson-Gegeo, K.A. & Boggs, S.T. (1977). From verbal play to talk-story: The role of routines in speech events among Hawaiian children. In Ervin-Tripp, S. & Mitchell-Kernan, C. (Eds.) *Child discourse.* New York: Academic Press.

Witkin, H.A. (1967). A cognitive-style approach to cross-cultural research. *International Journal of Psychology, 6,* 4–87.

Wong Fillmore, L. (1983). The language learner as an individual: Implications of research on individual differences for the ESL teacher. In Clarke, M.A. & Handscombe, J. (Eds.) *On TESOL '82: Pacific perspectives on language learning and teaching.* Washington, DC: TESOL.

Zanger, V.V. (1984). The social context of bilingual education: Bilingual and monolingual students' attitudes at a Boston high school. Unpublished manuscript, Boston University.

Zanger, V.V. (1987). The social context of second language learning: An examination of barriers to integration in five case studies. Unpublished doctoral dissertation, Boston University.

Zanger, V.V. (1989). The impact of racial hostility on linguistic minorities' achievement. Paper presented at the annual meeting of the American Educational Research Association, San Francisco, CA.

Zanger, V.V. (in press). "Not joined in": Intergroup relations and access to literacy for Hispanic youth. In Ferdman, B. & Ramírez, A. (Eds.) Albany, NY: SUNY Press.

Annotated Bibliography

Abi-Nader, J. (1990). "A house for my mother": Motivating Hispanic high school students. *Anthropology and Education Quarterly, 21*(1), 41–57.

Reports on an ethnographic study of successful Hispanic high school students enrolled in a program which motivated students by creating a vision of the future, redefining the image of self, and building a supportive community. The researcher used Vygotsky's theory of learning to explain the success of the program.

Alvarez, R.R. (1988). National politics and local responses: The nation's first successful school desegregation court case. In Trueba, H. & Delgado-Gaitan, C. (Eds.) *School and society: Learning content through culture.* New York: Praeger.

Documents the successful organizing efforts of Mexican parents in the 1930s in San Diego County. The parents attempted to change the policy of school segregation of Mexican-American children. Parents successfully challenged town and state segregationist policy in a local court decision handed down in 1931. The case is known as *Roberto Alvarez v. the Board of Trustees of the Lemon Grove School District.*

Arias, B. (1986). The context of education for Hispanic students: An overview. *American Journal of Education, 95*(1), 26–57.

Presents a summary of data on educational attainment of Hispanic students in K through 12, focusing on segregative patterns in schooling, partly as a result of housing demographics. Classifies three types of isolation in education and discusses the impact.

Clemant, R. (1980). Ethnicity, contact, and communicative competence in a second language. In Giles, H., Robinson, W.P., & Smith, P.M. (Eds.) *Language: Social psychological perspectives.* Oxford: Pergamon.

Proposes a model of second language acquisition in which primary and secondary motivational processes influence language learning. The former is a balance between a desire to integrate and a fear of assimilation, while the latter is the level of self-confidence arising from frequent and pleasant contact with members of the target language group. Distinguishes between language learning in a unicultural and multicultural setting.

Collier, V. (1989). Academic achievement, attitudes, and occupations among graduates of two-way bilingual classes. Paper presented at the annual meeting of the American Education Research Association, San Francisco, CA.

Presents findings from a descriptive study of Hispanic and Anglo graduates of an elementary two-way bilingual program. Subjects, now in their early twenties, were found to have maintained their bilingualism as well as a high level of social interactions with people from both cultural groups and had chosen work situations which utilized their bilingualism.

Cummins, J. (1986). Empowering minority students: A framework for intervention. *Harvard Education Review, 56,* 18–36.

Presents a theoretical framework for empowering minority students based on a socio-political analysis, with clear implications for pedagogy. The framework presents four dimensions in schooling which can lead to the empowerment or disablement of minorities: cultural/linguistic incorporation, community participation, pedagogy, and assessment.

Delgado-Gaitan, C. (1987). Traditions and transitions in the learning process of Mexican children: An ethnographic view. In Spindler, G. & Spindler, L. (Eds.) *Interpretive ethnography of education: At home and abroad.* Hillsdale, NJ: Lawrence Erlbaum Associates.

Describes an ethnographic study of Mexican children at home and at school in Los Portales, California. The discontinuity between the home, community, and school in three major areas is examined: collectivity-competitiveness, authoritarian-egalitarian, and multidimensional-unidimensional. The study concludes that these Mexican students' strengths are overlooked within the American classrooms.

Erickson, F. (1987). Transformation and school success: The politics and culture of educational achievement. *Anthropology and Education Quarterly, 18*(4), 335–356.

Reviews and critiques two theories on low academic achievement among minority students and attempts a synthesis. Calling for culturally responsive pedagogy, the article focuses on the central importance of student-teacher trust which is disrupted when teachers believe their mission is to impose cultural hegemony.

Fishman, J.A. (1989). *Language and ethnicity in minority sociolinguistic perspective.* Avon, England: Multilingual Matters.

A minority perspective on ethnicity and language, this work discusses the link between ethnicity and language, language maintenance and language shift, and language policy in the United States.

Gardner, R.C. & Lambert, W.E. (1972). *Attitudes and motivation in second language learning.* Rowley, MA: Newbury House.

A seminal work identifying ethnocentrism as a barrier to language learning. Twelve years of studies in the United States and Philippines are summarized. The main finding is that second language learners' attitudes toward the target language group influence ability to learn a second language. Distinguishes between integrative and instrumental motivational orientations. With the exception of Franco-Americans studying French, subjects in the studies were foreign language students.

Genesee, F. (1987). *Learning through two languages.* Cambridge, MA: Newbury House.

An overview of research on Canadian French immersion programs and some two-way bilingual programs in the U.S. Presents a sociocultural model of minority group education which takes into account both minority group factors and educational factors.

Genesee, F., Rogers, P., Holobow, N. (1983). The social psychology of second language learning: Another point of view. *Language Learning, 33*(2), 209–224.

Describes a Canadian study of adolescent English-speakers whose proficiency in French was found to correlate positively with their perception of support for their language learning from the French-speaking community and with their willingness to belong to social groups with French speakers.

Gougis, R.A. (1986). The effects of prejudice and stress on the academic performance of Black-Americans. In Neisser, U. (Ed.) *The school achievement of minority children.* Hillsdale, NJ: Lawrence Erlbaum Associates.

Describes findings from an experiment which suggest that exposure to a racist atmosphere can impair cognitive functioning among minority students. African American college students in an experimental group given a memorization task showed higher levels of anxiety, spent less time studying, and showed significantly less recall of the material than students in a control group who were not exposed to any racist behaviors.

Heath, S.B. (1983). *Ways with words*. Cambridge, England: Cambridge University Press.

An ethnographic study of communication between mothers and preschool children in three communities in a small Southern town: working-class white, working-class black, and middle-class white. Identifies differences in the way language is used by the respective groups, causing disorientation and discontinuity for the working-class children when they enter school.

Heath, S.B. (1986). Sociocultural contexts of language development. In *Beyond language: Social and cultural factors in schooling language minority students*. Los Angeles, CA: Evaluation, Dissemination and Assessment Center, California State University.

Presents the view that academic success depends less on the language children know than on the ways children use language, and that these are largely culturally determined. Summarizes research on how language is used in Mexican-American, Chinese-American, and Indochinese-American families and communities, and proposes that schools have a responsibility to adapt.

Hornberger, N. (1990). Extending enrichment bilingual education: Revisiting typologies and redirecting policy. Paper presented at the American Educational Research Association, Boston, MA.

Reviews existing bilingual education typologies, arguing for a framework consisting of three models: transition, maintenance, and enrichment. Presents a case study of enrichment bilingual education, a two-way bilingual school in Philadelphia which provides language majority and language minority (Spanish-speaking) students an integrated program with instruction in both languages.

Hurtado, A. & Rodríguez, R. (1989). Language as a social problem: The repression of Spanish in South Texas. *Journal of Multilingual and Multicultural Development*, *10*(5), 401–419.

Examines schools that define Spanish use by students as a social problem. According to this study, two major justifications are given for suppressing Spanish. One, the schools link students' English assimilation with economic and social mobility. Two, schools claim that English is the public language and Spanish should only be used in private.

Jacobs, L. (1990). An ethnographic study of four Hmong students: Implications for educators and schools. In Goldberg, S. (Ed.) *Readings of equal education: Critical issues for a new administration and Congress, Vol. 10*. New York: AMS Press.

Describes the deep frustration of Hmong students who mentally withdraw after failing to engage meaningfully in learning activities in the classroom.

The study points up the complexity of the cultural and linguistic differences and the task of adjustment.

Kagan, S. (1986). Cooperative learning and sociocultural factors in schooling. In *Beyond language: Social and cultural factors in schooling language minority students*. Los Angeles, CA: Evaluation, Dissemination and Assessment Center, California State University.

Reviews research on effectiveness of cooperative learning techniques in several areas: academic achievement, ethnic relations, and prosocial development, with a focus on findings related to minority students. Reasons for the particular success in raising black and Mexican-American student achievement are discussed. It is hypothesized that the method is culturally congruent because these and other minority groups are more cooperatively oriented.

Kanazawa, H. & Loveday, L. (1988). The Japanese immigrant community in Brazil: Language contact and shift. *Journal of Multilingual and Multicultural Development, 9*(5), 423–435.

Describes the language contact and language shift among different generations of Japanese immigrants in Brazil. The social factors involved in the abandonment of Japanese and its chances of survival are explored. The authors conclude that, in most cases, ethnic identity switch and mother tongue replacement with Portuguese occurs by the third generation.

Kaplan, R. (1988). Cultural thought patterns in inter-cultural education. In Wurzel, J. (Ed.) *Toward multiculturalism*. Yarmouth, ME: Intercultural Press.

Illustrates cross-cultural differences in rhetorical style, causing difficulties for non-native English-speaking students writing compositions at U.S. institutions.

Kiang, P. (1990). *Southeast Asian parent empowerment: The challenge of changing demographics in Lowell, Massachusetts*. Boston: Massachusetts Association for Bilingual Education (ERIC Document Reproduction Service No. UD 027534).

Presents a case study of Southeast Asian and Latino parents organizing successfully to challenge the segregative and inferior educational opportunities offered their children in Lowell, Massachusetts.

Liebkind, K. (1989) The identity of a minority. *Journal of Multilingual and Multicultural Development, 10*(1), 47–57.

Recent social psychological theories are presented on the predicaments of minority identity. The author offers a conflict perspective on society wherein values and definitions created by dominant groups are the cause of constant conflicts and negotiations.

Lindholm, K.J. (1987). *Directory of bilingual immersion programs: Two-way bilingual education for language minority and majority students.* Los Angeles: Center for Language Education and Research, University of California.

Provides a definition of two-way, or dual-language, instruction, and a directory of thirty programs in the United States in operation in 1987.

Macias, J. (1987). The hidden curriculum of Papago teachers: American Indian strategies for mitigating cultural discontinuity in early schooling. In Spindler, G. & Spindler, L. (Eds.) *Interpretive ethnography of education: At home and abroad.* Hillsdale, NJ: Lawrence Erlbaum Associates.

Identifies several sources of cultural discontinuity for Papago (Arizona) children entering tribal preschools with an emphasis on verbal performance and interference with autonomy. Describes the ways in which Papago teachers attempted to mitigate the discontinuity by introducing experiences of mainstream education while reinforcing children's native culture, language, and interactional styles.

Malik, A.M. (1990). A pscholinguistic analysis of the reading behavior of EFL-proficient readers using culturally familiar and culturally nonfamiliar expository texts. *American Educational Research Journal, 27*(1), 205–223.

Presents findings from a study of oral reading behavior of 15 Iranian college students studying in the United States. Subjects' reading comprehension and reading strategies such as predicting, confirming/correcting, and integrating were significantly enhanced when given text that was culturally familiar, compared to text that was not.

Massachusetts Department of Education, Office of Educational Equity (1990). *Two-way integrated bilingual education.* Quincy, MA: Massachusetts Department of Education.

Profiles in some depth four two-way bilingual programs operating in Massachusetts public schools. Concludes with an essay which analyzes the need for bilingual programs that are integrative in nature and identifies factors in successful integrated bilingual schools.

Montero-Sieburth, M. & Pérez, M. (1987). "Echar pa'lante," moving onward: The dilemmas and strategies of a bilingual teacher. *Anthropology and Education Quarterly, 18,* 180–189.

Reports on an ethnographic study of a Puerto Rican bilingual high school teacher, describing her culturally congruent relationships with students, handling of curricular issues, and definition of her own role.

Nelde, P.H. (1989). Ecological aspects of language contact or how to investigate linguistic minorities. *Journal of Multilingual and Multicultural Development*, *10*(1), 73–86.

Discusses minorities in danger of losing their languages in distinct sociolinguistic situations. Argues that an ecological approach is of prime importance in the analysis of linguistic/ethnic contact areas in which one or more languages are in danger of dying out. Discusses data collection methods to discover the real language situation in these areas, which conceal the linguistic realities. Emphasizes the sociological and psychological aspects of linguistic contact.

Nine Curt, C.J. (1984). *Non-verbal communication* (2nd ed.). Fall River, MA: Evaluation, Dissemination and Assessment Center.

Discusses variations in non-verbal communication patterns between Puerto Ricans and Anglos. Includes the report on a study among New York-born Puerto Rican children who retained the ability to understand Puerto Rican gestures even when they did not understand Spanish.

Ogbu, J. (1987a). Variability in minority responses to schooling: Non-immigrants vs. immigrants. In Spindler, G. & Spindler, L. (Eds.) *Interpretive ethnography of education: At home and abroad*. Hillsdale, NJ: Lawrence Erlbaum Associates.

Explains variations in academic achievement among minority students by differentiating between two kinds of minorities: immigrants and castelike minorities (blacks, Puerto Ricans, Native Americans, Chicanos). Although both groups encounter cultural discontinuities and racism in American educational settings, castelike minorities respond by developing a cultural frame of reference in opposition to the dominant group. This causes them to resist schooling because of perceived assimilationist pressures.

Orfield, G. (1986). Hispanic education: Challenges, research, and policies. *American Journal of Education*, *95*, 1–25.

Provides an overview of U.S. governmental policies toward Hispanic students in the twentieth century, from "Mexican" schools to bilingual education programs.

Oller, J., Baca, L., & Vigil, F. (1977). Attitudes and attained proficiency in ESL: A sociolinguistic study of Mexican Americans in the Southwest. *TESOL Quarterly*, *11*, 173–183.

Describes a study of Mexican American women which found that higher proficiency in English correlated with more negative attitudes about Americans. Disputes the validity of the Gardner and Lambert hypothesis that integrative orientation is associated with successful language learning.

Ortiz, F.I. (1988). Hispanic-American children's experiences in classrooms: A comparison between Hispanic and non-Hispanic children. In Weis, L. (Ed.) *Class, race, and gender in American education.* Albany, NY: SUNY Press.

Reports on a six-year study of observations in 96 elementary classrooms which identified the inferior quality of educational services received by Hispanic students, both in bilingual and non-bilingual classrooms. In the former, resources were more limited and teachers less competent and experienced. In the latter, Hispanic students experienced teacher bias and lowered expectations.

Philips, S. (1972). Participant structures and communicative competence: Warm Springs children in community and classroom. In Cazden, C., John, V., & Hymes, D. (Eds.) *Functions of language in the classroom.* New York: Teachers College Press.

Analyzes participant structures in a Native American community and in classrooms attended by the children, concluding that Native American students do not participate verbally in classrooms because the social conditions, particularly norms of participation, are unfamiliar.

Ramírez, M. (1988). Cognitive styles and cultural democracy in action. In Wurzel, J. (Ed.) *Toward multiculturalism.* Yarmouth, ME: Intercultural Press.

Presents a study supporting the theory of culturally determined learning styles. Concludes that the failure of many Mexican American children in American schools may be due to their field sensitive learning styles.

Sindell, P. (1988). Some discontinuities in the enculturation of Mistassini Cree children. In Wurzel, J. (Ed.) *Toward multiculturalism.* Yarmouth, ME: Intercultural Press.

Identifies some of the cultural discontinuities experienced by Cree children in Canadian government-run residential schools. Differences in role expectations, values, and interactional styles are discussed.

Suárez-Orozco, M. (1987). "Becoming somebody": Central American immigrants in U.S. inner-city schools. *Anthropology and Education Quarterly, 18*, 287–299.

Reports on an ethnographic study of recent Central American immigrants in American high schools, describing students' abilities to overcome numerous obstacles and achieve academic success. This is attributed in part to students' ties with relatives in their homelands and their tendency to make mental comparisons with the war-torn situations they left behind.

Tapia, M.R. (in press). Motivational orientations, learning, and the Puerto Rican child. In Ambert, A.N. & Alvarez, M.D. *Puerto Rican children on the mainland: Interdisciplinary perspectives.* New York: Garland.

Reports on a study comparing the motivational orientations of Puerto Rican and Anglo American students. The author found Puerto Rican children to be more cooperatively oriented and less competitively oriented than Anglo American children. She suggests that the structure of school activities exclusively on a competitive or individualistic basis may be hindering the emotional well-being and/or academic performance of Puerto Rican children. She offers specific suggestions for adapting classroom activities to promote learning in children who come from culturally diverse backgrounds.

Teitelbaum, H. & Hiller, R.J. (1977). Bilingual education: The legal mandate. *Harvard Education Review, 47,* 138–170.

Discusses the history of the legal mandate for bilingual education, as of 1977. Addresses the potential conflicts with desegregation legislation and argues that they need not be at odds.

Trueba, H. (1989). *Raising silent voices: Educating the linguistic minorities for the 21st century.* New York: Newbury House.

Presents an overview of effective schooling for linguistic minority students, using a Vygotskian theoretical framework. Of particular interest is a study describing students who had been labeled learning disabled but who, according to the Stress Hypothesis presented, had entered into a cycle of depression, withdrawal, and despair originally arising from culture shock.

Vogt, L., Jordan, C. & Tharp, R. (1987). Explaining school failure, Producing school success: Two cases. *Anthropology and Education Quarterly, 18*(4), 276–286.

Describes innovations and successes of the Project KEEP program for native Hawaiian children, using culturally congruent teaching methods. Describes attempts to replicate the model on a Navajo reservation, with only partial success, suggesting that specific cultural differences lead to school failure, and that culturally appropriate responses are necessary.

Zanger, V. V. (1987). The social context of second language learning: An examination of barriers to integration in five case studies. Unpublished doctoral dissertation, Boston University, 1987.

Presents five case studies of the acculturation experiences of Vietnamese and Puerto Rican adolescents enrolled in transitional bilingual education programs. Their isolation from the dominant culture is attributed to stigmatization, structural isolation, and acculturative patterns. Students' reactions to stigmatization are found to result in behaviors resulting in academic underachievement or in limited second language development.

Zanger, V.V. (in press). "Not joined in": Intergroup relations and access to literacy for Hispanic youth. In Ferdman, B. & Ramirez, A. (Eds.). Albany, NY: SUNY Press.

Analyzes perceptions of Hispanic high school students about intergroup relations. Concludes that at one school, access to conditions that promote literacy development are denied Hispanic students in three ways: the failure of the school to incorporate students' language and culture; the racist school climate; and the breakdown in trust between Hispanic students and many of their teachers.

CHAPTER II

The Acculturation of Ethnolinguistic Minorities

Nancy Cloud

Introduction

In the mid-1930s the study of acculturation was formally defined by the Social Science Research Council as part of the domain of cultural anthropology. It was defined as "those phenomena which result when groups of individuals having different cultures come into continuous first-hand contact with subsequent changes in the original pattern of either or both group" (Redfield, Linton & Herskovits, 1936, p. 149). Other definitions have also been advanced. Acculturation refers to changes in people's social and work activities as well as their thinking patterns, values, and self-identification (Gordon, 1964). Acculturation has also been defined as the acquisition of the values and behaviors of the majority culture by members of a minority group (culture) (García & Lega, 1979). Thus, the term acculturation implies a complex process of change brought about by the contact of one group with another. The process includes physical changes, biological changes, cultural changes, changes in social relationships, psychological changes, and behavioral changes (Lesley, 1988; Berry, Kim, Minde & Mok, 1987).

Acculturation Models

An acculturation continuum exists from totally unacculturated to highly acculturated (Olmedo, 1980; Padilla, 1980). According to this model, individual acculturation is a linear function of the amount of time, extent to which, and purposes for which a person has been exposed to the host culture (Berry, 1980; Leung, 1988). The rate at which the process takes place is a function of variables such as birthplace, generational level, educational level, proficiency in the host country's language, income level, personality characteristics, age, and sex of the acculturating individual. It is affected, as well, by the length of stay in the host country and the amount of social interaction with host country nationals. All of these variables have been studied in acculturation research.

While many Americans continue to view acculturation as a unidirectional process in concert with common metaphors for the process such as the "melting pot," this view of the process has been largely abandoned by researchers who see acculturation as a bidirectional and multi-leveled process.

Current models describe acculturation as a dynamic, multifaceted process (Cuellar, Harris & Jasso, 1980; Szapocznik & Kurtines, 1980) controlled by both extrinsic (physical and social proximity to the host culture) and intrinsic variables (gender and age of the acculturating individual; attitudes toward members of the host culture) (Franco, 1983; Padilla, 1980; Szapocznik & Kurtines, 1980). Researchers now seek to fully capture the multidimensional nature of acculturation in order to accurately establish relationships that might exist between an individual's level of acculturation and other important variables (psychological adjustment and stress level, for example).

Two major aspects of the acculturation process, one external and one internal, have been consistently differentiated in the literature: (1) the process as it takes place along an overt behavioral dimension of functioning, that is, language use, dress, foods consumed; and (2) the process as it takes place with respect to internalized value orientations, that is, preference of one cultural practice over another, normative standards, ethnic identity (Szapocznik & Kurtines, 1980). These variables are present in current models of acculturation and the scales designed to assess the construct.

The component variables of acculturation that are most frequently identified as defining the nature of acculturation fall into three major categories:

1. Linguistic: Language proficiency, preference, and use.
2. Psychological: Values, attitudes, knowledge, and behavior.
3. Sociocultural: Educational, occupational status, mobility, family size, and structure.

A good deal of the research on acculturation conducted to date has focused on defining and establishing valid methods of measuring the construct.

Implications for Educators

This area of inquiry is important to educators serving ethnolinguistic minority students for several reasons. First, level of acculturation is an important characteristic to study in evaluating mental health status, cognitive and personality development, and psychological and educational functioning of language minority students (Olmedo, 1980; Padilla, 1980). It can help explain some of the variance seen in these areas across the various populations of ethnolinguistic minority students. Beyond increasing our understanding of language minority students, level of acculturation is also useful in applied circumstances. For example, a student's level of acculturation is an important piece of information which can be used to improve the design and delivery of instructional interventions, counseling and other support services. In a recent book, Trueba (1989) urges educators to incorporate such information in their pedagogy, and to go beyond the current narrow educational focus on delivering English language development programs to such children to capitalize on language minority children's different experiences, cultural knowledge, and values in order to create "culturally congruent learning environments"—environments that offer the "structural and psychological contextual conditions that permit culturally diverse children to grow intellectually." Thus, this line of research provides essential information which can be used to guide educational policies and programs for acculturating individuals enrolled in U.S. schools.

Current Acculturation Research

The research to be described in this chapter covers a variety of populations: native peoples, identifiable ethnic groups born in the country of interest, as well as sojourners, refugees, immigrants and migrants who enter the country of interest. Each of these groups varies in important ways in terms of the nature of the relationship between the acculturating group and the dominant group and in terms of the level and permanence of contact with the dominant group of host country nationals (Berry, Kim, Minde & Mok, 1987). Both within group (married vs. unmarried immigrants; graduate vs. undergraduate international students) and between group differences (refugees vs. immigrants; migrants vs. reverse migrants) will be explored.

The review will cover research conducted in Australia, Canada, Europe, Greece, and the United States. Studies from North America predominate. The studies to be explored will focus on the acculturative process as experienced by children, adolescents, and adults. As will be seen, the nature of the issues addressed varies according to the age of the population of interest. In all cases, the research to be cited concentrates on a particular age group rather than comparing the process across age groups.

Organization of the Studies

The research reviewed is divided into three main parts: (1) Research which advances conceptualizations of the process or measurement of the construct. These studies are seen as theoretical in nature. (2) Research which looks at relationships between level of acculturation and another variable or variables, such as language proficiency, stress, and TV viewing practices, will be presented. The research will be presented according to type of population studied: sojourners, immigrants, refugees, and migrants and according to age group of the population: children, adolescents, and adults. (3) Research which evaluates intervention efforts. The latter two groups of studies are seen as having practical implications for service providers.

Conceptualizations or Measurement of the Process

The studies discussed in this section explore the conceptualization or measurement of acculturation.

In a study conducted by Wong-Rieger and Quintana (1987) with 434 adults (74 Southeast Asian immigrants, 80 Hispanic immigrants, 96 Southeast Asian sojourners, 94 Hispanic sojourners, and 90 Anglo-Americans), the researchers identified important pre- and postmigration factors that influence the acculturation process. In addition, they validated a non-cultural specific acculturation scale (the Multicultural Acculturation Scale), a 12-item self report scale of cognitive, behavioral, and self-identity changes and a 9-item values orientation scale.

According to the authors, individual premigration factors that influence acculturation are age, language, education, job skills, and previous contact. Sociocultural premigration factors that influence acculturation are religion, kinship structures, level of technology, and level of education. Regarding postmigration factors, the use of ethnic networks seems to play an important role in reducing ethnic assimilation for all groups. They assert that permanent immigrants are more motivated to assimilate than sojourners. The cultural adaptation process involves three levels of social-psychological functioning: cognition, behavior, and self-identity. Cultural similarity between the two, permanent immigrants and sojourners, also determines level of adjustment required. The authors found that ethnic maintenance was not mutually incompatible with Anglo orientation, suggesting that biculturalism is an additive process.

Utilizing previous conceptualizations of type of acculturation (assimilation vs. ethnic separation/ maintenance vs. marginality vs. bicultural integration), Wong-Rieger and Quintana found that Hispanic immigrants tended to be more assimilated than Southeast Asian immigrants, who tended to maintain a strong ethnic orientation. Both Hispanic and Southeast Asian sojourners were biculturally oriented. All groups were more assimilated in their work and place of residence than in friendships, daily activities, and self-identification. According to results of the study, biculturality seemed to be the most satisfying form of acculturation in contrast to early research which suggested that those who assimilated were best adjusted.

In a study of international students, predominantly from Asia, the Middle East, Africa, Europe, and North America, Chen (1988) established a relationship between level of acculturation and intercultural communication competence (effectiveness and appropriateness of communicative interactions). According to Chen, intercultural communication competence consists of four main dimensions: (1) personal attributes (self-concept, self-disclosure, self-awareness, and social relaxation); (2) communication skills (message skills, flexibility, interaction management, and social skills); (3) psychological adaptation (dealing with frustration and stress, alienation, and situational ambiguity); and (4) cultural awareness (social values, social customs, social norms, and the use of time and space). In this study, the international students were asked to rate themselves on the four different aspects enumerated. In addition, two raters from the United States were asked to rate the students' levels of intercultural communication. Results revealed significant correlations among measures of personal attributes, communication skills, psychological adaptation, and cultural awareness. This study is significant because it opens a new line of research into intercultural communicative competence as a measure of biculturality and establishes important interrelationships that need to be better understood between psychological adaptation, cross-cultural communication skills, cultural awareness, and a variety of personal attributes previously known to be important in the acculturation process.

Measurement of the construct has also been advanced through recent research efforts. In 1989, Mainous published a study describing the development of a 9-item index of acculturation based on an individual's role-identity or feelings of insiderness/outsiderness. He asserts that the role identity of an individual as an outsider or foreigner carries with it both a reality for the individual and implications for behavior. Furthermore, role identities have both interpersonal and societal expectations. In a 1979 survey of acculturating Hispanic adults (52 percent Spanish speaking and 48 percent English speaking; 40 percent male and 50 percent female), he found that three factors—language, self-identity as an insider, and self-identity as an outsider—correlated significantly with previously employed indicators of acculturation. He also found that the greater the use of Spanish, the less one conceives of him/herself as a member of the majority culture. This work extends the conceptualization of acculturation to include this heretofore absent aspect (insider/outsiderness) and suggests that perhaps this element can serve as an indicator of level of acculturation. His work is significant because it demonstrates the importance of one's role-identity in the process of acculturation and a relationship between how one sees oneself and one's corresponding behaviors and attitudes.

In a paper presented in 1990, Cloud provides an overview of the various conceptualizations of acculturation, discusses current difficulties in defining and measuring the construct, and reviews available acculturation measures for school-aged populations. This work is useful because it focuses on measurement concerns in relation to school-aged youngsters. In addition, the researcher describes her efforts in developing the Acculturation Questionnaire for Children, a measure designed to be directly administered to preadolescent Puerto Rican children. The measure consists of 33 items, 18 of which assess linguistic dimensions of acculturation (language characteristics of the parents, siblings, friends, and the student) and 15 of which assess sociocultural dimensions of acculturation (ethnic self-identification of the mother, father, and the student; food, music, TV, and movie preferences; church language;

ethnicity of the majority of the student's friends; birthplace of the mother, father and the student; whether the student has lived the majority of his/her life in Puerto Rico or the U.S. mainland and the frequency of travel to Spanish speaking locales). Factor analyses conducted indicate that the measure is based upon three factors: (1) student and sibling language, ethnic identification, and media preference; (2) parent language; and (3) friends' language. Thus, the social subsystems of the student from most intimate outward, seem to be measured by this scale. Analysis of behavior in each social subsystem of the individual may be another way of evaluating and understanding the acculturation process.

The author also reports on results of a pilot study conducted with the measure on the relationship between acculturation and adjustment in 35 urban, preadolescent Puerto Rican children, 18 male and 17 female. Results of the study indicate that the most acculturated group of students was the least well adjusted at home and has the most negative views of school and its importance in their lives. This finding is in concert with the conclusions of the Wong-Rieger and Quintana (1987) study previously cited.

Comparative Studies

An important comparative study of acculturative stress was conducted by Berry, Kim, Minde and Mok (1987). It is important, not only for the findings reported but also for advances in our conceptualizations of the process. The authors provide definitions of acculturation and acculturative stress and divide the types of changes experienced by those undergoing the acculturative process into five areas:

1. Physical changes: housing, climate, and living conditions.
2. Biological changes: nutritional status, diseases, and intermarriage.
3. Cultural changes: alteration or replacement of political, economic, technical, linguistic, religious, and social institutions.
4. Changes in social relationships: new sets of in/out groups and dominance patterns.
5. Physiological changes: behavioral changes and altered mental health status.

These categories assist in organizing studies that have been conducted to date and in assessing the depth of our understanding of the acculturation process for any particular group.

In addition to these theoretical contributions, a series of studies conducted in Canada during the period of 1969–1985 were reviewed by the authors in order to understand acculturation phenomena in terms of their origins and in variations across host societies, acculturating groups and their interactions. The studies they reviewed included native peoples (e.g., Cree, Ojibway), immigrants (e.g., Korean), refugees (e.g., Vietnamese), sojourners (e.g., Malaysian, Chinese), and ethnic groups (Northern and Eastern European groups) in Canada. Rarely have psychological studies of acculturation been comparative in nature across varying types of acculturating groups in a single society. The authors found substantial variation in stress phenomena across types of acculturating groups, across a number of individual difference variables (age, sex, education, attitudes, cognitive styles), and across a number of social variables (amount of contact, social support, and status). Those resisting acculturation, who feel marginalized by the process, tend to be the most stressed by the process, while those accepting a continuing, but not necessarily submissive relationship with the larger society tend to be least stressed. High stress groups included native peoples and refugees, intermediate stress groups were sojourners, and lower stress groups were immigrants and ethnic groups. In general, education, age, gender, cognitive style, prior intercultural experiences, contact experiences, and English knowledge were seen as mediators of stress. They also found greater female stress and more stress if the acculturating individual moved into a more tightly organized or stratified society. Education was a consistent predictor of low stress as was the availability of social support. In addition, forced change was found to create poor attitudes and feelings of resentment which lead to high stress. The greater the participation with the host society, the less stress.

The authors conclude that there may be an optimal level of acculturation stress which alerts a population to changes and motivates and facilitates an effective response, while too much or too little stress may prevent long term adaptation. This hypothesis should be tested in future research and research in other societies to see if the findings reported from the Canadian research are generalizable to other contexts.

Level of Acculturation and Other Variables

Sojourners. Several research studies assessed the adjustment of international students in institutions of higher education according to various indicators. These studies will be described in this section which addresses the acculturation issues of sojourners.

Zelmer and Johnson (1988) studied the employment and educational backgrounds, university and Canadian experiences, and subsequent occupations of a selected group of 28 financially assisted international students, overwhelmingly male, who had completed studies at the University of Alberta between 1972 and 1984. They found the following areas were frequently mentioned as problems in their adjustment to Canada: separation from family members during the period of study or family dislocation problems if the families accompanied the student; financial strains, especially in housing costs; and difficulty adjusting to the Canadian climate. Climate was mentioned most frequently by the sojourners as an aspect that caused serious adjustment difficulties. The students also mentioned language difficulties, racial prejudice, and the manner in which courses were taught and evaluated as problems they faced. In addition, they wished for more contact with faculty members and with Canadian nationals. Despite these challenges, the students felt that their experience added a new dimension to their personal lives and diminished their own intercultural ignorance and that these were valuable learning outcomes.

However, while the students valued the experience their studies abroad had provided, they felt despair and frustration upon return to their native countries. They reported serious reentry problems— a second traumatic transition—as they compared conditions at home to the conditions they had become accustomed to in Canada—and as they unsuccessfully attempted to apply the skills they had learned abroad in their home countries which were predominantly developing nations.

Another study examined directly the issue of reverse culture shock and reentry adjustments among 11 American college students who had been abroad from three months to one year and were returning to a U.S. college (Raschio, 1987). The study was designed to investigate the nature of reentry and the characteristics of readjustment. The author uses Uehara's (1983) definition of reverse shock as "temporary psychological difficulties that a returnee experiences in the initial state of the adjustment process at home after having lived abroad for some time." According to Raschio, reverse shock and the reentry problem are significant components of a sojourner's cross-cultural experience and reentry is often more difficult than the initial adjustment to the foreign culture. The students reported feelings of alienation and separateness on their return that ranged from mild emotional dissonance to a continuing sense of isolation and anomie.

Positive outcomes of the intercultural experience included a sense of personal change, a feeling of uniqueness or autonomy, language improvement, an opportunity for values clarification, and a sense of independence. Students who maintained contact with their families while away (to keep abreast of events at home) and those who had well-defined roles before the intercultural experience had an easier process of reentry than those who did not. Students expressed a need to interact with other returnees and to develop reentry support systems which could be used over a period of time after their return. At the same time 68 percent of colleges and universities surveyed did not offer any type of reentry program for returning students. The author points to the need to see the intercultural experience as a whole, encompassing preparation, time abroad, and reentry phases, for which appropriate supports would be provided by the sponsoring colleges and universities.

A study was done by Schram and Lauver (1988) comparing the alienation from university life felt by international and U.S. students. Alienation is defined by the authors as feelings of powerlessness, meaninglessness, and social estrangement. The authors state that many international students experience a painful adjustment period characterized by vulnerability, loneliness, loss of identity, helplessness, and alienation. A total of 266 international students, 19 percent undergraduate, 60 percent graduate, and 21 percent in special English programs were surveyed. Alienation from university life by international students was found to be more severe than that experienced by U.S. students.

The authors also found that alienation can be predicted on the basis of social contact with host country nationals, graduate status, and geographic home region. Students who had a high amount of social contact with U.S. students, who were pursuing graduate studies, and who were from urban European home regions experienced less alienation from university life than rural, non-European, undergraduate students who spent little time with host country nationals. This latter group is at a greater risk of feeling alienated, a condition which may affect their academic success, retention, and satisfaction with time spent in the United States.

A comprehensive study conducted by Lesley (1988) looked at acculturation and English as a second language (ESL) proficiency among

297 international students. The students were young, predominantly male, predominantly single, and predominantly from Asia, Southeast Asia, and the Middle East.

According to the author, in discussing the complex process known as acculturation, one must describe the preconditions, dimensions, stages, and probable results or effects of acculturation for a given individual or group. Preconditions, such as the level of contact between members of the two groups, must be described and the level of motivation to acculturate must be ascertained. The domains or dimensions of acculturation which must be assessed include: (1) sociocultural: age, ethnic group, length of residence in the U.S.; (2) cognitive: knowledge about various aspects of United States culture and language; (3) affective: attitudes toward U.S. natives and toward English; and (4) behavioral: social interactions with Anglos and use of English-language media. The stages of acculturation refer to where the person is in the process, for example, initial contact, conflict, adaptation.

Various sociocultural characteristics were associated with level of acculturation in the population studied. The author found that younger, single, and undergraduate students evidenced greater acculturation than older, married, and graduate students. Those who had traveled and lived abroad and those who lived longer in the U.S. were more acculturated than those with opposite characteristics. Christians were also more acculturated than members of other religious groups (Moslems, Buddhists, Jews).

Regarding a variety of behavioral characteristics studied, those with Anglo friends, boy/girlfriends, and roommates were more acculturated. This finding confirmed the importance of social interaction in the acculturation process. However, the researcher found that heavy TV watchers were less acculturated. While the extent of thinking in English and type of food eaten were significantly related to level of acculturation in this study, the type of clothing worn was not.

The main purpose of the study, however, was to test Schumann's acculturation hypothesis (1978) which states that the greater the level of acculturation in a particular individual, the greater the language learning will be for that individual. Results of a greater acculturation level in the advanced ESL group (after accounting for group differences in sociocultural characteristics) and the ability of the acculturation scales to predict ESL levels and grades provided empirical support for the claim that acculturation is a significant factor in second language learners. However, Lesley cautioned that no causative relationship can be interpreted from the data, as asserted by Schumann, and that acculturation, while important, is only one of the variables that influence the language learning process. Since it accounted for 7.34–23 percent of the variance in ESL level and grades, most of the variance would still have to be attributed to factors not measured in the study (e.g., aptitude and motivation). Another important finding of the study was that the more acculturated students perceived of themselves as better adjusted to life in the United States and socially better integrated with Anglos. Thus, international students appear to be acculturating at the same time they are learning language. The researcher concludes that acculturation activities deserve a place in the ESL curriculum, including the provision of information about American culture (cognitive change) and the provision of opportunities to meet and interact with Anglos (behavioral change).

An interesting difference between Schram and Lauver's findings and Lesley's is that the former found graduate students to be better adjusted, while the latter found undergraduate students to be better adjusted. This suggests that perhaps something else is controlling the outcome rather than level of study. This aspect requires clarification in future research with the sojourner population.

Immigrants and Ethnic Minorities

A second group of studies reported in current research concerned immigrants and/or ethnic minorities in the process of acculturation.

Adjustment. Adjustment factors in adult Asian Indian immigrants to the United States were reported by Sodowsky and Carey (1987). While only a small portion of their discussion was based on actual research conducted with this population, the article is one of the few sources of information about the acculturation process in Asian Indians, the fourth largest Asian population in the United States, following Chinese American, Filipino American, and Japanese American groups. The authors focus on mostly professional adults. The pilot research study cited involved Asian Indian university students. The authors describe Asian Indian immigrants' prior exposure to Western culture, the voluntariness of their migration, their higher socioeconomic status, and the ethnic social support offered from Asian Indians already in the host country as mediating variables which buffer acculturation stress and facilitate adjustment. The authors cite differences in Asian immigrants' world view and religion and in traditional family organization as sources of conflict that create ambiguity, role confusion, and feelings of marginality in the host society. They claim that Asian Indians have fewer intermarriages with Westerners than other Asians and that the maintenance of social distance from the dominant group sustains traditional cultural values. In addition, they report poorer assimilation into Western culture among Asian Indian women than among their parents created by the more rapid acculturation of children as compared to their parents.

Sources of stress cited include the stereotyping, discrimination, and polarization experienced by Asian Indians in the United States, where host nationals have superficial stereotypic knowledge of Asian Indian culture derived from media and books. They believe that poor self-acceptance, self-hatred, denial of ethnicity, alienation from their ethnic group, and antipathy toward Anglos may be greater among second generation Asian Indians. All of these findings appear to be based on personal observations. However, the authors do report the results of a preliminary study in which the Minnesota Multiphasic Personality Inventory was administered to Asian Indian university students in 1985. Little detail about the study is provided other than the results, which they claim provide strong evidence of hypomania (part of a manic-depressive cycle) among the population. According to the authors, this condition may reflect Asian Indians' drive to achieve and the stress experienced during the adaptation period.

Achievement. The achievement of adolescent immigrant students in Australia in relation to their acculturative status was reported by Bullivant (1988). In this study the author challenges the commonly held belief about immigrant disadvantages in education. He found that, in fact, many second generation high school students from non-English speaking ethnic groups were doing better academically than many Anglo-Australian high school students. He further claimed that "the 'ethnic success ethic' may be ubiquitous to western societies." He found evidence of an "aspiration-motivation hierarchy" at work in which the high aspirations and motivation of certain ethnic groups (groups that were hard working, academically motivated, self-disciplined, well-behaved, reliable, aspiring, and who experienced strong parental support) created academic advantages over other groups. These groups also tended to demonstrate resistance to the forces of "ethnocultural hegemony," where the dominant groups endeavor to maximize their life satisfaction and advantages over other groups by various methods of social closure or exclusion such as through the content and language of the curriculum. The hierarchy Bullivant established placed Melbourne high school students in the following order according to their academic achievement:

Asian (mainly Chinese) and Indo-Asian students, followed by Anglo-Australian middle and high socioeconomic status (SES) students, followed by non-English speaking students (Greeks, Yugoslavs, Italians), followed by Anglo-Australian middle and low SES students together with students from British and northern European immigrant backgrounds. Thus, he found that ethnic and cultural differences complemented by SES differences could be used to explain student achievement in an academic, examination-oriented education system.

He concludes that Anglo-Australians are a new risk category because of their lackadaisical attitudes toward the value of education and their disinclination to work hard to achieve future goals. He also found that as Chinese students acculturated to Australian society, they adopted these negative values and achievement declined.

While Bullivant found that the forces of ethnocultural hegemony were resisted by ethnolinguistic immigrant groups in Australia, he did document that these forces existed in the seven Melbourne high schools he studied. For example, he noted that lack of English proficiency was a barrier to career counseling and that entry into some programs was controlled by performance on exams conducted in English. At the classroom level he found that prejudice and discrimination were most likely to occur in learning interfaces in the transmission of the curriculum. This was especially so in relation to teacher attitudes and expectations which were largely guided by stereotypes about the various groups. He also documented interethnic prejudice and discrimination within the student population, both among the various ethnolinguistic immigrant groups (Asian, Indo-Asian, and non-English speaking) and among Anglo-Australian and the other ethnic groups. For example, the Anglo-Australians often rejected the Asians on the basis of their "braininess" and for "working too hard." Thus, his conclusion that there is no indication that immigrants are disadvantaged in Australian society must be tempered with these findings of widespread discrimination and interethnic tensions.

Biculturality. In a similar line of study, Landsman, Padilla, Clark, Liederman, Ritter and Dornbusch (1990) examined the relation between biculturality (low bicultural and high bicultural) and school grades, the amount of time spent on homework, and academic self-esteem among Chinese, Vietnamese, Mexican, and Central American adolescents. They found wide intragroup variability among Asian and Hispanic adolescents on these factors. They administered a self-report questionnaire to 7,000 students in San Francisco and conducted interviews with 144 adolescents. The quantitative data provided some evidence which showed that highly bicultural students from low- and mid-parent education backgrounds had higher grades and academic self-esteem than did their counterparts who were not bilingual.

Irrespective of level of acculturation, Chinese and Vietnamese students reported spending more time on homework and had higher grades than did Mexican and Central American students regardless of track (college preparation, general, remedial). A substantially larger proportion of Asian students were placed in higher track classes than were Hispanic students. The authors suggest that the student's cultural frame of reference influences achievement, with the Asian students demonstrating friendship patterns and behaviors that positively influence homework completion, academic achievement, and academic self-esteem. This finding is similar to Bullivant's finding that ethnic and cultural differences can be used to explain academic achievement. In addition, the researchers documented that parent education had significant effects on amount of time spent on homework, grades, and academic self-esteem across the student groups.

The case studies conducted provide evidence of a difficult transition for the adolescents, some of whom are estranged from their parents, some of whom feel distanced from native culture peers and at the same time do not identify with the host culture. The study is important, because the quantitative and qualitative data seem to show that bicultural adolescents have advantages over their less bicultural counterparts.

Schooling. Several recent investigative reports focus directly on the status of immigrant children in U.S. schools. First and Carrera (1988) conducted a national investigation to document the experiences of immigrant children and their families with public schools. They sought to identify barriers which impede the students' educational progress and to recommend policies to improve educational services for immigrant children. They conducted 180 structured interviews and 24 case studies with immigrant parents and students residing in the United States for less than five years. Participants came from Mexico, Central and South America, Southeast Asia, Haiti, the Philippines, Africa, and Eastern Europe. Additional immigrants testified at public hearings held around the country. Also, immigration and resettlement advocates, school personnel, and policymakers in heavily impacted states were interviewed. The report produced after this effort describes today's school-aged immigrant population, recounts their immigration experiences and the educational barriers they encounter in U.S. schools. The authors describe the acculturative process largely from the children's perspective and document a variety of problems encountered by children as they acculturate to their new environment. Some of these problems consist of language and cultural barriers, transformations in family roles, the psychological effects of the traumas of war and violence experienced by many prior to coming to the United States, difficulties created by family separation, economic pressures, lack of adequate housing and health care, social isolation often accompanied by racism, and fear of deportation or detention. The report warns of the potential negative outcomes for children that these unique stresses engender. Emotional adjustment problems which can lead to nervous breakdowns and suicide attempts, school failure and alarming drop out statistics, and the breakdown of family systems can result from the stresses experienced.

Another investigative report conducted in California was designed with the same purposes as the national study described above (Olsen, 1988). This report documented the needs and concerns of immigrant children, identified barriers to equal educational opportunity, documented the problems and resource needs of the schools in serving immigrant children, and provided recommendations for the communities, districts, and states to address these needs. There was active collaboration among the two projects and both reports were released simultaneously. The California report describes the state's immigrant population and discusses the data collected largely through personal interviews and public hearings. The researcher interviewed 360 recently arrived immigrant students, ages eleven to eighteen, and 187 community advocates, agency staff, teachers, researchers, and other experts from around the state. Administrators and school personnel in 29 school districts provided information on their programming efforts for immigrant students and programs were visited. In addition, state data on immigrant student achievement were analyzed.

Using first-hand testimony, this report documents the emotional and psychological costs to children who have experienced the disruption and trauma due to war, the confusion and sadness experienced by immigrant children during the acculturation process, unhealthy transformations in family roles experienced where children must negotiate the new environment for their parents, the cultural distancing that often emerges between children and their parents as the children acculturate more rapidly than their parents, the economic strains of life in California, and the hostilities experienced at school and in the surrounding community, including interracial tensions, conflict and social isolation. The report also documents the underachievement of this group using achievement data, dropout statistics, attendance rates, school suspensions, and enrollment figures in higher education. Thus, both qualitative and quantitative data collected point to a grave need for improving services for immigrant children in the process of acculturation in California's public schools.

These reports do not directly assess the acculturative status of the children surveyed, making it difficult to draw conclusions regarding the effect of level of acculturation on adjustment. However, they are important because they provide useful qualitative data regarding the acculturation process through the compilation of first-hand reports by immigrant children and their families. Data of this nature can be used to shape future empirical studies on the acculturation process in immigrant children.

Language use. Two additional studies conducted during this period concerned the use of Spanish by immigrants and the relationships between language use and acculturation.

Thompson (1988) designed a study to assess the impact of the increased publicly sanctioned use of Spanish in the United States on the linguistic assimilation of Hispanics. He looked at a neighborhood in Austin, Texas, which had been studied in 1971 when there was little use of Spanish in government agencies. This neighborhood was selected because of its demographic factors favoring maintenance. Evident in the area were stability, high fertility rate, large percentage of foreign born, wide availability of Spanish language media, and low educational and occupational levels. These factors were useful in assessing the impact of governmental uses of Spanish. Paradoxically, he found that while there was increased Spanish language media use (due to cable TV programming and a corresponding increase in broadcast channels), there was increased English language use in Hispanic homes. He also found that there was increased literacy in Spanish due to bilingual education programs, but that youngsters were speaking more English than before. Finally, he found that there was increased use of Spanish on the job by Hispanics, but that those with the credentials required by the employer to obtain the job had to relearn enough Spanish for use on the job. In summary, he found that the increased use of Spanish was not causing English to be replaced, instead English was interacting with Spanish and Spanish functioning as a social dialect of English. It seemed to be preferred for intimate and informal speech, otherwise English dominated. Another interesting finding reported by the author was that while language shift was evident in the homes, the parents felt that language use was not related to ethnic identity, as suggested by the literature.

A second study on language use was an ethnographic investigation of urban, first-generation Mexican American fifth graders from low-income, Spanish dominant homes (Commins, 1989). The researcher, through participant observation, documented how children's attitudes about themselves and their home language and culture (acquired through interaction in a larger social context) can affect progress in language development and academics. Commins explored the interaction of contextual variables with children's acculturative behaviors. In the study, a Spanish bilingual program had recently been implemented. Attitudes of mainstream teachers toward the new program were generally negative and the program was seen as compensatory in nature. Although limited English proficient children were placed in bilingual classes, Spanish seemed to be used only to clarify instruction, hence it was relegated to a subordinate or supplementary instructional role. Limited English proficient students were generally resistant to Spanish instruction. Instead, they opted for their less well mastered code and were reluctant to use Spanish in the academic context. This limited their opportunities to talk about abstract ideas and use higher cognitive skills at school. At home, the shift to English limited parents' ability to foster linguistic and cognitive development in their children, since parents were by and large Spanish dominant. The researcher documented that children were actively making choices about how they would function both in and out of school. She found that they acted as agents in their educational process both consciously and unconsciously based upon their internalized perceptions of themselves as linguistically different. Their decisions had a negative impact on their achievement. In addition, parents reported a sense of alienation and isolation from their children's schools due to language barriers and the ways in which the school related to non-middle class, non-majority parents. This was seen to further exacerbate the negative self-concepts of students. This study is an important complement to the Thompson study reported earlier. Together they demonstrate how language prestige affects language choice. In addition, these studies provide valuable insights on the process of linguistic acculturation in immigrant and ethnic minority groups.

Behavior. The following studies explore the impact of acculturation on the behavior of immigrant children and adults. The studies deal with the impact of acculturation on foreign children's television use, the effects of acculturation on Hispanic adults' knowledge of AIDS and HIV, and the effects of acculturation on the health behavior of elderly Hispanic women.

Television viewing. Zohoori (1988) reported on the use of television by foreign children in the United States and their Anglo counterparts. Participants were first through fifth grade students from 33 different countries, born outside of the United States, whose parents were not permanent residents or U.S. citizens. They had spent various amounts of time in the United States: 14.5 percent less than 6 months, 26.5 percent from 6 to 18 months, 32.5 percent from 19 to 54 months, and 26.5 percent more than 54 months. The sample was approximately equivalent in males and females surveyed. The researcher found that differences in cultural background lead to differences in TV viewing motivation, program preferences, exposure time, identification with TV characters and belief in the social reality portrayed by TV. Specifically, foreign children appeared to use TV more for learning about others and themselves, liked more educational/informational and adventure programs, exhibited greater identification with TV characters, and believed more strongly in the reality of TV events than the Anglo children studied. A larger number watched TV and they spent more time watching TV than their Anglo counterparts. This pattern was strongest in foreign children with shorter periods of residency. Cultivation effects (the proximity between the audience's perception of social reality and the portrayals of social reality presented by TV) were stronger among children with shorter periods of residency, as would be expected, since they have limited knowledge of their new culture against which to assess the images presented by TV programs. The author cautions that, while TV is an important source of education and information about the U.S. way of life, children who do not have access to alternative sources of information and who lack sufficient real-life experiences in the United States have no means of evaluating the televised portrayals of social reality and, therefore, tend to accept these portrayals without question.

Wu (1989) documented similar patterns in TV viewing habits among Chinese and Puerto Rican youngsters in New York City. She conducted a study to investigate the differences and similarities in television and videotape viewing patterns (amount of viewing and program preferences and parental supervision) among Chinese, Puerto Rican, and non-minority children in the United States. This information is fundamental in understanding how TV affects the socialization of minority children. Participants were 197 students, grades 4 to 6, from three different public schools (94 boys and 103 girls). The sample included 62 white, 77 Puerto Rican (35 born in Puerto Rico and 42 born on the mainland), and 58 Chinese children (28 immigrants and 30 born in the United

States). The results of the study indicated the Puerto Rican children spent about 6.5 hours on TV and videotape viewing per day, while non-minority children spent 3.7 hours, and Chinese children spent 2.1 hours on TV and videotape viewing. The researcher suggests that Hispanic parents may perceive TV viewing as an opportunity to learn English and for accelerating the acculturation process and, therefore, encourage their children to take advantage of TV viewing. She documented that TV was less accessible to the Chinese children because they had fewer TV sets at home compared to the other groups, their parents tended to implement more control over their TV viewing, and there was relatively limited programming available in their native language. Findings from the study indicted that the amount of TV viewing appears to be associated with the number of TV sets at home. Puerto Rican children who were born in Puerto Rico (presumably less acculturated) appeared to spend less time on TV viewing than did their mainland-born counterparts (in contrast to Zohoori's findings). Less acculturated children (migrant/immigrant in this study) also appeared to favor cartoons, which rely on motion and non-verbal communication to convey the plot. According to this study, there are important culturally determined differences between ethnic minority groups and within ethnic minority groups in TV viewing behavior. Cultural and acculturational differences appear to account for these patterns of behavior.

Health issues. A study conducted in San Francisco assessed the effects of gender and acculturation on knowledge of AIDS and HIV among Hispanic adults (Marin & Marin, 1990). The researchers interviewed 460 Hispanic adults (50 percent Central American, 30 percent Mexican American, and 5 percent Puerto Rican). The authors found that acculturation was significantly and strongly associated with knowledge about AIDS and HIV transmission. However, females showed a non-significant trend to have lower scores than males. The less acculturated Hispanics (defined in this study as those who preferred and used Spanish more) had many more erroneous beliefs about the casual transmission of AIDS and were less aware that someone could be affected without looking ill. These acculturation differences persisted even after controlling for level of education, since years of education showed a powerful association to more correct knowledge about AIDS and its transmission.

The highly acculturated Hispanic adults were more likely to correctly respond that someone with HIV can look healthy, that one can have the virus and not the disease and that teens can get AIDS. Less acculturated Hispanic adults were more likely to believe that HIV could be transmitted through casual contact, such as using public toilets, the cough or sneeze of someone with AIDS, contact with mosquitoes or other insects, a handshake, attending school or working with someone with AIDS, or eating in a restaurant where the cook has AIDS. This study has important implications for public health education efforts.

Marks, Solis, Richardson, Collins, Birba and Hisserich (1987) studied 603 elderly Hispanic females in Los Angeles to evaluate the usefulness of cultural factors as predictors of preventive health behavior, such as physical exams, screening for breast cancer, and pap smears. They found that no dimension of cultural assimilation (language familiarity, use, and preference; country of birth; contact with the homeland; attitudes regarding the ethnicity of children's friends) associated strongly or consistently with health behavior. They concluded that cultural factors may have little impact on the health behavior of Hispanics. Access to and availability of services, patients' affective reactions toward screening, and sociodemographic factors (education, age) are stronger determinants of Hispanic health practices and are more useful than cultural variables in understanding Hispanic health care behavior. The authors suggest that although lack of cultural assimilation has been discussed as a strong barrier to utilization of health services by Hispanics, their findings do not support this viewpoint.

The researchers did document, however, that positive health practices were somewhat greater among those who spoke English than among those who did not, but these effects were minimal. This may have been true due to the location of the study in Los Angeles, a large urban center where Spanish is widely spoken, a factor which might lower language and cultural barriers to health services.

When contrasted to the Marin and Marin (1990) study, this line of research raises interesting questions about the differences between the knowledge and behaviors of ethnic minority adults and the factors that influence both.

Refugees

By far the greatest amount of acculturation research reported during the last few years concerns refugee children, adolescents, and adults. Much of this research focuses on a better understanding of refugees' adjustment to this country. The studies explore refugees' psychological status, linguistic assimilation, and changes in cultural practices. Refugees must be distinguished from other immigrants because the motives for leaving their countries are different from other immigrants. Furthermore, persistent memories of the past, an acute sense of loss and trauma that accompanies forced, unplanned, and sudden uprooting, and the inability to return to the homeland, have negative long-term consequences for the psychological adjustment of refugees (Ima & Rumbaut, 1989). The consequences of migration are of greater severity for refugees because the feelings of loss and powerlessness are more intense (Mortland & Egan, 1987). Refugees experience serious disruption in their school and work lives, their family lives, and in their social support systems.

Psychosocial adjustment. Eisenbruch (1988) discussed the relationship of adequate (primary) cultural development to the mental health status of refugee children and their need to grieve and experience a sufficient bereavement process for their uprootedness. He claims that uprooting is not merely a phenomenon of physical relocation, rather, it disrupts the continuity of an individual's concept of selfhood and the "structure of meaning," that is, the conceptual organization of understanding one's surroundings. The greater the "cultural leap," the greater the difficulties, according to the author. Massive grief reactions, coupled with the absence of appropriate emotional and social support groups, have negative long-term effects, even after an apparently successful early adjustment. Children are seen as especially vulnerable because their personal equilibrium depends on the social equilibrium around them. Their individual health depends on their community's health.

While Eisenbruch stresses the long-term danger for those who have not really worked through who they were and who they are, he also discusses the resilience demonstrated by some children. He ascribes this resiliency to a positive personality disposition, a supportive family milieu, and an external societal agency that functions as a supply system to reinforce the child's coping efforts. Recommendations for practitioners include efforts designed to reduce alienation, increase the child's competence and personal resources to cope with the stress of cultural bereavement, and reinforce the child's identity as a member of a specific cultural group.

Lee (1988) presents an assessment framework for analyzing adjustment in Southeast Asian refugee adolescents. She has a special concern for this population since 40 percent to 50 percent of refugees are younger than eighteen years old, and she believes that adolescents are at particular risk because they are experiencing three types of stress simultaneously. These types of stress are physiological and emotional upheavals as adolescents, social and psychological adjustment problems as refugees, and intercultural conflicts caused by immense value system differences between Asian and Anglo cultures. Adolescent refugees have been documented to be significantly depressed and to manifest a variety of distress symptoms, such as somatic complaints, sleep disturbances, tantrums, violent antisocial behavior, and marked withdrawals. Suicide attempts, psychosis, disruptive behaviors, school crises, as well as difficulty in forming friendships, are also prevalent. A serious problem for this group is that of identity crisis or feeling of belonging to no culture.

Lee argues that the degree of acculturation of refugee adolescents depends on the number of years in the United States, cultural compatibility between their home culture and the host culture, age at the time of immigration, language use at home, the nature of the school environment, and the acculturation rate of parents and other family members. In working with this population, the author discusses the need to assess four major stressors: migration stress, acculturation stress, life cycle stress, and family stress (intergenerational conflicts). In addition, the service provider should assess the personal strengths and the culturally specific responses to mental health and psychiatric problems of the individual. Programmatic responses should be built around such an assessment.

A ten-year longitudinal study on the psychosocial adjustment of Hmong refugees was reported recently by Westermeyer, Neider and Callies (1989). It paints a bleak picture of the adjustment of Hmong refugee adults in this country. A self-rating scale and questionnaire were administered to Hmong individuals, sixteen years and older, living in Minnesota. The study assessed the acculturative skills and cultural affiliation of the population, that is, education, English speaking ability, and proximity/calls/visits to other Hmong. While the sample was predominantly employed, had attended some school, and could speak some English, a large number had no or limited English fluency and episodic rather than regular employment. Both males and females were isolated from the societal mainstream and were becoming even more isolated from their spouses and children as the latter adopted more U.S. mainstream culture social characteristics. The researchers concluded that Hmong adult refugees had acculturated less than other Southeast Asian groups. According to the authors, the picture is worsening, as Hmong refugees who arrived later than the group studied have been documented as less successful at acculturating than previous groups.

Mortland and Egan (1987) focused their ethnographic research on Vietnamese youth in foster care. There are over 4,000 foster youngsters from Vietnam in the United States. The majority are adolescents. The study was prompted by a review of the literature and previous research conducted by the authors which indicated that unaccompanied refugee minors in foster care in the United States had enormous adjustment difficulties and used specific strategies to cope with these difficulties.

Previous research had demonstrated that refugee adolescents experience a tremendous sense of loss, confusion over their sense of identity and self-worth, and an overwhelming sense of bewilderment at the new world and its demands. Therefore, they are at risk of physical and mental illness. The longer the migratory process endures and the greater the cultural distance between the old and new environments, the greater the adjustment difficulties. Since the support of family members is an important aid in adjusting to a new society, youngsters traveling without relatives are extremely vulnerable.

In this study, Mortland and Egan conducted interviews and acted as participant observers in 16 foster care families. They documented the adjustment difficulties of Vietnamese adolescents in foster homes caused by their experiences as refugees and exacerbated by efforts to place them in U.S. foster homes, which separated unaccompanied minors from the friends and others with whom they were traveling.

Deep level misunderstandings and conflicting expectations among the adolescents and their foster parents were documented. These problems were created, in large part, by the unrealistic ideas the youth held about the financial status of U.S. families, difficulties in accepting new parental figures (especially the foster mother), fear, a sense of helplessness and anger to be in such a situation, frustration, despair, feelings of loss, lack of self-worth, and experiences of loneliness and guilt. Unpredictable behavior in the adolescents and conflict between the adolescents and their foster families resulted. Arguments centered around several issues. Gender-based expectations related to food preparation and consumption were a source of conflict when male adolescents expected their foster mothers to prepare all their food and conform to their preferences, while the mothers expected the youth to prepare food for themselves and consume whatever was prepared. Arguments arose from the use of the monthly foster care stipend when the refugees saw their U.S. families as wealthy and not needing this money. The youth felt that the money was theirs and should be used as they saw fit rather than applied to their share of the expenses in the home. Conflicts also surfaced from differing expectations on health practices, degree of independence allowed (resistance to restrictions imposed by the foster family) and family organization (who does the chores). In general, the concept of foster care was foreign to the youth who were accustomed to extended family members assuming responsibility for individuals in need, rather than social institutions providing such services with a fee involved.

Adjustment strategies used by the youth were to: (1) use old information as a basis for interpreting events ("if you have a phone, you are rich, expense is not a problem, so I can call whomever I want for as long as I want"); (2) concentrate on the acquisition of high status material possessions (with corresponding expectations that the foster families should give them expensive high status items); (3) acquire information from every possible source, repeating questions to check accuracy and consistency across sources (peers of the same sex, age, nationality, and language with similar goals, adjustment difficulties, and living situations were seen as the most trusted); and (4) maintain previously established levels of independence (which created resentment of rules and requirements at home and at school). This study points to the need for intensive culturally appropriate programs which respond to the identified needs of unique populations of refugees, such as unaccompanied minors, and which provide support to the agents selected to facilitate their adjustment process for the benefit of all concerned.

Academic Achievement. Ima and Rumbaut (1989) examined the successes and problems of refugee youth in their educational and occupational attainments and aspirations, social adjustment, and prospects for economic self-sufficiency. The study was conducted by the Southeast Asian Refugee Youth Study in San Diego. Using data from the study, the authors identified the social background characteristics found to be most significantly associated with language status and academic achievement in Vietnamese, Chinese-Vietnamese, Lao, and Khmer speaking adolescents.

They found that Vietnamese and Chinese-Vietnamese speakers were extraordinarily high achievers in mathematics, while Lao and Khmer speakers had more modest math skills and were in the bottom quartile in reading. However, these groups surpassed the achievement of African Americans, Hispanics, and Pacific Islanders. The authors argue that there are cultural effects on patterns of learning and educational attainment and thus confirm studies by Bullivant (1988) and Landsman, Padilla, Clark, Liederman, Ritter and Dornbusch (1990).

They also found that among the various populations of refugees, ethnicity, age, time in the U.S. (an important correlate of the adaptive process), and parents' socioeconomic status accounted for 40 percent of the variance in reading achievement. The more educated the parents, the more time in the United States, and the younger the student, the greater the student's English reading skills when all other variables were controlled. The authors conclude that ethnicity and culture, family and social class background, age and time in the United States, the trauma of the refugee experience, the stress of the acculturation process, and the conditions of survival in this country must be accounted for in designing appropriate services. Furthermore, they suggest that those refugees entering U.S. schools after puberty will generally present more problems since they will have greater difficulties not only in learning English but also with acculturative stress and identity formation during the developmental transition of adolescence. This, of course, would be mediated by the quality of schooling in the home country or during the refugee camp period. This research is important because it highlights important differences within the various refugee populations and identifies some of the factors that contribute to those differences.

An ethnographic study done by Luce (1989) focused on the acculturative process in Vietnamese adolescent refugees. Daily participant observation with six students was conducted over a five-month period in a northeastern suburban high school setting. In addition, contact was maintained with the students over a five-year period. The study sought to determine the nature of cultural conflict experienced at school and in the life adjustment of these students, as well as the factors that seemed to account for their perceived successes and failures in acculturating to U.S. society. Participants agreed that their educational and life opportunities had been enhanced by emigrating to the United States. An underlying factor for their real or perceived success in U.S. schools was their optimistic perspective toward life in their new country. The students saw their new lives as an improvement over conditions that might have existed for them in their nation of origin. This motivated them to achieve. In addition, as a result of entering a new and very different culture, the students developed an inquiring mode of thought useful in problem solving, which helped them in school as well as in life in general. On the other hand, some of the students were not performing well in mainstream classes largely due to the oral and written demands of these classes. Both teachers and students were uncomfortable with the grading system in which ESL students were often graded on the basis of effort and intent rather than by "real achievement." Writing caused the most problems for the students. In addition, the students expressed resentment about being segregated to receive special educational services, such as ESL and tutoring, and devalued these services apparently because there was no differentiation between the services provided to new and continuing ESL students. Acculturation difficulties documented by the researcher appeared related to the students' culturally determined expectations formed on the basis of race, class, and gender which were challenged in their new environment.

Cultural changes. Changes in cultural practices among Southeast Asian refugees in the United States have also been analyzed in a recent research study on changes in food preferences, beliefs, and practices, explored within the context of the acculturation process.

Story and Harris (1988) analyzed the dietary changes among a group of recent Southeast Asian refugee adolescents in Minneapolis. A sample of 207 high school students, grades 10 to 12, all of whom had been in the United States for five years or less, were studied. Participants completed questionnaires to assess their meal and snack patterns, food practices and beliefs, and food preferences and frequencies. The purposes of the study were to understand the nutritional implications of any dietary changes experienced by the youth, obtain baseline information for the design of health curricula, and plan nutrition education programs for Southeast Asian students. There were 62 Vietnamese, 89 Hmong, and 56 Cambodian students in the sample (125 male and 82 female). The youths' households averaged seven individuals. In 56.5 percent of the households there was no father at home (due to death or imprisonment in Southeast Asia among other causes) and one-third were without mothers. Because of this, it was found that a large percentage of the students prepared meals and helped with grocery shopping. Rice was the preferred food among all three ethnic groups, followed by chicken, steak, and fruit (a high status food in Southeast Asia). Ice cream and soda pop were the best liked sweet foods. Cheese was the most disliked food. The ten disliked foods were those generally unavailable in Southeast Asia such as peanut butter, chocolate milk, hot dogs, spaghetti, and pizza. Native foods were preferred by 71 percent of the students overall, by 38 percent of the Hmong, 91 percent of the Vietnamese, and 85 percent of the Cambodians. The Hmong indicated a stronger desire to adopt American food preferences and practices than did the Cambodians and particularly more so than the Vietnamese. Like their U.S. counterparts, breakfast was found to be the most frequently missed meal. However, unlike their U.S. counterparts, less than 25 percent reported between meal snacking. The authors conclude that nutrition and health education programs are needed, since the youth were involved in food selection and preparation and were generally unaware of the food values of new U.S. foods or the effect of sugary foods on their teeth.

Sex differences in language use. Sex differences in English language acculturation and learning strategies among Vietnamese adult refugees in the United States, aged forty to ninety-two, were studied by Tran (1988). The author defined language acculturation as a process that requires immigrants and refugees to learn and use the host language in order to survive and adjust to the new environment. The author used data from the Southeast Asian Refugee Self-Sufficient Study to assess sex differences in English language acculturation and strategies used to improve English among 327 Vietnamese. An older population was used because age has been found to have a negative effect on both social and psychological adjustments among Vietnamese refugees in the United States. Knowledge of English was assessed because English proficiency has been shown to be a determinant of labor participation as well as a predictor of better social-psychological adjustment.

It was found that older Vietnamese women had more problems with the English language than older Vietnamese males. Half of the Vietnamese women were unable to speak English as compared to 13 percent of the males; 55 percent of the women could hardly read English or not at all, while 16.6 percent of males fell into the same category. Thirty-three percent of women did not know English well enough to shop for food; 58 percent did not read street signs; 84 percent could not use English to talk about health problems; 86 percent could not read the newspaper; 85 percent did not speak well enough to apply for aid; and 71 percent could not use English to call the police or fire departments. Overall, the researcher found that the majority of older Vietnamese did not have adequate skills in the English language to function normally in various social settings.

Males were also more likely than women to use various learning strategies to improve their English language skills. For example, men enrolled in ESL classes more frequently, practiced English with English speaking friends more, and watched more TV or listened to English radio stations more than women. Neither the men nor women surveyed used a tutor or lived in U.S. mainstream neighborhoods as a strategy for improving English language skills.

In addition, the author also documented communication barriers between grandchildren and grandparents and other intergenerational conflicts as the younger Vietnamese acculturate more rapidly than their older family members.

Tran argues that the gender differences documented might be attributed either to cultural beliefs and the differential socialization of males and females or to other factors, such as education, intelligence, language aptitude, motivation, and situational anxiety. The researcher concludes that language acculturation should be considered an intervening variable in examining the socioeconomic and social-psychological adjustment of older immigrants and refugees.

Migrants

The following studies are concerned with acculturation issues of migrants. The academic achievement of migrant children in European schools and migrant, reverse migrant, and circulatory migrant adolescents in Puerto Rico will be discussed.

Academic achievement. In a study done by the Organisation for Economic Co-operation and Development (1987), the children of migrants (such as Turkish children in Switzerland) were found to be underachieving and overrepresented in special education placements, largely due to lack of linguistic acculturation. The report states that in countries where streaming exists, foreign children represent the highest proportion of pupils in the slow, less "noble" streams, and that there are inequities in programming which leave migrants' children badly equipped to enter the labor market. Data such as those reported are useful in seeing overall trends on how acculturating children are faring educationally across wide geographic areas in order to stimulate major policy changes.

Adjustment. In a study of Puerto Rican migrants, return migrants, and circulatory migrants (Prewitt-Díaz & Seilhamer, 1987), the authors discuss the main reasons given in previous analyses for the high incidence of migration both to and out of Puerto Rico. These are, the short distance of emigration required to the mainland, changes in economic conditions, strong family ties, and homesickness. Most return migrants to the island are in intermediate and high schools. The children of return migrants have been reported as hating school, disliking their teachers, feeling a lack of identity (not knowing whether they are Puerto Ricans or Americans), facing language and cultural problems in both directions, feeling lost, and wanting to return to the United States. Previous findings cited by the authors concluded that these children lacked confidence, demonstrated feelings of inferiority and rejection, possessed low self-esteem, felt ambivalence as to their natural identity, and lacked understanding of the culture and customs of Puerto Rico even though they are of Puerto Rican heritage.

The Prewitt-Díaz and Seilhamer study was conducted in seven school districts in Puerto Rico with 273 randomly selected students, aged fifteen to eighteen years, in grades 10 to 12. Of the students sampled, 52 were non-migrants, 53 were migrants, 41 were return migrants, and 127 were circulatory migrants. The researchers found a relationship between the students physical adjustment and their cultural adjustment. As the level of cultural adjustment increased, evidence of physical adjustment became more noticeable and students more willing to verbalize physical symptoms. There was also a relationship between social adjustment and adjustment to school: The higher the social adjustment, the higher the adjustment to school. School adjustment was the best predictor of Spanish reading achievement. The authors report significant group differences between non-migrants and the three groups of migrant students on a reading achievement test. They argue that differences in vocabulary knowledge affected performance on tasks requiring reading ability.

Intervention Programs

While recommendations abound in the literature on intervention strategies to facilitate acculturation, few empirical studies exist that evaluate the effectiveness of recommended practices. A notable exception is a study conducted by Peterson and Peppas (1988) in which peer helpers were used to facilitate school adjustment of American sojourners in an overseas school. The study was conducted at the American Community School in Athens, Greece. The researchers selected 84 high school students, grades 9 to 12, and randomly assigned them to three groups: treatment, placebo, and control. Students were further assigned roles of helper or help recipient. Those in the treatment group learned how to provide peer support to acculturating sojourners. Students in the placebo group were placed in pairs and assigned roles of helper or help recipient, but no training was provided on how to provide support. The control group formed a base against which to test the effects of the other conditions. Dependent variables were achievement, adjustment, and self-control. Treatment group helpers showed significant increases in achievement over control group helpers but not in comparison with treatment group help recipients. Help recipients showed significant improvement in self-concept and adjustment compared with control group recipients. Placebo group recipients also showed a significant increase in achievement following nine weekly meetings with helpers, indicating that meeting with another student who wants to be helpful has a positive effect on achievement. The study showed that students can benefit from peer interaction and from peer helper training and that adjustment can be facilitated by trained and untrained peer helpers.

Given the wealth of unresearched recommendations made to practitioners, much more work is needed in this important area to establish effective intervention practices to facilitate the process of acculturation.

Conclusion

The research reported in this chapter has established important relationships between acculturation and the following variables: language proficiency, academic achievement, stress, social and emotional adjustment, self-concept/self-identity, and a variety of behaviors, such as TV viewing and health practices. These relationships have been found to be mediated by a range of sociodemographic characteristics, such as gender, age, level of education, previous intercultural experience, social distance between the home and the host countries, personality characteristics, and socioeconomic status.

Important differences have been noted across type of acculturating population. The needs of refugees are seen to be quite different from those of migrants and those of migrants are seen to be quite different from those of sojourners and immigrants. The social context into which these groups are acculturating is also important to the outcome.

Thus, the picture of the acculturation process is becoming increasingly complex. Each study contributes to our further understanding of the process and the issues it engenders for the individuals engaged in the process. Our ability to facilitate the process and provide an appropriate response will ultimately depend on a comprehensive understanding of the process in all its complexity.

Future Research Directions

Future research will need to clarify the stability of gender differences, especially in societies where the traditional roles of males and females are changing. Research is needed to provide more insight on the interactive nature of the process, where not only the effects on the subordinate group are studied but also the effects on the dominant group. The study of U.S. foster care families cited in this chapter shows a need to understand the effect such intercultural experiences have on groups that come in contact with one another. In addition, considerable research is needed to identify how contextual variables interact with the process. For example, we need to understand how language policies of the host country or attitudes of refugee sponsors affect the acculturation process. We currently have hypotheses about these relationships, but they are largely untested.

In addition, a host of other behaviors of acculturating individuals (for example, use of computers and other forms of technology, dietary practices, dating behavior, use of public transportation) need to be studied to see how level of acculturation affects behavior in a variety of spheres.

More emphasis on school-aged populations is warranted, with attention paid to specific ethnolinguistic groups underrepresented in the research reviewed for this volume, such as native peoples, Haitians, Dominicans, Central Americans, Middle Easterners, among others. In addition, the large numbers of Puerto Rican youngsters moving back and forth between the U.S. mainland and the island underscore the need for research such as the Prewitt-Díaz and Seilhamer study. Many pressing educational questions need to be answered in relation to the acculturation and reacculturation processes experienced by these youngsters. Research examining the family unit as a whole is needed to understand the acculturative and reacculturative processes as experienced by the Puerto Rican migrant, reverse migrant, and circulatory migrant families and the variables which mediate the stresses inherent in these processes. Such research is needed to shape the response of school personnel to the broad spectrum of acculturating populations present in today's schools.

References

Berry, J.W. (1980). Acculturation as varieties of adaptation. In Padilla, A.M., (Ed.). *Acculturation: Theory, models and some new findings* (pp. 9–26). Boulder, CO: Westview Press.

Berry, J.W., Kim, U., Minde, T., & Mok, D. (1987). Comparative studies of acculturative stress. *International Migration Review, 21*(30), 491–511.

Bullivant, B.M. (1988). The ethnic success ethic challenges conventional wisdom about immigrant disadvantages in education. *Australian Journal of Education, 32*(2), 223–243.

Chen, G. (1988). *Relationships of the dimensions of intercultural communication competence.* Paper presented at the annual meeting of the Eastern Communication Association, Baltimore, MD (ERIC Document Reproduction Service No. ED 297 381).

Cloud, N. (1990). *Measuring level of acculturation in bilingual bicultural children.* Paper presented at the annual meeting of the American Educational Research Association, Boston, MA.

Commins, N.L. (1989). Language and affect: Bilingual students at home and at school. *Language Arts, 66*(1), 29–43.

Cuellar, I., Harris, L.C. & Jasso, R. (1980). An acculturation scale for Mexican American normal and clinical populations. *Hispanic Journal of Behavioral Sciences, 2*(3), 199–217.

Eisenbruch, M. (1988). The mental health of refugee children and their cultural development. *International Migration Review, 22*(2), 282–300.

First, J.M. & Carrera, J.W. (1988). *New voices: Immigrant students in U.S. Public Schools.* Boston, MA: National Coalition of Advocates for Students.

Franco, J.N. (1983). *Acculturation levels of Mexican American children: Measurement issues and implications for mental health.* Paper presented at the Acculturation and Mental Health Among Hispanics Conference, Albuquerque, NM (ERIC Document Reproduction Service No. ED 254 359).

Garcia, M. & Lega, L.I. (1979). Development of a Cuban ethnic identity questionnaire. *Hispanic Journal of Behavioral Sciences, 1*(3), 247–261.

Gordon, M.M. (1964). *Assimilation in American life.* New York: Oxford University Press.

Ima, K. & Rumbaut, R.G. (1989). Southeast Asian refugees in American schools: A comparison of fluent-English-proficient and limited-English-proficient students. *Topics in Language Disorders, 9*(3), 54–75.

Johnson, P.J. (1989). Changes in financial practices: Southeast Asian refugees. *Home Economics Research Journal, 17*(3), 241–252.

Landsman, M., Padilla, A., Clark, C., Leiderman, H., Ritter, P., & Dornbusch, S. (1990). *Biculturality and academic achievement among Asian and Hispanic adolescents.* Paper presented at the National Association for Bilingual Education Conference, Tucson, AZ.

Lee, E. (1988). Cultural factors in working with southeast Asian refugee adolescents. *Journal of Adolescence, 11*, 167–179.

Lesley, T. (1988). Acculturation and ESL proficiency among international students. Unpublished doctoral dissertation, University of Southern California. *Dissertation Abstracts International,* 49/12A, 3642.

Leung, E.K. (1988). Cultural and acculturational commonalities and diversities among Asian Americans: Identification and programming considerations. In Ortiz, A.A., and Ramírez, B.A. (Eds.) *Schools and the Culturally Diverse Exceptional Student: Promising Practices and Future Directions* (pp. 86–95). Reston, VA: ERIC Clearinghouse on Handicapped and Gifted Children, Council for Exceptional Children.

Luce, E.F. (1990. *A case study of cultural adjustment: Vietnamese students in an American high school.* Paper presented at the University of Pennsylvania Ethnography in Education Research Forum, Philadelphia, PA.

Mainous A.G., III (1989). Self-concept as an indicator of acculturation in Mexican Americans. *Hispanic Journal of Behavior Sciences, 11*(2), 178–189.

Marin, B. & Marin, G. (1990). Effects of acculturation on knowledge of AIDS and HIV among Hispanics. *Hispanic Journal of Behavioral Sciences, 12*(2), 110–121.

Marks, G., Solis, J., Richardson, J.L., Collins, L.M., Birba, L. & Hisserich, J.C. (1987). Health behavior of elderly Hispanic women: Does cultural assimilation make a difference? *American Journal of Public Health, 77*(10), 1315–1319.

Mortland, C.A. & Egan, M.G. (1987). Vietnamese youth in American foster care. *Social Work, 32*(3), 240–245.

Olmedo, E.L. (1980). Quantitative models of acculturation: An overview. In Padilla, A.M. (Ed.). *Acculturation: Theory, models and some new findings* (pp. 27–46). Boulder, CO: Westview Press.

Olsen, L. (1988). *Crossing the schoolhouse border: Immigrant students and the California Public Schools.* San Francisco, CA: California Tomorrow.

Organisation for Economic Co-operation and Development (1987). Migrants' children at school. *OECD Observer, 146*, 16–18, 23.

Padilla, A.M. (1980). The role of cultural awareness and ethnic loyalty in acculturation. In Padilla, A.M. (Ed.) *Acculturation: Theory, models and some new findings* (pp. 47–84). Boulder, CO: Westview Press.

Peterson, A.V. & Peppas, G.W. (1988). Trained peer helpers facilitate school adjustment in an overseas school. *School Counselor, 36*(1), 67–73.

Prewitt-Díaz, J.O. & Seilhamer, E.S. (1987). The social psychological adjustment of migrant and non-migrant Puerto Rican adolescents. *Migration World, 15*(2), 7–11.

Raschio, R.A. (1987). College students' perceptions of reverse culture shock and reentry adjustments. *Journal of College Student Personnel, 28*(2), 156–162.

Redfield, R., Linton, R. & Herskovits, M.T. (1936). Memorandum for the study of acculturation. *American Anthropologist, 38*, 149–152.

Schumann, J.H. (1978). The acculturation model for second-language acquisition. In Gringas, R.C. (Ed.) *Second language acquisition and foreign language teaching* (pp. 27–50). Washington, DC: Center for Applied Linguistics.

Schram, J.L. & Lauver, P.J. (1988). Alienation in international students. *Journal of College Student Development, 29*(2), 146–150.

Sodowsky, G.R. & Carey, J.C. (1987). Asian Indian immigrants in America: Factors related to adjustment. *Journal of Multicultural Counseling & Development, 15*(3), 129–141.

Story, M. & Harris, L.J. (1988). Food preferences, beliefs and practices of Southeast Asian refugee adolescents. *Journal of School Health, 58*(7), 273–276.

Szapocznik, J. & Kurtines, W. (1980). Acculturation, biculturalism and adjustment among Cuban Americans. In Padilla, A.M. (Ed.). *Acculturation: Theory, models and some new findings* (pp. 139–160). Boulder, CO: Westview Press.

Thompson, R.M. (1988). *Does the public use of Spanish reverse linguistic assimilation?: A second look at Austin, Texas.* Paper presented at the annual University of Southern Florida Linguistics Club Conference on Second Language Acquisition and Second Language Teaching, Tampa, FL (ERIC Document Reproduction Service No. ED 297 597).

Tran, T.V. (1988). Sex differences in English language acculturation and learning strategies among Vietnamese adults aged 40 and over in the United States. *Sex Roles, 19*(11/12), 747–758.

Trueba, H. (1989). *Raising silent voices: Educating the linguistic minorities for the 21st century.* New York: Newbury House.

Uehara, A. (1983). The nature of American student re-entry adjustment and perceptions of the sojourner experience. Unpublished manuscript, University of Minnesota, Minneapolis.

Westermeyer, J., Neider, J. & Callies, A. (1989). Psychosocial adjustment of Hmong refugees during their first decade in the United States: A longitudinal study. *The Journal of Nervous and Mental Disease, 177*(3), 132–139.

Wong-Rieger, D. & Quintana, D. (1987). Comparative acculturation of Southeast Asian and Hispanic immigrants and sojourners. *Journal of Cross-cultural Psychology, 18*(3), 345–362.

Wu, S.T. (1989). *The forty-five hour alternative curriculum: A comparison of reported television and videotape viewing among Chinese, Puerto Rican, and white children.* Unpublished doctoral dissertation, Teachers College, Columbia University.

Zelmer, A.E. & Johnson, N.A. (1988). International students in higher education: A follow-up study of university graduates. *The Canadian Journal of Higher Education, XVIII*(3), 31–50.

Zohoori, A.R. (1988). A cross-cultural analysis of children's television use. *Journal of Broadcasting & Electronic Media, 32*(1), 105–113.

Annotated Bibliography

Annotations by Terese Brady-Méndez
ESL Specialist, Greenport School District

Berry, J.W., Kim, U., Minde, T., & Mok, D. (1987). Comparative studies of acculturative stress. *International Migration Review, 21*(3), 491–511.

Reports on a series of studies of acculturative stress involving 1,197 immigrants, refugees, native peoples, sojourners, and ethnic groups in Canada in the last decade and a half, using a common indicator of acculturative stress. Acculturative stress is defined as a reduction in health status (including psychological, somatic, and social aspects) of individuals who are undergoing acculturation, and for which there is evidence that these health phenomena are related systematically to acculturation phenomena. Results indicate substantial variation in stress phenomena across types of acculturating groups, across a number of individual difference variables (such as sex, age, education, attitudes, and cognitive styles), and across a number of social variables (such as contact, social support, and status). A need for further comparative studies is identified so that acculturation phenomena may be understood in terms of their origins in variations across host societies, acculturating groups and their interactions.

Bullivant, B.M. (1988). The ethnic success ethic challenges conventional wisdom about immigrant disadvantages in education. *Australian Journal of Education, 32*(2), 223–243.

Describes an ethnographic research project for the Australian Human Rights Commission to determine whether prejudice and discrimination were affecting the occupational socialization of senior students in seven Melbourne high schools. School curriculum, structure, and organization did not emerge as factors in discrimination. However, many teachers did favor non-English speaking (NES) students, especially Asian students, for valued traits, such as diligence, discipline, and achievement orientation. Intergroup prejudice within the school setting based on differing ethnic value systems emerged as a problem. Evidence was found that both ethnic groups and Anglo-Australians in the wider community discriminated against students in jobs. The author attempts to explicate the "ethnic success ethic" in terms of achievement for some groups and not for others, and cautions that success for these particular ethnic groups is often gained at considerable personal cost.

Cloud, N. (1990). *Measuring level of acculturation in bilingual bicultural children.* Paper presented at the annual meeting of the American Educational Research Association, Boston, MA.

Reports on a study of 35 low SES Puerto Rican youngsters, aged ten–fourteen, attending an inner city intermediate school in a large urban center. Utilizing a newly developed acculturation measure in Spanish and English, the

Acculturation Questionnaire for Children, as well as dual language versions of the Student Rating Scales of the Behavior Rating Profile and the Self Observation Scales—Intermediate Level, the children were questioned directly on variables from which a relationship between level of acculturation and adjustment could be established. Statistically significant results indicated that the most acculturated group appeared to be the least well adjusted in the home setting. In addition, the most acculturated group held the most negative views of school and placed least importance on it. Recommendations were made for improving acculturation measurement practice, particularly in measuring level of acculturation in children in culturally diverse populations.

Commins, N.L. (1989). Language and affect: Bilingual students at home and at school. *Language Arts, 66*(1), 29–43.

Describes how four Mexican-American elementary students' perceptions about school and the larger social environment affected their linguistic proficiency, school performance, and attitudes about learning and themselves. This participant-observer study took place in a newly instituted bilingual education program. The need for the school and the classroom setting to promote positive attitudes toward bilingualism in general is also discussed.

Eisenbruch, M. (1988). The mental health of refugee children and their cultural development. *International Migration Review, 22*(2), 282–300.

Suggests that uprooted Indochinese children may experience powerful grief, not only in response to personal loss of loved ones, but also to loss of their culture. Personal bereavement and cultural bereavement are viewed as complementary processes, and form the key variable in the refugee child's adjustment. The author refutes, in part, the notion of the stereotypical image of children's "natural resiliency" in dealing with transition crises and stresses. He points to the fact that many of these children do not have adequate support systems (immediate/extended family members, community resources) to work through the bereavement process, yet are expected to acculturate on an accelerated basis. These children, thus, become vulnerable to "disrupted development time" that can seed problems which only emerge after resettlement is completed. The role of the school in creating a comprehensive prevention program is outlined, with examples of successful programs cited. A major feature these programs share is that they provide a "moratorium" on acculturation by providing the children with a supportive place to examine how their cultural values and behavior differ from those of the mainstream United States, while helping the children to maintain a positive view of their own cultural identity.

First, J.M. & Carrera, J.W. (1988). *New voices: Immigrant students in U.S. public schools.* Boston, MA: The National Coalition of Advocates for Students.

Reports the results of an ambitious two-year in-depth examination of the status of immigrant children in the nation's public schools. The goals of the project were to: (1) investigate the experiences of immigrant children and families as they encounter the public schools in order to identify barriers which impede their educational progress; (2) develop and disseminate recommendations for changes in educational policy and practice which will benefit immigrant children; and (3) to create an informed constituency for immigrant children in the school. Data were gathered via 180 structured interviews and 24 case studies involving immigrant parents and students who resided in the United States for less than five years. The immigrants' national origins represented 15 countries in Central and South America, the Caribbean, Southeast and East Asia, Africa, and Eastern Europe. Information was also obtained from testimony of over 150 witnesses at public hearings held in five major cities. In addition, interviews were conducted with immigration and resettlement advocates at the federal, state, and local levels, as well as with school personnel and policymakers in seven states. A comprehensive review of relevant research was also conducted and reported.

Ima, K. & Rumbaut, R.G. (1989). Southeast Asian refugees in American schools: A comparison of fluent-English-proficient and limited-English-proficient students. *Topics in Language Disorders, 9*(3), 54–75.

Focuses on five Southeast Asian limited English proficient (LEP) and fluent English proficient (FEP) refugee ethnic groups: the Khmer from Cambodia, the Lao and Hmong from Laos, and the Chinese and Vietnamese from Vietnam. Documents fundamental differences among various immigrant and refugees experiences in American schools. Two sets of quantitative data (N = 5,472 and N = 239) were used, both of which contain information on secondary school students' age, gender, ethnicity, years in school, active/inactive status, and LEP/FEP language status. Measures of educational attainment, such as cumulative grade point averages and test scores on the Comprehensive Test of Basic Skills (CTBS), were also used. Findings indicated that students' social background characteristics were most significantly associated with language status and academic attainment. The authors argue that consideration must be given to ethnicity and culture, family and social class background, age and time in the United States, the trauma of the refugee experience, the stress of acculturation processes, and the conditions of survival in the country. Controversial issues about assigning Southeast Asian students to special education programs are also addressed.

Lee, E. (1988). Cultural factors in working with Southeast Asian refugee adolescents. *Journal of Adolescence, 11,* 167–179.

Discusses some of the unique socio-political and socio-cultural factors affecting the psychological development of Southeast Asian refugees, and describes problems the adolescents relate to their developmental crises as adolescents, adjustment problems as refugees, and intercultural conflicts caused by value differences between Eastern and Western cultures. Suggests a framework for intervention which includes: (1) assessment of major stresses (i.e., migration stress, acculturation stress, life cycle stress, and family stress); (2) assessment of strengths; and (3) assessment of culturally specific responses to mental health and psychiatric problems. Recommends specific treatment modalities for dealing with this population. Provides an insightful analysis of specific issues relevant to this population which could be useful to service professionals who come in contact with Southeast Asian refugee youths.

Leung, E.K. (1988). Cultural and acculturational commonalities and diversities among Asian Americans: Identification and programming considerations. In Ortiz, A.A. & Ramírez, B.A. (Eds.) *Schools and the culturally diverse exceptional student: Promising practices and future directions* (pp. 86–95). Reston: VA: ERIC Clearinghouse on Handicapped and Gifted Children, Council for Exceptional Children.

Presents an overview of the commonalities and diversities of Asian Americans in terms of their cultural and acculturational experiences. Succinctly describes how this population differs in origin, immigration and settlement history, degree and type of acculturation, and current status. Summarizes the commonalities of their culture in terms of world views, values, beliefs, lifestyles, traditions, and customs. Suggests ways in which these facets of Asian American experience can be used in special education for identification and programming, as well as ways to enhance family involvement.

Luce, E.F. (1990). *A case study of cultural adjustment: Vietnamese students in an American high school.* Paper presented at the University of Pennsylvania Ethnography in Education Research Forum, Philadelphia, PA.

Describes an ethnographic, participant-observer study of how six Vietnamese students perceived their American educational experiences in a suburban high school setting. The author attempted to discover which values, cultural conflicts, and other factors affected their acculturation process. The author found that: (1) there is an educational paradox of implementing an ambitious ESL program to enhance the students' skills, but which students may devalue both for its segregational or stigmatizing aspects, as well as for the difficulty of addressing the wide variety of needs of the students that it intends to help; (2) literacy needs for this group of immigrants differed greatly, and teachers and administrators may overvalue literacy in the high school curriculum; (3) Asian American students achieve real or perceived success because of strong motivation provided by an optimistic perspective toward life opportunities in their new country; (4) as a result of entering a new and very different culture, these students developed a skeptical and inquiring mode of thought useful in problem solving; and (5) some of the difficulties of adaptation may have resulted from class, race, and gender-based expectations brought from their native land.

Mortland, C.A. & Egan, M.G. (1987). Vietnamese youth in American foster
    care. *Social Work, 32*(3), 240–245.

Presents the results of an ethnographic study of unaccompanied minor
refugees from Vietnam placed in American foster homes in the United States.
Through formal and informal interviews with foster parents, refugee youth,
caseworkers, and interpreters, a number of adjustment strategies employed by
the youth were identified and described within a cultural, psychosocial, and
historical frame of reference. Implications of the study included suggestions
about how these youth may be better understood and what services could be
developed to mediate the conflicts and difficulties arising in the foster care
placement setting.

Olsen, L. (1987). *Crossing the schoolhouse border: Immigrant students and
    the California Public Schools.* San Francisco, CA: California Tomorrow.

Contains a comprehensive report on the status of limited English proficient
(LEP) and fluent English proficient (FEP) children in California schools who
represent seven major immigrant groups in the state: Mexican, Central American,
Filipino, Southeast Asian, Korean, Japanese, and Chinese. Three hundred sixty
children, between the ages of eleven and nineteen, were interviewed in 33
communities. Interviews, consisting of 83 structured items, were conducted in
either the native language, English, or a combination of languages. In-depth
interviews focusing on identifying problems facing immigrant children were
conducted with community advocates, youth-serving agency staff, educators,
and researchers. A total of 29 school districts, which made their statistics and
materials available for the study, were visited by the researchers. Data also
include information obtained from two full days of public hearings in which
55 witnesses presented testimony on the needs and experiences of immigrant
students. The report is divided into three major sections: (1) demographic data
and background information on immigrant children and their immigration
experience; (2) information about the content and structure of school programs,
school experiences of immigrant children, and data on the achievement and
school success of immigrant students; and (3) suggestions for steps that can
be taken at the state, local, school site, and community level to create a school
experience more responsible to the needs of immigrant children.

Organisation for Economic Co-operation and Development (1987). Migrants'
    children at school. *OECD Observer, 146*(23), 16–18.

Presents a statistical picture of the presence of immigrant children in
Western European schools. Attempts to explain reasons for overall poor school
performance and the prevalence of these children in special education programs.
Raises questions about how educational systems can integrate foreign children
into the mainstream of the dominant culture without alienating them from their
own.

Peterson, A.V. & Peppas, G.J. (1988). Trained peer helpers facilitate student adjustment in an overseas school. *The School Counselor, 36*(1), 67–73.

Describes the effects of peer helpers paired with newly arrived students at the American Community School of Athens, Greece. Results of the study indicated that peer counseling helped the students improve self-concept, social adjustment, and academic achievement.

Prewitt-Díaz, J.O. & Seilhamer, E.S. (1987). The social psychological adjustment of migrant and non-migrant Puerto Rican adolescents. *Migration World, 15*(2), 7–11.

Discusses patterns of Puerto Rican migration since the 1950's and explores the relationship of these patterns on current reading achievement and physical, social and school adjustment among 273 randomly selected migrant, return migrant, circulatory migrant, and non-migrant high school students in seven school districts in Puerto Rico.

Thompson, R.M. (1988). Does the public use of Spanish reverse linguistic assimilation?: A second look at Austin, Texas. Paper presented at the annual University of Southern Florida Linguistics Club Conference on Second Language Acquisition and Second Language Teaching, Tampa, FL (ERIC Document Reproduction Service Center No. ED 297 597).

Compares the results of the author's 1971 investigation of 136 male headed households with a second study completed in 1982 in which 44 of the participants were available and reinterviewed. Despite the government's official adoption of Spanish for use in education and social welfare programs in the intervening years, the author found that earlier patterns of assimilation had not been reversed. However, the increased public use of Spanish created cultural and linguistic paradoxes which resulted in a new interaction of the two languages for intimate and formal speech.

Wu, S.T. (1989). The forty-five hour alternative curriculum: A comparison of reported television and videotape viewing among Chinese, Puerto Rican, and white children. Unpublished doctoral dissertation, Teachers College, Columbia University, 1989.

Examines the TV and videotape viewing patterns of 197 fourth to sixth grade students in three public schools in a metropolitan city, using three questionnaires. The study group contained 62 white, 77 Puerto Rican and 58 Chinese children. Data were analyzed along the following dimensions: (1) TV and videotape viewing time; (2) TV program and videotape preferences; and (3) parental control of TV and videotape viewing. Significant differences in the amount of TV viewing among the three ethnic groups were found. Program preferences tended to reflect the types of programs available in the time slots selected for investigation. Differences among the three groups were also found in the amount and quality of parental control over TV viewing practices. Videotape watching constituted a very small proportion of TV viewing time; however, preferences in videotapes reflected a highly disproportionate amount of PG-13 and R-rated videos. The study confirmed that children are attracted to TV programs and videotapes regardless of ethnicity, and that for some children, TV and videotape viewing are their second curriculum.

Zohoori, A.R. (1988). A cross-cultural analysis of children's television use. *Journal of Broadcasting and Electronic Media*, *32*(1), 105–113.

Compares uses of U.S. television by 83 foreign born children from 33 different countries with 276 U.S. classmates in a Midwest public school in light of theories of acculturation, cultivation and uses, and gratification. Examined how differences in cultural backgrounds of children could lead to differences in viewing motivations, television program preferences, exposure time, identification with television characters, and belief in the social reality portrayed by television. It was found that as foreign children become acculturated to U.S. society, television appears to be an important source of education and information about the U.S. way of life. It was further suggested that the cultivation effects of television (i.e., television's impact in cultivating social reality) should be stronger among children with shorter periods of residency in the U.S. than among those with longer periods of residency. This impact is more salient when the audience does not have access to alternative sources of information and lacks sufficient real-life experience upon which to evaluate social reality as portrayed on television.

CHAPTER III

Bilingualism and Second Language Acquisition in Academic Contexts

Eugene E. García

Introduction

Our understanding of language continues to expand in the utilization of diverse theories of linguistics, cognition, and socialization (August & García, 1988). What was once considered the study of habits and structure (Skinner, 1957; Chomsky, 1959) has become today an interlocking study of linguistic, psychological, and social domains, each independently significant, but converging in a singular attempt to reconstruct the nature of language. It is this multifaceted phenomenon which confronts an educator when addressing the educational appropriation of knowledge in classrooms. For the educator of language minority students, the issue of language becomes particularly important.

Within the last few years, research in language acquisition has shifted from the study of one language (Brown, 1973; González, 1970) to the comparative study of children from diverse linguistic societies (Bowerman, 1975; Braine, 1976) and to the study of children acquiring more than one language (Krashen, 1981; García, 1983; McLaughlin, 1984; Hakuta, 1986; Hakuta & García, 1988; Ambert, in press). The following discussion introduces the theoretical and empirical knowledge bases necessary to understand bilingualism and second language acquisition in school contexts. The linguistic, cognitive, and social research and theory developed over the last two decades in the fields of bilingualism and second language acquisition will be addressed. Such contributions have dramatically reshaped our view of bilingualism. At the turn of the century, bilingualism in children was considered a linguistic, cognitive, and academic liability (Hakuta, 1986). However, our understanding of bilingualism today indicates that bilingualism is not a linguistic liability. In fact, bilingualism may be a cognitive advantage.

School initiatives targeted at limited English speaking students in the United States will be the focus of this chapter. As González (1990) has documented, children who speak a different language and hold values significantly different from those of the American mainstream are usually perceived as "foreigners," "intruders," and "immigrants." This perspective has lead policymakers (including the U.S. Supreme Court) to highlight the most salient characteristic of the student, the language difference, in their attempts to address the historical academic underachievement of this population.

This chapter will include an expanded discussion of the research, theory, educational practice, and educational policy of significance to limited English proficiency students. Specifically, the chapter will address the bilingual character of these students. Bilingualism, however, is much more than a linguistic phenomenon. Therefore, the chapter includes linguistic, psycholinguistic, and sociolinguistic treatments of this widespread phenomenon. In addition, since many language minority students embark on the course of bilingualism only after a non-English native language is well developed, the chapter addresses the many variables linked to the second language acquisition process. Lastly, but most significantly, the chapter addresses the educational response, in policy and practice, of U.S. schools to the linguistic diversity of students—a policy and practice which has recognized the linguistic difference of a segment of the population. Recommendations related to educational practices and further research are offered which recognize previous failures and the emerging research discussed in this chapter.

Bilingual Acquisition

Little systematic research is available on the native language (L1) acquisition of children who are acquiring more than one language, simultaneously, during early childhood. However, recent work in this area has centered separately on the linguistic (García & González, 1984), cognitive (Cummins, 1979), and social/communicative aspects (Moll, 1988) of the bilingual child. That is, research with young bilingual populations has concentrated independently on three areas: (a) the developmental nature of phonology, morphology, and syntax;

(b) Piagetian and related cognitive attributes of bilingualism; and (c) the social/discourse characteristics of bilingual development. This section reviews research in these areas with an attempt to highlight similar and disparate theoretical conceptualizations and empirical findings generated by these research endeavors.

Bilingualism Defined

It remains difficult to define any term to the satisfaction of the theoretician, researcher, and educator. The term bilingualism used here suggests the acquisition of two languages during the first five to seven years of life. This definition includes the following conditions:

1. Children are able to *comprehend and produce* aspects (lexicon, morphology, and syntax) of each language.
2. Children *function "naturally" in the two languages* as they are used in the form of social interaction. This condition requires a substantive bilingual environment in the child's first three to seven years of life. In many cases this exposure comes from within a nuclear and extended family network, but this need not be the case (visitors and extended visits to foreign countries are examples of alternative environments).
3. The *simultaneous character of development* must be apparent in both languages. This is contrasted with the case of a native speaker of one language, who after mastering that one language, begins the acquisition of the second language.

The preceding combined conditions define a bilingual population. It is clear from this definition that an attempt is made to include both the child's linguistic abilities and the social environment during an important psychological "segment" of life (August & García, 1988).

Linguistic Development

It is now clear that a child can learn more than one linguistic form for communicative purposes in many societies throughout the world. Sorenson (1967) describes the acquisition of three to four languages by young children who live in the Northwest Amazon region of South America. In this Brazilian-Colombian border region, the Tukano tribal language serves as a *lingua franca*, but some 25 clearly distinguishable linguistic groups continue to exist. European colleagues Skutnabb-Kangas (1979) and Baetens Beardsmore (1982) have provided expanded discussions on the international proliferation of multilingualism. Skrabanek (1970), Waggoner (1984), and Hakuta (1986) report on school age children in the United States who continue to be bilingual with no indication that this phenomenon will be disrupted.

One of the first systematic linguistic investigations of bilingualism in young children was reported by Leopold (1939, 1947, 1949a, 1949b). This author set out to study the simultaneous acquisition of English and German in his own daughter. His initial descriptive reports indicate that as the child was exposed to both languages during infancy, she seemed to weld both languages into one system during initial language production periods. For instance, early language forms were characterized by free mixing. Language production during later periods seem to indicate that the use of English and German grammatical forms developed independently.

In the United States, Padilla and Liebman (1975) report a longitudinal linguistic analysis of Spanish-English acquisition in two 3-year-old children. The researchers followed Brown's (1973) model in recording linguistic interactions of children over a five month period. By an analysis of several dependent linguistic variables (phonological, morphological, and syntactic characteristics) over this time period, they observed gains in both languages, although several English forms were in evidence while similar Spanish forms were not. They also report the differentiation of linguistic systems at phonological, lexical and syntactic levels. They conclude:

> the appropriate use of both languages in mixed utterances was evident; that is, correct word order was preserved. For example, there were no occurrences of *raining está* or *a baby es,* but there was evidence for such utterances as *está raining* and *es a baby.* There was also an absence of the redundance of unnecessary words which might tend to confuse meaning. (p. 51)

García (1983) reports developmental data on the acquisition of Spanish and English for Chicano preschoolers (3–4 years old) and the acquisition of English by a group of matched English-only speakers. The results of that study can be summarized as follows: (a) acquisition of both Spanish and English was evident at complex morphological levels in bilingual Spanish/English four year-old children; (b) English was more advanced in the bilingual children studied, based on the quantity and quality of obtained morphological instances of language productions; and (c) there was no quantitative or qualitative difference between Spanish/English bilingual children and matched English-only controls on English language morphological productions.

Huerta (1977) conducted a longitudinal analysis of a Spanish/English two-year-old child. She reports a similar pattern of continuous Spanish/English development, although identifiable stages appeared in which one language forged ahead of the other. Moreover, she reports the significant occurrence of mixed language utterance, which made use of both Spanish and English vocabulary as well as Spanish and English morphology. In all such cases, these mixed linguistic utterances were well formed and communicative.

In a study of Spanish/English four-, five-, and six-year-old bilingual children throughout the United States, García, Maez, and González (1983) found regional differences in the relative occurrence of switched language utterances. That is, bilingual Spanish/English children from Texas, Arizona, Colorado, and New Mexico, showed higher (15 percent–20 percent) incidences of language switched utterances than children from California or Illinois, especially at pre-kindergarten levels. These findings suggest that some children may very well develop an "interlanguage" in addition to the acquisition of two independent language systems later in development.

However, in a study of 30 Puerto Rican kindergarten children attending bilingual programs in Hartford, Connecticut, Ambert (in press) found that the children were developing Spanish at developmental levels similar to Puerto Rican children acquiring language in monolingual settings in Puerto Rico. They had developed syntactic and grammatical structures consistent with their age and they had also developed conversational skills that demonstrated their communicative competence in verbal interaction. Furthermore, the English language influence present in their language was insignificant and limited to vocabulary. No English influence was found in the children's syntactical development.

The above "developmental" linguistic findings can be summarized as follows for bilingual children:

1. The acquisition of two languages can be parallel but need not be. That is, the qualitative character of one language may lag behind, surge ahead, or develop equally with the other language (Huerta, 1977; Padilla & Liebman, 1975).

2. The acquisition of two languages may result in an interlanguage, incorporating the attributes (lexicon, morphology, and syntax) of both languages. But, this not need be the case. Languages may develop independently (Huerta, 1977; García, González, & Maez, 1983).

3. The acquisition of two languages need not hamper structurally
    the acquisition of either language (García, 1983; Hakuta, 1986;
    Ambert, in press).

Intelligence, Cognition, and Bilingualism

A separate but significant research approach to the understanding
of bilingualism and its effects has focused on the cognitive (intellectual)
character of the bilingual. Based on correlational studies indicating a
negative relationship between childhood bilingualism and performance
on standardized tests of intelligence, a causal statement linking
bilingualism to "depressed" intelligence was tempting and this negative
conclusion characterized much early work (Darcy, 1953). Due to the
myriad of methodological problems with the studies investigating this
relationship, any conclusions concerning bilingualism and intellectual
functioning (as measured by standardized individual or group intelligence
tests) are extremely tentative in nature (Darcy, 1963; Díaz, 1983).

With a general shift away from standardized measures of
intelligence, the cognitive character of bilingual children has received
attention. In one of the first investigations of bilingual acquisition,
Leopold (1939) reported a general cognitive plasticity for his young
bilingual daughter. He suggested that linguistic flexibility (in the form
of bilingualism) was related to a number of non-linguistic cognitive
tasks such as categorization, verbal signal discrimination, and creativity.
In a summary of their work with French/English bilingual and English
monolinguals, Peal and Lambert (1962) suggested that the intellectual
experience of acquiring two languages contributed to advantageous
mental flexibility, superior concept formation, and a generally diversified
set of mental abilities.

Other researchers provide relevant evidence regarding such
flexibility. Feldman and Shen (1971) report differential responding
between Chicano Spanish/English bilingual and English monolinguals
across three separate tasks reflecting Piagetian-like problem solving
and metalinguistic awareness (that is, conscious awareness and
knowledge of language construction and use). Results indicated
significantly increased cognitive flexibility for Chicano bilinguals. Ianco-
Worral (1972) compared matched bilinguals (Afrikaan/English) and
monolinguals (either Afrikaan or English) on metalinguistic tasks
requiring separation of word-sounds and word meanings. Comparison
of scores on these tasks indicated that bilinguals concentrated more on

attaching meaning to words rather than sounds. Ben-Zeev's (1977) work with Hebrew-English bilingual children is also related to the metalinguistic abilities of these children. Subjects in these studies showed superiority in symbol substitution and verbal transformational tasks. Ben-Zeev summarizes:

> Two strategies characterized by thinking patterns of the bilingual in relation to verbal material: readiness to impute structure and readiness to reorganize. (p. 1017)

More recent research findings on Chicano bilinguals reported by Kessler and Quinn (1986, 1987) supply additional empirical support for the emerging understanding that, all things being equal, bilingual children outperform monolingual children on specific measures of cognitive and metalinguistic awareness. In Kessler and Quinn's 1987 study, bilingual and monolingual children engaged in a variety of symbolic categorization tasks which required their attention to abstract verbal features of concrete objects. Spanish/English Chicano bilinguals from low SES backgrounds outperformed low SES English-speaking monolinguals and high SES English-speaking monolinguals on these tasks. Findings of metalinguistic advantages have been reported for low SES Puerto Rican students as well (Galambos & Hakuta, 1988). Such findings are particularly significant given the criticism by McNab (1979) that many bilingual "cognitive advantage" studies utilized only high SES subjects of non-U.S. minority backgrounds.

Theoretical attempts linking bilingualism to cognitive attributes have emerged. In an attempt to identify more specifically the relationship between cognition and bilingualism, Cummins (1979, 1981, 1984) has proposed an interactive theoretical proposition: that children who do not achieve balanced proficiency in two languages (but who are immersed in a bilingual environment) may be cognitively "different" and possibly "disadvantaged."

Any detailed conclusions concerning the relationship between the bilingual character of children and cognitive functioning must continue to remain tentative (Díaz, 1983). However, it is the case that:

1. Bilingual children have been found to score lower than monolingual children on standardized measures of cognitive development, intelligence, and school achievement.
2. Bilingual children have been found to score higher on specific Piagetian, metalinguistic, concept-formation, and creative cognitive tasks.

3. "Balanced" bilingual children have outperformed monolinguals and "unbalanced" bilingual children on specific cognitive and metalinguistic tasks.

Social/Communicative Aspects of Bilingualism

Language is a critical social repertoire. The linguistic component of any social interaction most often determines the general quality of that interaction (Hymes, 1974; Halliday, 1975; Bates, 1976; Shantz, 1977; Cole, Dore, Hall, & Dowley, 1978; Canales, 1983; Ramírez, 1985). Therefore, language carries special importance for the bilingual child where social tasks include language choice. Moreover, like other children who acquire the ability to differentially employ linguistic codes determined by social attributes of the speaking context (Phillips, 1972; Ervin-Tripp & Mitchell-Kernan, 1977), bilingual children face the task of multiple code differentiation. Implicit in this discussion is the general notion that languages must not only be mastered in a structural sense and operate in conjunction with cognitive processes, they must be utilized as a social instrument.

The study of language acquisition in context is known as pragmatics (Bates, 1976). This approach demands that we think of the context of communication as involving information about the speaker, the listener, the speaker's goal in using a particular utterance, the information assumed to be true in a particular speech context, and the rules governing discourse. For example, in considering the conventional rules for discourse, three aspects of language may be considered important: (a) how the child establishes a topic; (b) maintains a topic; or (c) changes the topic across "turns" in a conversation. Adult speakers are generally adept at introducing a new topic into a conversation, by using such conventional routines as "Let me tell you about X" or "You'll never guess what happened today" or "I want to talk about Y." Adults can also maintain a topic across many turns in conversation, even when the other person participating is not particularly cooperative.

Interest in social contexts has generated studies in bilingual mother-child, teacher-child, and child-child interaction. García (1983) reports an investigation of Chicano mother-child interaction including the description of Spanish/English use by children and adults (the childrens' mothers) in three different contexts: (a) preschool instruction periods; (b) preschool freeplay periods; and (c) the home. These descriptions pointed out very consistently that children, in particular, were "choosing" to initiate an interaction in either Spanish or English as a function of the language the mother was using to initiate that interaction. A closer qualitative examination of the same mothers and children interacting is reported by García and Carrasco (1981). This analysis suggested that almost 90 percent of mother-child interactions were initiated by the mother, most often in Spanish. That is, mothers most often did not allow children to initiate. For those small number of instances in which children did initiate, the topic determined language choice. That is, "what" the child spoke about was highly correlated with the language in which he/she chose to speak.

The richest data on topic initiation by bilingual children come from child-child interactions. While investigating the use of Spanish and English among first-graders, Ginishi (1981) concluded that the general language initiation rule for these students was: "Speak to the listener in his/her best language." Her analysis suggests that when speaking with peers, children first made a choice on language of initiation based on their previous language use history with their fellow students. Zentella (1981) agrees that bilingual students do make these decisions. However, she found another discourse rule operating: "you can speak to me in either English or Spanish." Although Genishi's (1981) and Zentella's (1981) discourse rules differ, each observation suggests that bilingual students make use of their social and language use history to construct guidelines in discourse initiation. These studies suggest that particular sociolinguistic environments cause bilingual students to be aware of language choice issues in discourse initiation.

A comprehensive understanding of early childhood bilingualism must, therefore, take into consideration more than the linguistic nature of the bilingual or the child's cognitive attributes. It must consider the child's surrounding environment. Recent data tentatively suggest that social context will determine:

1. The specific social language rules for each language.
2. The roles assigned to each language.

Summary

The linguistic, cognitive, and social domains of the bilingual experience have been demonstrated as individually important in understanding the essence of the bilingual child. But, the interaction of these would seem to more clearly describe the ongoing developmental quality of this phenomenon. This interactive conclusion suggests the following:

1. The linguistic, cognitive, and social characteristics of the bilingual child are developing simultaneously.
2. Linguistic, cognitive, and social development are interrelated. That is, cognitive processing factors may act to influence linguistic and social development. Linguistic development (the ability to operate within the structural aspects of language(s)) may act to influence social and potential cognitive functioning. In turn, the development of social competence influences directly the acquisition of linguistic and cognitive repertoires.

This interactive conceptualization is meant to reflect the interrelationship among linguistic, cognitive, and social aspects of bilingual development often missing in educational programming for bilingual students. Changes in each of these domains may be attributed to changes in other domains, and in turn, may further alter the qualitative character of the bilingual. It is recent linguistic, cognitive, and social discourse data related to bilingualism that have transformed the phenomenon from a purely linguistic framework into one which requires an integrative conceptualization.

Second Language Acquisition

McLaughlin (1985) traces the reported scholarly interest in second language acquisition to the third millennium B.C., when Sumerian scholars received the task of translating their Arkadian conquerers' language into their own. Egyptian historical records indicate that by 1500 B.C., multilingual dictionaries were available. According to McLaughlin (1985), Egyptians and Jews received educational experiences in Greek. Furthermore, Jewish scholars developed the comparative study of Semitic and non-Semitic languages, the scholarly foundation for modern comparative linguistics.

McLaughlin (1985) and Richards and Rodgers (1986) provide incisive updated reviews of the development of theoretical and instructional contributions to the study of second language acquisition. (These reviews contain a more extended discussion of second language acquisition.) These authors agree that several themes characterize the historical treatment of second language (L2) acquisition in language minority students. These themes include:

1. An interest in the relationship between first language and second language acquisition and input.
2. An understanding that the individual and social circumstances within which a second language is acquired can determine the course of second language acquisition.
3. A concern for psychological/cognitive processes utilized during second language acquisition.

The following discussion will explore these themes in recent research and theoretical contexts.

First and Second Language Acquisition

Learners' errors have been considered significant in proving an understanding of the strategies and processes the learner employs during second language acquisition. Dulay and Burt (1974b) studied the errors in the natural speech of 179 five– to eight-year-olds learning English as a second language. They classified errors as either related to first language ("interference" errors) or related to normal language development ("developmental" errors). Their analysis indicated that "interference" accounted for only 4.7 percent of the errors while 87.1 percent of the errors were similar to those made by children learning English as a first language. They postulated that a universal "creative construction process" accounts for second language acquisition. The process was creative because no one models the type of sentences children produce when acquiring a second language. The researchers suggested that innate mechanisms cause children to use certain strategies to organize linguistic input. Dulay and Burt did not claim that they could define the specific nature of the innate mechanisms. They did claim, however, that these mechanisms have certain definable characteristics that cause children to use a limited set of hypotheses to deal with the knowledge they are acquiring. The strategies parallel those identified for first-language acquisition.

Krashen (1981) has developed a conceptualization of second language acquisition which considers as fundamental this innate creative construction process. His "natural order" hypothesis indicates that the acquisition of grammatical structures by the second language learner proceeds in a predictable "natural" order, independent of first language experiences and/or proficiency. Such acquisition occurs unconsciously without the learner's concern for recognizing or utilizing structural rules. However, his "monitor" hypothesis suggests that conscious learning of a second language can occur when the learner has achieved a significant knowledge of structural rules and has the time to apply those rules in a second language learning situation. Krashen, therefore, extends Dulay and Burts' creative construction and natural order conceptualizations by introducing the notion of the "monitor" hypothesis. That is, a second language can be learned by first understanding the grammatical structure and having the time to apply that grammatical knowledge. He concludes however, that conscious learning of a second language is not as efficient or functional as the natural acquisition of a second language.

Other research has documented a distinct interrelationship between first language and second acquisition. Ervin-Tripp (1974) conducted a study of 31 English-speaking children between the ages of four and nine who were living in Geneva and were attending French schools. She found that the errors these children made in French, their second language, were a result of their application of the same strategies that they had used in acquiring a first language. Such strategies as overgeneralization, production simplification, and loss of sentence medial items, all predicted the kinds of errors that appeared. In overgeneralization, the American children acquiring French applied a subject-verb-object strategy to all sentences in French, and thus systematically misunderstood French passives. In production simplification, they resisted using two forms if they felt that two forms had the same meaning. Also, medial pronouns were less often imitated than initial or final pronouns. She believed that interference errors occurred only when the second-language learner was forced to generate sentences about semantically difficult material or concepts unfamiliar in the new culture. Moreover, the strategies children use in acquiring a second language (L2) may change as they become more proficient in the second language. At the beginning of L2 acquisition, imitation plays an important role in language learning. As children acquire more of the target language they begin to use first-language acquisition strategies to analyze this input.

Hakuta (1974) demonstrated that a child, through rote memorization, acquired segments of speech called prefabricated patterns. Examples of these prefabricated patterns are various allomorphs of the copula, the segment "do you" as employed in questions, and the segment "how to" as embedded in how questions. These patterns are very useful in communication. The child uses these patterns without understanding their structure but with knowledge of which particular situations call for what patterns in order to communicate in the target language.

Wong Fillmore (1976) spent a year observing five Spanish-speaking Chicano children acquiring English naturally and she noticed the same phenomena. The first thing the children did was to figure out what was being said by observing the relationship between certain expressions and the situational context. They inferred the meaning of certain words which they began to use as 'formulaic expressions.' (These expressions were acquired and used as analyzed wholes.) The formulaic expressions became the raw material used by the children in order to figure out the structure of the language. Wong Fillmore gave two examples of how children use first-language acquisition strategies to begin to analyze these expressions:

1. Children notice how parts of expressions used by others vary in accordance with changes in the speech situation in which they occur.
2. Children notice which parts of the formulaic expressions are like other utterances in the speech of others.

As the children figured out which formulas in their speech could be varied, they were able to "free" the constituents they contained and use them in productive speech.

In addition, at the beginning of L2 acquisition, children seem to depend much more on first-language transfer strategies. As learners acquire more of the second language, they depend less on these strategies and more on such strategies characteristic of first-language acquisition, such as over-generalizations (August & García, 1988).

Children acquiring a second language may depend initially on transfer from the first language and on imitation and rote memorization of the second language. In more practical terms, the less interaction a second learner has with native speakers, the more likely transfer from the first language to the second language will be observed. As the second language is acquired many of the strategies that children use to acquire the second language seem to be the same as those used in first-language acquisition (McLaughlin, 1984, 1985).

The Importance of Target-Language Input

It is apparent that target-language input provides children with the raw material necessary for language acquisition. In addition, the frequency and salience of forms in the input data influence the presence of these forms in the output. Hatch (1974) found that the frequency of morphemes in the input data appears to influence the sequential acquisition of these morphemes. For example, the order of acquisition of question words appears to parallel their frequency in what children heard. She also noted that there is an interaction between frequency of forms and semantic importance. A form appearing frequently, though of low semantic importance, will be acquired later. Larsen-Freeman (1976) found that in-class teacher-talk of ESL teachers showed a rank order for frequency of morphemes similar to that found in the learner output. Hakuta (1975) discovered that the auxiliary most often omitted by learners in utterances involving the catenative "gonna" was "are." He found such a construction less perceptually salient to the learner because of its absence. The auxiliary, because of its absence in the input, resulted in its omission in the learner's output.

These observations make researchers (Hatch,1974; Larsen-Freeman, 1976; Hakuta, 1975) question whether the invariant order of morpheme acquisition (Dulay & Burt, 1974) is a reaction to the input to which the learner was exposed. The correspondence between input and output suggests that interaction between speakers might be important in structuring language output. Even Krashen (1981), a proponent of the natural order of grammatical acquisition, suggests in his "input" hypothesis that second language learning is enhanced under conditions in which the learner is provided with input that contains "the next level of linguistic competence." Krashen (1981) identifies this enhancement strategy as "providing comprehensible input." Paradoxically, however, he cautions against any conscious strategy to provide "comprehensible input" and instead suggests natural interaction which focuses on meaning. Therefore, even though second language learning may be enriched by providing "comprehensible input," any attempt to do so without the "natural" concern for conveying meaning could be linguistically disruptive.

Conversely, Keenan (1976) hypothesizes that the interactions from which syntactic structures develop are determined by the rules of discourse. As indicated earlier in this chapter, certain rules are generally followed in order to carry on a conversation. One must get the attention of the conversational partner. The speaker then nominates a topic and develops it. Partners take turns. Topic clarification, shifting, avoidance, and interruption characterize interactions. Finally the topic is terminated.

Adult-child and child-child conversations are very difficult. Each genre of conversation follows the rules of discourse but the rules are applied differently. As a consequence, the child acquiring another language learns different things from each type of conversation. In adult-child conversations the rules of discourse put both the child and the adult under certain constraints (Hatch, 1978; McLaughlin, 1985; García, 1986). These constraints structure the interaction and consequently also the output. The child must first get the adult's attention. Once this is accomplished by gestures and verbalizations, the child must nominate a topic. The adult is also constrained by the rules of discourse in that the response must be relevant. For the response to be relevant, the information about the topic must be shared by both child and adult. The adult's response usually clarifies the topic that has been nominated by labeling it or asking for more information about it. *What, where, whose, what color, how many, what is x doing, can x verb, is x verbing* are the kinds of questions adults can use in response to the child's topic nomination and be relevant. The child's response in turn must also be relevant. As a result there is a great deal of what, where, whose, who is verbing, etc. Hatch (1978) hypothesized that this accounted for the order of acquisition of these forms in previous studies. If the child is unable to say something relevant he or she can just repeat what the adult has said but with the appropriate intonation. He or she will answer a question with rising intonation and a statement with falling intonation.

In summary, current research suggests that natural communication situations must be provided for second-language acquisition to occur. Regardless of the differences in emphasis in the theories discussed above, recent theoretical propositions on second language acquisition propose that through natural conversations the learner receives the necessary input and structures which promote second language acquisition.

Social Factors in Second Language Acquisition

There are sociocultural variables that contribute to a child's motivation to communicate in the target language. The attitude that the learner has towards members of the cultural group whose language he or she is learning influences language acquisition. Gardner and Lambert

(1972) found that the positive attitude of English-speaking Canadians toward French-speaking Canadians led to high integrative motivation to learn French. Ramírez (1985) reports a series of studies which investigated the relationship between Chinese, Japanese, and Hispanic students' achievement in English and their attitude toward the foreign-language group. Positive attitudes toward the target-language group corresponded to higher language proficiency.

Schumann (1976) found that children are more motivated to learn a second language if they do not perceive this learning process as alienation from their own culture. If a child belongs to a family whose integration pattern is preservation of the native language and culture rather than assimilation or acculturation, the child may be less motivated to acquire the second language. There may be less impetus for a cultural group to assimilate or acculturate if that group has its own community in the host country or if the duration of residence in the foreign country is short.

Not only is the individual's attitude toward the target culture important, but the relationship between the two cultures influences second-language acquisition. Schumann (1976) hypothesized that the greater the social distance between the two cultures, the greater the difficulty the second-language learner will have in learning the target language, and conversely, the smaller the social distance, the better the language learning situation will be. Social distance is determined in part by the relative status of two cultures. Two cultures that are politically, culturally, and technically equal in status have less social distance than two cultures whose relationship is characterized by dominance or subordination. In addition, there is less social distance if the cultures of the two groups are congruent.

A child, motivated to learn a second language, still needs certain social skills to facilitate his or her ability to establish and maintain contact with speakers of the target language. Wong Fillmore (1976) and Wong Fillmore and Valadez (1985) suggest that individual differences in the social skills of the child influence the rate of second-language acquisition. Second language learners who seem most successful employ specific social strategies. They will:

1. Join a group and act as if they understand what's going on even if they don't. Learners must initiate interactions and pretend to know what is going on. As a result, they will be included in conversations and activities.

2. Give the impression with a few well chosen words that they can speak the language. Children must be willing to use

whatever language they have and as a result, other children will keep trying to communicate with them.

3. Count on their friends for help. The acquisition of language depends on the participation of both the learner and someone who already speaks the language—a friend. The children's friends may help in several ways. They show faith in the learner's ability to learn the language, and by including the learner in their activities, they make a real effort to understand what the learner says. Friends also provide the learner with natural linguistic input that he or she can understand.

High-input generators are the most successful second language learners. High-input generators are learners who place themselves in situations in which they are exposed to the target language and are willing to use it for communication. Therefore, they receive the necessary input as well as the opportunity for practice (Seliger, 1977).

In summary, children acquire a second language naturally. Although the underlying cognitive processes used by children in acquiring a second language may be similar in all children, social factors seem to influence second language acquisition.

Summary

From the above review of second language acquisition theory and research, it appears that second language acquisition is:

1. Characterized as *related* and *not related* to acquisition of first language linguistic structures;
2. related to specific rules of discourse;
3. influenced by the motivation to learn a second language; and,
4. related to social factors.

Hammerly (1985) has also suggested that it is useful to indicate what second language acquisition is *not*:

1. An intellectual exercise involving the understanding and memorization of grammar;
2. translation;
3. memorization of sentences;
4. mechanical conditioning; and/or,
5. application of abstract rules.

Our understanding of second language acquisition requires cognizance of similar interrelationships identified in this chapter when discussing the nature of bilingualism. Each phenomenon has been "diagnosed" as dependent on L1–L2 crosslinguistic effects in combination with the social aspects of language use and the psychological/cognitive processes which serve and guide learning. Certain theoretical emphases and contradictions discussed in this chapter continue to remind us that our understanding of second language acquisition remains incomplete. This is not to suggest that little is known. The above discussion has presented a large body of research and various sophisticated conceptualizations to guide our understanding of this phenomenon.

From Bilingual Education to Language Minority Education

The debate regarding the education of language minority students in the United States has centered on the instructional use of the two languages of the bilingual. With regard to the schooling process, the broader issue has been the effective instruction of a growing population of ethnic minority students who do not speak English. Discussion of this issue has included cross disciplinary dialogues involving psychology, linguistics, sociology, politics, and education. [For a more thorough discussion of these issues see Cummins (1979); Troike (1981); Baker & deKanter (1983); García (1983); Willig (1985); Rossell & Ross (1986); Hakuta & Gould (1987); and August & García (1988)]. The central theme of these discussions has to do with the specific instructional role of the native language. At one extreme of this discussion, the utilization of the native language is recommended for a significant part of the non-English speaking student's elementary school years, from 4–6 years, with a concern for native language communicative and academic "mastery" prior to immersion into the English curriculum. At the other extreme, immersion into an English curriculum is recommended early, as early as preschool, with minimal use of the native language and English language "leveling" by instructional staff to facilitate understanding on behalf of the limited English speaking student.

Each of these disparate approaches argues that the result of its implementation brings psychological, linguistic, social, political, and educational benefits. The "native language" approach suggests that competencies in the native language, particularly in academic learning, provide important psychological and linguistic foundations for second language learning and academic learning in general ("you really only learn to read once"). Native language instruction builds on social and cultural experiences and serves to politically empower students from communities which have been historically limited to meaningful participation in majority educational institutions. The "immersion" approach suggests that the sooner a child receives instruction in English, the more likely that student will acquire English proficiency ("more time on task, better proficiency"). English proficiency will in turn mitigate against educational failure, social separation and segregation, and ultimate economic disparity.

As this discussion has unfolded, it is clear that the education of students who come to our schools speaking a language other than English has received considerable research, policy, and practice attention in the last two decades. Public agencies as well as private foundations have supported specific demographic studies and instructional research related to this population of students, preschool through college. Congress has authorized legislation targeted directly at these students on five separate occasions (1968, 1974, 1984, and 1987) while numerous states have enacted legislation and developed explicit program guidelines. Moreover, the courts have concluded adjudication proceedings which directly influence the educational treatment of language minority students. This significant attention has allowed answers to some questions of importance which were unanswerable less than a decade ago. The following discussion will highlight these questions and their respective treatment in light of emerging information regarding "bilingual" students.

Who Are These Students?

As one searches for a comprehensive definition of the "language minority" student, a continuum of definitional attempts unfolds. At one end of the continuum are general definitions such as "students who come from homes in which a language other than English is spoken." At the other end of that continuum are highly operationalized definitions, "students scored in the first quartile on a standardized test of English language proficiency." Regardless of the definition adopted, it is apparent that these students come in a variety of linguistic shapes and forms. The language minority population in the United States continues to be linguistically heterogeneous with over 100 distinct language groups identified. Even among Hispanic students, there are monolingual Spanish speakers, monolingual English speakers, while others are to some degree bilingual. Other non-English speaking minority groups are similarly heterogeneous. Not inconsequential are the related cultural attributes of language minority, making this population not only linguistically distinct but also culturally distinct. Describing the "typical" language minority student is highly problematic. However, we might agree that the student is one who (a) is characterized by substantive participation in a non-English speaking social environment; (b) has acquired the normal communicative abilities of that social environment; and, (c) is exposed to a substantive English speaking environment, more than likely for the first time, during the formal schooling process.

Estimates of the number of language minority students have been compiled by the federal government on several occasions (O'Malley, 1981; Development Associates 1984). These estimates differ because of the definition adopted for identifying these students, the particular measure utilized to obtain the estimate, and the statistical treatment utilized to generalize beyond the actual sample obtained. For example, O'Malley (1981) defined the language minority student population by utilizing a specific cutoff score on an English language proficiency test administered to a stratified sample of students. Development Associates (1984) estimated the population by utilizing reports from a stratified sample of local school districts. Therefore, estimates of language minority students have ranged between 1,300,000 (Development Associates, 1984) to 3,600,000 (O'Malley, 1981) with the following attributes:

1. The total number of language minority children, ages five–fourteen, in 1976 approximated 2.52 million, with a drop to 2.39 million in 1980 and a projected gradual increase to 3.40 million in the year 2000 (Waggoner, 1984). In 1983, this population was more conservatively estimated to be 1.29 million (Development Associates, 1984). Recall that this divergence in estimates reflects the procedures used to obtain language minority "counts" and estimates.
2. The majority of these children reside throughout the United States, but with distinct geographical clustering. For example, about 62 percent of language minority children are Chicano students found in Arizona, Colorado, California, New Mexico, and Texas (O'Malley, 1981; Development Associates, 1984; Wagoner, 1984).
3. Of the estimated number of language minority children in 1978, 72 percent were of Spanish language background, 22 percent

other European languages, 5 percent Asians, and 1 percent Native American. However, such distributions will change due to differential growth rates, and by the year 2000, the proportion of Spanish language background children is projected to be about 77 percent of the total (O'Malley, 1981). Estimates by Development Associates (1984) for students in grades K-6 indicate that 76 percent are Spanish language background; 8 percent Southeast Asian (Vietnamese, Cambodian, Hmong, etc.); 5 percent other European; 5 percent East Asian (Chinese, Korean, etc.); and, 5 percent other (Arabic, Navajo, etc.).

4. For the national school districts sample in the 19 most highly impacted states utilized by Development Associates (1984), 17 percent of the total K-6 student population was estimated as language minority in these states.

Regardless of differing estimates, a significant number of students from language backgrounds other than English are served by U.S. schools. Moreover, this population is expected to increase steadily in the future. The challenge these students present to U.S. educational institutions will continue to increase concomitantly.

What Types of Educational Programs Serve These Students?

For a school district staff with language minority students there are many possible program options: transitional bilingual education, maintenance bilingual education, English as a second language (ESL), immersion, sheltered English, submersion, etc. (Government Accounting Office, 1987). Ultimately, staff will reject program labels and instead answer the following questions:

1. What are the native language (L1) and second language (L2) characteristics of the students, families, and community(ies) we serve?
2. What model of instruction is desired?:
    (a) How do we choose to utilize L1 and L2 *as mediums of instruction*?
    (b) How do we choose to handle the *instruction* of L1 and L2?
3. What is the nature of staff and resources necessary to implement the desired instruction?

Program initiatives can be differentiated by the way they utilize the native language and English during instruction. A recent report by Development Associates (1984) surveyed 333 school districts in the 19 states which serve over 80 percent of language minority students in the United States. For grades K-5, they report the following salient features in the use of language(s) during the instruction of language minority students:

1. The use of English predominated in the programs of 93 percent of the schools; conversely, 7 percent indicated that the use of the native language predominated.
2. Of the sampled schools, 60 percent reported that both the native language and English were utilized during instruction.
3. Minimal or no use of the native language during instruction was reported by 30 percent of the schools.

Two-thirds of the schools surveyed have chosen to utilize some form of bilingual curriculum to serve this population of students. However, some one-third of these schools minimize or altogether ignore native language use in their instruction of language minority students. Recall that some two-thirds to three-fourths of language minority students in this country are of Spanish-speaking backgrounds. Programs which serve these students have been characterized primarily as "Bilingual Transitional Education." These programs transition students from early-grade, Spanish-emphasis instruction to later-grade, English-emphasis instruction, and, eventually, to English-only instruction.

Recent research in transition type schools suggests that language minority students can be served effectively. Effective schools develop educational structures and processes which take into consideration both the broader aspects of effective schools reported for English speaking students (Purkey & Smith, 1983) and specific attributes relevant to language minority students (Tikunoff, 1983; Carter & Chatfield, 1986; García, 1988). Of particular importance has been the positive effect of intensive instruction in the native language on literacy development (Wong Fillmore & Valadez, 1985). Hakuta and Gould (1987) and Hudelson (1987) maintain that skills and concepts learned in the native language provide a "scaffold" for acquisition of new knowledge in the second language.

For the one-third of the students receiving little or no instruction in the native language, two alternative types of instructional approaches likely predominate: English as a Second Language (ESL) and immersion. Each of these program types depends on the primary utilization of

English during instruction but does not ignore the fact that the students served are limited in English proficiency. However, these programs do not require instructional personnel who speak the native language of the student. Moreover, these programs are suited to classrooms in which there is no substantial number of students from one non-English speaking group but may have a heterogeneous non-English background student population (Ovando & Collier, 1985).

Both ESL and immersion programs have been particularly influenced by recent theoretical developments in the instruction of a second language (Krashen, 1984; Chamot & O'Malley, 1986). These developments suggest that effective second language learning is best accomplished under conditions which simulate natural communicative interactions and minimize the formal instruction of linguistic structures, e.g., memorization drills, learning grammatical rules, etc. Although ESL programs continue to involve "pull-out" sessions in which students are removed from the regular classroom to spend time on concentrated language learning activities with specially trained educational staff, the recent theoretical and practice consensus is that such language learning experiences should be communicative and centered around academic content areas (Chamot & O'Malley, 1986).

School district staff have been creative in developing a wide range of language minority student programs. They have answered the above questions differentially for (a) different language groups (Spanish, Vietnamese, Chinese, etc.); (b) different grade levels within a school; (c) different subgroups of language minority students within a classroom; and (d) even different levels of language proficiency. The result has been a broad and at times perplexing variety of program models.

Federal and State Policies Generated

The immediately preceding discussion has attempted to lay a foundation for understanding *who* the language minority student is and *how* that student has been served. This discussion turns now to educational policy: first, federal legislative and legal initiatives, and second, state initiatives.

Federal legislative initiatives. The U.S. Congress set a minimum standard for the education of language minority students in public educational institutions in its passage of Title VI of the Civil Rights Act of 1964 prohibiting discrimination by educational institutions on the basis of race, color, sex, or national origin and by subsequent Equal

Educational Opportunity Act of 1974 (EEOA). The EEOA was an effort by Congress to specifically define what constitutes a denial of constitutionally guaranteed equal educational opportunity. The EEOA provides in part:

> No state shall deny equal educational opportunities to an individual on account of his or her race, color, sex, or national origin, by . . . the failure by an educational agency to take appropriate action to overcome language barriers that impede equal participation by students in its instructional programs. 20 U.S.C. ss 1703 (f).

This statute does not mandate specific education treatment, but it does require public educational agencies to sustain programs to meet the language needs of their students.

On five occasions (1968, 1974, 1978, 1984, and 1987) the U.S. Congress has passed specific legislation related to the education of language minority students. The Bilingual Education Act (BEA) of 1968 was intended as a demonstration program designed to meet the educational needs of low-income limited English speaking children. Grants were awarded to local educational agencies, institutions of higher education, or regional research facilities to: (a) develop and operate bilingual education programs, native history and culture programs, early childhood education programs, adult education programs, and programs to train bilingual aides; (b) make efforts to attract and retain as teachers individuals from non-English-speaking backgrounds; and (c) establish cooperation between the home and the school.

Four major reauthorizations of the BEA have occurred since 1968— in 1974, 1978, 1984 and 1987. As a consequence of the 1974 Amendments (Public Law 93–380), a bilingual education program was defined for the first time as "instruction given in, and study of English to the extent necessary to allow a child to progress effectively through the education system, the native language" (Schneider, 1976). The goal of bilingual education continued to be a transition to English rather than maintenance of the native language. Children no longer had to be low income to participate. New programs were funded, including a graduate fellowship program for study in the field of training teachers for bilingual educational programs and a program for the development, assessment, and dissemination of classroom materials.

In the Bilingual Education Amendments of 1978 (Public Law 95-561), program eligibility was expanded to include students with limited English academic proficiency as well as students with limited English-speaking ability. Parents were given a greater role in program planning and operation. Teachers were required to be proficient in both English and the native language of the children in the program. Grant recipients were required to demonstrate how they would continue the program when federal funds were withdrawn.

The Bilingual Education Act of 1984 created new program options including special alternative instructional programs that did not require use of the child's native language. These program alternatives were expanded in 1987. State and local agency program staff were required to collect data to identify the population served and describe program effectiveness.

Over one billion federal dollars have been appropriated through Title VII legislation for educational activities (program development, program implementation, professional training, and research) for language minority students. In addition, other congressional appropriations (e.g., Vocational Education, Chapter I, etc.) explicitly target language minority students.

Federal legal initiatives. The 1974 U.S. Supreme Court decision in *Lau v. Nichols* (414 U.S. 563) is the landmark statement of the rights of language minority students, indicating that limited English proficient students must be provided with language support:

> [T]here is no equality of treatment merely by providing students with the same facilities, textbooks, teachers, and curriculum: for students who do not understand English are effectively foreclosed from any meaningful discourse.

> Basic English skills are at the very core of what these public schools teach. Imposition of a requirement that, before a child can effectively participate in the education program he must already have acquired those basic skills is to make a mockery of public education. We know that those who do not understand English are certain to find their classroom experiences wholly incomprehensible and in no way meaningful.

The Fifth Circuit *Castaneda v. Pickard* (1981) court set three requirements which constitute an appropriate program for language minority students:

(1) The theory must be based on a sound educational theory.
(2) The program must be "reasonably calculated to implement effectively" the chosen theory.
(3) The program must produce results in a reasonable time.

The courts have also required appropriate action to overcome language barriers. "Measures which will actually overcome the problem" are called for by the *U.S. v. Texas* court (506 F. Supp. at 433), or "results indicating that the language barriers confronting students are actually being overcome" are mandated by the *Castaneda* court (628 F 2nd at 1010). Therefore, local school districts and state education agencies have a burden to assess the effectiveness of special language programs on an ongoing basis. Other court decisions have delineated staff professional training attributes and the particular role of standardized tests.

State initiatives. Through state legislation, 12 states mandated special educational services for language minority students, 12 states permit these services, and one state prohibits them. Twenty-six states have no legislation which directly addresses language minority students.

State program policy for language minority students can be characterized as follows:

1. Implementing instructional programs which allow or require instruction in a language other than English (17 states).
2. Establishing special qualifications for the certification of professional instructional staff (15 states).
3. Providing school districts supplementary funds in support of educational programs (15 states).
4. Mandating a cultural component (15 states).
5. Requiring parental consent for enrollment of students (11 states).

Eight states (Arizona, California, Colorado, Illinois, Indiana, Massachusetts, Rhode Island, and Texas) impose all of the above requirements concurrently. Such a pattern suggests continued attention by states to issues related to language minority students (see August & García, 1988) for details).

General Implications for Education and Research

The previous discussions of bilingual acquisition and second language acquisition have attempted to highlight important data and theory which serve to provide an understanding of these phenomena. The same data and theory, however, have influenced the educational treatment of language minority students. As indicated previously, the knowledge base in this area continues to expand but is in no way to be considered complete or overly comprehensive. In addition, it would be an error to conclude that the data and theory which have emerged are the primary factors in determining the educational treatment of language minority students. However, it does seem appropriate to identify the possible program, policy, and future research implications derived from research and theory as highlighted by the present discussion and that of Hakuta and Snow (1986); August and García (1988); and Hakuta and García (1988).

1.   One major goal of language minority education should be the development of the full repertoire of linguistic skills in English in preparation for participation in mainstream classes. Future research should delineate alternative routes which will allow for effective achievement of this goal.

2.   Time spent learning the native language is not time lost in developing English. Children can become fluent in a second language without losing the first language and can maintain the first language without retarding the development of the second language. Presently, it is not clear what processes or mechanisms facilitate this positive transfer. Identifying such processes is the challenge awaiting future research.

3.   There is no cognitive cost to the development of bilingualism in children; very possibly bilingualism enhances children's thinking skills. Further research which explores specific cognitive/academic functioning of bilingual children is necessary.

4.   Language minority education programs should have the flexibility of adjusting to individual and cultural differences among children. Furthermore, educators should develop the expectation that it is not abnormal for some students to need instruction in two languages for relatively long periods of time. We do not yet know how much time spent in negative language instruction positively influences academic outcomes in the second language. This type of research will greatly enhance the educational outcomes for language minority students.

5.   Educators should expect that young children will take several years to learn a second language to the level of a native speaker. At the same time, they should not have lower expectations of older learners, who can learn languages quite quickly, and often end up speaking them just as well as younger learners. The clear distinction between "young" and "older" learners requires further research.

6.   Children who are at risk for reading failure should be taught to read in the native language. Reading skills acquired in the native language transfer readily and quickly to English and will result in higher

reading achievement in English. Future research must make the link between overall literacy in the native language and overall literacy in the second language.

7. A major problem for language minority children is that young English speaking children share the negative stereotypes of their parents and the society at large. Any action that upgrades the status of the language minority children and their language contributes to the children's opportunities for friendship with native English speaking children. Future research with these children must link issues of ethnic identity, general self-concept, and specific academic self-concept.

In summary, theoretical and, to some extent, research support can be identified for educational interventions which choose to utilize language in a variety of distinct ways within an educational program for language minority students. It seems necessary to conclude that the present state of research and theory on the language and the education of language minority students does allow for some specific conclusions. Of course, we would recommend that educational professionals, in their quest to intervene for the betterment of language minority students, carefully scrutinize relevant theory and research and utilize that analysis to design, implement, and evaluate interventions of significance to their particular educational circumstances. It is fair to request from such designers and implementors a clear theoretical and research foundation, one which can in turn receive the necessary careful scrutiny.

References

Ambert, A.N. (in press). The enriched language of Puerto Rican children. In Ambert, A.N. & Alvarez, M.D. (Eds.). *Puerto Rican children on the mainland: Interdisciplinary perspectives.* New York: Garland.

August, D. & García, E. (1988). *Language minority education in the United States: Research, policy and practice.* Chicago, IL: Charles C. Thomas Publisher.

Baetens Beardsmore, H. (1982). *Bilingualism: Basic principles.* Clevedon, England: Tieto.

Baker, K.A. & de Kanter, A.A. (1983). An answer from research on bilingual education. *American Education,* 48–88.

Bates, E. (1976). *Language in context: The acquisition of pragmatics.* New York: Academic Press.

Ben-Zeev, S. (1977). The influence of bilingualism on cognitive strategy and cognitive development. *Child Development, 48,* 1009–1018.

Bowerman, M. (1975). Crosslinguistic similarities at two stages of syntactic development. In Lennenberg, E. and Lennenberg, E. (Eds.) *Foundations of language development*. London: UNESCO Press.

Braine, M.D.S. (1976). Children's first word combination. *Monographs of the Society for Research in Child Development*. New York: Wiley.

Brown, R.A. (1973). *A first language: The early stages*. Cambridge: Harvard University Press.

Canale, M. (1983). From communicative complete to communicative pedagogy. In Richards, J., & Schmidt, R. (Eds.) *Language and communication*. London: Longman.

Carringer, D.C. (1974). Creative thinking abilities of Mexican youth: The relationship of bilingualism. *Journal of Cross Cultural Psychology, 5,* 492–504.

Carter, T.P. & Chatfield, M.L. (1986). Effective bilingual schools: Implications for policy and practice. *American Journal of Education, 95*(1), 200–234.

Castaneda vs. Pickard, 648 F.2d 989, 1007 5th Cir. 1981; 103 S.ct. 3321 (1983).

Chamot, A.U. & O'Maley, J.M. (1986). *A cognitive academic language learning approach: An ESL content based curriculum*. Wheaton, MD: National Clearinghouse for Bilingual Education.

Chomsky, N. (1959). Review of B.F. Skinner, *Verbal Behavior and Language, 35,* 116–128.

Cole, M., Dore, J., Hall, W. & Dowley, G. (1978). Situation and task in children's talk. *Discourse Process, 1,* 119–126.

Cummins, J. (1979). Linguistic interdependence of the educational development of bilingual children. *Review of Educational Research, 19,* 222–251.

Cummins, J. (1981). The role of primary language development in promoting educational success for language minority students. In California State Department of Education (Ed.) *Schooling and language minority students: A theoretical framework*. Los Angeles, CA: Evaluation, Dissemination, and Assessment Center, 3–50.

Cummins, J. (1984). *Bilingualism and Special Education*. San Diego. CA: College Hill Press.

Cummins, J. & Gulatson, M. (1974). Bilingual education and cognition. *Alberta Journal of Education Research, 20,* 259–269.

Darcy, N.T. (1953). A review of the literature of the effects of bilingualism upon the measurement of intelligence. *Journal of Genetic Psychology, 82,* 21–57.

Darcy, N.T. (1963). Bilingualism and the measurement of intelligence: Review of a decade of research. *Journal of Genetic Psychology, 103,* 259–282.

Development Associates (December 1984). *Final report of the descriptive study phase of the national longitudinal evaluation of the effectiveness of services for language minority limited English proficient students*. Arlington, VA: Development Associates.

Díaz, R.M. (1983). The impact of bilingualism on cognitive development. In Gordon, E.W. (Ed.) *Review of research in education, Vol. X*. Washington, DC: American Educational Research Association, 23–54.

Dulay, H. & Burt, M. (1974). Natural sequence in child second language acquisition. *Working papers on bilingualism*. Toronto: The Ontario Institute for Studies in Education.

Duran, R. (Ed.). (1981). *Latino language and communicative behavior*. Norwood, NJ: Ablex.

Ervin-Tripp, S.M. (1974). Is second language learning like the first? *TESOL Quarterly, 8*(2)., 111–127.

Ervin-Tripp, S. & Mitchell-Kernan, C. (1977). *Child discourse*. New York: Academic Press.

Feldman, F.C., & Shen, M. (1971). Some language-related cognitive advantages of bilingual five-year-olds. *Journal of Genetic Psychology, 118*, 235–234.

Galambos, S.J. & Hakuta, K. (1988). Subject-specific and task-specific characteristics of metalinguistic awareness in bilingual children. *Applied Linguistics, 9*, 141–162.

García, E. (1983). *Bilingualism in early childhood*. Albuquerque, NM: University of New Mexico Press.

García, E. (1986). Bilingual development and the education of bilingual children during early childhood. *American Journal of Education, 95*, 96–121.

García, E. (1988). Effective schooling for language minority students. In National Clearinghouse for Bilingual Education (Ed.) *New Focus*. Arlington, VA: National Clearinghouse for Bilingual Education.

García, E. & Carrasco, R. (1981). An analysis of bilingual mother-child discourse. In Duran (Ed.) *Latino discourse*. New York: Ablex (173–189).

García, E. & González, G. (1984). Spanish and Spanish-English development in the Hispanic child. In Martinez, S.V. & Mendoza, R.H. (Eds.) *Chicano Psychology*. New York: Academic Press.

García, E., Maez, L., & González, G. (1983). Language switching in bilingual children: A national perspective. In García, E. (Ed.) *The Mexican-American child: Language, cognition and social development*. Tempe: Arizona State University (56–73)..

Gardner, R.C. & Lambert, E. (1972). *Attitudes and motivation in second language learning*. Rowley, MA: Newbury House.

Ginishi, C. (1981). Code switching in Chicano six year olds. In Duran, R., (Ed.) *Latino language and communicative behavior*. Norwood, NJ: Ablex (133–152).

González, G. (1970). The acquisition of Spanish grammar by native Spanish speakers. Unpublished doctoral dissertation, University of Texas, Austin.

González, G. (1988). *The education of Mexican students during the era of segregation*. Tucson, AZ: University of Arizona Press.

González, G. (1990). *Chicano education in the segregation era: 1915–1945*. Tucson, AZ: University of Arizona Press.

Hakuta, K. (1974). A preliminary report on the development of grammatical morphemes in a Japanese girl learning English as a second language. *Working Papers in Bilingualism.* Toronto: The Ontario Institute for studies in Education, *3,* 294–316.

Hakuta, K. (1975). Learning to speak a second language: What exactly does the child learn? In Dato, D.P. (Ed.) *Georgetown University Round Table on Language and Linguistics.* Washington, DC: Georgetown University Press.

Hakuta, K. (1986). *Mirror of language: The debate on bilingualism.* New York: Basic Books.

Hakuta, K. & García, E. (1988). Bilingualism and bilingual education. *American Psychologist.*

Hakuta, K. & Gould, L.J. (1987). Synthesis of research on bilingual education. *Educational Leadership, 44*(6), 39–45.

Hakuta, K. & Snow, C. (1986). The role of research in policy decisions about bilingual education. Washington, DC: U.S. House of Representatives, Education and Labor Committee (Testimony: January).

Halliday, M. (1975). *Learning how to mean: Explorations in the development of language.* London: Dover.

Hammerly, H. (1985). *An integrated theory of language teaching.* Burnby, Canada: Second Language Publications.

Hatch, E. (1974). Is second language learning universal? *Working Papers on Bilingualism.* Toronto: The Ontario Institute for Studies in Education, *3,* 1–16.

Hatch, E. (1978). *Second language acquisition: A book of readings.* Rowley, MA: Newbury House.

Hudelson, S. (1987). The role of native language literacy in the education of language minority children. *Language Arts, 64*(8), 827–841.

Huerta, A. (1977). The development of codeswitching in a young bilingual. *Working Papers in Sociolinguistics* (21).

Hymes, D. (1974). *Foundations in sociolinguistics: An ethnographic approach.* Philadelphia: University of Pennsylvania.

Ianco-Worral, A. (1972). Bilingualism and cognitive development. *Child Development, 43,* 1390–1400.

Kennan, E. (1976). Conversational competence in children. *Journal of Child Language, 1,* 163–183.

Kessler, C. & Quinn, M.E. (1986). Positive effects of bilingualism on science problem-solving abilities. In Alatis, J.E. and Staczek, J.J. (Eds.) *Perspectives on Bilingual Education.* Washington, DC: Georgetown University Press, 289–296.

Kessler, C. & Quinn, M.E. (1987). Language Minority children's linguistic and cognitive creativity. *Journal of Multilingual and Multicultural Development, 8*(1), 173–185.

Krashen, S.D. (1981). Bilingual education and second language acquisition theory. In California State Department of Education (Ed.) *Schooling and language minority students.* Dissemination and Assessment Center, California State University, Los Angeles, 3–50.

Krashen, S.D. (1984). *Principles and practices in second language acquisition.* Oxford: Pergamon.

Larsen-Freeman, D. (1976). An explanation of the morpheme acquisition order of second language learners. *Language Learning, 26,* 125–134.

Lau vs. Nichols (1974). U.S. Supreme Court, 414 U.S. 563.

Leopold, W.F. (1939). *Speech development of a bilingual child: A linguist's record, Vol. I. Vocabulary growth in the first two years.* Evanston, IL: Northwestern University Press.

Leopold, W.F. (1947). *Speech development of a bilingual child: A linguist's record, Vol. II. Second learning in the first two years.* Evanston, IL: Northwestern University Press.

Leopold, W.F. (1949a). *Speech development of a bilingual child: A linguist's record, Vol. III. Grammars and general problems in the first two years.* Evanston, IL: Northwestern University Press.

Leopold, W.F. (1949b). *Speech development of a bilingual child: A linguist's record, Vol. IV. Diary from age two.* Evanston, IL: Northwestern University Press.

MacNab, G. (1979). Cognition and bilingualism: A re-analysis of studies. *Linguistics, 17,* 231–255.

McLaughlin, B. (1984). *Second language acquisition in childhood, Vol. I: Preschool children.* Hillsdale, NJ: Lawrence Erlbaum.

McLaughlin, B. (1985). *Second language acquisition in childhood, Vol. II: School age children.* Hillsdale, NJ: Lawrence Erlbaum.

Moll, L. (1988). Educating Latino students. *Language Arts, 64*(10), 315–324.

O'Malley, M.J. (1981). *Children's services study: Language minority children with limited English proficiency in the United States.* Rosslyn, VA: National Clearinghouse for Bilingual Education.

Ovando, C. & Collier, V. (1985). *Bilingual and ESL classrooms: Teaching in multicultural contexts.* New York: McGraw-Hill.

Padilla, A.M. & Liebman, E. (1975). Language acquisition in the bilingual child. *The Bilingual Review/La Revista Bilingüe, 2,* 34–55.

Peal, E. & Lambert, W.E. (1962). The relation of bilingualism to intelligence. *Psychological Monographs: General and Applied, 76*(546), 1–23.

Phillips, S.U. (1972). Participant structures and communication incompetence: Warm Springs children in community and classroom. In Cazden, C., Hymes, D. & John, W.J. (Eds.) *Language functions in the classroom.* New York: Teachers College Press.

Purkey, S.C. & Smith, M.S. (1983). Effective schools: A review. *Elementary School Journal, 83,* 52–78.

Ramírez, A. (1985). *Bilingualism through schooling.* Albany, NY: State University of New York Press.

Richards, J. & Rodgers, T.S. (1986). *Approaches and methods in language teaching*. Cambridge: Cambridge University Press.

Rossell, C. & Ross, J.M. (1985). *The social science evidence on bilingual education*. Boston: Boston University.

Schneider, S.G. (1976). *Revolution, reaction or reform: The 1974 Bilingual Education Act*. New York: Las Americas.

Schumann, J.H. (1976). Affective factors and the problem of age in second language acquisition. *Language Learning, 25*, 209–239.

Seliger, H.W. (1977). Does practice make perfect? A study of interactional patterns and L2 competence. *Language Learning, 27*(2), 263–278.

Shantz, C. (1977). The development of social cognition. In Hetherington, E.M. (Ed.) *Review of child development research*. Chicago, IL: University of Chicago Press.

Skinner, B.F. (1957). *Verbal behavior*. Englewood Cliffs, NJ: Prentice-Hall.

Skrabanek, R.L. (1970). Language maintenance among Mexican Americans. *International Journal of Comparative Sociology, 11*, 272–282.

Skutnab-Kangas, T. (1979). *Language in the process of cultural assimilation and structural incoporation of linguistic minorities*. Rosslyn, VA: National Clearinghouse for Bilingual Education.

Sorenson, A.P. (1967). Multilingualism in the Northwest Amazon. *American Anthropologist, 69*, 67–68.

Tikunoff, W.J. (1983). *Compatibility of the SBIF features with other research on instruction of LEP students*. San Francisco, CA: Far West Laboratory (SBIF-83-4.8/10).

Trioke, R.C. (1981). Synthesis of research in bilingual education. *Educational Leadership, 38*, 498–504.

U.S. General Accounting Office (1987, March). *Research evidence on bilingual education*. Washington, DC: U.S. General Accounting Office, GAO/PEMD-87–12BR.

U.S. v. Texas Court, 506 F.Supp. at 433 (1984).

Waggoner, D. (1984). The need for bilingual education: Estimates from the 1980 census. *NABE Journal, 8*, 1–14.

Willig, A. (1985). A meta-analysis of selected studies on the effectiveness of bilingual education. *Review of Educational Research, 55*, 269–317.

Wong Fillmore, L. (1976). The second time around: Cognitive and social strategies in second language acquisition. Unpublished doctoral dissertation, Stanford University.

Wong Fillmore, S. & Valadez, C. (1985). Teaching bilingual learners. In Wittrock, M.S. (Ed.) *Handbook on research on teaching*. Washington, DC: AERA.

Zentella, A.C. (1981). Ta bien you could answer me en cualquier idioma: Puerto Rican code switching in bilingual classrooms. In Duran, R. (Ed.) *Latino language and communicative behavior*. Norwood, NJ: Ablex (109–112).

Annotated Bibliography

Appel, R. (1989). Bilingualism and cognitive-linguisitic development: Evidence from a word association task and a sorting task. *Journal of Multilingual and Multicultural Development, 10*(3), 183–196.

Reports the results of a study on the influence of bilingualism on the cognitive-linguistic development of monolingual Dutch and bilingual Turkish, Moroccan, and Surinamese children living in The Netherlands. Word association and sorting tasks were administered to the children. No differences were found among the four groups of children on the variables studied. The author concluded that bilingualism does not affect cognitive-linguistic development negatively.

August, D. & Garcia, E. (1988). *Language minority education in the United States: Research, policy and practice.* Chicago: Charles C. Thomas.

Provides a succinct overview of bilingual and second language research in concert with research directly related to the education of language minority students in the United States. Of particular significance is the discussion of the federal, state, and court related educational policy generated over the past two decades.

Baetens Beardsmore, H. & Kohls, J. (1988). Immediate pertinence in the acquisition of multilingual proficiency: The European Schools. *The Canadian Modern Language Review, 44*(4), 680–701.

Describes the European School phenomenon, that is, worldwide multilingualism in an educational context, through a case study. The authors argue that this case study offers an alternative model to societies that must deal with educating populations coming from different linguistic backgrounds. Provides theoretical explanations for the linguistic outcome produced by the European School system.

Baker, C. (1988). *Key issues in bilingualism and bilingual education.* Avon, England: Multilingual Matters.

Discusses a variety of issues in the field of bilingual education, including bilingualism and intelligence, cognitive functioning, attitudes, motivation, current research, and the application of theory to practice.

Bild, E.R. & Swain, M. (1989). Minority language students in a French programme: Their French proficiency. *Journal of Multilingual and Multicultural Development, 10*(3), 255–274.

The French proficiency of bilingual and monolingual students in an eighth grade English/French bilingual program in Ontario was compared. The students' first languages were English, Italian, or a non-Romance language. French proficiency was assessed using written cloze tests and oral story-telling activities. Bilinguals were found to perform significantly better than monolinguals on almost all measures. The authors conclude that knowing a second language facilitates learning a third language. Therefore, bilingual children are excellent candidates for French immersion programs.

Britton, J., Shafer, R.E., & Watson, K. (1990). *Teaching and learning English worldwide.* Avon, England: Multilingual Matters.

Contains historical studies of the teaching of English as a native, second and, in some cases, a third language in 13 different countries, including the United States.

Danesi, M. & Mollica, A. (1988). Second-language pedagogy in the eighties: An annotated index of the CMLR/RCLV Volumes 38–42 (1981–1985). *The Canadian Modern Language Review, 44*(3), 431–522.

A very useful annotated bibliography of articles appearing in *The Canadian Modern Review/La Revue canadienne des langues vivantes* from 1981 to 1985 on the topics of second language acquisition, learning, and teaching. It includes articles concerning ongoing research, instructional practices, theoretical developments, and technological innovations. The bibliography is divided into the following sections: (1) Psychology of Language Learning; (2) Applied Linguistics; (3) Methodology; (4) Equipment and Media; (5) Curriculum; (6) Testing and Evaluation; (7) Teacher Education; (8) Materials Development; (9) Culture; and (10) General.

Fagan, W.T. & Hayden, H.R. (1988). *The Canadian Modern Language Review, 44*(4), 653–668.

Ten fifth grade Anglo students, who had participated in a French immersion program since the first grade, were selected for this study to examine three processes in the writing process in both English and French: planning, composing, and editing. The authors found that there was great variation in language performance. However, results of the study indicate that writing processing behaviors in English transferred from instruction in French.

Faltis, C.J. (1988). Code-switching and bilingual schooling: An examination of Jacobson's new concurrent approach. *Journal of Multilingual and Multicultural Development, 10*(2), 117–127.

Describes the New Concurrent Approach to bilingual instruction. This approach incorporates intersentential code-switching in the teaching of content to limited English proficient children living in a bilingual setting. Examines how code-switching can be incorporated and adapted for instruction and how the adaptation contributes to the balanced distribution of the two codes. Presents evidence to show that fears about the use of code-switching for instructional purposes are unfounded.

García, E. (1988). Effective schooling for language minority students. In National Clearinghouse for Bilingual Education (Ed.) *New Focus*. Arlington, VA: National Clearinghouse for Bilingual Education.

Describes the work of several researchers who have attempted to document the attributes of effective educational programs for Spanish/English bilingual populations in the Southwestern United States. Specific instructional, staffing, and administrative aspects of these programs are identified.

Gass, S., Madden, C., Preston, D., & Selinker, L. (1989). *Variation in second language acquisition. Volumes I and II*. Avon, England: Multilingual Matters.

These two volumes present the issues of variability in second language acquisition. Discourse and pragmatics are analyzed in the first volume and the second volume discusses psycholinguistic issues.

González, G. (1990). *Chicano education in the segregation era: 1915–1945*. Tucson, AZ: University of Arizona Press.

Provides an overview of the educational segregation of Mexican-American students in the Southwest from the turn of the century through World War II. Instructional practices and educational policy during the period are analyzed.

Hakuta, K. & García. E. (1989). Bilingualism and education. *American Psychologist*, 44(2), 374–379.

A discussion of the concept of bilingualism applied to bilingual children. Reviews the history of research on bilingual children and bilingual education in the United States. Future research directions are suggested.

Hakuta, K. & Gould, L.J. (1987). Synthesis of research on bilingual education. *Educational Leadership*, 44(6), 39–45.

A comprehensive and easy to read overview of educational research assessing the effects of bilingual education. The effects of native language instruction are a particular focus of discussion along with the complex issue of doing sound, empirical, comparative educational research with language minority populations.

Hamers, J.F. & Blanc, M. (1988). *Bilinguality and bilingualism*. Cambridge, England: Cambridge University Press.

Examines the way bilingualism develops in childhood and later and its social, neurological, and psychological foundations. Also analyzes the social and cultural consequences of bilingualism. The authors explore the wider issues of language contact and the applications of bilingual research to language teaching and language planning.

Hansen, D. (1989). Locating learning: Second language gains and language use in family, peer, and classroom contexts. *NABE Journal*, *13*(2), 161–180.

Discusses a study of 117 elementary school students from Spanish-dominant homes to determine the relationship between second language gains to language use in the classroom, at home, and with peers. Students were tested for reading comprehension skills and auditory vocabulary skills. According to the author, schooling interrupts peer influences while stimulating family influences on second language learning and the places in which second language learning occur are more specific and delimited for skills that require greater intention and effort.

Hudelson, S. (1987). The role of native language literacy in the education of language minority children. *Language Arts*, *64*(8), 827–841.

Explores the link between native language literacy development and literacy development in a second language. Recent theoretical and empirical contributions suggest that "you only learn how to read once." Specific instructional suggestions are given regarding the transfer of literacy skills.

Kessler, C. & Quinn, M.E. (1987). Language minority children's linguistic and cognitive creativity. *Journal of Multilingual and Multicultural Development*, *8*(1), 173–185.

Provides empirical evidence for the link between bilingualism and cognitive advantages in elementary level, economically disadvantaged students. Experimental verifications of the effects are provided.

Lee, E. (1989). Chinese American fluent English proficient students and school achievement. *NABE Journal*, *13*(2), 95–111.

Describes a study to compare the academic performance in reading, language, and mathematics of two groups: (1) Chinese American LEP students initially identified and then reclassified as fluent English proficient (FEP) and (2) non-minority native English speakers. Results of the study indicated significantly higher scores in language and mathematics achievement for Chinese American FEP students when compared with the native English speakers. An interesting finding was that the socio-economic status of the Chinese American students affected the achievement levels. Students from low SES backgrounds and from Viet Nam did less well in reading, language, and mathematics achievement than non-minority English speakers.

Leung, C. & Franson, C. (1989). The multilingual classroom: The case for minority language pupils. *Journal of Multilingual and Multicultural Development*, *10*(6), 461–472.

Describes the differences between majority language learners learning a second language and minority language learners learning a second language.

The authors emphasize the difficulties faced by minority language speakers and the need for the development of more effective teaching practices.

McGroarty, M. (1989). The benefits of cooperative learning arrangements in second language instruction. *NABE Journal, 13*(2), 127–143.

Describes the six advantages of cooperative learning arrangements in bilingual and second language instruction: (1) increased frequency and variety of second language practice through variety of interaction; (2) possibililty for use of the first language to support cognitive development and increase second language development; (3) opportunities to integrate language with content area learning; (4) use of a greater variety of curricular materials for language and concept development; (5) possibility for language teachers to master new communication teaching skills; and (6) opportunities for students to serve as resources and asume a more active learning role.

Moll, L. (1988). Educating latino students. *Language Arts, 64*(10), 315–324.

Describes literacy programs operating in several effective elementary classrooms populated primarily by Hispanic Spanish/English bilingual students. An ethnographic approach is utilized to describe the roles of the teacher and students in their classrooms.

Morren, R.C. (1988). Bilingual education curriculum development in Guatemala. *Journal of Multilingual and Multicultural Development, 9*(4), 353–370.

Describes the process of developing a bilingual curriculum for Guatemala's four largest Mayan language groups. It also discusses the direction of bilingual education in Guatemala which has been designed to maintain the distinct linguistic and cultural identity of the Mayans while developing Spanish language skills.

Nadeau, A. & Miramontes, O. (1988). The reclassification of limited English proficient students: Assessing the inter-relationship of selected variables. *NABE Journal, 12*(3), 219–242.

Discusses a study of 2,100 students in a four-stage bilingual program in a California urban school district. The purpose of the study was to determine whether primary language achievement data provide useful information in the reclassification of LEP students, whether there are significant differences in achievement in English reading between the primary and intermediate grades or between oral English achievement groups, and whether there are significant discrepancies between teacher judgment and other selected variables influencing the reclassification process. The authors conclude that primary language achievement, instructional level, and oral English performance may be important indicators of achievement in English.

Oksaar, E. (1989). Psycholinguistic aspects of bilingualism. *Journal of Multilingual and Multicultural Development, 10*(1), 33–46.

According to the author, there are many more bilingual people in the world than monolingual. Monolingualism, the author contends, is the problem in the present day world, not bilingualism. However, psycholinguistics continues to approach language from a monolingual point of view. The author argues that it is necessary to broaden the frame of psycholinguistics to give bilingualism the place it deserves in the field. The article discusses a variety of issues on bilingualism from a psycholinguistic point of view and its relation to biculturalism.

San Miguel, Jr., G. (1988). Bilingual education policy development: The Reagan years, 1980–1987. *NABE Journal, 12*(2), 97–112.

Describes the federal government's policies toward bilingual education under the Reagan administration. The author argues that bilingual education programs have suffered as a result of federal policies.

Saunders, G. (1988). *Bilingual children: From birth to teens.* Avon, England: Multilingual Matters.

A sequel to the author's previous book, *Bilingual children: Guidance for the family*, it continues exploring the issue of bringing up bilingual children successfully to the age of thirteen.

Singleton, D. (1989). *Language acquisition: The age factor.* Avon, England: Multilingual Matters.

Examines the evidence for an age factor in language acquisition and explores the educational implications of the age question, with particular emphasis on formal second language teaching.

Skutnabb-Kangas, T. & Cummins, J. (1988). *Minority education: From shame to struggle.* Avon, England: Multilingual Matters.

Analyzes policy issues on the education of minority students in western industrialized societies. Presents case studies of programs that have been successful in reversing the pattern of minority students' academic failure. According to the authors, the academic difficulties of minority students are rooted in the power relations between dominant and subordinate groups in society. Schools reflect and reinforce these power relations through strategies such as punishment of children for speaking their native language in school, thereby depriving children of confidence in their own cultural identity and academic abilities. Successful programs are described in which minority students and communities are empowered to reverse this trend.

Spener, D. (1988). Transitional bilingual education and the socialization of immigrants. *Harvard Educational Review, 58*(2), 133–153.

The author argues that educational policies in the United States reflect an economic need to socialize immigrants and language minorities to fill low-status jobs. Transitional bilingual education programs, which provide only a limited period of native language instruction and do not ensure English mastery, prevent language minority children from attaining academic success in either their native language or in English. This academic failure reinforces negative stereotypes and serves to legitimize limited access to better jobs.

Strouse, J. (1988). Immigration and education policy in the United States. *NABE Journal, 12*(2), 113–132.

Examines the factors which characterize immigration to the United States with an emphasis on new immigrants and refugees. Describes the educational policies that affect refugee children.

Thomas, J. (1988). The role played by metalinguistic awareness in second and third language learning. *Journal of Multilingual and Multicultural Development, 9*(3), 235–246.

Compares bilingual students learning a third language with monolinguals learning a second language. Participants of the study were bilingual in English and Spanish and learning French as a third language. Results indicate that English-speaking students with prior knowledge of Spanish have an advantage over monolinguals when performing activities usually associated with learning French formally in a classroom. According to the author, the English-Spanish bilinguals who had received a minimum of two years' formal training in Spanish had developed a conscious awareness of language as a system that provided them with advantages over bilinguals who had acquired Spanish informally. The author concluded that developing the metalinguistic awareness of students may increase the potential advantage of knowing two languages when learning a third.

Torres, M. Attitudes of bilingual education parents toward language learning and curriculum and instruction. *NABE Journal, 12*(2), 171–185.

Reports on a study on parent attitudes toward bilingual education and the school participation of Hispanic parents. Participants of the study were Chicano parents with children in bilingual education programs. Results of the study indicated that Chicano parents have positive attitudes toward bilingual education. In addition, parents felt that English should be taught in school because of the economic benefits of knowing English but that Spanish should also be taught for both social and economic reasons.

VanPatten, B. & Lee, J.F. (Eds.) (1990). *Second language acquisition/Foreign language learning*. Avon, England: Multilingual Matters.

A resource for researchers, teachers, and teachers in training, the volume explores the discipline of second language acquisition and foreign language learning. The authors argue that both fields of inquiry come together.

Vásquez, J. (1989). Building instructional strategies from student traits. *NABE Journal, 13*(2), 145–160.

Presents a model of an instructional process which allows teachers to observe student traits and incorporate them into instructional strategies. The model is geared to teachers of linguistically and culturally distinct children.

Yamamoto, M. & Swan, J. (1989). Connotative differences between foreign and Japanese English teachers in Japan. *Journal of Multilingual and Multicultural Development, 10*(3), 233–253.

Describes a study in the connotative level of meaning. A survey was developed and used to sample populations of foreign and Japanese English teachers. Results of the study indicate that teachers immersed in one cultural background, native-speakers as well as non-native speakers, may, without realizing it, transmit images that do not correspond to the connotations understood in other societies.

Yu, V.W.S. & Atkinson, P.A. (1988). An investigation of the language difficulties experienced by Hong Kong secondary school students in English-medium schools: Some causal factors. *Journal of Multilingual and Multicultural Development*, 9(4), 307–322.

A study of 118 Chinese speaking high school students in Hong Kong schools where the language of instruction was English. The purpose of the study was to investigate the subjects' language, educational and social background, and opinions on the two languages and the medium of instruction. Responses to the questionnaire designed for this purpose indicated that a number of factors contributed to the ineffectiveness of the English-medium education in Hong Kong. These are students' lack of exposure to English outside school, the absence of the Hawthorne effect which has positive influence on new second-language immersion programs, and the possibility that students suffer from subtractive bilingualism. These factors appear to prevent the students in the present study from learning English effectively.

CHAPTER IV

Early Childhood Education:
The Effects of Language on Learning

Evangeline Harris Stefanakis

Introduction

Researchers are challenging the narrow linguistic definition of bilingualism and suggest a definition encompassing ethnographic, psychosocial, political, and cultural aspects of bilingualism. Many misconceptions about bilingualism have arisen because of failure to calculate the complexity of the bilingual phenomenon. According to researchers, policymakers must reconsider the goals of bilingual education and focus on more than just English language output. Research and policymakers have often focused on educationally vulnerable populations of students and ignored the increasing reality of bilingualism as a need for all children (Hakuta & García, 1989). A broad view of bilingualism informed by expert research findings should have a positive impact on the development of successful programs for young language minority children.

The current political, social, and economic climate poses a need to develop the learning capacities of an evergrowing young bilingual population. The changing demographic reality in the United States, where the language minority population is constantly growing, requires a closer look at the education of young children and presents a challenge to offer an education which will enhance their educational opportunities. In their review of the literature on bilingualism and education, Hakuta and García (1989) set the stage for this effort:

> The controversy surrounding bilingualism is magnified by a sense of urgency generated by the changing demographic picture. In the United States, there are over 30 million individuals for whom English is not

the primary language of the home. Of those, 2.5 million are children
in the school age range and this number is expected to double in the
year 2000. (p. 374)

The under education of at-risk youth is a critical issue overlooked
by the education reform movement of the 1980's (Rodríguez, in press).
At risk youth, who are for the most part economically, culturally, racially,
and ethnically disadvantaged, are leaving school unprepared for further
education or available work. Workers' lack of basic skills is creating
an inadequate labor force for the United States to compete in a world
economy. Federal aid to education has declined in real dollars by 23
percent and is now insufficient to serve (a) low income children in need
of preschool education; (b) students in need of remedial programs; (c)
students in need of bilingual education; and (d) youth in need of job
training (Smith & Lincoln, 1988).

This chapter presents an analysis of the most recent research efforts
focusing on the education of young language minority children.

Overview of Current Research

Current research on the education of young bilingual children
continues to address the effects of language on learning. Research results
indicate that second language learners are academically disadvantaged
in monolingual school settings. Studies have also confirmed the
advantages of the bilingual school experience for young children. Most
research in the field continues to focus on the effects of traditional
methods of instruction and appropriate assessment strategies for children
with linguistic differences. The current literature gives strong support
to whole language and natural experience approaches to second language
instruction.

Overall the thread connecting these inquiry efforts is the challenge
of isolating the effects of language differences on the early learning
of children. The research explores this idea by focusing on two major
themes: (a) ways to understand young bilingual children; and (b) ways
to foster their learning through effective teaching.

In the context of these two themes, the literature continues to
examine factors which affect the achievement of bilingual children.
The factors consistently discussed are:

1. cognitive ability
2. assessment
3. home experience and parental involvement
4. program models
5. successful learning techniques

This chapter will analyze each of these factors in light of current research findings focusing on bilingual early childhood.

Cognitive Ability

Cognitive ability is one of the predominate factors noted by researchers as impacting the achievement of the bilingual learner. As we will see, current studies focus on the positive impact of bilingualism on young children's cognitive abilities.

In a study of 75 eight-year-old Yugoslavian children, in five second grade classes, Vilke (1988) investigated the advantages of introducing linguistic familiarity at an early school age, including its beneficial effects on cognitive growth. The study focused on understanding the difficulties in foreign language acquisition in young children. The children were offered two periods of English as a second language (ESL) training per week, working in groups of 12 to 15. A control group began ESL training in the fourth grade in the same schools under the same conditions. Pre- and post-test interviews were conducted with the children and parents to determine their respective attitudes toward learning English. Vilke collected data on the groups over a period of six years using observation and assessment of English language competency. Preliminary findings show that:

1. An early start in ESL training created a positive attitude toward the English language in both children and their parents.
2. Students had patterns of performance difficulties in learning English related to the negative effects of transfer from their native language (L1) to their new foreign language (L2).
3. Vocabulary in L2 that was not in L1 was more difficult to learn.
4. Students showed difficulties in learning the structural elements of English as a result of interference of L1 with L2 (e.g. articles are used in L2, but not in Serbian, the native language).
5. Interference from L1 manifests itself at both a linguistic and conceptual level.

6. In 75 percent of the cases, student IQ was a predictor of success in learning English.

To conclude, Vilke found that bilingualism increases motivation for learning and prevents enthnocentrism. She also points out that early bilingualism has beneficial effects upon attitude, more directly than observable cognitive growth. Such effects stem from a very high motivation in children this young to make use of the native language and new language in general, especially when contrasted with postpubescent learners. Vilke's work sets a framework for seeing both native language learning and bilingualism as essential goals for early childhood education.

As a result of her longitudinal studies of preschool children in Japan, Chang (1988) argues for preschool level intervention in order to foster balanced cognitive development between learning of the English language and other academic tasks. Chang started a nine-year longitudinal project to study the cognitive and social development of preschool children in Singapore. Phase 1 of her work collected baseline data on a random sample of children, ages 3 to 6 years, from 40 local private and public preschool centers. The children were tested on a range of language, mathematics, cognitive, and social tasks. Children attending private kindergartens scored better on most tasks than those children in public centers. This was especially true in English language tasks.

Phase 2 of the project focused on center-based intervention strategies for cognitive and social development. During the implementation of Phase 2, the gap narrowed in cognitive and mathematical tasks between private and public center learners. This was not true, however, in their performance on English language tasks. Chang asserts that the results of this study strongly support intervention in learning English at a preschool level. Phase 3 of the project, to be completed in 1992, will involve parents in center activities.

In a study on the effects of total L2 immersion on cognitive development, Dodson and Thomas (1988) studied 200 children, aged five to seven, attending 65 infant schools in Wales. The sample consisted of monolinguals, developing bilinguals, and competent bilinguals. The categories were based on teacher and parent reports on the children's language abilities. The children attended five types of schools: Welsh native language, mixed language (unstreamed), mixed language (streamed Welsh), bilingual education schools, and English language schools. Over a three year period, children were tested in their preferred language each year to determine the effect of total immersion programs on concept development. The tests included 40 tasks to assess the children's concept development. Tests results show that:

1. On Piagetian conservation tasks, five-and six-year-old English speakers did better than Welsh speakers, but by the age of seven, the Welsh speakers catch up to their English speaking counterparts.
2. When the samples of children were controlled for socioeconomic status and educational background of parents, English speakers performed better than Welsh speakers in classification tasks.
3. When children in each of the five schools were compared, significant differences were found on the Piagetian conservation tasks. Children in monolingual English and bilingual education schools did better than native Welsh and mixed language schools.
4. At the end of three years, the children in Welsh schools catch up to children in the English schools and perform better than children in the mixed language schools.

Dodson and Thomas concluded that overall total immersion programs only temporarily retard measurable concept development in participating students. The study supports the contention that total L2 immersion education (the exclusion of the students' preferred language to transmit ideas or to aid second language acquisition) gives pupils the best chance to gain a fluent and accurate command of the target language in a short period of time. Any initial delay in the development of some concepts is of no permanent consequence according to this study. They suggest that message-oriented activities in the preferred language be introduced to prevent delayed concept development.

If individuals' preferred language is ignored, especially during the early stages of second language acquisition, they will never become competent bilinguals. On the other hand, if their preferred language is not merely tolerated, but *actively built into* the language and learning acquisition process for meaning, their accuracy and fluency will be accelerated (p. 483).

After examining the influence of early bilingualism (German/Italian) on the personality, social behavior, perception, and linguistic competence of 65 bilingual and monolingual, four- to six-year-old Italian preschoolers, Gallerano (1987) found no difference in social behavior. However, she found positive effects in terms of self-confidence, self-control, memory, and oral skills in the young bilingual children she studied.

García (1988) addressed the information processing of bilingual children as it is related to specific areas of cognitive development. He culled the findings of many studies and posited that bilinguals have significantly increased cognitive flexibility. García presented the historical research findings that bilinguals have added mental flexibility. According to García, bilinguals are able to process information in one language and provide allied information in another language. He cites methodologically sound studies that find balanced bilinguals cognitively advantaged. (A balanced bilingual is someone who is a competent speaker of two languages.) However, he stressed that this conclusion should be held tentative pending further study.

Research in early childhood education continues to point out significant advantages of early bilingualism in preschool learners. Furthermore, it appears that young bilingual children benefit in areas of motivation and attitude, as well as in increased cognitive and social-emotional growth by their dual language exposure.

Assessment

The controversy regarding language and learning continues to come to the forefront in assessing the abilities of young second language learners. The problems of assessment continue as specialists attempt to distinguish between "handicapping conditions" and the normal characteristics of language acquisition.

Test validity. Test validity is an issue frequently examined in the literature. The following discussion centers around the limits and distorted perspective of some methods of testing which are brought to the fore in current research inquiries. Specific guidelines and resources to achieve non-discriminatory assessment are identified. A significant body of the research continues to point to the need for native language proficiency as a baseline for all other efforts of assessment of the abilities of bilingual children. A unique approach, suggesting preliminary use of a process oriented portfolio for more comprehensive assessment of young children is presented.

In preliminary findings with preschool and primary aged children, Bracken and Fouyad (1987) conclude that the Spanish translation of the Bracken Basic Concept Scale is adequate in content validity. This is a first step in examining the effectiveness of this test in translation for use with bilingual learners.

Padilla, Valadez, and Chang (1988) examined the Woodcock

Johnson Psychoeducational Battery (Woodcock & Johnson, 1978, revised in 1989) and its effectiveness as an assessment tool. The Woodcock Johnson is an individually administered set of diagnostic tools which measure achievement in mathematics, reading, written language, as well as broad knowledge of science, social studies, and humanities. It also measures skills in letter-word identification, applied problems in math, and dictation. In the present study, the researchers evaluated 22 English speaking, 23 Spanish speaking, and 26 bilingual (Spanish/English) children at the beginning of kindergarten and Grade 1. They concluded that group differences in Spanish-English oral language and reading competencies were more related to differences in language proficiency and lack of formal English instruction than to differences in cognitive ability and home experience. Results also show that Spanish-speaking monolingual children acquire some proficiency in English but at levels below other groups. Behavioral observations that may be significant for professionals to use when evaluating bilingual learners in particular testing environments are described. Issues related to semantic functioning (word definitions and the understanding of word relationships) in bilingual young children were also examined. Results of this study indicate that in young bilingual children, tasks requiring understanding word relationships may be less likely to be self-initiated than other efforts at communicative competence. That is, young children are driven to produce meaningful output in language and may be initially less concerned with the exact definition of individual words they use. This may be mistakenly perceived as a learning deficit when it is actually a learning strength.

Wilcox and Aasby (1988) present normative data for the Spanish version of the Test for Auditory Comprehension of Language (TACL) (Carrow, 1985). The data were collected from a sample of 60 Mexican children in three age groups: 4.0 to 4.5 years, 6.0 to 6.5 years, and 8.6 to 8.11 years. Half of the sample were monolingual Spanish speaking children residing in a government orphanage and were therefore of low SES. The other half of the children sampled were high SES children attending private schools where instruction was in English. Students were judged monolingual or bilingual according to parent and teacher reports on questionnaires.

Although with both monolingual and bilingual children TACL scores increased with age, at all ages the performance of the bilingual children was superior to that of the monolingual Spanish speakers. The authors conclude that:

1. There is an age related increase in scores across all groups indicating that the Spanish version of the TACL is measuring some developmental aspect of language ability in all subjects.
2. For all age groups, high SES bilingual speakers outperformed the low SES monolingual speakers. Therefore, second language learning does not inhibit native language acquisition in high SES learners.
3. Comparison of scores on the English and Spanish versions of the test indicate inconsistent results. For all Spanish-speaking groups, except high SES six-year-olds, age related scores fall below the corresponding mean chronologically for English speaking children. This finding suggests the non-equivalency of the two versions of the test.
4. Subsections of the TACL allow comparison of group performance on morphology, vocabulary, and syntax. For all children, vocabulary scores consistently increased with age. Also, all children showed a marked increase in syntactic and morphological auditory comprehension skills following enrollment in school regardless of the setting or language of instruction.

In summary, all subjects made a distinct increase in syntactic, morphological, and auditory comprehension abilities after school enrollment, not affected by setting or language of instruction. Wilcox and Aasby (1988) conclude that the Spanish version of the TACL is measuring a developmental aspect of language ability in all subjects. They clearly suggest the non-equivalency of the two versions of the test (English/Spanish) and point to the need for separate norms for each version.

Several researchers point to the particular variables that will continue to plague assessment of young bilingual children. Koopmans (1987) and Wilkinson and Holzman (1988) identify factors that appear in evaluating children whose native language is not English. They note that conclusions must be held tentative when testing linguistically and culturally different children because particular variables will continue to be problematic in the assessment of young bilingual children. According to the authors, variables evident from the research that are important in the assessment of language minority children are:

1. Task time: The amount of task time may negatively influence assessment results.

2. Reasoning skills: The type of task reasoning used can further influence results because different cultural groups use different reasoning processes.
3. Language proficiency: The aspects of linguistic proficiency measured may not be clearly identified. Measures of linguistic proficiency should include semantic functioning, everyday communication competence, reading ability, reading aptitude, and oral language competence.

Assessment of language proficiency. The measurement of language competency and proficiency is heavily emphasized in the literature. Detailed analyses of all aspects of language competency are included in recent studies. Researchers emphasize the continued need to assess the level of bilingualism of language minority children, from monolingual to partially fluent to fully fluent in both languages in order to plan appropriate educational programs. Native language competency is also of paramount importance in recent research studies.

Wilkinson and Holzman (1989) emphasize the need to consider native language assessment for all bilingual children. In addition, they point to the continued overidentification of linguistically different children as needing special education services. In their study of 40 bilingual Hispanic children, Wilkinson and Holzman studied the relationship between language proficiency of bilingual children and their scores on tests administered in one or both of their languages. The Hispanic students were in grades two to four and were referred for special education because of suspected learning disabilities. In this study, only a moderate relationship was found between language proficiency and IQ and achievement scores. Most important was the fact that 9 percent to 17 percent of the group qualified for learning disabilities programs on the basis of their English, *not their Spanish*, scores. This underscores the need to test bilingual children in their native language.

The implications of assessment of handicapped limited English proficient (LEP) students were researched by Ortiz and Polyzoi (1988). The major purpose of this study was to identify the best combination of techniques which effectively distinguish between LEP students who are truly handicapped and those who may be showing characteristics of normal second language acquisition. Of special interest to the researchers was whether pragmatic criteria are better alternatives than the use of standardized language assessment instruments to distinguish between normal and abnormal development in language minority students.

The authors, through the Minority Handicapped Research Institute, are currently conducting a longitudinal study of the oral language of 120 kindergarten students classified as speech and language handicapped (SLH), learning disabled (LD), and non-handicapped achievers (NA), and non-handicapped underachievers (NU). Thirty students were asssigned to each of the four groups. In this three year study of Hispanic LEP kindergarteners, Ortiz and Polyzoi point out the need to use language proficiency as a basis for assessment. They discuss specific instrumentation, including use of standardized language measures, achievement testing, and options for oral language sampling. They recommend using specific language measures that in preliminary findings seem most appropriate for diagnostic purposes.

In their report, the authors analyze the complexities of assessing language skills. Results indicated that the analysis of Hispanic LEP students' relative proficiency in English and in Spanish provides an essential set of information useful in determining the choice of assessment procedures and the language in which to conduct future testing. Recommendations on a specific testing battery for the accurate special education assessment of LEP students will be forthcoming upon completion of the study.

Special education screening. To address the continued need for more comprehensive and complete assessment of language minority children, Harris Stefanakis (in press) suggested using a "Portfolio Approach" to assess young children with linguistic differences. In a pilot project with urban school systems in the United States, Harris Stefanakis and collaborating school assessment teams have designed a process oriented procedure for compiling information on young children. This assessment procedure is for the early identification of children with special needs. Early identification of special needs facilitates early intervention to foster normal growth and development in children. The conceptual idea behind a Portfolio Approach is to combine formal and informal assessment material and use a variety of observational sources to create a more complete picture of the strengths and weaknesses of a young child. Since special education regulations require screening of young children for early identification of potential learning problems, a more complete and culturally relevant look at linguistically different children can impact potential over identification.

Before the children are involved in the screening process, parent interviews help determine the preferred language of the child. In limited English proficient children, language dominance testing is done by a speech and language specialist. All observations, tests, and interviews are then administered in the child's dominant language.

The process includes collecting a portfolio of information on linguistically different children that includes observations, questionnaires, a preschool screening instrument, a parental interview, and a behavioral checklist, along with collecting feedback from the assessment team on the performance of other children who are from the same culture of origin as the child in question. By compiling various sources of information about a child—academic performance, play behavior, parents' behavioral observations, work samples, teacher reports—a more comprehensive idea about the child can be ascertained.

Pilot programs in Boston, Chelsea, and Somerville, Massachusetts, have been initiated to develop procedures for implementing a portfolio approach to screening young children for special needs. Under the auspices of the Greater Boston Regional Education Center, the three school systems modified their existing team procedures and trained personnel in adapting their evaluation techniques.

Since the portfolio approach is more labor intensive than other assessment procedures, the urban school systems that have adopted it use the portfolio for linguistically different children who fail normal screening procedures. However, the author suggests that this approach be used for all children to help determine the learning strengths and styles of children and facilitate more appropriate program placement.

Teams of special education personnel, including administrators, team facilitators, special educators, speech and language pathologists, occupational therapists, parent liaisons, and kindergarten teachers worked for six months in collaborative groups to develop each school system's customized "Portfolio Approach for Preschool Screening." In the Somerville and Boston schools, testing is done in the native language by English and Spanish speaking teams. For children who speak languages other than Spanish, native language speaking translators are used with English speaking testers.

The basic framework for each school system's procedures includes the following components:

1. Observation of play behavior by three individuals, including a classroom teacher.
2. Observation of group interaction, using a formal checklist.
3. A preschool screening instrument (each school system uses different tests, recognizing the limitations of particular tests for non-English speakers).

4. Parental questionnaire and follow-up interview.
5. Evaluation team feedback on culture of origin of a specific child.

After one year of using the Portfolio Approach as a screening procedure, evaluation teams from Somerville and Chelsea report greater satisfaction in the reliability of assessment of linguistically different children. In these two systems, administrators, teachers and specialists indicate that using a portfolio helps identify areas of strengths in each child not easily found in previous screening or testing and helps provide multiple perspectives on each child thereby validating learning areas that may show culturally based differences. As a preliminary effort, the use of a portfolio approach in preschool screening may offer a means for assessment that can more carefully discern language from learning problems. If linguistically different children are not mislabeled as special education students early, they stand a better chance to begin their school experience in a mainstream academic environment.

Home Experiences and Parental Involvement

The effect of home experiences and parental involvement is another concern of research studies on the young bilingual learner. There appears to be consensus among researchers in this field that it is beneficial to increase parental involvement in the language learning process of young bilingual children.

Observing three-year-olds in their home environments, Ferhadi (1988) noted differences in speech patterns according to whom the child addresses. In a descriptive study, Ferhadi examined the adjustment made in an individual's speech according to the age and the native language of the person being addressed. The researcher compared the results of the descriptive study with previous findings on the characteristics of "foreigner talk" and "mother talk" observed in children and adults.

In this study, an adult native speaker addressed four people: (1) an adult native English speaker; (2) an adult non-native English speaker; (3) a three-year-old native speaker; and (4) an adult non-native English speaker. The dialogues were recorded and analyzed for rate of speech, non-fluencies, references, redundancies and paraphrases, and number of interaction elements. Additional aspects were examined including simplification strategies used with children, spatial orientation, and confirming responses. Ferhadi concluded that variation in speech does occur depending on the linguistic competence of the person being addressed. The results support the existence of reduced registers such as "foreign talk" and "mother talk." Ferhadi found more evidence of simplified and repetitive speech exchange between adult and child in this case study.

In a study of children in Australia, Rado and Foster (1987) focused on cases in which parents addressed their children in an interlanguage of English (a mixture of their native language and English). The researchers compared grammatical and discourse features of the language of native English (NES) and non-native English speaking parents and their primary school children. The study focused on how non-NESs alternate between the native language, English, and interlanguage (a combination of the two languages). Language samples were analyzed for code switching, number of words, routine utterances, connective error patterns, message restoration, and omissions. The study showed that those children whose parents addressed them in interlanguage often needed to repair their parent's language to make it intelligible.

In another article Rado (1986) reported that native English-speaking parents impose a very heavy listening burden on their children and are not as hearer oriented as non-native English speaking parents. The implication of this study is that bilingualism in the family does not necessarily enhance language awareness in young children.

Vargas (1988) recommended parental involvement as a way to improve the Smart Start early intervention program for young children from different linguistic backgrounds. Vargas suggested both parent training and parent support as critical elements in fostering early home-school partnership for LEP children and their families in the US.

In a position paper Rodríguez (1988) argued that Mexican Americans make poor progress in special education programs as they are currently structured in U.S. schools. Emphasizing comments made by other researchers, he stresses that overidentification of LEP children with learning problems is still a major educational issue. Poorly trained personnel also hamper service delivery. Instruction for LEP students is hampered by school personnel's limited knowledge of differing learning styles and the cognitive development of linguistic minority children. Rodríguez calls for a more comprehensive evaluation of special education programs coupled with added dissemination of techniques that have proven successful with minority learners. Rodríguez suggests parent involvement as a key intervention strategy in the education of language minorities.

A strong body of international research speaks to the importance of early parental support in the language learning process of young children.

In New Zealand, Susan Shafer (1988) supports parental involvement in Maori schools through the use of language nests. These language nests are preschools offering the usual early learning activities, but having the children's mothers present in the schools. The mothers are primarily English speakers who learn the Maori native language and culture within the context of the language nest. They are taught by Maori women who are well versed in teaching language and native cultural traditions. The mothers, in turn, pass their learning on to their offspring. The language nest setting also offers mothers background knowledge in child-rearing and child development. Shafer concluded that native language competency benefits both the Maori mothers and their children by helping both comprehend and preserve the Maori culture.

Several studies advocate parental involvement in the schools and in the community, as well as at home. In the Chang (1988) study reported earlier with Singaporan children, the author supported engaging parents in preschool center activities. As a result of her work with preschool children in Italy, Gallerano (1987) recommended the involvement of parents in preschool education in order to foster stronger language modeling and better early socialization.

Program Models

Although parental involvement is clearly recommended by researchers of early childhood education in the United States and in other countries, little consensus exists on how to develop program models. Recommendations for early childhood programs vary greatly within the United States and in research that appears from international settings. A survey of perspectives presented in this chapter suggests the diversity of opinions present in this body of research activity.

Ariza's (1988) research examined the effect of a pilot instructional program named Bilingual Basic Curriculum (BBC) on two cohorts of Hispanic kindergartners in six Florida schools which she followed for two years. She compared pre- and post-test results of the groups using content achievement tests in English and Spanish at the end of grades 1 and 2. Achievement test results showed no appreciable improvement in the achievement of students in the BBC program. Students in the control curriculum scored no worse than their BBC counterparts. Ariza suggested that the amount of time devoted to native language instruction should be increased to make bilingual curricular content more effective. She argued that the methodology and materials in the bilingual curriculum should be examined.

Jarvis, Opperman, and Taleporos (1988) evaluated early childhood programming in New York City. The study analyzed early childhood interventions and their impact in New York City. They asserted that the investment in early childhood education (pre-K to Grade 3) can have a long term effect on academic and social/emotional behavior. Early childhood education can also strengthen a child's opportunity for future success. The authors examined achievement testing in New York City, and the results suggested that children profit from current early childhood intervention. Children who had been in all day kindergartens and reduced class size in grade 3 registered an increase in achievement. They scored above grade level in reading (+4.0 percent) and math (+4.3 percent) on national achievement testing. On state math tests the percent of grade 3 children scoring above state minimum standards jumped 8.6 percent. The vast majority of the children who, on the basis of testing, were considered limited English proficient (LEP) when they entered, passed the grade 2 English proficiency test. Of the children who entered all day bilingual kindergarten, 20 percent were LEP, but 5 percent acquired enough basic English by the end of grade 2 to pass proficiency tests and no longer qualified for bilingual education.

The authors contended that simply realigning resources does not guarantee positive educational results in young children. The New York City project implemented full day kindergarten and reduced class size in primary grades in order to assist young language minority children. This extensive evaluation offers policy suggestions and strategies for planning relevant early childhood programs for young bilingual children in the United States.

The authors provided a set of questions that can help guide practitioners in program development and pedagogy that follows a strong developmental base. They suggested the use of the following questions to direct future programming efforts:

1. How can schools marshal resources best to strengthen early childhood education?
2. What type of programs are likely to pay off for a given population of young bilingual children?
3. Which existing programs deserve more financial support?

4.   Which teaching strategies are likely to succeed?

In the Dodson and Thomas (1988) longitudinal study reviewed earlier in the chapter, the effects of different types of programs (native language, bilingual, English immersion, and mixed language) on the concept development of young Welsh children are analyzed. The study focused on children who are monolingual, developing bilingual, or competent bilingual, kindergarten to grade 3. Preliminary findings suggested that immersion programs may temporarily retard concept development of second language learners. The authors supported the idea of early second language training to foster linguistic competency in specific populations of young children.

Successful Learning Techniques

Twelve studies in the most recent research focus on instructional techniques as key elements in bilingual education. The consensus of the research is that more naturalistic opportunities for language and literacy learning prove successful. The positive effect of cooperative learning on language and literacy development is also highlighted. Franklin (1988) examined how Hispanic kindergarten and first grade children express personal meaning. She noted that children express personal meaning by drawing parts of stories read aloud, then by dictating their own responses, and finally by writing their own original narratives. Her descriptive research analyzes story writing in a group of three kindergarten and three first grade Hispanic bilingual children. These six children were involved in a summer reading program for migrant children. In the program teachers read stories and the children were encouraged to create personal meaning through participation in art and language activities (p. 184). The children were also given opportunities to write stories in which they could explore their vision of the world: home, school, nature, and imagination. The author concluded that reading and writing stories based on personal experiences helps children learn more about the functions, the processes, and the conventions of literacy. She also suggested that literacy activities can promote the development of thinking skills.

In a review of studies on the literacy development of Spanish speaking children, Freeman (1988) analyzed different methods of teaching reading in Spanish. In addition to the whole language approach, the reading methods described are the onomatopeic method, the phonics method, the syllabic method, the language experience method, and the eclectic method. Based on her analysis of the research, the author urges the use of the whole language approach for Spanish speaking children. She argues that Spanish reading fluency is enabled by reading materials that reflect current knowledge of the reading process.

> Research on reading in Spanish point out that present methods of teaching Spanish which are based on a word approach to reading are not taking into account children's language knowledge and natural tendency to make sense out of text. The researchers recommend that materials and methods used to teach Spanish reading should focus on language in context, student interests and content areas rather than decoding and skill building. . . . The whole language approach draws upon the child's strengths and background . . . [it] helps children make sense of their own world through reading. (pp. 657 and 661)

Freeman stresses the use of authentic Spanish literature, not translated English literature digested into basal readers, as the basis for reading development for young children.

According to the author, research on reading in Spanish supports the use of the whole language method because it is a learner centered approach; uses all language modes of reading, writing, speaking, and writing; and acknowledges the social and personal experiences of students.

The success of cooperative learning in early childhood classrooms is reflected in the work of Lindholm (1988). Lindholm conducted a study of the process with 112 children, 58 in kindergarten and 54 in grade 1, in a California immersion program after its first year of implementation. Participants were monolingual English speaking children and Spanish speaking children in a Spanish immersion program. The study was designed to determine levels of first and second language proficiency and whether there were gains after one year; the levels of math and reading achievement in Spanish and in English and whether there were achievement differences according to language background; levels of students' perceived academic, peer, and physical development competencies; and the attitudes toward immersion programs among parents and staff. A control group of 20 kindergarteners and 19 first graders not in the immersion program was also tested in reading and math.

It was found that all students in the immersion program made gains in Spanish and in English, with Spanish dominant children achieving greater fluency in both languages. Both monolingual English speakers and Spanish speaking students in the program scored above average in content area achievement. Students' perceived interpersonal competence was high and parents and staff displayed positive attitudes toward the program.

Lindholm's work has some important implications. Despite a small amount of English instruction, both Spanish and English speakers made significant gains in English proficiency. This supports the premise of bilingual immersion programs, which is that Spanish speakers increase their Spanish abilities and gain English proficiency. English speakers maintain their English and gain Spanish proficiency. More importantly, achievement results show positive gains for both English and Spanish spakers. After one year of instruction English speakers scored above average on tests normed for native Spanish speakers. Spanish speakers were average to above average on Spanish achievement testing. Both the English kindergarteners and Spanish first graders scored average to above average in reading, language, and math testing. The fact that these students were able to score this high in English reading and math despite having received instruction in Spanish demonstrates that the students were acquiring the concepts in Spanish and transferring the concepts into English. These results validate achievement assumptions supporting the bilingual model which assumes that content learned in Spanish will be available to students in English.

In the international arena, several authors describe methods of instruction for young children that focus on naturalistic settings, home environments, and direct teaching.

In her work in Australia, Schafer (1988) examined formal school efforts in the Maori language. Commenting on instruction, she found that the flexible approach being used in primary immersion programs helps to support cultural preservation and social integration. Maori language immersion programs happen in the first years of formal school for young children. "Language Assistants" join primary teachers in early childhood classrooms. These assistants are similar to LEP teachers in the United States, but are not originally trained as teachers. They are selected for their knowledge of the Maori language and culture. They learn their teaching skills on the job with a head teacher.

The educational program for the Maori immersion classroom compares to any language enriched environment that may appear in other preschool settings. For the Maori, immersion classroom routine starts with a morning ritual time, including prayer and greetings. Then follows storytelling, reading in Maori, and writing stories in Maori. A formal language lesson also takes place daily. Only English and math are taught in English and the remainder of the program activities are carried out in Maori.

Chang and Watson (1988) investigated the effects of prediction strategies and materials on teaching ethnic Chinese children in the United States how to read in Chinese. They studied four kindergarten children who were developing literacy skills in Chinese. One child was bilingual in English and Chinese. The others were English speaking ethnic Chinese. The children were exposed to 30 two hour sessions once a week over one school year. Data were collected by video, teacher report, children interviews, and an informal assessment of literacy behavior.

Five teaching strategies were used with the children in developing their literacy skills in Chinese:

1. Talking about background knowledge.
2. Questioning story content and story message.
3. Watching the teacher demonstrate reading.
4. Allowing children to independently read aloud in small groups.
5. Relating predictable Chinese stories to drawing and writing activities.

They found that the use of predicable materials and prediction strategies encourages children's use of natural language abilities and general life knowledge and increases the awareness of the direct link between what children know about language and what they see in print. The authors noted that reading instruction that focused on meaning occurred in similar ways for English as for Chinese. The children in this study performed the same cognitive activities—predicting, confirming, and integrating information—to construct meaning, using Chinese text in a simulated whole language approach as do English speaking children. The authors point to the positive results in the study which support the assumption that reading instruction that focuses on meaning occurs in similar ways for English and Chinese. Chang and Watson support a whole language approach to reading instruction in Chinese.

In a recent commentary on methods of teaching reading in Spanish, Freeman (1988) presented a different perspective. Noting that some educators are calling for a whole language approach to replace a word approach, she supported the use of a variety of methods of instruction. Although Freeman cautioned practitioners against adapting the whole language approach as the sole reading method, she did outline the benefits of the whole language approach and suggested that it is a more naturalistic method. By naturalistic Freeman refers to an approach to literacy that parallels the process of natural language acquisition in young children. She also offered guidelines and materials for teachers who use the whole language reading approach. In conclusion, she argued that the whole language approach uses children's language strengths and helps children understand their world through reading. However, it is not the only solution to reading instruction.

In a paper presented at the International Conference on Language Teaching, Byong Won Kim (1988) reported on a study of barriers to success in learning English as a second language (ESL). The study incorporated data gathered from three sources: a case study of five- and seven-year-old Korean children; English reading and writing tests of academically successful Korean high school students; and language proficiency achievement levels of Korean college freshmen taught English by either the oral or written method. The author compared the young Korean children with successful English language learners in high school and the college students. Her findings suggest that the secret to learning English is to effectively accumulate naturalistic experiences in oral communication with peers. The paper outlines English as a second language approaches that promote naturalistic oral and written expressions.

In a review of the literature on bilingualism and early childhood, García (1989) offered general guidelines that summarize the essential components of a strong language learning program. He discussed the Significant Bilingual Instructional Feature Study (SBIF), reported by Tikunoff (1983), as a baseline for early bilingual instructional practice. The SBIF study focused on 58 classrooms in six sites which were judged to be effective bilingual programs. The SBIF study described instructional features that were common to bilingual and monolingual settings (shared instructional features) and instructional features which were unique to bilingual settings. The shared instructional features indicated that successful teachers of limited English proficient (LEP) students: (a) specify what students are expected to do to complete a task competently; (b) communicate high expectations and confidence in their teaching abilities; and (c) use active teaching techniques which include communicating clearly when giving directions, specifying new tasks, presenting new information, pacing lessons, keeping students on-task, monitoring student progress and giving students timely corrective feedback. Unique instructional features include both teacher and student characteristics. Successful teachers of LEP students mediate instruction for the students by using the students' native language (L1) and English (L2) for instruction, alternating between the two to ensure comprehension. Students learn the language of instruction when engaged in instructional activities in a regular classroom rather than a pull-out program.

The SBIF researchers found three ways in which home and community culture can be incorporated into classroom life for young children:

1. Cultural referents are used to communicate instructional demands. That is, classroom rules and teaching instructions respect verbal and non-verbal cultural norms of representative groups.
2. Teaching practices are sensitive to and compatible with student/ teacher interaction patterns within the context of students' cultural backgrounds. Teachers are aware of culturally determined behavior and modify their teaching practices accordingly.
3. The values and norms of the native culture are respected by those who work in the schools. (p. 36)

Clearly, no one instructional approach seems to be a panacea for language and literacy needs of young bilingual children. It appears that current research points to the importance of creating a learning environment that nurtures naturalistic language learning and literacy development.

Conclusions

Overall recent research literature in early childhood bilingual education indicates a need for the continued study of young bilingual children and ways to teach them. Some tentative conclusions can be gleaned from the above discussion.

First, research supports the assertion that young bilingual children are cognitively flexible and may have unrecognized learning strengths in monocultural environments. Educators must understand that language minority children have different learning strengths from monolingual children and work to discover these positive learning styles.

Second, anecdotal references as well as the research point to the overidentification of young bilingual children for special education programs. Traditional assessment practices continue to discriminate against children with cultural and linguistic differences. Some basic insights need to be recognized by the educational community. These are:

• Linguistically different children may take more time to complete tasks, so their performance on timed tests may be negatively affected.

• Test results may be influenced by the type of reasoning used by culturally different children. Young language minority children may not have yet adapted to a more systematic, sequential approach to problem solving which many assessment tools require.

• Careful evaluation of native language proficiency is critical in any attempt at assessment of learning potential.

• The concept of a portfolio approach in the assessment of young bilingual children presents a promising alternative to traditional testing practices (Harris Stefanakis, in press). Combining observation, teacher and parent interviews, and test results gives a more complete picture of the young child.

Third, characteristics of successful bilingual programs have been identified in recent research studies. The specific components that have proven successful in bilingual programs for young children follow:

• Teachers mediate instruction for LEP students by using the student's native language and English to clarify instruction.

• Successful programs use information from a child's home culture to promote engagement in instructional tasks and contribute to a feeling of mutual trust between teacher and students.

• Naturalistic or whole language approaches to literacy development provide positive results in young bilingual learners. This approach can be adapted to languages other than English and has proven successful in Spanish and Chinese.

• Students appear to learn a language when engaged in tasks expressed in that language. Cooperative groups appear to positively affect student language learning.

A Research Agenda

A future research agenda for bilingualism and bilingual education has been outlined by Hakuta and García (1989). They point to five directions:

1. *The language-cognition-affect connection.* The relationship between language and thinking should be explored and how both language and thinking are related to affective issues, such as attitudes, self awareness, and identity formation in bilingual children. Studies should focus on the intricate interrelationships of emotion, cognition, and language learning.

2. *Individual and societal roles in bilingualism.* A question that remains to be explored is how native language can be maintained in some social groups. Lower levels of language vitality at the community level presumably affect the language proficiency of individuals. Close examination of comparative social groups should be undertaken to help clarify how the community or the environment affects the maintanenance of a native language and learning a second language. More research on the relationship between the social milieu of the bilingual child and learning is needed.

3. *The research, practice, and policy interface.* Quality research needs to be generated on the processes of bilingualism and the nature and effectiveness of educational programs that serve linguistic minority populations. A merging of researchers, practitioners, and policymakers is necessary to maintain an ongoing dialogue in the formation of policy and practice in bilingual education.

4. *Linguistic minorities and linguistic majorities.* A major research question that needs to be addressed is whether second language acquisition is the same in language majority and language minority children. How is learning English different for a Cambodian refugee in Minnesota and a French child learning English in Quebec? Further research needs to explore the effectiveness of language immersion programs for English-speaking children learning a second language in conjunction with Spanish-speaking children. Two-way bilingual education programs with the participation of English-speaking children provide an important continuity among diverse cultural groups and can address an important societal need for bilingualism in the workforce.

5. *Understanding the complexity of bilingualism.* An interdisciplinary perspective is needed to fully understand the complexities of issues in the education of bilingual children. This complexity must be addressed by future research efforts.

References

Ariza, M. (1988). Evaluating limited English proficient students' achievement: Does curriculum content in home language make a difference? Paper presented at the annual meeting of the American Educational Research Association.

Bracken, B. & Fouyad, N. (1987). Spanish translation and validation of the Bracken Basic Concept Scale. *School Psychology Review, 16*(1), 94–102.

Carrow, E. (1985). *Test for Auditory Comprehension of Language (English and Spanish)*. Allen, TX: Developmental Learning Materials-Teaching Resources.

Chang, A.S.C. (1988). A study of cognitive development of preschool children and its implications for intervention in Singapore. Paper presented at the Australian Development Conference.

Chang, Y.L. & Watson, D. (1988). Adaptations of prediction strategies and materials in a Chinese-English bilingual classroom. *Reading Teacher, 42*(1), 36–44.

Dodson, C.J. & Thomas, S. J. (1988). The effect of total L2 immersion education on concept development. *Journal of Multilingual and Multicultural Development, 9*(6), 467–485.

Ferhadi, A. (1988). Impact of Adults and Children on the Addressor. Paper presented at the Annual Meeting of the Teachers of English to Speakers of Other Languages.

Franklin, E.A. (1988). Reading and writing stories: Children creating meaning. *Reading Teacher, 42*(3), 184–190.

Freeman, Y. (1988). Do Spanish methods and materials reflect current understanding of the reading process? *Reading Teacher, 41*(7), 654–662.

Gallerano, B.H. (1987). The effect of bilingualism on child development: An investigation in South Tyrol. *Rassegna Italiana di linguistica applicata, 18*(3), 29–62.

García, E. (1988). Bilingual education in early childhood programs. *Teacher Education and Practice, 41*(1), 31–46.

Goldman, S. & Rueda, R. (1988). Developing writing skills in bilingual exceptional children. *Exceptional Children, 54*(6), 543–551.

Hakuta, K. & Garcia, E.E. (1989). Bilingualism and education. *American Psychologist, 44*(2), 374–379.

Harris Stefanakis, E. (in press). *A portfolio approach to preschool screening*. Boston: Greater Boston Regional Center.

Jarvis, C., Opperman, P. & Taleporos, B. (1988). *Shaping the future: Teaching our youngest students. Research brief.* New York: New York Board of Education Office of Assessment.

Kim, B.W. (1988). Why students fail in ESL and what should be done. Paper presented at the annual meeting of the Japan Association of Language Teachers International Conference on Language Teaching and Learning.

Linholm, K.J. (1988) *The Edison Elementary School bilingual immersion program: Student progress after one year of implementation.* CLEAR Technical Report Series. Los Angeles: California University Center for Language Education and Research.

Koopmans, M. (1987). The difference between task understanding and reasoning skills in children's syllogistic performance. Paper presented at the American Educational Research Association.

Ortiz, A. & Polyzoi, E. (1988). Language assessment of Hispanic learning disabled and speech and language handicapped students: Research in progress. In *Schools and the culturally diverse exceptional student: Promising and future dimensions.* Reston, VA: Council for Exceptional Children.

Padilla, A. M., Valadez, C. & Chang, M. (1988). *Young children's oral language proficiency and reading ability in Spanish and English.* CLEAR Technical Report. Los Angeles, CA: California State University Center for Language Education and Research.

Rado, M. & Foster, L. (1987). The language environment of children with a non-English speaking background. Paper presented at the Ethnicity and Multiculturalism National Conference, Melbourne, Australia.

Rodríguez, A. (in press). On to college: Drop out prevention is possible. In Ambert, A.N. & Alvarez, M.D. (Eds.) *Puerto Rican children on the mainland: Interdisciplinary perspectives.* New York: Garland.

Rodríguez, R. (1988). Bilingual special education is appropriate for Mexican American Children with mildly handicapping conditions. *ERIC Digest.*

Roden, G. (1988). Handicapped immigrant preschool children in Sweden. *Western European Education, 20*(3), 95–107.

Shafer, S.M. Bilingual bicultural education for Maori: Cultural preservation in New Zealand. *Journal of Multilingual and Multicultural Development, 9*(6), 487–501.

Smith, R.C. & Lincoln, C. (1988). *America's hope: Twelve million youth at risk.* Chapel Hill, NC: Educational Resources Information Center.

Tikonoff, W.J. (1983). *Compatibility of the SBIF features with other research on instruction of LEP students.* San Francisco, CA: Far West Laboratory.

Vilke, M. (1988). Some aspects of early second-language acquistion. *Journal of Multilingual and Multicultural Development, 9*(1–2), 115–128.

Wilcox, K.A. & Aasby, S. (1988). The performance of monolingual and bilingual Mexican children on the TACL. *Language, Speech and Hearing Services in Schools, 19*, 34–41.

Wilkinson, C. & Holzman, W. (1988). Relationships among language proficiency, language test administration and special education eligibility for bilingual Hispanic students with suspected learning disabilities. Paper presented at the American Educational Research Association.

Woodcock, R. & Johnson, B. (1989). *The Woodcock Johnson Psychoeducational Battery.* Allen, TX: DLM Teaching Resources.

Vargas, A. (1988). Testimony on Smart Start: The Community Collaborative Act, Early Childhood Development Act of 1988 before the Senate Committee on Labor and Human Resources. National Council of La Raza.

Annotated Bibliography

Ambert, A.N. (in press). The enriched language of Puerto Rican children. In Ambert, A.N. and Alvarez, M.D. *Puerto Rican Children on the Mainland: Interdisciplinary perspectives.* New York: Garland.

Reports on a study on the native language development of Puerto Rican children attending bilingual kindergartens. Results of the research study indicate that contrary to popular beliefs about the language limitations of Puerto Rican children, participants in the study were developing language normally. Furthermore, it was found that, though the children were living in bilingual settings, English did not have a negative impact on their native language development.

Ariza, M. (1988) Evaluating limited English proficient students' achievement: Does curriculum content in home language make a difference? Paper presented at the American Educational Research Association.

A report of longitudinal achievement results of LEP Hispanic (K-2) students who participated in a pilot instructional program. Bilingual Basic Curriculum (BBC) in the native language was used from 1984–1987. Six elementary schools were randomly assigned to BBC or non-BBC groups. Students were followed from kindergarten to the end of grade 2. Achievement tests were administered in English and Spanish. No difference was noted in BBC or non-BBC groups. The author recommends that the amount of time devoted to native language should be increased and the BBC curriculum revised. The report contains descriptions of the achievement tests and data collected.

Chang, A.S.C. (1988). A study of cognitive development of preschool children and its implications for intervention in Singapore. Paper presented at the Australian Development Conference, Melbourne, Australia.

A longitudinal report of the Institute of Education in Singapore's study of cognitive and social development of preschool children. A three phased program concentrated on collecting baseline data to formulate intervention strategies, using center-based intervention strategies for young children and involving parents in center activities with their young children. Data were collected from 40 preschool centers using a sample of children from 3.5 to 6 years old. Children were tested on a range of language, math, cognitive, and social tasks. Children who attended private kindergartens scored better on English language tasks than children in public centers. On cognitive and math tasks the gap narrowed as children got older. Results suggest intervention in English at a preschool level is beneficial.

Dodson, C.J. & Thomas, S.J. (1988). The effect of total L2 immersion education on concept development. *Journal of Multilingual and Multicultural Development*, *9*(6), 467–485.

Reports on a longitudinal examination of the effects of certain forms of schooling (bilingual, immersion, mixed-language) on the concept development of monolingual, developing bilingual, or compentent bilingual children. Studying children in the primary grades in Wales, the study indicates that immersion programs temporarily retard concept development of second language learners.

Franklin, E.A. (1988). Reading and writing stories: Children creating meaning. *Reading Teacher*, *42*(3), 184–190.

Discusses the story writing experience of a group of kindergarten and first grade Hispanic bilingual students and notes some specific behavioral observations. The author contends that young bilingual children create and express personal meaning through story writing and drawing. The author suggests using story writing paired with art as an instructional technique to create a curriculum tied to children's interests and knowledge. The author concludes that reading and writing stories helped the children participating in the study learn more about the functions, process, and conventions of literacy while helping them become more informed about their own learning environment.

Freeman, Y. (1988). Do Spanish methods and materials reflect current understanding of the reading process? *Reading Teacher*, *41*(7), 654–662.

Reviews different methods of teaching reading in Spanish. It examines how these methods reflect research results. It also outlines a whole language approach and suggested materials to accompany it. The author concludes that to best help Hispanic students become confident, fluent readers in their native language, bilingual reading methods and materials need to reflect research findings on the reading process. Of all the reading methods discussed, only the whole language approach is based on psycholinguistics and reflects an understanding of research done on the reading process in Spanish. The author cites specific materials that can serve as an alternative to Spanish language basal readers.

García, E. (1988). Bilingual education in early childhood programs. *Teacher Education and Practice*, *41*(1), 31–46.

A survey of the research based on several early childhood bilingual education programs. It provides guidelines for the development of successful programs for young language minority children.

Goldman, S. & Rueda, R. (1988). Developing writing skills in bilingual exceptional children. *Exceptional Children*, *54*(6), 543–551.

This article claims that literacy does not follow a pattern of linear development from listening to speaking to reading then to writing. The authors do not support the idea of introducing a set of techniques for writing separate from thematic and organizational aspects of other literacy skills. Two theoretical perspectives for instruction are presented: the cognitive developmental and the functional interactive. Recommendations for writing curricula are presented for each of these. For bilingual exceptional children, the authors contend, the two approaches should be used. Instructional approaches for these children should stress the use of goal-directed and meaningful writing tasks, such as dialogue journals and narrative writing, in which the teacher provides interactive scaffolding for learning activities.

Hamayan, E. & Pfleger, M. (1987). Developing literacy in English as a second language: Guidelines for teachers of young children from non-literate backgrounds. *Teacher Resource Guide*. Washington, DC: Center for Applied Linguistics.

An invaluable resource guide for English as a second language teachers of the young children of non-literate parents. The guide presents a diverse approach to language arts instruction. It provides a theoretical base in second language learning for young children. The focus of the guide is on adapting whole language methods for classroom use. The methods presented are those that promote reading and those that promote writing. Suggested classroom techniques include using the language experience approach, shared reading, dictated stories, story completion, and dialogue journals with young children. Projects that support these findings are reviewed.

Jarvis, C., Opperman, P. & Taleporos, B. (1988). Shaping the future: Teaching our youngest *students*. *Research brief*. New York: Board of Education Office of Assessment.

Presents findings from evaluations of New York early childhood programs. It describes New York City's efforts to implement all day kindergarten, decreasing class size of primary grades, and providing pre-kindergarten classes for four-year-old children. It appears that simply realigning resources does not guarantee positive results. By drawing on the Office of Educational Assessment's evaluation of recent early childhood initiatives, this research brief suggests that particular attention should be paid to curriculum and professional development in early childhood education. These findings are particulary relevant to policymakers and specific strategies for planning early childhood programs.

Koopmans, M. (1987). The difference between task understanding and reasoning skills in children's syllogistic performance. Paper presented at the American Educational Research Association.

This study reports on response time related to bilingual student performance on reasoning tasks. Thirty-nine Puerto-Rican students in grades 3–6 were asked to solve problems in both languages. Response times were recorded and students were asked to justify their answers to assess to what extent reasoning lead to success in the tasks given. Response times were found to be longer if the justification given reflected reasoning, but it was also found that students needed more time to give an answer in their stronger language than in their weaker language. The study indicates that students have different reasoning strategies at different age levels. Younger students successfully solve problems if they understand what is expected. Older students appear to use a default strategy which often takes more time. The key implication of this research is that student strategies, not success in task performance, is a better guage of learning.

Lindholm, K.J. (1988). *The Edison Elementary School Bilingual Immersion Program: Student progress after one year of implementation.* CLEAR Technical Report Series. Los Angeles: University of California, Center for Language Education and Research.

A progress report on a bilingual immersion program after its first year of implementation. A total of 58 kindergarteners and 54 first graders participated. Pre- and post-test comparisons of achievement tests show that all students made gains in both English and Spanish with more Spanish dominant students fluent in both languages. Measures of interpersonal competence and attitudes toward the program were found to be positive. Follow-up recommendations focus on developing a Spanish and English language arts curriculum and fostering group work among the children.

Reetz, L. & Cerny, M. (1988). *Acres cross cultural bibliography for rural special educators*, ERIC Document, February 1988.

Cites thirty-four articles on non-discriminatory assessment in their cross-cultural bibliography designed for rural special educators. This bibliography is an important source of cross-cultural writing, including articles, books, court cases, and government reports focused on rural populations. Under the non-discriminatory assessment sections are three noteworthy articles: (1) "A Three Tiered Model for the Assessment of Culturally and Linguistically Different Children; (2) "Pluralistic Assessment in Speech-Language: Use of Dual Norms in the Placement process"; and (3) "19 Steps for Assuring Non-Biased Placement of Students in Special Education." The bibliography contains 437 citations on diverse populations, such as black Americans, Hawaiians, Hispanics, and Native Americans.

Rodríguez, R. (1988). Bilingual special education is appropriate for Mexican American children with mildly handicapping conditions. *ERIC Digest.*

Mexican Americans, according to this article, make poor progress in special education programs as they are currently structured. Mislabeling and misplacing of these students continue to exist. Lack of trained personnel and inadequate knowledge of successful instructional programs hamper service delivery to this population. The author recommends further study on the differences in learning styles and cognitive development of bilingual children. Parental involvement in a child's total educational program is suggested as a key factor for intervention.

Tobin, J.J., Wu, D.Y.H., & Davidson, D.H. (1989). *Preschool in three cultures.* New Haven: Yale University Press.

A study of a Japanese, a Chinese, and an American preschool using ethnographic techniques wherein participants, who included teachers, administrators, and parents, commented on their preconceptions, attitudes, and practices in relation to preschools in their cultures.

Vilke, M. (1988). Some aspects of early second-language acquistion. *Journal of Multilingual and Multicultural Development, 9*(1–2), 115–28.

Presents an argument for early introduction of bilingual instruction. It is a study of eight-year-old students' acquisition of English during formal classroom instruction. The author finds that beneficial effects include increased motivation for language learning and positive cognitive growth. The author also points to the secondary gain in learning two languages.

Wilkinson, C. & Holzman, W. (1988). Relationships among language proficiency language test administration and special education eligibility for bilingual Hispanic students with suspected learning disabilities. Paper presented at the American Educational Research Association.

Examines the relationship between the relative language proficiency of bilingual students and their scores on tests among a group referred for special education. Bilingual Hispanic students (25 males and 15 females) were referred to special education and were considered of limited English proficiency. Most tests showed a moderate relationship between language proficiency and achievement. Most test means did not differentiate between English dominant and Spanish dominant children. However, between 9 percent and 17 percent of the group qualified for learning disabilities services on the basis of English, *but not Spanish* test scores. This study underscores the need to consider native language aseessment for all children as the primary vehicle in program placement.

Vargas, A. (1988). Testimony on Smart Start: The Community Collaborative Act, Early Childhood Development Act of 1988, before the Senate Committee on Labor and Human Resources. National Council of Raza.

Presents the views of the Hispanic community which supports federal legislation focusing on early childhood education. Education is the single most important issue of concern listed in surveys of the Hispanic community. Early childhood development legislation is important to Hispanics because it seeks to prevent early enrollment below grade level, usually caused by a child's failure to pass to the next grade; it lowers the drop out rate and improves the educational attainment of Hispanics. The testimony includes recommendations for staff training in second language acquisition and multicultural education; parental involvement in all phases of programs; the composition of state task forces and policy groups which should reflect the ethnic composition of the groups affected; and data collection on groups remaining on waiting lists for early childhood services.

CHAPTER V

Native and Second Language Literacy: The Promise of a New Decade

Carmen I. Mercado

Introduction

The purpose of this chapter is to present a synthesis of the most current research and theoretical literature on the development of native and second language literacy in bilingual and English as a second language (ESL) settings. Recent developments reflect movements and trends that have been evident during the past decade, some dating back further. However, it is distinctive in the emphasis it gives to (a) examining the development of literacy in adolescent learners from different language groups and instructional settings; (b) collaborative-intervention research in which teachers, students, parents, and researchers work together to create effective practices; and (c) activity-based learning in which the development of literacy occurs within the learning or academic content— a concept that is distinct from and not to be confused with content area reading.

As literacy and biliteracy are complex social, political, and cognitive phenomena, research and theory presented in this chapter reflect the influence of the various disciplines that inform our understanding of these. In particular, insights gained from the disciplines of anthropology and sociology have become increasingly important as classrooms grow

I am grateful to Minerva Gorena and Rosario Gingras of the National Clearinghouse for Bilingual Education as well as to David Spenner of the National Clearinghouse on Literacy Education for their assistance in locating current sources of information. I am especially grateful to Cristina Andre for her assistance in the preparation of this manuscript.

more and more diverse, culturally, linguistically, and socioeconomically.

In an effort to be representative, data for this review have been obtained from a variety of sources, including (a) journal articles; (b) technical reports resulting from federally funded research projects; (c) ERIC documents; (d) books; (e) reviews of the research literature; and (f) unpublished manuscripts from the past two years. Excluded from this review are studies that relate to college-age students acquiring literacy in a foreign language and adult literacy programs, unless related to the development of literacy in school-age populations.

In the narrative which follows, attention will be given to ethnographic classroom and community research within the context of current notions and theories of literacy and biliteracy, thereby highlighting what is distinctive about current research. Two questions will guide this discussion: (1) What does it mean to be bilerate? and (2) Under what conditions do students for whom English is a second language learn to read and write more effectively in school settings? It is expected that this information will be of value to researchers but also to teachers and administrators involved in the education of second language learners, whether or not they are in bilingual/ESL settings.

The Nature of Literacy and Biliteracy

Conceptions of literacy/biliteracy influence how literacy is assessed and developed or practiced in schools as well as how literacy is researched in monolingual and bilingual settings. In her review of research on literacy, Langer (1988) notes that "multiple uses of the term literacy have created misunderstandings and confusion" as the term has been "used interchangeably to denote a skill, a state, and an action, each use stemming from a different set of research questions and a different tradition in research and instruction" (p. 42). She proposes that these are three complementary, rather than competing uses reflective of the complex nature of literacy. Scribner (1988) agrees that conflicts and contradictions are inevitable when literacy is not viewed as "a many-meaninged thing" (p. 73). Yet these different meanings also reflect changes in emphasis that have become evident through time. Scribner makes the point that social literacy practices vary in time and space and what counts as literacy vary with them (p. 72).

William and Snipper (1990) describe three broad categories or varieties of literacy "that count" in the United States today: (1) Functional literacy refers to basic writing (coding) and reading (decoding) skills that allow people to produce and understand simple texts. (2) Cultural literacy emphasizes the shared body of knowledge and experiences or background knowledge needed to comprehend texts. (3) Critical literacy is related to the political component inherent in reading and writing.

Similarly, Scribner (1988) describes literacy in three metaphors: literacy as adaptation, literacy as power, and literacy as grace. Literacy as adaptation emphasizes the survival or pragmatic function of literacy, enabling the individual to adapt effectively to a range of settings and routine activities. This is a far broader notion than the one suggested by William and Snipper as functional literacy. Literacy as power emphasizes the importance of literacy as a tool for the social and political advancement of poor and powerless groups/communities in society, analogous to "critical literacy." Literacy as a state of grace emphasizes the tendency in many societies to confer upon literate individuals special powers or virtues, not unlike William and Snipper's notion of cultural literacy. However, Scribner's emphasis that literacy is an activity or practice, not a quality of an individual, is significant. Currently, a distinct trend in research on literacy in monolingual and bilingual settings with school-age children reflects this notion of literacy as an activity, as evident in studies by Chang and Wells, 1989; Mercado, 1990; Warren, Rosebery, and Conant, 1990; Moll, Vélez-Ibáñez and Greenberg, 1989.

There is general agreement that varieties of literacies are the norm, however, it is also recognized that not all literacies are equally powerful in society. Wells (1990) suggests that literate thinking is essential to academic pursuits and to function in a technologically advanced society. Accordingly, literacy and thinking are intertwined in the notion of "literate thinking." While Wells argues that writing is essential to constructing and critically evaluating one's own interpretation of texts, he also maintains that literate thinking is not dependent on texts which involve only letters and words. All modes of symbolic representation constitute a text, including oral accounts. Chang and Wells (1989) explain the connection between writing, reading, and thinking as follows. It is through writing, reading, and re-writing that we can work on our thinking—or interpretation of text—in a conscious and deliberate manner. Although Scribner (1988) would say that you cannot become literate in a society that does not have a writing system, Wells suggests otherwise. This view of literacy makes clear the relationships between and among literacy and oral uses of language; literacy and writing; and literacy and thinking. The notion that literacy mediates and is developed through social learning is the foundation of activity-based, whole language approaches now being used in an increasing number of settings with concentrations of second language learners (Hudelson, 1989). This notion is based on the thinking of Russian psychologist Vygotsky, who emerges as the single, most influential theorist of this decade. Although Vygotsky's theory of cognitive development was initially formulated in the late 1920's, it was not until a half-century later that English translations of his ideas on the development of higher psychological processes were made accessible to a wider public in the United States (Vygotsky, 1978).

The Development of Literacy

Langer (1987) draws upon Vygotskian theory to articulate a sociocognitive perspective on the development of literacy which has clear instructional implications. Its three basic principles are as follows. (1) literacy learning results from understandings that grow in social settings where learners see models of literate behavior as other people engage in literacy activities. In effect, children learn about culturally appropriate ways to communicate in oral and written modes and to interpret written texts. They also develop preferred ways of communicating. (2) In becoming literate, people assume control over and internalize new skills and understandings by understanding how the skills and ideas work toward some end in the social context and by learning how to use them toward that end. However, the development of literacy is an interactional accomplishment. Growth is promoted when there are opportunities to collaborate with others in the accomplishment of tasks too difficult to accomplish independently but where procedures are instituted to promote gradual independence. (3) The context in which literacy is used and learned leads to particular ways of thinking and doing. Metalinguistic and metacognitive skills are learned through the interactive events that are at the heart of literacy learning. Like other aspects of literacy learning, these strategies can be broader or narrower depending upon the context in which they are learned (Langer, 1987, pp. 11–12). This explains the variations in the uses of literacy that are evident within and across cultures and the influence of context in the development of literacy. Langer emphasizes the important role of instruction in extending the range of experiences students have with literacy, but Wells (1990) reminds us that there is no prerequisite age nor state of "readiness" that must be reached before this learning can commence. The notion of "emergent literacy" emphasizes that reading and writing develop concurrently and are interdependent.

This discussion, which emphasizes the primacy of thinking and writing in literate behavior, provides a context for interpreting recent developments in the literature on literacy and second language learning, also referred to as biliteracy, which is discussed in the following section.

Biliteracy

Current developments in the study of literacy in bilingual and ESL settings mirror developments in the field of literacy in general, not surprisingly in light of the increased communication across areas of inquiry that characterize research today. A dominant theme reflected in the literature today is the notion that monolingualism and bilingualism are more alike than different (Hakuta, 1990; Hornberger, 1989). Specifically, recent studies (Hall, 1990; Verhoeven, 1990; Chang & Watson, 1988; Hudelson, 1989; Lasisi, Falodun & Onyehalu, 1988) with students varying in terms of the languages spoken, the degree of proficiency in two languages, age, and sociocultural orientation suggest that becoming literate in a second language is not separate from becoming literate in a first language. Studies have employed a broad range of methods and procedures, such as analysis of oral reading "errors" or miscues (Freeman, 1988), think-aloud protocols obtained during oral interviews (Swaffar, 1988); and response patterns on written tasks and during instructional activities (Lasisi, Falodun & Onyehalu, 1988; Verhoeven, 1990). This finding is significant not only because it relates to the issue of transference but also because it has implications for the way teachers, especially mainstream teachers, may help second language learners develop literacy in English. However, Chang and Watson (1988) remind us that, while it is important to understand the commonalities, this does not deny the fact that differences exist. "Any language learning must be concerned with cultural, linguistic, and orthographic differences" (p. 38). The literature continues to explore such differences.

While reading and writing processes may be universal, not all students have the opportunity to decode or produce written texts in two languages and develop their biliterate potential to its fullest. Simich-Dudgeon (1989) reports that school-age children may or may not be exposed to print in their native language because "[m]any of the world's languages lack a written form," as is the case with speakers of Hmong, spoken in Southeast Asia (p. 2). The range of languages represented in schools today is far more extensive than ever before, thereby exacerbating the problem (Weber, 1989). Moreover, Hakuta (1990) argues that even with high incidence languages, as with Spanish in the United States, only a small portion of the bilingual programs have continued to maintain students' first language as an explicit goal. For this reason, Hornberger (1989) characterizes biliteracy as a continuation of literacy development in one language which may or may not result in the complete development of the biliterate potential of an individual. Accordingly, biliteracy refers to any and all instances in which communication occurs in two (or more) languages in and around writing (Hornberger, 1990, p. 2).

Hornberger employs the notion of continuum as a device for organizing and situating current research in biliterate contexts in terms of three interrelated dimensions: (1) the contexts of use; (2) individual development; and (3) media of biliteracy. This framework will be used to present research reported by Hornberger but also other studies and theoretical discussions which appear in the current literature.

The contexts of biliteracy. The contexts of biliteracy are defined in terms of three continua. The micro-macro continuum characterizes continuities in the functions and uses of reading and writing within and across individuals and societies who speak different languages. The oral-literate continuum characterizes continuities between these two modalities of use, within and across languages. The monolingual-bilingual continuum characterizes continuities regarding functions and uses to which different varieties and styles are put within and across languages.

Two insightful sets of findings with respect to contexts of use merit attention. One, biliteracy often occurs in a context of unequal power relations, with one or another literacy becoming marginalized, as has occurred with languages other than English in the United States (Hakuta, 1990; Hornberger, 1989). Furthermore, Weber (1989) makes the point that even when students are learning to read the language of their household, they may encounter difficulties, if they receive negative evaluations because the variety used in school-related literacy differs from the one used by the students. Two, there are barriers and consequences to the development of literacy, for the group as well as the individual. At the societal level, the introduction of literacy may result in undermining traditional societal structures, as Hornberger reports occurred with the Ute (Native Americans) in Utah and their habitual ways of passing down knowledge from one generation to another. At the level of the individual, literacy is potentially alienating because it may create resentment and distance between family members, as Harman and Edelsky (1989) argue. Ferdman (1990) agrees that people's perceptions of themselves in relation to their ethnic group and the larger society can change and be changed by the process of becoming and being literate. Both he and Harmon and Edelsky call for more sensitive models of literacy acquisition "that take into account the social contexts in which literacy is defined and expressed" (Ferdman, 1990, p. 201).

Biliterate development. Hornberger characterizes biliterate development in terms of three continua: the reception-production continuum which includes listening and speaking, and reading and writing; the oral language-written language continuum; and the L1–L2 transfer continuum. She reports that biliterate development occurs along all three continua simultaneously and that development along one continuum is crucially affected by development along the others, and "is likely to zigzag across points within the three dimensional space defined by the three continua" (p. 286). Therefore, development occurs along a continuum beginning at any point and proceeding cumulatively or in spurts in any direction, and it also occurs in response to environmental demands.

Studies of young children in "print-oriented" societies indicate that children interact with print, hypothesize as to how the written language works, and engage in reading and writing, long before they are exposed to it in school (Hudelson, 1989). In her study of literacy development in young second language learners, Hudelson (1987) found that children moved themselves from monoliteracy in Spanish to biliteracy in Spanish and English on their own initiative (p. 834). That is, she found that young students developed literacy in the second language without being formally introduced to it, suggesting the possibility that transference occurs automatically, whether through direct instruction in the first language, exposure to the second language in school settings and out, or both. Wald (1987) emphasizes that for the adolescent second language learner, writing (meaning composing) may be the primary means through which skills in other areas, such as reading, are developed. "Write first" instructional approaches may be more effective for developing literacy in older learners than "speak first" or "read first" approaches. "Writing first" approaches also provide an important means of self-expression, circumventing concerns over pronunciation to which students are especially sensitive at this age. Thus, several significant trends are evident. It is recognized that the notion of developmental sequence is illusory and that writing plays an important role in the development of reading as well as thinking. Clearly, these findings challenge enduring beliefs and practices, such as the belief that language develops sequentially from listening to speaking, to reading, and finally to writing. Goldenberg (1989) suggests that these assumptions, which have tended to dominate instruction for second language learners in general and for children in lower-level reading groups in particular, are at the heart of the bottom-up approach to reading instruction which emphasizes that reading develops sequentially from the recognition of letters and words to higher level processes such as those involved in textual comprehension. As all of the language processes develop simultaneously, practices such as those of delaying instruction in reading and writing until there is oral mastery of what is to be read in English as a second language are of questionable value, serving to limit the learning opportunities made available to second language learners. Indeed, studies in progress document how activity-based learning is accomplishing the development of all language skills simultaneously, as will be discussed in the section on instructional practices.

These findings also provide insights on the relationship between oral and written language that relate to the view of literacy proposed by Wells. It suggests that it is possible to develop literacy through the oral mode in a language that has no written tradition as well as for older students who are said to be illiterate.

The media of biliteracy. The continua that characterize the media through which the biliterate individual communicates are: simultaneous-successive exposure, similar-dissimilar structures, and convergent-divergent scripts. Although relatively fewer studies on these dimensions are cited in this review, one point is noteworthy. It is emphasized that the student's first language does not have to be fully developed before the second one is introduced. That is, it is possible to promote the development of literacy in the second language with minimal literacy skills in the first, although greater benefits may be accrued when literacy development continues in the student's native language. Thus, a number of configurations exist as to the simultaneous or successive development of biliteracy involving varying degrees of development of the first language.

Hornberger's framework helps us understand and assess the accomplishments that have been made during the past decade in the study of biliteracy, but it also gives direction for future research by exposing areas that require careful examination or re-examination through systematic inquiry. Additionally, this framework has instructional implications (Hornberger, 1990). As Hornberger states, "the more the learning contexts allow students to draw on the three continua of biliterate development, that is, both oral and written, both receptive and productive, both first and second language skills, the greater the chances for their biliterate development" (p. 3). In the following section, specific attention will be given to research on instructional practices which reflect insights derived from Hornberger's framework.

Research on Instructional Practices

Although current studies of instructional practices in bilingual/ESL settings result from different lines of inquiry, studies highlighted in this section represent a distinct trend in the literature that is worthy of attention. Collaborative research projects constitute a significant response to the concern to improve the conditions of school learning by involving teachers directly in the transformation of practice, as suggested by Moll and Díaz (1987). In so doing, collaborative research incorporates more than the perspective of teachers. This approach to research includes teachers as partners working and learning together with other members of the research team, including students and parents. As research and practice become interwoven in this manner, traditional distinctions between the two become obviated, as is the need to seek instructional implications for research or to bridge the gap between research and practice.

As previously stated, the notion of literacy as an action or activity, a way of thinking, is also guiding much of this effort. Moll, Vélez-Ibáñez and Greenberg state that "activity-based approaches highlight children as active learners using and applying literacy as a tool for communication and for thinking . . . activities which involve students as thoughtful learners in socially meaningful tasks" (p. 2). This is important to note as many of these projects do not have the characteristic features of traditional literacy programs because students use literacy to mediate learning activities rather than as the direct focus of instruction. Some of the projects presented are small-scale independent efforts and others are large-scale collaborative research projects that are federally funded. As research has tended to be costly, the federal government has played a major role in giving direction to and sponsoring research on bilingual/ESL instruction, which may account for the general emphasis that is evident in the research on English language literacy.

Federally Sponsored Research

The Innovative Approaches Research Project (IARP) was funded by the Office of Bilingual Education and Language Minority Affairs (OBEMLA) and is "intended to develop and assess innovative instructional approaches designed for language minority students." Within this umbrella project, four individual research and demonstration projects are presently under way, two of which are of particular interest given the focus of this chapter. These are:

1. Community Knowledge and Classroom Practice: Combining Resources for Literacy Instruction which includes the research team of Moll, Vélez-Ibáñez, and Greenberg from the University of Arizona; and

2. Cheche Konnen: Science and Literacy in Language Minority Classrooms which includes the research team of Warren, Rosebery, and Conant from Bolt, Beranek, and Newman, in Massachusetts.

In the narrative which follows each of these ongoing projects will be described individually, the first as the Arizona Project and the second as the Massachusetts Project.

The Arizona Project. As described by the researchers, the goal of the Arizona Project "is to produce change in literacy practices *through* the development of joint activities with teachers and students" (Moll, Vélez-Ibáñez, & Greenberg, 1989, p. 37). The project involves primarily Mexican students of varying levels of proficiency in English and Spanish in grades 4 through 6. It is comprised of two major and related components. One, the heart of the project in that it feeds instruction-related activities, is a community study of the transmission of knowledge and skills among households in a Hispanic community of Tucson. As this study can stand on its own and because it relates to the discussion of home/community influences, it will be described in greater detail in a forthcoming section of this chapter. Two, the instructional component occurs in two distinct settings: an after-school lab and school-based classrooms. The lab serves as a mediating structure between these classrooms and the community, and provides a more relaxed setting where researchers, teachers, and students may learn and work together to experiment with literacy instruction that includes social and cultural practices identified in the household study. Classroom settings are used to carry out collaborative activities within traditional arrangements, that is, they enable the research team to monitor the application of practices created in the lab in these real settings with attendant constraints.

During the first year of this study, researchers and teachers collaborated to develop literacy modules or instructional activities which take into account the specifics of each classroom—the characteristics of the participants, the instructional goals and objectives, and instructional constraints. These modules were said to allow for indepth study of a topic or theme and provided for multiple opportunities to use reading and writing. Literacy modules were generated around the themes of "writing," a concern of one of the teachers, and "construction," of interest to students. A third theme on "career development" was initiated and developed independently by one of the participants, an insightful outcome. Ideas for modules resulted from activities in the lab as well as activities in the classroom, thereby exemplifying the mutual influence of these two settings.

Findings on instructional practices described in the year one progress report indicate that it is possible to increase the opportunities to engage students in meaningful uses of reading and writing in English and in Spanish. It is also possible to "develop literacy activities that exceed in sophistication, intellectual level, and scope of what is currently being taught in schools" (Moll, Vélez-Ibáñez, & Greenberg, 1989, p. 37). However, the researchers acknowledged that they have gained a greater appreciation of the difficulties involved in introducing innovation into classroom practice from these activities. In effect, while research had informed practice, practice had also informed research.

The Massachusetts Project. In the Massachusetts Project, researchers and teachers of primarily Haitian-Creole students in bilingual programs at the junior and senior high school level are collaborating to develop an investigation approach to science for language minority students (Warren, Rosebery, & Conant, 1990). "Cheche Konnen," which means search for knowledge in Haitian Creole, has as its goal the development of scientific literacy, conceptualized as "a socially and culturally produced way of thinking and knowing that evolves gradually through engagement in authentic scientific activities" (Warren, Rosebery & Conant, 1990, p. 2). The researchers emphasize that language plays a central role in this process in that it is essential for thinking and talking about science and for communicating and sharing ideas. Students learn about science by doing science the way practicing scientists do. They formulate questions about phenomena that interest them; they build and criticize theories; they collect data; they evaluate hypotheses through experimentation, observation, measurement, and simulation; they interpret data; and they communicate their feelings (p. 7). The theme for the first year of the project, "water," resulted in two major investigations: The Water Taste Test and the Black Nook Pond Investigation.

Through these activities, students are expected to learn the reasoning and conceptual knowledge required for scientific activity but also the social and language processes that mediate these. Similarly, through their collaboration with practicing scientists, teachers are expected to learn about the scientific enterprise and to reflect this understanding in the way they organize literacy and science instruction. Preliminary findings suggest that the model and the goals of each teacher interacted to produce different interpretations of science, not only influencing the teaching and learning of science but also the teaching and learning of literacy. In the seventh and eighth grade classroom, students engaged in "purposeful and multidisciplinary uses of literacy in the class" (p. 22). In the high school setting, the model's goals were not met initially, but "a transformation took place in the kind of science and literacy that were practiced" later on in the year (p. 23). These findings suggest the interactive nature of instruction and the need to examine carefully the way individual students and teachers react to instructional procedures that are considered to be innovative. Clearly, not all respond in the same way.

Independent Research Efforts

Building upon these two research and development projects as well as earlier work by Brice-Heath (1985), Mercado (1990) initiated a collaborative partnership with a classroom teacher with the purpose of introducing African American and Hispanic sixth graders in an intermediate school in the Bronx, New York, into the world of educational research. During regularly scheduled visits, the teacher educator modeled ethnographic research practices she was using to document classroom activities *as* students engaged in examining issues of personal significance to them. This explains the name for the project: "Researching Research: A Student-Teacher-Researcher Collaborative Project." That is, students learned about research while doing research, in keeping with principles of activity-based theory. During the 1989–90 school year, students worked in collaborative partnerships with peers to study topics such as teenage pregnancy, AIDS, drugs, and the homeless—topics which represented lived experiences for many of the students. Trueba (1987) found similar concerns in his ethnographic study of the English writing abilities of Mexican-American high school students in San Diego. Through their involvement in these activities, students were expected to develop further their communication skills in English and in particular produce a great deal of writing, a major goal of the Arizona and Massachusetts projects. What is distinctive about the Bronx Project is that classroom participants were members of a research team which had numerous opportunities to share their work through oral and written reports at authentic research conferences and within two teacher education programs at local colleges. That is, they became enculturated to the world of research. One of the highlights of the year was the presentation made at the Ethnography in Education Forum, a first for the students and a first for the Conference.

Through these activities, the sixth graders in the Bronx Project have been challenged to do more advanced work than students are typically assigned at this level. As they expressed it, "research is hard but fun," and they can do "college work." "By focusing their attention on one topic over a period of time, students gained greater knowledge about their topic, which is evident from the effortless manner in which they were able to conduct themselves during formal presentations" (Mercado, 1990, p. 12). Preliminary analysis of the scores on the New York Public Schools system reading test (the DPR's) revealed dramatic gains in reading, exceeding the 4–point increment considered to be significant by school standards by as many as 16 points. While these findings need to be subjected to further analysis, they suggest exciting possibilities.

The common thread which unites these three projects, other than the fact that all three involved collaborative partnerships with teachers, is that "the learning of English is subsumed to a higher order goal of academic learning" (Moll, Vélez-Ibáñez, & Greenberg, 1989, p. 36). To a greater or lesser extent, all three projects capitalize on community resources for the development of literacy. Specific efforts in this area, which constitute a new trend in the research, will be described in the next section.

Ethnographic and Descriptive Research on
Home-Community Influences

The household study that is part of the Arizona Project, referred to in the previous section, makes a significant contribution to helping us understand the positive influences of the home on the development of literacy. In initiating this study, the researchers were guided by the belief that every household is an educational setting which has as a major function the transmission of information so as to enhance the survival of its members. The content and manner of this transmission were identified as central features of this ethnographic study of households.

The study was undertaken in 28 households, equally divided between treatment and comparison groups. Data on literacy practices in Spanish and English as well as data on the structure and functions of social networks within the community were obtained from (1) Self-Report Questionnaires; (2) Literacy Checklists; and (3) Ethnographic Field Notes taken by members of the research team during pre-arranged visits to the homes.

Although the analysis is still in progress, preliminary findings suggest that (1) poor and working class households contain cognitive resources with great utility for instruction but which schools tend to ignore or underestimate; and that (2) these resources or "funds of knowledge" form an essential part of a broader set of activities, social relationships, related to the households' functioning and survival within harsh social conditions. Specifically, a variety of reading and writing materials and activities were observed and reported. In addition, direct examination and analysis of social networks revealed at least nine domains of knowledge. These included the following: (1) agricultural information; (2) marketing; (3) material and scientific knowledge; (4) economic and strategic knowledge; (5) arts; (6) social exchange and culture; (7) ritual and religion; (8) medicine; and (9) education. Working in collaboration with teachers, these researchers are demonstrating how these funds of knowledge may be utilized as resources for instruction to promote the development of school-related literacy.

The three naturalistic, ethnographic case studies described in this section are intended to be suggestive of current trends. Clearly, the emphasis is on providing higher quality learning environments than typically exist by drawing upon the resources second language learners bring to the classroom.

Conclusions

This review, which intended to highlight new research approaches concerned with literacy development in bilingual/ESL settings, suggests the following conclusions.

1. Literacy mediates and is an outgrowth of engagement in collaborative learning activities that are purposeful and meaningful to learners.
2. The classroom environment is a major influence on the types of literacies students develop.
3. Instruction can be modified, through direct and indirect intervention, in ways to capitalize on the cognitive, linguistic, and cultural resources of students, so as to better prepare second language learners to compete successfully in academic settings.
4. Second language learners, especially students from poor and working class homes, can become literate thinkers in English through involvement in challenging and meaningful learning activities, not just through direct instruction.
5. Poor and working class households contain cognitive resources of great utility to learning.

These developments continue to extend our understanding of the complexities of promoting literacy/biliteracy in a range of public school settings and with a greater variety of culturally and linguistically diverse students, referred to in the literature as limited English proficient or LEP, bilinguals, students of English as a second language, students-at-risk, and language minority students. In particular, we now know more than ever before about the character of instruction which promotes growth in the literate uses of two or more languages and the contributions of the home-community in the development of literacy/biliteracy.

Instructional Implications

As a major trend in current classroom research emanates from collaborative partnerships with teachers, insights thus gained have clear implications for instruction. Teachers of second language learners in other settings should find it helpful to learn about how colleagues in other settings are experimenting with different learning environments, capitalizing on the resources students bring to the classroom so as to accomplish academic excellence.

Directions for Future Research

This research synthesis provides an opportunity to pause, reflect on, and put into perspective recent developments and to gain fresh insights to continue to work toward positive change. We have reason to be optimistic in view of the many advances that are being made toward this goal, but there is much that remains to be done, as evident from the contents of this review. Specifically, we need to continue to study with different populations and in different settings the following:

1. The forms and functions of literacy in the home and the community.
2. The cognitive resources available within distinct ethnolinguistic communities which may be used to promote the development of biliteracy in school settings.
3. How teachers and peers assist and guide students to accomplish tasks beyond the students' independent level as well as the learners' cognitive development under these conditions.
4. The role of the students' native language in the development and assessment of English literacy.
5. How reading in English influences growth in and knowledge of the spoken language.
6. Longitudinal studies of the development of biliteracy in second language learners.
7. How technology is being used to promote the development of biliteracy, for example, the use of word processing programs for composing or writing.

However, it would be foolish to omit or deny the fact that the context for research in these areas is, as it has always been, charged with a great deal of controversy. The reality is that in the United States certain groups of students continue to be less successful than others in acquiring and developing literacy in and for school purposes. Or, to phrase it differently, schools have tended to be less successful with some students than with others in promoting school-related literacy. Secada (1990) summarizes current research concerns succinctly when he says that many see "bilingual education as related to issues of social oppression and struggle by diverse groups against the processes by which inequality is transmitted in our society." (p. 21) This being the case, we are moving toward a broader understanding of what it means to be biliterate today, which has positive consequences for how teachers may create more effective learning environments for the development of literacy/biliteracy in their classrooms.

References

Brice-Heath, S. (1985). Literacy or literate skills? Considerations for ESL/EFL learners. In Larson, P., Judd, E.L., & Messerschmidt, L. (Eds.) *On TESOL '84: A brave new world for TESOL.* Washington, DC: TESOL.

Chang, G.L. & Wells, G. (1989). Conceptions of literacy and their consequences for children's potential as learners. In Norris, S.P. & Philips, L.M. (Eds.) *The breadth and depth of literacy: Political and educational perspectives* (in press).

Chang, Y.L. & Watson, D.J. (1988). Adaptation of prediction strategies and materials in a Chinese/English bilingual classroom. *Reading Teacher, 42,* 36–44.

Ferdman, B. (1990). Literacy and cultural identity. *Harvard Educational Review, 60*(2), 181–204.

Freeman, Y.S. (1988). The contemporary Spanish basal reader in the United States: How does it reflect current knowledge of the reading process? *NABE Journal, 13*(1), 59–81.

Goldenberg, C.N. (1989). Parents' effects on academic grouping for reading: Three case studies. *American Educational Research Journal, 26*(3), 329–352.

Hakuta, K. (1990). *Bilingualism and bilingual education: A research perspective.* Occasional papers in bilingual education, 1. Washington, DC: National Clearinghouse for Bilingual Education.

Hall, C. (1990). Managing the complexities of revising across languages. *TESOL Quarterly, 24*(1), 43–60.

Harmon, S. & Edelsky, C. (1989). The risks of whole language literacy: Alienation and connection. *Language Arts, 66*(4), 392–406.

Hornberger, N.H. (1990). Creating successful learning contexts for biliteracy. *Penn Working Papers in Educational Linguistics, 6*(1).

Hornberger, N.H. (1989). Creating successful learning contexts for biliteracy. Alienation and connection. *Language Arts, 66*(4), 392–406.

Hudelson, S. (1989). *Write on: Children writing in ESL*. Englewood Cliffs, NJ: Prentice Hall Regents.

Hudelson, S. (1987). The role of native language literacy in the education of language minority students. *Language Arts, 64*, 827–841.

Kreeft, J.P., Staton, J., Richardson, G., & Wolfram, W. (1990). The influence of writing task on ESL students' written production. *Research in the Teaching of English, 24*(2), 142–171.

Langer, J.A. (1988). The state of research on literacy. *Educational Researcher, 17*(3), 42–46.

Langer, J.A. (1987). A sociocognitive perspective on literacy. In Langer, J. (Ed.) *Language, literacy and culture: Issues in society and schooling* (pp. 1–20). Norwood, NJ: Ablex.

Lasisi, M.J., Falodun, S., & Onyehalu, A.S. (1988). The comprehension of first and second language prose. *Journal of Research in Reading, 11*, 26–35.

Mercado, C.I. (1990). Researching research: A student, teacher, researcher collaborative project at Hunter College of CUNY. (Unpublished paper presented at the Ethnography in Education Conference, Philadelphia, PA, March 1990).

Moll, L.C. & Díaz, S. (1987). Change as a goal of educational research. *Anthropology and Education Quarterly, 18*(4), 300–311.

Moll, L.C., Vélez-Ibáñez, C., & Greenberg, J. (1989). Year One Progress Report. Community knowledge and classroom practice: Combining resources for literacy instruction. Unpublished report.

Scribner, S. (1988). Literacy in three metaphors. In Kintgen, E.R., Kroll, B.M., & Rose, M. (Eds.) *Perspectives on literacy* (pp. 71–81) Carbondale, IL: Southern Illinois University.

Secada, W. (1990). Supporting research in bilingual education. *NABE News, 13*(7), 21–22.

Simich-Dudgeon, C. (1989). English literacy development: Approaches and strategies that work with limited English proficient children and adults. *New Focus*, Occasional papers in bilingual eduction, 12, Summer 1989. Washington, DC: The National Clearinghouse for Bilingual Education.

Swaffar, J.K. (1988). Readers, texts, and second languages. *Modern Language Journal, 72*, 123–149.

Trueba, H.T. (1987). Organizing classroom instruction in specific sociocultural contexts: Teaching Mexican youth to write. In Goldman, S.R. & Trueba, H.T. (Eds.) *Becoming literate in English as a second language* (pp. 235–252). Norwood, NJ: Ablex.

Verhoeven, L.T. (1990). Acquisition of reading in a second language. *Reading Research Quarterly, 25*(2), 90–114.

Vygotsky, L.S. (1978). *Mind in society*. Cambridge, MA: Harvard University Press.

Wald, B. (1987). The development of writing skills among high school students. In Goldman, S.G. & Trueba, H.T. (Eds.) *Becoming literate in English as a second language* (pp. 155–186). Norwood, NJ: Ablex.

Warren, B., Rosebery, A., & Conant, F.R. (1990). Cheche konnen: Science and literacy in language minority classrooms. Unpublished monograph.

Weber, R.M. (1989). Linguistic diversity and reading in American society. Unpublished monograph to appear in *Handbook of reading research II*.

Wells, G. (1990). Creating the conditions to encourage literate thinking. *Educational Leadership*, 47(6), 13–17.

William, J.D. & Snipper, G.C. (1990). *Literacy and bilingualism*. New York: Longman.

Annotated Bibliography

Blosser, B. (1988). Television, reading and oral language development. The case of the Hispanic child. *NABE Journal*, 21–42.

Although previous studies have found an inverse relationship between TV viewing and reading among native English speakers, this study re-examined that relationship with 168 Mexican and Puerto Rican children in grades 2, 4, and 7. Of additional concern was the influence of TV viewing on oral language development. Data were obtained from (1) a media-use questionnaire, completed by students, with assistance when needed; (2) scores on the English and Spanish versions of the Language Assessment Scales (LAS); and (3) grade equivalent vocabulary and reading comprehension scores from the Iowa Test of Basic Skills (ITBS). Analyses suggested a positive relationship between reading scores and TV viewing, but the relationship differed by (1) ethnicity; and (2) the time of the day when viewing occurred. Content analyses of programs are necessary to explore the influence of specific programs on oral language use, particularly vocabulary knowledge, an essential component of reading comprehension.

Buriel, R. & Cardoza, D. (1988). Sociocultural correlates of achievement among three generations of Mexican American High School seniors. *American Educational Research Journal*, 25, 177–192.

Drawing upon data obtained from a national survey, the High School and Beyond Study, this investigation examined the academic achievement of three generations of Mexican-American high school seniors. Academic achievement was analyzed in relation to several variables, including students' Spanish language background, that is, students' self-report of their proficiency in and use of Spanish for speaking, reading, and writing. Findings suggest that the use of the Spanish language has a time-related inverse effect on achievement, but personal aspiration is a more potent predictor. The researchers acknowledge that students represented in the sample are those determined to survive in high school, unlike the 60 percent who drop out by the 10th grade.

Carell, P.L., Pharis, B.G., & Liberto, J.C. (1989). Metacognitive strategy training for ESL readers. *TESOL Quarterly, 23*(4), 647–669.

This study was designed to ascertain whether metacognitive strategy training enhances reading in a second language and how the effectiveness of this training is related to the learning styles of the students. Twenty-six ESL students enrolled in level 4 of an intensive ESL program and varying in terms of age, native language backgrounds, and educational experiences received training in semantic mapping or ETR (the experience-text-relationship) method. Training occurred during a brief four day period, and data were obtained from the same pre- and post-tests, administered within a nine day interval. Findings suggest that (1) metacognitive training in semantic mapping and ETR does enhance second language reading comprehension and (2) the effectiveness of strategies seems related to differences in learning styles. The researchers admit that results should be interpreted with caution in view of the short period involved.

Chang, Y.L. & Watson, D.J. (1988). Adaptation of prediction strategies and materials in a Chinese/English bilingual classroom. *Reading Teacher, 42*, 36–44.

This study explored the adaptation of prediction strategies with four ethnic Chinese kindergarten children learning to read and write in English and Chinese simultaneously. The teacher employed six activities to encourage students to use prediction strategies with predictable materials: (1) initial language experience; (2) questioning and semantic expectation; (3) demonstration of reading; (4) assisted reading; (5) independent reading; and (6) extensive literature work. Audio and videotaped data and field notes taken by the teacher and interview data were collected to ascertain students' responses over a span of two terms or 30 two-hour sessions. According to the researchers, the findings indicate that reading for meaning occurs in similar ways for beginning readers of Chinese and English.

Cummins, J. (1989). Language and literacy acquisition in bilingual contexts. *Journal of Multilingual and Multicultural Development, 10*(1), 17–31.

Discusses the role of research and theory in language and literacy acquisition planning for bilingual programs involving less used languages. Outlines three psychoeducational principles: the additive bilingual enrichment principle, the interdependence principle, and the sufficient communicative interaction principle. Discusses the role of these principles in the educational language planning process and offers a procedural framework for problem-solving in educational contexts.

Eagen, R. & Cashion, M. (1988). Second year report of a longitudinal study of spontaneous reading in English by students in early French immersion classes. *The Canadian Modern Language Review*, *44*(3), 523–526.

Reports on an ongoing study investigating the development of English reading and writing skills in twelve Anglo-Canadian children enrolled in French immersion classes. At this point in the study, four children are excellent readers, that is, they are fluent English readers; four children are promising readers, that is, learning to read but not yet fluent; and three children are unsuccessful readers, that is, they are not reading well in English. Among the group of unsuccessful readers there is the greatest correspondence between their French and English reading competence. Useful information is given by the authors on the characteristics of excellent, promising, and unsuccessful readers.

Ferdman, B. (1990). Literacy and cultural identity. *Harvard Educational Review*, *60*(2), 181–204.

Concerns over ethnic differences in school performance motivate this social psychological analysis of the way literacy and culture influence each other within a multiethnic setting such as the United States. It is emphasized that becoming literate means developing mastery not only over processes, but also over the media of the culture—the ways in which cultural values, beliefs, and norms are represented. Being literate implies maintaining contact with collective symbols and the processes by which they are presented. However, in situations in which there are mismatches between definitions and significance of literacy, as represented in a person's cultural identity and in the learning situation, decisions must be made as to whether to adopt or resist particular forms of literacy, both of which have consequences for the individual. This analysis generates several important questions for future research, such as, for example, What significance do particular texts have for the individual's cultural identity?

Freeman, Y. (1988). The contemporary Spanish basal reader in the United States: How does it reflect current knowledge of the reading process? *NABE Journal*, 59–81.

Six Spanish basal programs (K-5) published in the United States by 1980 were examined using instruments specifically developed for this purpose. Findings indicate that these basals did not seem to consider variations within language and viewed the learner as passive and dependent on the materials. In turn, teachers were viewed as technicians with little flexibility in accomplishing instructional goals. It was concluded that the Spanish basals reflected little understanding of the reading process and urged teachers and administrators to be well informed about materials before making these available for classroom use.

Goldenberg, C.N. (1989). Parents' effects on academic grouping for reading: Three case studies. *American Educational Research Journal*, *26*(3), 329–352.

This study examines how the home environment influences the opportunities second language learners of English have to be exposed to literacy activities that are intellectually challenging. A naturalistic case study approach was used to document, over a 15 month period, how parents of three Hispanic first graders at-risk of reading failure influenced their children's reading achievement by what they did at home to support school learning. Data were gathered from (1) classroom observation; (2) teacher ratings; (3) parent interviews, and (4) testing of children. Findings suggest that parents can have a positive, indirect influence on student achievement by influencing teachers' perceptions of students. That is, teachers' perceptions influence students' placement in reading groups, which in turn influences the types of exposures students have to different types of learning opportunities. Students in lower-level reading groups are typically exposed to less intellectually demanding materials than students in higher groups. This important study would have been strengthened by actual examination of the home learning environment.

Hall, C. (1990). Managing the complexities of revising across languages. *TESOL Quarterly, 24*(1), 43–80.

A descriptive study of revising processes across languages was conducted with four advanced ESL writers, from 21 to 38 years of age and with differing linguistic, cultural, and educational backgrounds. Data were collected from four writing tasks designed to elicit argumentative texts on topics of academic life. Analysis included examining the data in terms of stages, levels, type, and purpose of revision. The results show similarities in revision across languages, but revising in a second language was not simply a mirror image of revision processes in the first. Several instructional implications are presented which emphasize that the ability to revise develops when ESL writers confront problems in their own writing and, therefore, should not be treated as a separate topic of study.

Harmon, S. & Edelsky, C. (1989). The risks of whole language literacy: Alienation and connection. *Language Arts, 66*(4), 392–406.

This thought-provoking article argues that the acquisition of literacy, particularly literacy acquired by means of the whole language approach, may have unanticipated repercussions in the lives of students. Literacy may be potentially alienating because students learn new ways of viewing the world, in addition to new ways of comprehending text. It suggests that teachers may deal with this situation by having students (1) examine and compare status and non-status discourses; (2) act upon the findings of their investigation; (3) express their voices through legitimate outlets; and (4) re-connect themselves with their communities.

Hayes, E.B. (1988). Encoding strategies used by native and non-native readers of Chinese Mandarin. *Modern Language Journal, 72*, 188–195.

Two experiments were designed to investigate phonological, visual, and semantic processing strategies among native and non-native readers of Chinese Mandarin, with the assumption that errors in the recognition of words/characters revealed underlying strategies. Seventeen native Chinese from Taiwan and seventeen non-native, proficient American readers of Chinese Mandarin completed each experiment. Findings indicate that phonological encoding was a primary strategy used by native readers at the word (character) level, whereas non-native readers seemed to use a mixed strategy of phonological and graphic encoding. At the sentence level, non-native readers made more graphic errors than natives, and significantly more graphic errors than phonological or semantic errors. The predominant strategy for natives at the sentence level appeared to be a mix of graphic and semantic. Instructional implications are presented.

Hornberger, N.H. (1990). Creating successful learning contexts for biliteracy. *Penn Working Papers in Educational Linguistics, 6*(1), 1–21.

Drawing upon data obtained during a comparative ethnographic study on school community literacy in two languages, this monograph compares and contrasts how two elementary school teachers create successful learning contexts for the biliterate development of primarily Puerto Rican and Cambodian students, in ways that go beyond what is considered to be "good teaching." The two settings are distinct in that one is in a two-way maintenance bilingual program in Spanish and English, and the other is in a pull-out ESL program. Each learning context is described in terms of four themes that surface from the literature: motivation, purpose, text, and interaction. Despite contextual differences, both teachers give special emphasis to using required basals in challenging ways, thereby extending the limitations these may impose. Students engage in a variety of reading and writing activities and are encouraged to examine written language critically. Activities are accomplished as a result of the sense of community that both teachers have created in their classrooms.

Hudelson, S. (1989). *Write-on—Children writing in ESL*. Englewood Cliffs, NJ: Prentice Hall.

This publication presents research, theory, and practice as it relates to the development of writing among young English as a second language learners. Chapter one reviews research trends over the past 25 years and concludes that writing ability is acquired and developed through meaningful and continued writing. The second chapter discusses the positive role of native language in the development of writing in a second language. The third chapter provides suggestions for involving students in a variety of writing activities and for the assessment of growth in writing. Written in clear and concise prose, teachers should find this an informative and practical reference.

Kreeft, J.P., Staton, J., Richardson, G., & Wolfram, W. (1990). The influence of writing task on ESL students' written production. *Research in the Teaching of English, 24*(2), 142–171.

Reports findings of a study which examined how writing task influenced the written expression of 12 sixth-grade Asian and Hispanic students with high to low levels of proficiency in English. Data, generally derived from assigned and unassigned writings produced during a period of one week, included (1) unassigned dialogue journal entries; (2) assigned and unassigned letters; (3) an assigned essay comparing and contrasting the deserts and grasslands. Analysis included comparisons between assigned and unassigned writings in terms of quantity, complexity, focus, and cohesive qualities. Although acknowledging the limitations of drawing conclusions from limited samples, findings suggest that students demonstrate a wider range of writing abilities in unassigned tasks.

Lasisi, M.J., Falodun, S., & Onyehalu, A.S. (1988). The comprehension of first and second language prose. *Journal of Research in Reading, 11*, 26–35.

This study tests the hypothesis generated from schema-theoretical views that culture influences reading comprehension with seventh-grade Nigerian students having a reasonable level of reading ability in English. Approximately 300 students were administered reading passages containing familiar content but different cultural context, as some passages were "culturally based" and others were "foreign-based." Passages were written in English and Yoruba. Analyses of scores on multiple-choice questions indicate that students obtained higher scores on English texts with culturally-familiar content. The procedures used in this study have implications for instructional practice in any setting.

Medina, M., Jr., & de la Garza, J. (1989). Initial language proficiency and bilingual reading achievement in transitional bilingual educational programs. *NABE Journal*, 113–125.

A longitudinal study of two groups of Mexican Americans, first through third graders, was done. One was a Spanish monolingual group and the other was English dominant. The results from testing on SAT and CAT tests showed that the two groups did not vary significantly, although the Spanish monolinguals outperformed the English dominant group on the CAT in the vocabulary subtest after one year of bilingual instruction in reading. Findings suggest that students with low SES who are exposed to bilingual instruction may have an easier time transferring information to the second language. Language minority students who do not do well linguistically may be transferring prematurely, resulting in a drop of test scores which may indicate that further bilingual instruction is needed.

Swaffar, J.K. (1988). Readers, texts, and second languages. *Modern Language Journal, 72*, 123–149.

Provides an intensive, though somewhat technical, examination of cognitive studies of second language literacy which reflect the notion of reading comprehension as an interactive, constructive process involving "top-down" and "bottom-up" influences. Findings presented suggest that second language learners of English play an active role in constructing meaning from text from which they learn both language as well as subject matter. Swaffar also provides instructional application generated by the research, which includes using the native language to ascertain textual comprehension as well as techniques for developing vocabulary knowledge in context.

Verhoeven, L.T. (1990). Acquisition of reading in a second language. *Reading Research Quarterly, 25*(2), 90–114.

A longitudinal study which examines the processes of literacy acquisition of Turkish working class children during the first two grades of primary school in the Netherlands. The responses of Dutch and Turkish children exposed to the same "eclectic" initial reading program were compared on the following tasks: (1) an oral reading of a list of words; (2) a coherence (sequencing), anaphora (referential relations), and inferencing (implied relations) tasks of reading comprehension; and (3) a receptive and productive vocabulary and sentence imitation tasks of oral language. Data on sociocultural orientation were obtained by means of teacher ratings and interviews with students. Although findings suggest that Turkish children were generally less efficient in word recognition and reading comprehension than their Dutch counterparts, both groups rely on comparable strategies. Intralingual differences as well as oral language proficiency may account for some of these results. The researchers are uncertain as to the generalizability of these findings to similar students in the United States.

Weber, R.M. (1989). Linguistic diversity and reading in American society. Unpublished monograph to appear in *Handbook of reading research II.*

Describes trends in reading research emanating from studies in bilingual education and second language learning, appropriately grounding these in a historical and political context. This review provides a direction for continued inquiry, calling for examination of how reading in a second language influences oral language development in that language and longitudinal studies of the growth or reading ability in a second language.

CHAPTER VI

Literature and the Language Minority Child: A Multicultural Perspective

Milga Morales-Nadal

Introduction

Language minority children are found in any of several educational environments in the United States: a native language dominant self-contained bilingual class, a sheltered English classroom, or in a so-called "mainstream" setting. While this type of diversity exists in academic placements, the range of books and materials reflecting the cultural heritage and linguistic diversity of these students appears to be limited. The purpose of this chapter is to discuss recent research on children's literature for the language minority child in the United States and future research needs. In addition, a listing of selected titles and professional resources appropriate for those doing research in the field is included.

Empowering Language Minority Children

While many educators agree that reading is the key to academic success, there is still some controversy as to the most effective way of increasing children's desire to read in and out of school. This is a significant issue for language minority children who are learning to read in order to learn. What is the best approach to teaching language minority children to read? Are the goals different for language minority children? Should we also be concerned with developing readers for pleasure among these children? Which books and materials are available to children for whom English is not the dominant language? Will learning to read in and of itself empower children or does the content of the literature affect children's perceptions of themselves in relation to the world?

These questions have been addressed recently by some of the most acclaimed researchers in the areas of bilingual education, second language acquisition, psycholinguistics, and reading. Jim Cummins (1989) has developed a framework which may provide the necessary context for an analysis and discussion of these "empowerment" issues. Cummins affirms that it is difficult to separate the cognitive/academic and social/emotional factors in addressing the notion of empowerment. He is concerned with: (1) the incorporation of minority students' language and culture in the school program; (2) community participation in the schools; (3) the extent to which the "pedagogy promotes intrinsic motivation on the part of the students to use language actively in order to generate their own knowledge"; and (4) the advocacy role of those involved in the assessment of minority students. Cummins suggests that the extent to which minority students' language and culture are incorporated in the school curriculum is a factor in predicting academic success.

Two of the programs that appeared to do this successfully are the Kamehameha Early Education Program in Hawaii and the Carpinteria School District near Santa Barbara, California. In the Kamehameha program the reading program was changed to incorporate the collaborative learning styles of the students and to encourage the active generating of language by having children create and publish their own texts. In the Carpinteria program, language was also used to promote conceptual development, vocabulary, learning new ideas, and problem solving. In both programs, the children were involved in meaningful linguistic interactions in their native language.

Another approach to the empowerment of language minority children is offered by Bowman (1989). She suggests that bridging the gap between children's cultural backgrounds and the school's objectives may be accomplished by attending to developmentally equivalent patterns of behavior. This includes observing children in a variety of contexts; not penalizing young children for appearing reluctant to give up their language; becoming familiar with a child's primary language and culturally appropriate styles of address; and encouraging the teacher to be affectionate, interested, and responsive in the classroom.

Brauer (1989) was concerned with the effective teaching of mainstreamed language minority students in a Framingham, Massachusetts, secondary school. She identifies and recommends four basic premises for the improvement of the instructional programs for recently mainstreamed Hispanic students: (1) involving the Hispanic community in the classroom; (2) raising expectations; (3) forming mixed cooperative learning groups; and (4) basing the curriculum on meaning rather than isolated skills development.

Genishi (1989) and Nathenson-Mejía (1989) are also concerned with developing a meaningful curriculum for language minority children. Genishi asks teachers to spend time observing second language learners before making assumptions about their knowledge base in the new language. She relates the story of a child from Morocco who appeared to be producing very little language in school until he became thoroughly comfortable and familiar with the "animal" theme studied in school through a visit to the zoo where he actually saw everything that had been discussed in class. Nathenson-Mejía found that reading original literary works allowed students to learn through language instead of memorizing rules. She spent 90 minutes a week, for nine weeks, with 12 first graders in a bilingual school in Puebla, Mexico, reading from a *trade book* written in English and discussing the story with the children in English and Spanish. In this case, the children negotiated meaning from their phonological knowledge of Spanish and the teacher noted how the children would use this information to write about the stories read to them.

The use of the native language in the classroom as a tool of empowerment has been addressed by other researchers as well. Wallace and Goodman (1989) review evidence indicating the importance of knowing that the special abilities of language minority children may be masked due to the lack of clarity of their oral English. Furthermore, books and materials for language minority children should not be chosen based only on language proficiency in English.

Teaching Language Minority Children to Read

Approaches

It has often been stated that a child's love for reading is nurtured by family and friends who read to the child, answer questions about interesting stories, and provide books and materials which stimulate the child's desire to "experience" the world. According to Reyhner and García (1989), to read well in any language young students must also be fluent speakers of the language. Therefore, their initial reading experiences should be in the native tongue. In addition, children should also be exposed to good examples of culturally appropriate reading materials so they can select books and magazines that interest them. Sustained silent reading time may be allocated in the classroom as well. These researchers are critical of "scripted" curriculum materials such as the teachers' guides to basal reading.

Freeman (1988a), Pugh (1989), and Sutton (1989) have responded to these concerns by suggesting, as Reyhner and García have done, that the whole language approach is more relevant to the needs of the language minority child. This approach, as put forth by Kenneth S. Goodman (1989),

> is a philosophy of curriculum, of learning, of teaching, and of language. Whole language redefines reading and writing as processes for making sense out of and through written language. It redefines the teacher as professional decision maker, the curriculum leader in the classroom. It redefines the learner as someone who is strong, active, and already launched on the road to literacy before school begins. It redefines the relationship between teacher and learner as one of supporting development rather than controlling it. Whole language redefines the curriculum; it unifies and integrates oral and written language development with the development of thinking and building knowledge. Students learn to read and write *while* they read and write to learn and solve problems. (p. 69)

After carefully analyzing six basal programs in Spanish, Freeman notes that these programs do not reflect the recent research and knowledge about the reading process.

Freeman's analysis suggests that traditional methods of teaching Spanish emphasize a word recognition approach. She reviewed several basal texts and found that they emphasized one of several reading methodologies: *el método alfabético, el método onomatopéyico, el método fonético, el método silábico, el método global, el método ideovisual, el método ecléctico, y el método integral.* Freeman found that each of these methodologies provided for very little student-centered meaningful reading and writing activities. She recommended that only the whole language approach, which allows students to experience the reading process through authentic Spanish literature, was an alternative.

Pugh (1989) underscores this point and adds that literature should be selected for both thematic relevance and linguistic accessibility. This concern is similarly expressed by Sutton (1989) and expanded to include several guidelines which should be followed in implementing a literature-based whole language approach in the classroom:

1. Use the language experience approach.
2. Read aloud to students.
3. Expose them to different styles of writing.
4. Select well-illustrated texts.
5. Incorporate creative dramatics and dialogues.
6. Use reading for enjoyment; poetry, jokes, riddles.
7. Include folktales and stories from the student's native culture.

Another advocate of the whole language approach for language learning and for increasing language competence is Pickering (1989). He asserts that the whole language curriculum is not driven by worksheets and "contrived techniques for teaching so-called skills" (p. 146). The materials for learning are books, trade books, as well as textbooks and stories written by the children. Language skills will develop as long as students have something interesting to read, write, and think about.

While the whole language advocates have their critics (Heymsfeld, 1989; Harman & Edelsky, 1989), few reject the philosophy outright. Heymsfeld, for example, is concerned with filling what she perceives as the hole in the whole language. She would "add" to such a reading program some direct instruction in skill strategies and would not throw out basal readers because they often contain familiar poetry and excerpts from children's literature. Harman and Edelsky want to make sure that all discourses become part of the classroom and "objects of examination" for strengths and weaknesses. The voices of the different groups outside the classroom must also have a forum in the mainstream, otherwise only the dominant language will be validated.

A kindergarten teacher from Ohio, Jeanette Throne (1988) has brought the bedtime story into the classroom. She does not use the prepackaged versions of *The Three Billy Goats Gruff*, for example, because, as her children have put it, this version had probably been copied from the original but made more boring.

Tunnell and Jacobs (1989) found that original literature used with limited English proficient children did in fact yield positive results in reading. They studied The Open Sesame Program in New York City, where 225 kindergarten children were provided with books for "pleasure." Neither workbooks nor basals were used. As the year concluded, all 225 children could read their dictated stories and many of the picture books used in the classroom. According to the authors, some of the children were even able to read at the second grade level. In a prior study, Tunnell (1986) had employed a similar literature-based approach with an entire class for seven months. When standardized tests were administered, students in the class improved their reading scores. Attitudes toward reading were improved as well. Commercial publishers, particularly those that have catered to the bilingual programs in the elementary schools, are beginning to supply the whole language advocates and practitioners with literature-based reading programs. Freeman (1988b), however, has been critical of the badly adapted translations of children's literature which are tacked on to basal reading programs. The question remains: Are the materials and books to be used in the whole language approach meaningful to language minority children? Does the literature available allow children to reflect on the world through meaningful, culturally familiar stories?

Cultural Diversity in Children's Literature

In a review of children's books, Minderman (1990) states that "by exposing students to the varied works of writers from all over the world, you'll help them develop a lifelong respect for the contributions that people from different cultures have made to America" (p. 22). Even with the exhaustive research carried out by the diversity of library services and librarians as well as educators interested in the availability of children's books and materials that truly reflect the ethnic and racial mosaic that is the United States there is genuine concern about the quality and quantity of this genre.

In an article published in the *Bulletin on Interracial Books for Children*, García, Hadaway and Beal (1988) indicated that in the 1980s there has been some movement toward a broader examination of multiethnic themes and minority and ethnic group characters with more universal characteristics. But they report that in at least one study, an examination of 57 trade books revealed only 22 nonfiction selections that were adequate representations of multicultural literature. *Happily May I Walk* was one of the few selections that challenged the stereotypical notion that Native Americans are a monolithic cultural group, for example. The authors affirmed the lack of contemporary multicultural children's literature while suggesting a list of strategies to effectively deal with this serious situation, including putting pressure on publishers.

In a section devoted to the representation of Hispanics in children's literature, Cullinan (1989) states that the "number of books portraying Hispanic characters stands in stark contrast to the numbers of Hispanics in the population." She reports on a study which found that only 2 percent of all children's books published represent the Hispanic culture. Cullinan adds that "considering the numbers of Hispanic American children (approximately 17 million people of Spanish origin live in America today) who need to see themselves represented in books, there is a dearth of books available" (p. 597).

A multicultural list of children's literature that is easily accessible has been compiled by Tiedt and Tiedt (1988). The invaluable Council on Interracial Books for Children, an organization that has been attending to issues of stereotypes, omissions, and distortions in children's literature since the 1960s, continues to update and critically evaluate books and materials with multicultural themes and topics. With the help of a diverse staff and contributors, the Council has focused on books that promote cultural diversity, positive images, self-esteem, and positive identity. The books also include a diversity of characters and topics reflecting tolerance toward differences in race, gender, class, lifestyles and sexual orientation, ethnicity, and language.

Issues of assimilation vs. cultural affirmation are addressed in particular in a less recent work by Sonia Nieto (1983). The dated yet informative articles researched by Nieto are pertinent to the study of children's literature for the language minority child, particularly with respect to Puerto Rican/Latino children.

Addressing Linguistic Diversity Among Language Minority Children

While in many cases language minority children are in the process of acquiring English as a second language, they, nonetheless, are anxious to learn about the world around them and want to become familiar with the stories, the folklore and folktales native English speakers are exposed to. Travers (1988) states that the "exposure to a wide variety of good children's literature provides an effective expedient for the absorption and integration of new vocabulary and structures. Stories, especially those with repetitive, predictable, and rhythmic patterns, establish an engaging setting for simultaneously promoting the meaning and melody of the language" (p. 1). Travers has constructed a well-researched bibliography of children's books that allow children at different levels of English language acquisition to enjoy literature as they develop the confidence to use language meaningfully. He adds that "the myriad of spontaneous details that good stories allow instills in second language learners the language to mean what they say and say what they mean" (p. 5).

"Good stories," or good literature, have been defined in a recent book which also addresses the linguistic diversity among language minority children (Ada, 1990). The author describes literature as good when "it broadens the reader's horizon, validates his or her experiences, invites reflection, and awakens an aesthetic sense" (p. 3). With that definition in mind, she has prepared a resource to allow teachers and parents to: (1) help each child reclaim or revitalize his or her sense of self; (2) recognize the social value of language; (3) recognize the importance of technology; (4) understand that children are protagonists in their own lives; (5) use children's literature to provide opportunities for cooperative group work. The activities she proposes in *Spanish Language Children's Literature in the Classroom* and the guidelines cited above are based on Paulo Freire's critical pedagogy. Ada asserts that children's literature has the capacity to transform, therefore the activities and the selections correspond to that belief. In the book, she includes a variety of stories in Spanish for the lower and upper grades (K–3 and 4–6).

Conclusion and Recommendations for Research

The most recent research in the area of children's literature and the language minority child demonstrates that while there is a strong movement toward literature-based instruction in the schools, articles on the topic and stories appropriate for language minority children do not abound. Moreover, multiethnic literature reflecting the diversity of U.S. society is not readily available. Stories with universal themes which project the images of children's different voices and different lives have yet to be written in the variety and in the quantity which will ensure that language minority children have choices when and if the basal or "scripted" reading curricula have been banished from the schools.

Qualitative studies which focus on the response of language minority children to a variety of themes, to stories written bilingually vs. monolingually, to a variety of illustrated texts, and to children's original works will be helpful for both publishers and teachers in their selection of curriculum materials and books to be used in classrooms.

The annotated bibliography provided at the end of this chapter has been compiled to facilitate this type of research. To that end, it will be divided in two parts. The first will be a selected list of professional references for those interested in children's literature and the language minority child of Hispanic/Latino heritage. The second part will be a list of recently published books that should be part of all children's libraries because of the universality of the stories, the familiar themes or topics, and the inclusive nature of the books. In these stories, people are represented in a diversity of lifestyles, and common stereotypes, omissions and distortions have been avoided.

References

Ada, A.F. (1990). *A magical encounter: Spanish language children's literature in the classroom.* San Francisco: Santillana.

Bowman, B.T. (1989). Educating language minority children: Challenges and opportunities. *Phi Delta Kappan, 71,* 118–20.

Brauer, J.Z. (1989). Empowering Hispanics in the mainstream. *Equity and Choice, 6,* 42–48.

Cullinan, B.E. (1989). *Literature and the child.* New York: Harcourt Brace Jovanovich.

Cummins, J. (1989). *More possibilities: fewer failures: Instructional interventions for limited English proficient students.* New York: New York City Board of Education, Division of Special Education.

Freeman, Y. (1988a). The contemporary Spanish basal reader in the U.S.: How does it reflect current knowledge of the reading process? *NABE, 13,* 59–78.

Freeman, Y. (1988b). Do Spanish methods and materials reflect current understanding of the reading process? *The Reading Teacher, 41,* 654–662.

García, J., Hadaway, N., & Beal, G. (1988). Cultural pluralism in recent nonfiction trade books for children. *The Social Studies,* Nov./Dec. 1988, 252–555.

Genishi, C. (1989). Observing the second language learner: An example of teachers' learning. *Language Arts, 66,* 509–515.

Goodman, K. (1989). Whole language is whole: A response to Hemsfeld. *Educational Leadership, 46,* 69–70.

Harman, S. & Edelsky, C. (1989). The risks of whole language literacy: Alienation and connection. *Language Arts, 66,* 392–406.

Heymsfeld, C. (1989). Filling the hole in whole language. *Educational Leadership, 46,* 668.

Minderman, L. (1990). Literature and multicultural education. *Instructor,* March 1990, 22–23.

Nieto, S. (1983). Children's literature on Puerto Rican themes. *Interracial Books for Children Bulletin, 14,* 10–16.

Nathenson-Mejía, S. (1989). Writing in a second language: Negotiating meaning through invented spelling. *Language Arts, 66,* 516–526.

Pickering, C.T. (1989). Whole language: A new signal for expanding literacy. *Reading Improvement, 26,* 144–149.

Pugh, S. L. (1989). Literature, culture, and ESL: A natural convergence. *Journal of Reading, 32,* 320–329.

Reyhner, J. & García, R.L. (1989). Helping minorities read better: Problems and promises. *Reading Research and Instruction, 28,* 84–91.

Sutton, C. (1989). Helping the nonnative English speaker with reading. *The Reading Teacher, 42,* 684–688.

Throne, J. (1988). Becoming a kindergarten of readers? *Young Children, 43,* 10–16.

Tiedt, P.L. & Tiedt, I.M. (1990). *Multicultural teaching: A handbook of activities, information, and resources.* Boston: Allyn and Bacon.

Travers, J.P. (1988). Tunes for bears to dance to. Paper presented at the 22nd Annual TESOL Convention. Chicago, Illinois, March 8–13.

Tunnell, M.O. & Jacobs, J.S. (1989). Using "real" books: Research and findings on literature-based reading instruction. *The Reading Teacher, 42,* 470–477.

Wallace, C. & Goodman, Y. (1989). Research currents: Language and literacy development of multilingual learners. *Language Arts, 66,* 542–551.

Annotated Bibliography

Professional References

Ada, A.F. (1990). *A magical encounter: Spanish language children's literature in the classroom.* San Francisco: Santillana.

The author provides us with ideas for integrating Spanish language children's literature in the classroom. While the book is written in English, Spanish is used to further enrich the content of the book. Ada gives examples of stories that may be used for a variety of purposes. For example, Leo Lionni's "Nadarin" (which has been translated into English) demonstrates that "en la unión está la fuerza" because the story is about a school of fish joining together to ward off bigger fish. A bibliography of recent publications for lower (K– 3) and upper grades (4–6) includes seven of Ada's own contributions to Spanish literature for children.

Canales, M. (1989). To serve the Spanish-speaking: A sampler of Spanish language titles from Latin America. *Libraries, 20,* 455–58.

Conceived at the 1988 Guadalajara Book Fair in Mexico, this is a comprehensive listing of recent publications from Mexico and Argentina. Includes selections appropriate for older readers as well. One of the titles reviewed, for example, is a biography of filmmaker Luis Buñuel. All the references contain a short synopsis. Some of the illustrations from the selected titles are reproduced as well.

Cullinen, B. (1989). *Literature and the child.* (2nd Ed.) Orlando, FL: Harcourt Brace Jovanovich.

Chapter 11 of this text is "Literature of many cultures." The author discusses and gives examples of titles that exemplify the poetry, fiction, and nonfiction of different groups: African Americans, Asian Americans, Hispanics, Jewish Americans, Native Americans. A section on peace education books and materials is offered as well. A list of professional resources is included. For each ethnic and racial group, suggestions are made to the teacher for activities that the children would enjoy and learn from.

Hickman, J. (1989). Bookwatching: Notes on children's books. *Language Arts, 66,* 564–570.

The author has selected notable books with multicultural and/or multilingual themes from the titles available in early 1989. Several groups are represented, including African Americans, Hispanic/Latinos, and Native Americans. Hickman includes an extensive summary of each book, indicating why it is noteworthy for those interested in providing multicultural literature-based reading. The author also provides the ages for which the books are appropriate and the number of pages for each title.

Ohanian, S. (1990). The best of the new books. *Learning '90: Creative Ideas and Insights for Teachers, 18,* 29–33.

A listing of over 60 titles appropriate for all grades. The section titled "Words About Cultural Richness" includes several selections particularly appropriate for children who are interested in the folklore and in the history of the United States. "What Should We Tell Our Children about Vietnam?" and "The Log of Christopher Columbus' First Voyage to America" (written by Bartolomeo de las Casas) are two examples of the books that are reviewed by the author.

Quezada, S. (1988). Spanish books for children. *Booklist, 80,* 361–363.

Highlights 24 books written in Spanish by well-known children's authors such as Alma Flor Ada, Alma Flora, James DeSauza, Richard Brown, and Harriet Rohmer. The author included the ages and grades for which the books are appropriate as well as a publisher's price. A list of publishers of Hispanic books is also included.

Sale, L. (1988). Spanish books. *The Horn Book Magazine, 64,* 89–91.

Bilingual (Spanish/English) books translated by Alma Flor Ada and Rosalma Zubizarreta are reviewed by the author. The selections included are by noted children's authors. Harriet Rohmer, who has adapted the folklore of Spanish-speaking countries and has published them through Children's Book Press, is included. Four titles for younger and intermediate readers, who are either speakers of Spanish or are interested in acquiring the language, are also included.

Schon, I. (1988). Recent children's books in Spanish: The best of the best. *Hispania, 71,* 418–422.

More than 28 references of picture books, fiction, and nonfiction books recently published in Spain, Mexico, Argentina, Venezuela, and the United States. Included are translations from the English of several science books, as well as a new version of *The Three Bears and Goldilocks (Los tres osos y ricitos de oro).* The author has included titles which may be appropriate to secondary school as well. In addition to a detailed summary and analysis of each selection, the author includes the translations of each title and the appropriate grade.

Schon, I. (1988). Hispanic books (Libros hispánicos). *Young Children, 43,* 81–85.

Schon provides us with two excellent resources: an annotated bibliography of professional resources and a listing of books published in Spanish for young children. Of the most recent entries included in the list of professional resources is *Library Services for Hispanic Children,* published by Oryx in 1987 and edited by A. Allen. Schon also includes professional resources in Spanish. The *Historia y Antología de la Literatura Infantil Iberoamericana* (History and Anthology of Latin American Children's Literature), published in Madrid in 1982 by Editorial Doncel and edited by C. Bravo-Villasante, includes children's literature from Latin America, Portugal, and the Philippines.

Schon, I. (1989). Recent children's books about Hispanics. *Journal of Youth Services in Libraries, 2,* 157–161.

Schon describes 19 titles selected for their "objective" portrayal of Hispanics/Latinos from the Caribbean, Central, and South America. The review features many nonfiction titles such as *Venezuela in Pictures* and *Ecuador in Pictures*. None of the books was published before 1986. Except for some bias toward modernization vis-a-vis emphasis on deteriorated housing, the authors attempted to reflect the reality of those countries. Schon evaluates each selection with an eye toward pointing out the socio-historical gaps. Fiction works focusing on the myths and legends of these countries are also included.

Schon, I. (1989). Recent notable books in Spanish for the very young. *Journal of Youth Services in Libraries, 2,* 162–164.

Schon has selected 13 titles appropriate for very young Spanish readers. The books have been published recently in Spain, Mexico, and the United States. Almost all of the books reviewed have been translated from the English but are stories by authors that have delighted children all over the world. She includes, for example, *La Cocina de Noche* (The Night Kitchen) by Maurice Sendak, which has been translated into Spanish. The selections range from books appropriate for pre-kindergarten children up to the third grade.

Schon, I., Hopkins, K, & Woodruff, M. (1988). Spanish language books for young readers in public libraries: National survey of practices and attitudes. *Journal of Youth Services in Libraries, 1,* 444–450.

The authors surveyed 160 librarians, asking them to respond to questions about library services for Hispanics, materials and book selection processes, and other questions. The most disturbing result reported was the percentage of circulation of books in Spanish. Almost half of the librarians indicated that circulation of Spanish books for children and young adults constituted only 1 percent of the total circulation. However, it should be noted that over 85 percent of those responding indicated that books written in Spanish were needed in their libraries. This informative study should be read by all those interested in increasing the publication of books in Spanish or in other languages, since it reflects the attitudes of librarians toward materials and books in other languages in public libraries.

Taylor, M. (1990). Bookshelf. *Interracial Books for Children, 19,* 11–17.

A review of a multicultural selection of books with a focus on African American children and themes. Ten books with minority themes have been carefully reviewed as evaluated by members of the respective minority groups.

Tiedt, P.L. & Tiedt, I.M. (1990). *Multicultural teaching: A handbook of activities, information, and resources.* Boston: Allyn and Bacon.

The authors have updated their extensive bibliography of books and materials as well as professional resources that may be used in multicultural settings or by educators and parents who want to expose children to a diversity of cultures and cultural experiences. Included in the appendix of this most recent edition are selections about Africa, Asia, Canada, and South America, in addition to books and materials about African Americans, Asian Americans (Chinese, Japanese, and Korean), Hispanic Americans, Native Americans, and Jewish Americans. While some of the books are dated, they represent a great deal of what has been published to date. Folklore, fiction, and nonfiction entries are included but not annotated. The sections are divided into general resources, books for students, and books for adults.

Travers, J. P. (1988). Tunes for bears to dance to. Paper presented at the annual meeting of the Teachers of English to Speakers of Other Languages, Chicago, IL, March 8–13.

The author has prepared a selected bibliography of children's literature for English as a second language classrooms. Over 80 entries are included but not annotated. Nonetheless, in the accompanying article Travers discusses his use of stories written in English with limited English proficient children. It is a compilation that, according to the author, is purposeful and pleasurable while allowing the children to gain confidence and competence in English. The selections appear more appropriate for younger children but the themes, if of interest, may make the books pleasurable for any age. *The Snowy Day*, *Leo the Late Bloomer*, and *The Very Hungry Caterpillar* are among those classics that are listed.

Multicultural and Multilingual Selections for Children

Ada, A.F. (1989). *Amigos*. Northvale, NJ: Santillana.

Illustrated by Barry Koch. *Amigos* is much more than a book about shapes, colors, and sizes. It allows children to express their ideas about differences while they become familiar with the concepts of triangles, rectangles, squares, and circles. Children will understand that a triangle can remain a triangle, but it is fun to find out what the circles are doing and even to collaborate with them. Children in the lower grades will love reading or having someone read this book to them.

Agard, J. (1989). *The Calypso alphabet*. New York: Holt.

Illustrated by Jennifer Bent. Contains the alphabet, reflecting a diversity of expressions from the Caribbean. Words from Anancy to Zombie are included. Children will ask questions at each page about the beautiful illustrations and will be quick to point out what is familiar to their culture. For language minority children (K–3) from the English Caribbean as well as for others that are beginning to enjoy multicultural books in English.

Bunting, E. (1989). *The Wednesday surprise*. New York: Holt.

Illustrated by D. Carrick. Literacy can emerge at any age. Grandmother is learning to read with the help of her granddaughter. A wonderful way of helping children to understand that reading at home can take place even when parents are not literate. For young speakers and readers of English, this book promotes warm and nurturing relationships among family members.

Delacre, L. (1989). *Arroz con leche*. New York: Scholastic.

Illustrated by Lulu Delacre. Included are popular songs and rhymes from Latin America that are well known in Puerto Rico. Raised in the United States, some Hispanic/Latino parents may not remember their parents singing "*Qué linda manita.*" This book will serve to jar their memories as well as to teach non-Latinos about the folklore of Latin America. Translations from the Spanish to the English are included.

De Paola, T. (1989). *The art lesson*. New York: Putnam.

A story about growing up in a society that may try to constrict your ambitions and goals. Tommie wants to be an artist, but in school the rules must be followed. He learns to compromise and yet to keep his individuality. He loves his Irish and Italian grandparents and draws for them. Children who comprehend English in the lower grades (K–2) will enjoy reading and re-reading this story.

Garaway, M.K. (1989). *Ashkii and his grandfather*. Tucson: Treasure Chest Publications.

Illustrated by Harry Warren. Ashkii is waiting for grandfather. He knows he will learn about sheepherding, something Ashkii looks forward to doing in the future on the Navajo reservation. But grandfather wants Ashkii to go to school. The story reflects respect for culture and for the folkways of the Navajo people. The illustrations can tell the story, but for children in pre-K to 2nd grade, teachers, or parents may share the story and children learn to read it themselves.

Goble, P. (1989). *Iktoni and the berries*. New York: Orchard Books.

A Native-American trickster tale. Iktoni tries different ways of getting berries except for the most obvious. It is a story that can be read aloud to children in an intermediate English as a second language class or for the upper grades for the native speakers of English.

Havill, J. (1989). *Jamaica Tag-along*. Boston: Houghton Mifflin.

Jamaica is an African-American girl who is being left out of fun games by her brother Ossie because she is a girl. She knows that this is unfair, but when she plays with her sandcastle she does not want to be bothered either, especially by little Berto. All children face being left out because of gender, race, language, etc. Intermediate students in English as a second language classes in the second or third grades will readily identify with Jamaica, particularly girls.

Hayes, S. (1990). *Eat up Gemma.* New York: Lothrop, Lee & Shepard Books.

Illustrated by Jan Ormerod. Gemma won't eat, and everyone in this African American family is trying to find a way to get her to eat. Her brother, who is only a few years older, observes what Gemma does like to put in her mouth. He constructs a plan which works and Gemma eats up. Very young children will love the pictures of baby Gemma and the story could be read to two to six-year-old children with some translation to the native language for the children who are in the process of acquiring English.

Hurwitz, J. (1990) *Class president.* New York: Morrow.

Children who face challenges constantly will identify with Julio Sánchez as he runs for class president. English-speaking children of Puerto Rican heritage, grades 2–5, will identify with and enjoy this story.

Jacobs, W.J. (1990). *Ellis Island: New hope in a new land.* New York: Scribners.

The use of historical and contemporary portraits of immigrants arriving at Ellis Island will help second and third generation children understand the struggle of their grandparents and great-grandparents. Advanced English as a second language students will find this book informative and stimulating, and many that have arrived recently will find it relates to their own lives as well.

Kurusa, B. (1988). *La calle es libre.* Caracas: Ediciones Ekare-Banco del Libro.

Illustrated by Monika Doppert. The diversity of the people in a barrio in Venezuela is clearly depicted in this story. They are of all colors, with a variety of hair textures and physical features. The story is about children fighting for a park. It is written in Spanish and would be appropriate for children in Spanish-dominant classes or for children in the upper grades (4–6) that speak and read Spanish.

Leaf, M. (1988). *El cuento de Ferdinando.* New York: Penguin (Edición Española).

Illustrated by Roberto Lawson. This story for young emerging readers of Spanish was translated from the English by the acclaimed author of Puerto Rican folktales, Pura Belpré. Ferdinando is a bull (*toro*) that aspires to be happy under a tree with flowers. But a freak accident leads him to the bull ring. Ferdinando does not want to fight. Eventually he gets his way and loses the title of "El Toro Feroz," but he is content.

Levine, H. (1989). *I hate English*. New York: Scholastic.

Children learning English will love this story of a Chinese girl who does not want to stop speaking Chinese, her native language, and does not want to learn English. How she finally comes to accept the importance of becoming bilingual is the focus of this tale for the upper grades (4–6).

McKissack, P. (1989). *Nettie Jo's friends*. New York: Knopf.

Nettie Jo's story about her favorite doll and her cousin's wedding is set in the southern part of the United States. It reflects the extended family and is written in Black southern dialect. Advanced English as a second language students in upper grades (3–5) will become more aware of language varieties in the United States by reading or having this wonderful tale read to them.

Rice, E. (1989). *Peter's pockets*. New York: Greenwillow Books.

The relationship between Peter and his uncle is remarkable in this story about a little boy who needs pockets to put his "treasures" in but instead must use his uncle Nick's. A picture book to be read aloud to children in the younger grades (K–2) who enjoy the cacophony of "Peter's pockets" throughout the story.

Rohmer, H. & Achondo, M. (1988). *How we came to the fifth world. (¿Cómo vinimos al quinto mundo?)*. San Francisco: Children's Books Press.

Illustrated by Graciela Carrillo. This is an Aztec myth recounting the creation and destruction of the world by the deities representing each of the four elements of the world: water, air, fire, and earth. Intermediate and advanced students in English as a second language classes may be introduced to the genre of legends and myths through this bilingual (Spanish and English) book.

Rohmer, H. & Guerreo Rea, J. (1988) *Atariba/Niguayona* (revised edition). San Francisco: Children's Books Press.

Illustrated by Consuelo Méndez. This is a bilingual version of a Taíno legend. Spanish-speaking and native speakers of English in the upper grades (3–6) will enjoy this story about the indigenous peoples of the Caribbean.

CHAPTER VII

Bilingual Gifted and Talented Students

Deborah M. Harris and Jeanne Weismantel

Introduction

Nations around the world are experiencing the need to educate students from diverse cultural and linguistic backgrounds for careers in increasingly complex fields. In times of change and complexity, societies are dependent on those who can master technology, develop creative responses to intercultural situations and new needs, and provide avenues of verbal, visual, and artistic means of communication. The persons who are most likely to possess such abilities and to offer the leadership necessary to move from thinking to products, service, and action are those gifted with broad outlooks, keen observation skills, ability to perceive relationships, willingness to commit to tasks, high degree of intelligence in one or a number of areas, and a capacity for creativity (Sisk, 1987). The need for students who possess gifts and talents to develop their potential and become productive members of their societies has been recognized worldwide. In response to this need, a World Council for the Gifted and Talented was established in the 1970s.

Although there is growing awareness of the need for gifted and talented students to reach their potential, there is also a paradox in the attitudes of societies toward this population. In an address to the World Council (quoted in Imison, Endean, & Smith, 1986), Dr. James Gallagher, then president of the Council, commented on the love-hate relationship that he saw cross-culturally between most societies and their gifted individuals. While there may be pride in the gifted person's achievements, there may be the feeling that the gifted are fortunate students who do not need special assistance. Offering programs for gifted and talented students is sometimes termed elitist.

The issue of whether to serve the gifted and talented in special programs is also seen as a matter of equity. All students should have the opportunity to reach the upper limits of their potential. The problem for gifted and talented students is that there may not be enough challenge in school systems geared to the needs of average learners (Fetterman, 1988). How to identify gifted and talented students, especially among minority populations, and how to provide these students with a meaningful, challenging education are questions confronting educators. The issue of whether to offer special programming to gifted and talented students is answered differently among school systems according to the desires of their constituencies. If special assistance is offered, then the question is to whom should the services be given. Who are the gifted?

Definition of Gifted

Interest in gifted students as an identifiable group was spurred by Terman's research with highly able students (Terman, 1925). His definition of gifted was the top 1 percent in general intellectual ability as measured by the Stanford Binet Intelligence Scales (1925). Since Terman's work, experts have called for a broadening of the definition. The trend has been an expansion of the definition of gifted from students who earn a single high score on an IQ test to students whose gifts lie in areas other than those of traditional academic emphasis generally measured by an intelligence test (Maker, 1986). Expansion of the definition of gifted has been supported by research, particularly in the areas of creativity and the multifaceted nature of human intelligence.

Creativity

Possession of intelligence(s) in itself does not define giftedness. The evidence of ability to produce or to perform is also important. A great deal of research has been directed toward the relationship between creativity and giftedness. Researchers have recognized the interrelatedness of creativity and intelligence (Torrance, 1969). In a review of the research, Greenlaw and McIntosh (1988) pointed out that it is difficult to give a specific definition of creativity. The creative person is a producer, rather than a reproducer, a divergent thinker who is original in approach, quick in association, and able to elaborate.

Creativity along with intelligence is needed in every field of endeavor if problems are to be solved. In modern definitions of giftedness superior intelligence and a measure of creativity which can be developed are common ingredients.

Intelligence(s)

Researchers have also directed attention to the nature of human intelligence. Intelligence was seen as a unitary ability, manifested in different ways. The unitary ability could be measured by an IQ test. Thus, the student who possessed gifted intelligence was the one who scored two deviations above the mean on an individually administered test of intelligence. A definition of gifted was scoring above 130 on an IQ test (Shaughnessy, 1990). However, in 1956 Guilford veered away from this unitary view of intelligence and developed a model of the structure of the intellect which had three dimensions: operations, contents, and products. Subsequently, researchers applied various experimental techniques to the study of intelligence and assimilated the knowledge about information processing that was available in cognitive psychology research and the concept of intelligence changed. G, or general intelligence theory, has been termed inadequate (Keating & MacLean, 1987). Researchers now look at the different types of intellectual abilities people appear to demonstrate. Possessing different intelligences seems to be more responsive to what is perceived in the real world (Matthews, 1988). The theory of triarchic intelligence was developed by Sternberg (1985). According to this theory, three main areas of competency appear consistently: verbal ability, problem solving, and social competence. The gifted child has superior vocabulary, allowing rapid knowledge acquisition; superior information processing, allowing problem identification and solving; and superior social competencies, allowing the application of findings to specific domains (Shaughnessy, 1990).

Another view of intelligence as multifaceted was introduced by Gardner (1983, 1987), who drew on neuropsychology, biology, and anthropology studies for evidence of seven distinct areas of human competencies. According to his theory, the multiple intelligences (MI) are linguistic, logico-mathematical, musical, spatial, kinesthetic, interpersonal, and intrapersonal. Gifted children may demonstrate superior competence in one or any combination of these intelligences.

The particular competencies of an individual depend on personal, societal, and cultural factors.

Current research has enabled the construction of pluralistic frameworks of intelligence that provide a theoretical basis for the broad definitions of giftedness. These frameworks allow the incorporation of students who exhibit superior abilities in any or a number of domains to be admitted into the category of gifted and talented students (Richert, 1985). This is important for minority language and culture students who may not exhibit their superior gifts in the combination of abilities or in the domains recognized as gifted by the majority.

Educational Definitions

Research findings on intelligence have had a crucial impact on the current definitions of giftedness developed at the federal and local educational levels. The U.S. Office of Education (OSOE, 1972) defined gifted students as those with outstanding ability who are capable of high performance in one or more of six areas indicating the need for differentiated education: general intellectual ability, specific academic aptitude, creative or productive thinking, leadership capability, visual and performing arts, and psychomotor ability. (The last criterion was later excluded because there were specialized athletic programs in most schools.) The definition was revised in 1978 to emphasize the importance of early identification and differentiated instruction. Giftedness must be identified by professionally qualified persons (Marland, 1972).

Another influential definition is that of Renzulli (1978), who defined giftedness as "the intersection among three basic clusters of human traits—these clusters being above average general abilities, high levels of task commitment, and high levels of creativity." These three traits interact and are brought to bear upon a valuable area of human endeavor. When students demonstrate that they can develop an interaction among the three clusters, they require instructional services beyond the regular curriculum (p. 261). Renzulli's definition allows for the admission of students whose abilities and talents lie in many areas to be considered for individualized educational programs for gifted students.

Characteristics

In their review of the literature, Greenlaw and McIntosh (1988) describe the characteristics of giftedness. Early and accurate use of a large vocabulary, ability to work alone, mastery of a wide range of subjects, persistence on task, and a high level of social concern are common to lists of characteristics. Generally, gifted children move through the expected stages of development in a field of learning quickly. Gifted children have been described as developmentally advanced (Silverman, in press).

It is important to emphasize that a gifted child is an individual who may not demonstrate all the characteristics or even many of them (Greenlaw and McIntosh, 1988). There is a wide range of variablility among individuals in particular combinations of gifts and talents. The term talented is often used to indicate the individual who is advanced, persistent, committed, and creative in one area (such as art, music, or psychomotor abilities). Generally, students who are talented in one area but who do not exhibit a high level of intellectual ability are served in special schools with faculty who have the necessary professional level of expertise. In this chapter and in accordance to the work reviewed, the term talented is applied to students who are advanced in one area and also are capable of high level academic work. These students would be eligible for and able to carry out the academic studies required in programs for gifted students.

Bilingual Gifted and Talented Students

Bilingual gifted students are native speakers of a language other than English whose English language proficiency ranges from limited (LEP) to fluent (FEP) and possess cognitive ability that is markedly advanced beyond that of their peers. This cognitive ability is combined with a high level of creativity. Bilingual talented students have a dual language background, are academically above average, and show outstanding ability in one or more areas. That is, the student performs beyond expectations for age level in an area such as art, music, dance. However, bilingual gifted and talented students may not be able due to distinct linguistic and cultural factors to demonstrate their superior capabilities since they may not fit the giftedness identification criteria established by school systems serving mainstream students.

One of the major factors limiting the inclusion of minority culture and language students into programs for the gifted has been that the definitions of giftedness commonly used in schools have tended to reflect majority culture values and perceptions. Much emphasis is placed on verbal ability as measured by tests that reflect mainstream cultural values. The patterns of intellectual activities, thinking styles, interests, and values of minority culture members are not reflected in the definition of giftedness (Maker, 1986).

While the definition of giftedness has broadened, there remains a strong tendency among school systems to retain the requirements that are considered important by the mainstream, such as a high score on an IQ test. The cultural bias in the definition of giftedness was stated by Bothmer (1988), who said that being gifted is possessing the rare, valuable qualities and abilities recognized by a society at a particular time and place. For example, the Eskimo values spatial acuity, the Pacific Islander values the ability to navigate, and U.S. educators continue to value and favor skills measurable by IQ tests. Intelligence tests, developed for mainstream students and standardized with native English-speaking populations bar students of minority language and culture from participating in programs for the gifted. It is no coincidence that Native Americans, considered in proportion to their mainstream peers, are underrepresented in classes for the gifted. They have seldom been identified as gifted (Tonemah, 1987).

Identification is the crucial first step within school systems to develop appropriate programs to realize gifted students' potential. Therefore, the proper identification of gifted and talented students has been studied intensively. In the cases of language minority students, the issue of appropriate identification is critical because of the linguistic and cultural factors involved.

Identification

In the U.S. there is no one model for the identification of gifted students. The traditional method of identification consists of nomination through teacher referral and an assessment process consisting of screening and selecting. The referral is generally based on a checklist of gifted student characteristics filled out by the teacher. A major component of assessment has been the IQ test, usually administered by a school psychologist. Each of these procedures is described below, along with criticisms levied in terms of the identification of gifted minority language and culture students. Recommendations mentioned in the literature for proper identification are given.

Nomination. The teacher identifies gifted students by using a checklist of about 20 items. The criteria on the checklist include characteristics, such as learning behaviors, intellectual abilities, and creativity. However, language minority students may come from families that retain a high degree of ethnicity and native language use and may not share the values, beliefs, learning styles, and behaviors of the dominant culture. Therefore, language minority students are less likely to demonstrate the characteristics of giftedness usually found on teacher checklists. These students may have styles of thinking and learning that differ culturally from the mainstream students, making identification of the gifted among them a complex task (Bernstein, 1988). If the students are limited in English or speak a dialect, then they are even more likely to be overlooked in the process of identification of giftedness (Eby, 1989). Coordinators and classroom teachers who work with gifted students may not understand the time required for second language acquisition, and English as a second language (ESL) teachers may not be familiar with characteristics of gifted students. Further, students from culturally and linguistically diverse families may also live in poverty. Because of the low expectations teachers have of children who come from poverty backgrounds, they may not believe that the children could be gifted and have special instructional needs to reach their potential (Frasier, cited in Sisk, 1988a).

The following recommendations (adapted from Sisk, 1988a) are useful for the non-biased identification of giftedness in language minority students:

- Use a broad base of persons for nomination. Nomination forms could be placed in the community where persons who work with children could make recommendations to schools.
- Provide information to teachers about cultural and linguistic characteristics of the diverse populations within the school.
- Provide information about the particular strengths the students might have.
- Provide situations where students can display skills and abilities other than verbal/logical.
- Provide a broader checklist which includes characteristics that have been shown to be positive traits for minority and disadvantaged students.
- Observe students in different settings in and out of school.

Assessment. Students are first screened for possible inclusion in the gifted program. Often the process involves a group administered IQ test, or the process may be individual testing through standardized tests. Testing may also be carried out in the final placement of students. A commonly given group test is the Otis-Lennon. The most common individual tests used are the Wechsler Intelligence Scale for Children-Revised (WISC-R), Kaufman Assessment Battery for Children (K-ABC), and Stanford-Binet Intelligence Scale (4th ed). At times combinations of these are used.

Testing has been frequently examined by researchers. As early as the 1930s, researchers were commenting on the inappropriate use of standardized tests for identification of giftedness with Hispanic students due to cultural and linguistic barriers (Ortiz & Volloff, 1987). Tests were not normed on the population tested and, in addition, demanded a high level of verbal ability and culturally determined information. Other researchers have noted discrepancies in scores among cultural groups. For example, Native American children score differently on the WISC-R than do other groups. They tend to score higher on subtests assessing perceptual organization and lower on those assessing verbal conceptualization (Kirschenbaum, 1988).

Tests that measure achievement, such as reading tests, also present problems to students from minority culture and language backgrounds. Lack of familiarity with the topics that are familiar to students of the mainstream culture makes achievement tests more difficult for minority culture students. For limited English proficient (LEP) students achievement tests demand a level of syntactic and semantic information even the bright language minority child may lack, due to limited English language proficiency. When LEP students speak in the language they are less proficient in, they often use context to supply meaning to their conversation. The standardized reading test is difficult for them because of ambiguous vocabulary without contextual support. The bright bilingual will use strategies, such as reasoning from what is already known, to determine meaning.

Low achievement scores do not necessarily indicate low cognitive ability. If tests developed specifically for language minority students are administered in students' native languages, then testing can provide more information about students' true abilities.

Recommendations. Recommendations have led to some improvements. Over time there have been efforts to increase validity and reliability in testing students of minority culture and language backgrounds.

1. Development of appropriate tests. Although tests have been developed for use with Hispanic populations, because school personnel may not be familiar with these tests, they are often not used. Furthermore, appropriate tests are not available for use with all linguistic and cultural groups. Tests have not been normed on Native Americans, for instance (Tonemah, 1987).

2. Use of testing methods appropriate to the particular cultural group tested. Different cultural groups may experience problems with test requirements, such as speed. Hispanics and Native American students appear to achieve less success on tests with strict time requirements, which puts them at odds with their cultural inclination to carefully consider a problem before answering. Therefore, test translation is not adequate to fairly assess the skills of language minority students.

3. Examination of variations in scores across tests. Researchers have tested Hispanic students with various instruments and compared results. Discrepancies occurred among students' scores on various tests. Hispanic students achieved higher scores on the WISC-R than on certain other tests (Ortiz & Volloff, 1987). Some discrepancies may have been due to ecological differences. It is important to note, therefore, that some tests may be more biased than others against language minorities.

4. Evaluation of achievement tests used in the particular school in relation to cultural groups. School personnel should be trained in the evaluation of tests used with culturally and linguistically different students to identify biases inherent in tests developed for language majority students.

5. Inclusion of different types of tests. A variety of tests have been developed for the purpose of providing a fairer means of identification (Sisk, 1988a). Examples are nonverbal tests, such as drawing tests, and culture-specific tests that attempt to measure abilities that are specific to a particular group.

6. Consideration of ecological factors. More awareness of ecological factors that may influence test scores is needed. Knowledge of a cultural group is important in this area. Studies based on research with linguistically and culturally different groups have found significant differences in cognitive styles (field-dependence and field-independence, for example) and motivational orientations (Ramírez, 1988; Ramírez & Castañeda, 1977; Tapia, in press) between Hispanics and Anglo Americans. During the past two decades, the multidimensional concept of learning styles has been incorporated into educational models. There are cross-cultural differences in preferred learning styles. Furthermore, studies have indicated that gifted students also have preferred learning

styles. When students are in environments and in classrooms where their learning styles are acknowledged and complemented, they achieve higher scores (Anderson, 1988). Minority language and culture students may not be in situations that favor their preferred learning styles.

7.   Development of teachers' identification skills. Teachers should be assisted in devising observational and instructional criteria and classroom instruction-based tests that allow minority culture and language students to demonstrate their knowledge and skills.

8.   Use of trained test administrators. The complexities of testing language minority students require that the administration and scoring of tests be done by trained persons familiar with the culture and language of the groups represented in the school community. All school personnel involved in identification of gifted and talented students need to be aware of the extent to which linguistic, ethnic, and cultural differences influence learning and achievement (Dunn, Gemake, Jalali, & Zenhausern, 1990). They must also be aware that minority groups are not homogenous. Even when students come from the same ethnic category as Hispanics do, there are major differences among them. Mexican Americans, Puerto Ricans, and Cubans, for instance, have different knowledge bases because of historical, cultural, and linguistic differences. The cognitive ability of an individual student or of a group of minority language and culture students will be affected by linguistic and cultural differences and the environment in which they live and learn. A complex situation such as that of language minorities should be addressed by trained personnel, familiar with the languages and cultures of the students in their schools.

9.   More reliance on tests of creativity. Some researchers have recommended the use of tests for creativity as part of the identification of gifted students. These tests are especially valuable with culturally and linguistically different students. The Torrance Tests of Creative Thinking are examples of this type of test and are still frequently used. According to Torrance (1969, 1977), the discovery of giftedness among culturally different students depends on the school personnel's ability to look for "positives." Some of these positive characteristics are the ability to express feelings and emotions; articulateness in role playing, sociodrama, and storytelling; the use of expressive speech; and emotional responsiveness.

Multicriteria identification. Although educators have not rejected standardized tests, they have been warned of the dangers of overdependence on and misuse of these instruments. Because of the problems involved in dependence on standardized tests with minority culture and language students, researchers have pointed to the use of multicriteria as the preferred way to identify gifted and talented students. The criteria, which usually include the use of appropriate tests, should be considered as opportunities for students to demonstrate their potential. Such criteria include: teacher checklists, achievement tests, aptitude tests, student performance in differing domains, interviews, grades, student products, parental information, peer interviews, community member information, and appropriate standardized tests (Richert, 1985). The use of multicriteria has provided a basis for selection of minority students into gifted programs.

Selection

Despite the development of multicriteria as a basis for the selection of gifted minority students, problems persist. Many U.S. school systems use the 130 IQ score as a major criterion. Furthermore, students selected for gifted programs still tend to be typically first or only children, English speaking, from white, middle class families, have both parents who both have higher than average levels of education (Greenlaw & McIntosh, 1988).

Recommendations. Suggestions have been made to increase selection of minority children for the gifted programs. Commitment on the part of school personnel to include culturally and linguistically different children is a major factor. Fortunately, attitudes are slowly changing. There is more recognition that there are many unrecognized gifted minority students, even among dropouts (Baldwin, 1987).

Inclusion of parents and community members in the referral and selection processes is a second important factor. When parents are from diverse cultural and linguistic backgrounds, they may need assistance in understanding language and procedures. If the particular culture is preliterate or occupies low status, adult members may need to realize that their children are gifted and require special instruction.

Involved parents and community members are assets to the program. As persons familiar with the characteristics of a culture, they can provide information and insights that help school personnel understand and validate culturally diverse student products and performance.

Another vital factor in selecting minority students for gifted programs is to set up an eligibility process. One such process is a nurturing program where students are placed because they have potential to be identified as gifted. In nurturing programs, students are provided with experiences designed to develop their potential. Family and community members frequently are part of these programs, helping to provide cultural and linguistic information and to design experiences appropriate for the particular cultural group.

A number of program models have been designed and implemented in an attempt to include more minority students in the gifted category. The following models have been selected for review because each has features that seemed worthy of note.

Program Models

A Nurturing Model

The Program of Assessment, Diagnosis, and Instruction (PADI) was designed to explore ability among a large group of minority students, those not yet at the level defined as gifted (Gregory, 1987). The goal of this program is to assist students to become capable learners, then select those able to enter gifted classes.

A battery of seven assessment activities was developed and testing personnel trained. (Approximately 400 children participating in the original testing also took the WISC-R, which served as the single criterion measure. Activities that did not predict score on the WISC-R were dropped.) The seven types of activities that were retained included tasks related to non-verbal assessment, interviews with referred students, and surveys of their peers. In 1985–1986, the students enrolled in PADI were 45 percent African American, 18 percent Hispanic, 26 percent white, and 11 percent Asian. At the same time, the ethnic makeup of elementary gifted and talented programs was 76 percent white, 12.1 percent Asian, 8.1 percent African American, and 3 percent Hispanic.

PADI does not identify gifted minority students, but those who may be gifted. By providing students with experiences that expand their capabilities but which students may have lacked because of their backgrounds, PADI offers an opportunity to minority language and culture students to be identified as gifted.

A Behavior Model

A multicriteria model developed by Eby (1989) synthesized the attributes identified in 32 studies of creativity, intelligence, talent development, productivity, inventiveness, achievement, and giftedness. The attributes—perceptiveness, active interaction with the environment, reflectiveness, persistence, independence, goal orientation, originality, productivity, self-evaluation, and effective communication of feelings— are described and operationalized in a set of instruments, the Eby Gifted Behavior Index (GBI). The GBI assesses six different content or talent areas: verbal, math/science/problem solving, music, visual and spatial arts, social/leadership, and mechanical/technical inventiveness (1989). Students who are limited in English or have not had time to develop a broad information base in the mainstream culture can demonstrate gifted behaviors in a wide range of areas.

A Revolving Door Model

Minority students have more opportunities to be identified as gifted when the percent of students admitted into enrichment programs is raised. The Revolving Door Identification Model (RDIM) provides various types and levels of enrichment to more students than the 3 percent to 5 percent percent served in most traditional programs (Renzulli, 1987). From 15 percent to 20 percent of the school population is identified rather than the 3 percent to 5 percent often identifed when students are measured by intelligence tests. The assessment process involves the use of one or more ability test scores, nominations and ratings by teachers, and other criteria. A larger focus group, the talent pool, is eventually created by naming one-half selected on the basis of test scores at or above the 92 percent percentile; approximately one-half on the basis of non-test criteria, teacher nominations, any alternate pathways the district chooses to use; and a special nomination procedure designed to incorporate those who might be overlooked. Students in the talent pool are assisted in realizing their potential. Parents and community members participate (Renzulli & Reis, 1987).

Secondary School Models

Secondary students are frequently not served by specific programs for giftedness but by some form of Advanced Placement classes designed for academically superior students. These classes provide more intensive academic work and cover a wider scope of information than regular classes. Renzulli and Reis (1987) described problems in setting up differentiated classes for gifted students in high schools. Problems exist in scheduling and finding time for creative work in classes already heavy with content.

The Secondary Triad Model. This is a revolving door model developed for high school students which identifies 15 percent to 20 percent of students for inclusion in a Talent Pool (Renzulli & Reis, 1987) as described above.

The Secondary School Experiential Learning Community. Another model, implemented in Richmond, Virginia, is the Secondary School Experiential Learning Community (SSELC) project, a full time alternative school (Dabney, 1988). One of the major goals of the school is to admit minority students who demonstrate potential into a program for gifted students. Students enter by meeting one or more of the criteria which include performance on aptitute, achievement, creativity, and motivation tests, writing samples, interviews, adaptability, and demonstration of leadership skills.

An important feature of this model is that students may be admitted into the gifted program if they demonstrate high ability in some areas. The purpose of the assessment is to look for student's strengths. If the only basis for admission had been standardized tests with a high cut-off point, a number of students who have been successful in the program would not have been admitted.

A Model for Native Americans

There are 278 identified Native American tribes in the United States who speak a multitude of languages and have different cultures. Yet, there are commonalities that tie the tribes together. Native Americans follow traditions, transmit knowledge verbally from old to young, believe in cooperation with nature as well as with persons, share family responsibilities in child rearing, and on the whole, desire to maintain their cultures, languages, and religions. This desire is more respected in schools today than in the past (Daniels, 1988). Development of leadership among young Native Americans who can assist their people to achieve economic and social progress in the mainstream society, while preserving tribal traditions, is a major goal.

Not much research attention has been given to the assessment of Native American students. Some of the difficulties these students encounter include a wide variation in English proficiency and in level of acculturation among individuals and tribes and an awareness of the poor image of Native Americans in the mainstream culture, including the media, where they are stereotyped, negatively portrayed, and oversimplified (Daniels, 1988). Educators should be concerned that gifted Native Americans participate in culturally appropriate programs.

American Indian Research and Development. Identification of gifted Native Americans who can assume leadership roles is an objective of American Indian Research and Development (Tonemah, 1987). AIRD has developed the American Indian Gifted and Talented Assessment Model (AIGTAM) that tries to incorporate aspects appropriate to common cultural values and desires of the tribes. Tribal peoples were surveyed to determine what characteristics they perceived as indicating giftedness. While participants listed high intelligence, creativity, and problem solving as top characteristics, they also included in the top ten being respectful of tribal leaders, high leadership qualities, respect toward others, and a high degree of artistic talent. Farther down on the list were knowledge of tribal culture and storytelling ability.

The identified characteristics were grouped into several categories, including aesthetic values, language, tribal/cultural understanding, and personal/human qualities. Recommended means of assessment of Native American students is multicriterial. Information from many sources is collected, including self-reports, a test of nonverbal reasoning (Ravens Progressive Matrices has been a valid indicator of general intelligence), Torrance tests of creative thinking, student products, and performance, especially in art and dance. Various standardized tests may be included, with the understanding that Native American children's scores may be different from mainstream children's.

The North Wind Warriors Program. Begun in Minneapolis, Minnesota, in 1977, this program serves gifted Native American students in grades 3 to 6. The screening procedure relies upon Native American values, nationally accepted checklists, and achievement tests in math and science. Teachers must be familiar with resources of community people and have training in teaching the gifted. The program was described as being sensitive to the traditions of its students and academically strong (Neubeck, cited by Daniels, 1988).

Zuni Revolving Door Model. Another model for Native American gifted education, patterned after the Renzulli Revolving Door Model, was implemented on the Zuni reservation in New Mexico. Only .6 percent of Native American students had met the state criterion of two standard deviations beyond the mean on approved intelligence and achievement tests. Reservation schools were exempted from meeting that criterion. The model described by Kirschenbaum (1988) allows entrance of students nominated by teachers who either meet state criteria or who score at or above the 80th percentile on any subtotal of the California Tests of Basic Skills, i.e., total reading, total math, or total language. Regardless of the test scores, if a student is nominated by a teacher at least twice in the previous three years, the student enters the program. One of the impressive results of the program is that students nominated by teachers have done as well as those who met state criteria.

Generally, exemptions from meeting criteria have not been accepted by many states. The overall process of identification is often tied to requirements that are difficult for minority populations to meet. Once they meet the requirements, they may face difficulties in gifted classes designed for language majority children. It is essential, then, that language minority children identified as gifted receive instruction that takes into account their linguistic and cultural background.

The key to the identification of giftedness in Native American students in the above models is the assessor. Assessors must possess knowledge of the particular tribe(s) from which students come and are able to evaluate student products such as poetry sensitively and ably.

Instructional Methods

For culturally diverse students, it is necessary to ascertain what types of special programming they need in order to reach their potential and then provide the appropriate programs. In other words, programs must be tailored to meet the needs of the students (Greenlaw & McIntosh, 1988). Once students from culturally and linguistically different backgrounds are identified as gifted, they participate in differentiated instruction, that is, qualitatively different from the curriculum of the school (Maker, 1986). Planning such instruction for these students requires knowledge and adaptation that takes into account the level of language and acculturation of the students.

There are many delivery models for serving gifted and talented students with differentiated instruction in the United States: summer sessions, special schools, special programs within a school where students attend all day, pullout models in which students go for a portion of time, and special groups within classrooms. In some schools, a consulting teacher works with classroom teachers. Bilingual/ESL teachers may give instruction to students with limited English proficiency. School counselors and psychologists are also involved in working with bilingual gifted and talented students.

Given the types of programs and the varied personnel involved, it is not surprising that instructional methods and content vary. Some general concepts related to instructional planning for these students follow.

Individualization

Some states consider gifted education as part of special education services and an Individualized Education Plan (IEP) is required. Parents participate and their consent is necessary for student participation. In general, attention to individual needs is a major part of instructional programming for the gifted and talented. Emphasis is placed on developing individual creative responses. Talented students need special instuction by persons qualified in the area of the students' ability.

A difficulty in planning for students from diverse backgrounds is that the teacher may not have the knowledge necessary to judge products and performance of students from other cultures or be able to incorporate information from the students' culture in instruction.

Programs

Acceleration. Gifted students move through instructional components swiftly and may benefit from advancing through courses or grades. Early college entrance is another example of acceleration. Because their development may be unequal—emotional and social development may lag behind intellectual development—acceleration is not always recommended. Accelerating students from diverse backgrounds might be problematic. Such factors as degree of acculturation, language proficiency, and achievement orientation would have to be considered.

Enrichment. Gifted and talented students have needs beyond what is supplied in standard instruction. There are various ways of providing enrichment which extend and advance the regular curriculum. In a pullout program, for instance, students might investigate local history, use the local library for research, and then write papers. An example of an activity for multicultural students might be finding influences from their country of origin in their new environment. At the secondary level, students might enter an internship program where they work on a research project along with executives and leaders. Mentors and community persons with special ability are invaluable for gifted and talented students. Reaching into the communities of minority language and culture students for mentors who can provide assistance is helpful to students from these backgrounds. The Latino Adopt-A-Class Program which functions in New York City schools   with high concentrations of Hispanics is a good example of this type of approach. The goal of the program is to provide students with role models and a vision of opportunities available to them after they successfully finish school (Mercado, 1991).

Curriculum compacting. This method uses a combination of acceleration, enrichment, and individual plans. The purposes are to eliminate the unnecessary, that is, what is known; subsititute what is not known; and in extra time, provide enrichment. In the areas of their particular gifts and talents, students spend less time on basics (Renzulli, 1988). Through careful diagnosis and documenting of mastery, teachers plan curriculum to advance gifted students rapidly as compared to peers. Students from diverse backgrounds may lack academic vocabulary and factual information about the mainstream culture that their mainstream peers have. Therefore, curriculum compacting for minority language and culture students requires a high level of skill and awareness on the part of the teacher.

Curriculum Planning

A number of models exist for curriculum planning. One model that incorporates different aspects of enrichment is Renzulli's (1988). The model is adapted for both elementary and secondary schools and emphasizes participation of parents and community. There are three types of curriculum planning models in Renzulli's enrichment program.

Type I enrichment. Talent pool students are supplied with a variety of experiences in different fields of study that may stimulate them towards further study. An enrichment team of teachers, parents, and administrators plans and carries out this level of enrichment, encouraging the participation of the whole school body and community. This builds positive school-community relationships, valuable in bridging the gap between mainstream school and minority community members.

Type II enrichment. Talent pool students are instructed in methods, materials, and techniques designed to develop higher level thinking processes, research and reference skills, and processes related to personal and social development. These skills prepare students for optional advanced inquiry in areas of personal interest.

Type III enrichment. Students who demonstrate a stong interest in a problem develop a contract to carry out a plan of research. A mentor is often used to teach the methodology of the discipline and to determine in advance the nature of the product.

The Renzulli model, as noted in the section on identification, has been implemented successfully for Zuni Indians because it allows for flexibility and the bringing in of multicultural components.

A Bilingual/Bicultural Curriculum Component

Adapting advanced curriculum for students from culturally and linguistically different backgrounds presents a challenge to teachers. The students are, however, a great resource. Having an ethnic mix in classes for gifted and talented students is now a social and political responsibility in a period when intensive study of the contributions of various cultures is essential (Maker, in an interview with Balsamo, 1989). Within any model of instruction for gifted and talented students, multicultural components should be included. There are numerous sources of such materials currently available. Parents and community members are sources of information about the arts, for instance, in which members of their culture excel. Gifted and talented students can research and share information about their backgrounds. Family interviews are good techniques even for the very young.

For gifted students from diverse backgrounds a relevant curriculum should have some focus on the achievements of persons from minority backgrounds, presented in continuous, orderly sequence. In middle school, for instance, the curriculum should provide opportunities for risk taking, such as visualizing (drawing a mental picture of an ethnic role model, then discussing the circumstances of that person's actions), role plays, and debates. Such methods provide ways to demonstrate creativity and empathy for others. Writing for a newspaper and judging a performance also allow students to analyze, synthesize, and evaluate with the overall purpose of extending their views beyond their minority status (Bernstein, 1988).

Culture sensitive curriculum should also include special coursework designed to meet needs of students from differing backgrounds. For Native Americans, for example, features identified as important were time to think before initiating a task, opportunities to explore values of tribe, family and self, opportunites to compare these values to those of other cultures, and experiences in storytelling (George, cited in Daniels, 1988). Specific science activities that addressed the students' needs were field trips to varied outdoor locations, collections of plant life, construction of weather stations, and participation in science fairs (Catmull et al., cited by Daniels, 1988). Independent projects that Native American students would become involved in might be centered on themes taken from books that present fair treatments of Native American history (Project Necessity, a guide for secondary level Native American students in social study, reviewed by Daniels, 1988).

Leadership Development

In the World Council for the Gifted, interest is high in developing leadership. Curriculum for gifted students is frequently designed to include elements of leadership training. Five trends that have been considered promising in leadership education were experience in predicting, planning, and extrapolating; explicit leadership training; thinking skills; experience in problem finding and problem solving; and study of major concepts, themes, issues, and ideas (Feldhusen & Kennedy, 1988). Other areas of importance listed were the study of one or more foreign languages, mentoring experiences with creative adults who work in students' talent areas, and examination of values in ethical systems. Such a curriculum is demanding and students with limited experience in mainstream life would be able to carry out the work if the curriculum incorporates ideas from students' cultures and teachers invite adults who come from the students' cultures and are familiar with materials from the cultures to participate. In this approach, mainstream students benefit as well because their horizons are widened.

Language Learning

If provided with opportunities in class, bilingual students can interest other students in the process of language learning. In the United States there has been lingering doubt about the advisability of learning more than one language because of the supposed added cognitive load. This myth has been discredited by the research in the field (Hakuta, 1986). Language is learned through use and bilingual instruction for gifted students is an opportunity for cooperation and sharing. There is great need for bilingual, biliterate persons in the country. Gifted students could change the nation's monolingualism (Brickman, 1988) in two-way programs where LEP gifted students and native English speaking students learn in two languages.

Resources

The general scope of curriculum planning for this special population is to provide enough content, challenge, practice, and opportunity to encourage bilingual gifted students to develop their abilities to the maximum. These are students who move through the curriculum quickly. Identifying resources is a need. Incorporating materials from various cultures is time consuming and in some areas very difficult. Often, the gifted teacher is alone in a school. Collaborating with university faculty, librarians, and other teachers in schools with similar populations helps build knowledge. Collaboration is facilitated by networking through meetings, conferences, and newsletters, allowing dissemination of information. Sharing resources and combining in-service training for teachers in a district are recommended (Dodd, Nelson, & Peralez, 1988–1989).

Information from other programs can be another valuable resource. Some examples of programs have been described in recent issues of *International School Journal*. The programs described are theory-based multiple talent models, designed to develop higher order and critical thinking skills for gifted and talented students. They include a sequentially ordered curriculum that teaches a creative problem solving process. Investigating the programs in such schools offers insight into possibilities for instruction. Other information can be gained from looking at programs in schools outside the United States.

Gifted Programs in Other Countries

The latter part of the twentieth century has been a time of understanding and provision for services to gifted students (Thomas, 1987). A plethora of nations now have policies and programs for the gifted. The decision to offer such programs, who will be included, and what type of instruction will be offered depends on the particular country. Political and economic conditions affect the choice.

International. One program that sets up universal criteria is the International Baccalaureate (IB). Offered in schools in different parts of the world, the program provides advanced classes for secondary school students who have to complete six subjects and pass examinations. Requirements include the Extended Essay, the Theory of Knowledge, and the Creative Aesthetic courses. The IB program is content oriented and planned for highly motivated academically achieving students.

Australia. In Australia a growing IB program indicates interest in academically talented students. One area of emphasis is foreign language learning, especially European and Asian languages. Australia has a multicultural society. In 1984 over 20 percent of the population had birthplaces other than Australia. Birthplaces included Yugoslavia, Greece, Vietnam, and Malta. Australia, like the United States, is finding it imperative to develop ways to work with a multicultural population (Schlesinger, 1987).

The states control education in Australia within certain limits. Programs vary across states. In New South Wales, a 1983 survey revealed that 23 percent of the students were from non-English speaking backgrounds and a wide range of English proficiency existed. There was a need to identify and instruct the students with exceptional talents among the minority language populations. The government is committed to meeting this need (Schlesinger, 1987).

The three areas of importance that Australian schools had to consider were:

1. *Culture.* Culture specific talents (the word "talents" is equivalent to giftedness) that may not be traditionally valued by the school must be considered. This may necessitate working with parents and community members to identify those talents and develop curricula in which these talents are used. This may mean having to convince minority group members that possession of these abilities indicates superior capacities in the children.

2. *Individuality.* School personnel need to consider that the variables within the cultural, linguistic, and socioeconomic factors which contribute to the uniqueness of the child will differ markedly in their relationship to each other. A disproportionate number of students from minority language backgrounds are seen as disadvantaged.

3. *Language.* The role of language in the instruction of the talented child is important. Based on the aims of the Multicultural Education Policy adopted in 1983, the value of maintenance of the mother tongue was acknowledged, while the importance of the use of English to participate fully in national life was affirmed. The problem was that limited English proficiency could inhibit recognition of talented students who would not be able to demonstrate superior performance. The desire was to avoid what Eby (1989) described as the risk for gifted LEP students in the United States who are assigned work on the basis of their ability in English. In New South Wales the schools considered that a student's performance might not necessarily be an indication of potential, especially if the measure is performance in English.

Schools in Australia consider that talented students may be found in one or more of the following categories:

- The student who is proficient in English and displays talent valued by the school.
- The underachieving student who experiences handicapping conditions, such as inability of the school to identify the student and/or to provide a supportive school environment for the child and the parent.
- The student from the non-English speaking background who may only demonstrate linear acceleration in learning English and so become an underachiever if not offered enrichment.
- The student who may possess culture-specific talent and be invisible because school personnel lack the knowledge to recognize the talent. (Schlesinger, 1987)

It was recommended that schools take these factors into consideration in the beginning stages of planning school programs. School personnel needed to look for opportunities in which multicultural students can display abilities.

Britain, China, and Indonesia. There are similarities and differences in exceptional child education in the three countries. All three have programs for academically able students (Thomas, 1987). Education of the gifted and talented is part of special education services in Britain. In the 1980s, Indonesia also included the gifted within the category of special education. In China there has been a great deal of attention given to the gifted as the nation has searched for talent to hasten socioeconomic development. Competitions are held to honor students who are high achievers, especially in science. These students attend key schools that offer scholarships.

Techniques for assessment vary, however. In Britain intellectually gifted children are usually identified through their achievement on tests administered throughout the school system at certain times in their school careers. These achievement tests are sometimes supplemented by intelligence tests.

In China there are four requirements to enter the key schools: high marks on the national examinations in subject-matter areas, high-level marks in past schooling, faithful political moral awareness as defined by the Chinese Communist Party, and good physical health.

In Indonesia the procedures for identifying gifted students appear less advanced than in Britain or China. Indonesia apparently intends to offer special learning opportunities to gifted students but is in the early stages of developing a system for such training.

Taiwan. In Taiwan 15 percent of the national budget is spent on education. All the cost of teacher training is borne by the national government. Children who demonstrate high ability are placed in resource rooms for special educational services (Gallagher, 1988).

Japan and Germany. In comparison to the United States, Japanese schools maintain mixed ability classrooms, with no acceleration for students who demonstrate superior ability. The emphasis is on student effort. Teachers are highly respected. Screening of able students is carried out through tests in secondary school that determine admission to universities (Fortner, 1988).

In Germany differentiated education for gifted students is a matter of dispute. Testing at the secondary level is a means of routing students either to trade schools or university (Fortner, 1988). Recently, changes have occurred. Programs for advanced students, especially those in mathematics, have been implemented (Fetterman, 1988).

Attitudes toward the gifted in different countries tend to reflect the economic, political, and cultural framework of the national society. In a survey of Ghana, Kenya, Uganda, Indonesia, Nigeria, and Oman, attitudes toward the gifted varied according to political ideology, economic situation, and aim of the educational programs (Baldwin, 1989). If the aim was to identify and train gifted students in science and technology, there was more acceptance among the public. Overall, the researcher found that there were advocates for active selection of children for special programs, but interest was tentative. Among the general population, attitudes were usually negative. High academic achievement and being articulate in oral/written language were considered identifying characteristics of superior students. Creative problem solving and graphics arts abilities were of less interest. In some developing nations interest may lie more in providing classes for all students. In contrast, highly developed nations have facilities and resources allowing provision of differentiated education for students of differing capabilities and the training of faculty to meet different needs.

Teachers of Bilingual Gifted Students

Increasingly, teachers will work with students from diverse cultural and linguistic backgrounds. Those who work with gifted and talented students from diverse backgrounds have complex teaching assignments in which they need the skills and knowledge of teachers of the gifted and of teachers of bilingual/ESL students. In both areas, gifted and talented and bilingual/ESL, there is emphasis on matching instruction to the individual's need. Both areas emphasize the skills needed to work on assessment teams and to communicate with parents who are involved in the planning. The ESL teacher, like the teacher of the gifted and talented, frequently has no counterpart within a school setting, and so must be a person of independence. The recommended characteristics of teachers of the gifted, however, differ in emphasis placed on intellectual and creative abilities.

Teachers of the Gifted

Teachers of the gifted need to be highly intelligent, resourceful, and have mastery of content. They need energy, humor, and self-confidence to deal with their highly demanding students. Enthusiasm for learning, strong preparation, and development of creative activities are necessary (Maker, 1986). In terms of professional knowledge, they need to be familiar with characteristics of giftedness, have knowledge of and practice in curriculum design, and be familiar with research. It is safe to say that these teachers are challenged to stay ahead of their students (Greenlaw & McIntosh, 1988).

Teachers of Bilingual/ESL Special Education Students

Teachers of bilingual students who may be unfamiliar with a mainstream classroom need to be empathetic, to tolerate differences, to be able to establish and maintain a warm, affective atmosphere. In the 1980s interest grew in training teachers to work in the field of bilingual special education. A survey of 77 teachers working with special needs students from diverse backgrounds in the Southwest was carried out (Reuda, Rodríguez, & Prieto, 1981). Teachers were asked to rank 18 competencies taken from the literature. They identified 13 competencies that were desirable in working with bilingual multicultural exceptional children. The competencies deemed most important were ways to involve parents in the education process, skill in criterion based assessment, and methods for working with these children in the classroom. Familiarity with language of children, ability to interpret and use data from normative tests, and acting as a resource/consulting teacher were slightly less important, while examining roles of parents, current research, other programs, legal issues, and cultural backgrounds followed. The last competency ranked was ability to evaluate commercially developed materials for bilingual/exceptional students.

Building on this study researchers surveyed 102 teachers in rural areas and 102 teachers in urban areas who worked with special needs populations from diverse backgrounds in California during the 1986–87 academic year. Teachers were asked to rate their present skill level and desired skill level in relation to each of the 13 competencies in the earlier study. A majority of teachers (over 50 percent) reported they possessed low present level skills and desired higher skills in all 13 competencies (Chávez, Burton, & López, 1986-1987).

A comparison of relative highs and lows among the 13 competencies revealed that both groups identified low skill levels in acting as a resource consultant, in evaluating materials, and familiarizing other teachers with languages and dialects. Both groups selected parent training skills as competencies they wished to have. Rural teachers indicated that examining family roles and interpreting normative assessment data were desired high priority competencies. Urban teachers gave greater precedence to defining bilingual multicultural special education students, using specific methods, and involving parents.

These findings indicated that teachers continue to need training to acquire specific skills for working with language minority children and their families. The researchers pointed out that while teachers desired to work with families, they assigned lower priority to becoming familiar with language and in acquiring consulting skills. Yet, these two competencies apply to working with families and with minority populations as well as collaborating with other faculty members. The researchers suggested that with more information teachers might see more need for language and consulting skills training (Chávez, Burton, & López, 1986–1987).

While this research was carried out with teachers of students who have handicapping conditions, there is relevance for teachers of gifted students. In many places gifted students are part of special education because they are exceptional, that is, generally they are in the upper 3 percent of the population in intellectual ability. Often schools must provide Individualized Education Plans for them, which involve working with parents. The teacher of the gifted student is often alone in the school and is consultant, interpreter of assessment and achievement, collaborator, and informant to other faculty. When minority population students are either not identified in the program or experience difficulties, the teacher of those students should be able to work with school personnel at local and higher levels, with parents and community to develop a program addressing the needs of the particular school and its cultural mix. It appears that teachers of bilingual gifted and talented students are themselves a special population!

Teachers of Bilingual Gifted and Talented

The intersection of these two areas involves the teacher having the ability to create a warm affective atmosphere while providing a high level of intellectual stimulation. The teacher needs to be able to see student ability manifested in different ways and to develop curriculum that is appropriate both to the level of language ability and to the cognitive ability of the students. How to challenge students with potential ability but who lack the common knowledge base of the dominant culture is a challenging question. The teacher must blend *general education curriculum*, that is, the knowledge needed to participate effectively in the society; *specialized curriculum*, that is, the instructional needs that will allow the gifted student to grow; the *covert/subliminal curriculum*, that is, what the students receive from the climate and environment that affects their self-concepts and relationships; and the *non-school curriculum*, that is, the learning acquired in all the institutions in which the students are involved (Passow, 1989). When gifted students are from diverse family backgrounds, their teacher is indeed challenged.

Finally, the bilingual gifted and talented teacher is an advocate for students individually and as part of a program that usually has to be defended. There probably will never be a point where the need for gifted programs will not have to be defended (Passow, 1988).

While there was no comprehensive discussion in which characteristics and competencies of teachers of gifted students of diverse backgrounds were found, there was one consistent theme presented in the literature. Teachers of gifted multicultural students have great respect for the culture of the students. Respect begins with understanding of students and their families. Parenting gifted children is often difficult. In a new culture, the difficulties may be compounded. Teachers need to understand these difficulties.

Parenting Gifted and Talented Bilingual Children

Cultural Differences

The paradoxical feelings that societies experience toward their gifted members are reflected in the feelings of parents with gifted children. While they feel pleasure and pride in their children's abilities, they also may find the parenting of children who differ from the norm so markedly a difficult task (Smutny, Veenker, & Veenker, 1989).

Gifted and talented children challenge parents because these children move through developmental stages more rapidly, require more stimulation, and experience more difficulties in self-acceptance than their peers. Gifted and talented children are likely to be absorbed in what interests them and to persist beyond what seems reasonable in their chosen tasks. What may be admirable traits in pursuing learning and solving problems may make these children seem difficult and demanding in the home.

A comprehensive understanding of the emergence of abilities and how these abilities change over time is needed (Roedell, 1989). The situation becomes even more complex when these changes occur in a new cultural environment. Parents are the most knowledgeable persons about the emergence of abilties in their children. School personnel need to compose questions about specific achievements, ask these questions to parents in interviews, and actively listen to the parents of students who may be gifted, especially the highly gifted (Roedell, 1989). In identification and carrying out of the instructional plan for a gifted student, parents should be part of the procedure. When the parents are limited in English, an interpreter will be needed (Perlman & Chamberlain, 1988). Intercultural communication is time consuming and can be uncomfortable but essential to the equitable application of educational procedures.

When the parents do not have the same values as the values of mainstream culture expressed by the school, they may feel threatened. In the United States, for example, mainstream parents and professionals place high value on fostering independence, the belief that one can control one's environment and help oneself, and an orientation to change and direct action to accomplish that change. These values are reflected in classes for gifted students. Parents from other cultural orientations may not agree with these values (Hanson, Lynch, & Wayman, 1990). Patterns of parenting differ from culture to culture.

The parenting patterns reflect the values held in the culture. Asian and Hispanic (these terms used here only indicate general characteristics exhibited among some peoples who belong to the cultural groups mentioned) parents nurture their very young children by gratification of needs and physical warmth expressed through touch. As the children grow older, differences in the patterns emerge. Many factors influence the achievement of a particular child. These child-rearing practices may seem unusual to school personnel not familiar with other cultures and judgments detrimental to the children may be based on this lack of knowledge.

The following discussion is not intended as an illustration of the failure of some forms of parental guidance but to indicate that cultural values of minority parents may differ from those of the mainstream. If schools could incorporate students and their families from differing backgrounds in planning and implementing educational processes and assign value to their cultural behaviors, more gifted minority students might be identified and achieve at their potential. For example, developing educational activities and providing cooperative games where winning is shared (instead of exclusively competitive games) might be important to Hispanic students (Tapia, 1991).

Asians. As their children mature, Asian parents expect them to behave in conforming and adult ways (Chan, 1986). These parents expect to be in control, to restrict their children, and to protect them. Long hours of study are expected even for first graders. Asian American children are overrepresented in classes for the gifted, especially in science and math programs, in numbers and percentage beyond what would be predicted from the numbers and percentage of Asians in the United States (Maker, 1986).

Hispanics. Hispanic families maintain close relationships among family members. Cooperation and affiliation are preferred orientations among Puerto Ricans (Tapia, 1991), for example, rather than competition. Placing family needs above career needs may make Hispanic students' decisions incomprehensible to school personnel who work with the gifted and talented. Hispanic students are underrepresented in gifted programs (Maker, 1986).

Many studies have documented cultural differences in child rearing. It is important for school personnel to respect diversity and to seek to recognize potential (Hanson, Lynch, & Wayman, 1990). The challenge is to learn to obtain and to provide family information in culturally sensitive ways.

School's Role in Parental Participation

Parents wish to receive information from schools, but communication across language and culture is difficult (Hanson, Lynch, & Wayman, 1990). It may take time to understand how people communicate within a culture, to work with an interpreter to be certain that meaning is maintained, to learn about the native country and the customs and values parents from other cultures might have. School personnel need to take into consideration the significant impact of social and environmental factors such as immigration and discrimination on minority language and culture students, especially those who are racially different from the mainstream. Ethnic competence is being able to interact in ways expected by members of the other culture. In regard to gifted and talented students, school personnel need to understand family structure, (including the extended family), parents' expectations, the value they place on achievement, the level of their understanding of the host country's programs for the gifted, how parents express affection or how they discipline, what attributes parents value, and whether parents understand what the label "gifted" means. School personnel can expect parents from different cultures to need time to understand the expectations of U.S. schools (Hanson, Lynch, & Wayman, 1990).

The best mentors for the gifted and talented children are informed parents (Smutny, Veenker, & Veenker, 1989). U.S. schools have at times provided linguistic minority parents with information, in their language if necessary (Perlman & Chamberlain, 1988). The parents of bilingual gifted and talented students may experience difficulties as their bright youngsters become part of the new cultural surroundings. School counselors can assist families to cope with change.

Counseling

Culturally diverse gifted and talented students, their families, and their teachers have counseling needs. Gifted students may experience conflict between the psychosocial drive toward intimacy and the desire for acceptance by family and peers and the need to achieve and excel beyond their average peers (Gross, 1989). It may appear to culturally diverse students that they must give up some of their cultural identity if they become one of the mainstream achievers (Colangelo, 1985).

The Counselor's Role

Values validation. Counselors need to be sensitive to demands of family and cultural values. Gifted and talented students who choose intimacy at the cost of achievement are not realizing their potential; they may experience frustration, alienation, and lowered self-esteem (Gross, 1989). If they choose achievement at the cost of their close personal associations, they are lonely. Their feelings are especially acute when they encounter racism and prejudice (Aramen & Berry, 1987). Overcoming loneliness is aided by bringing gifted and talented students into contact with each other.

Parental guidance. Counseling parents is often necessary because parents who themselves are outside the mainstream may not realize the potential of their child and may not be aware of the career choices possible to them. An area of sensitivity develops when the gifted child speaks the new language and the parents do not. Parents as well as children can benefit from support and discussion groups. Counselors can interact between school and community, demonstrating acceptance of minority langauge and values by being visible (Colangelo, 1985).

Emotional support. Gifted and talented children may have problems with self-acceptance, especially when their appearance differs from that of their mainstream peers. Awareness of the needs of students from other cultures and development of skills in counseling them are being addressed. The use of books and of literary materials appropriate to the culture and to gifted and talented students' problems is one method. Cuento therapy, in which folktales are used as a strategy for counseling Puerto Rican students is an example (Costantino, Malgady, & Rogler, 1985). Bibliotherapy, which involves the use of stories and poetry organized around themes for discussion in groups, is another method (Adderholt-Elliott & Eller, 1989).

Counselors can also provide leadership in schools which enroll students from diverse backgrounds. By encouraging cross-cultural groups and by providing support to teachers, counselors can help to promote communication and acceptance of the minority culture members.

Academic support. As members of student assistance teams, counselors can also participate in the education of culturally diverse students. Teams formed from school personnel gather data on referred students, review data, and make recommendations. Counselors can assist in goal setting in the school with the aim of providing an academic environment in which students are well. A well student is one who is achieving at a rate commensurate with his or her ability (Maker, 1986).

Career counseling. Counselors provide a vital role in assisting gifted minority culture and language students in making appropriate career choices. Most important, counselors can be advocates for the at-risk students, such as gifted and talented bilinguals who, if allowed to demonstrate their abilities and provided with classes and materials, develop into leaders (Ogden & Germinario, 1988).

Advocacy

Advocates for the culturally diverse gifted and talented students such as school counselors, teachers, and parents are needed if students are to realize their potential. Advocacy groups form at the individual school level and at district level, where teachers, parents and community persons may advocate for a program. An example of a local group is the North Central Florida Association for Gifted. Parents and school personnel join in arranging programs, attending conferences, and working to achieve instructional opportunities for gifted students. Organizations that support education for gifted and talented students also form at state and national levels. Effective advocacy may lead to court actions. Parents may sue if they think that their children are not receiving the education to which they are entitled.

Court Decisions

A landmark decision was handed down by the Pennsylvania State Supreme Court which held that if a state provides gifted education and requires procedural safeguards, then the whole thrust of the system is to provide individualized, appropriate instruction for each gifted child. The state does not have to go beyond its resources but must provide whatever resources are in place for gifted students (Karnes & Marquardt, 1988).

In this case the parents were the advocates. The state association for the gifted supported the parents by filing briefs and underwriting the cost of the attorney. Advocacy workshops were held around the state to provide training for teachers and parents for the gifted. The association efforts served as a model for other cases (Karnes & Marquardt, 1988).

Advocacy Organizations

There are advocacy groups at the national and international levels. The National Association of Gifted Children is one group that has been active in the United States. Advocacy efforts at the national level have been effective. In 1989 the Jacob K. Javits Gifted and Talented Act charged the U.S. Department of Education to provide leadership in developing new ways to seek out and to serve high ability students from various backgrounds. Other nations such as Australia have associations to advocate for the gifted. On the international level the World Council for the Gifted and Talented is providing an arena for interaction among advocates from many nations.

Conclusions

Interest in the education of the gifted and talented has been more intense because of the need for persons who can process information and master complex technology in all countries of the world. Schools in many countries are enrolling large populations of students of diverse backgrounds. Educators are challenged to find equitable means of identification of and instruction for gifted and talented students from families of linguistic and cultural backgrounds that differ from those of the school systems which tend to reflect language, beliefs, values, and information of the mainstream.

Education of this population is also made more complex by the lingering feeling that gifted students do not need special assistance; they are capable of educating themselves. After reviewing and annotating a great number of books and articles about gifted and talented students, Greenlaw and McIntosh (1988) concluded that these students cannot educate themselves; they need advocates to ensure that they will receive the opportunities for learning that will assist them to become the leaders of tomorrow. There are gifted students among every population. In societies with increasing diversity, the need to identify and educate gifted and talented students from all backgrounds is pressing. The blending of cultural groups, under the leadership of these students, is important to the future of the nation (Sisk, 1988b).

Directions for Research

A powerful theme throughout the literature reviewed for this chapter is the need to develop leaders for the future. Gifted and talented students are our resources, our hope for a good future in an increasingly complex world society. They are the potential leaders who could see relationships, build bridges, speak, read, and write more than one language well. In many nations demographic changes have brought about the need to identify and instruct leaders from minority populations. Research is needed in many directions if leadership is to be developed among cultural and linguistic minorities. In an article on this subject, Young (1986) discussed some of the major issues.

1.   There is the question of how to motivate the nontraditional populations to seek and to accept leadership roles. In the United States

such populations include women, African Americans, Hispanics, Asian Americans, Native Americans, and people with handicapping conditions. These groups are still disproportionately underrepresented in high level, elected, appointed, and corporate roles. They are not, in proportion to their numbers, developing leadership skills. Research is needed to explore effective mechanisms to foster leadership skills in language minority children.

2.   Schools can be gateways to leadership positions. Early identification of potential leaders within nontraditional groups and provision of programs for them are the steps needed. Despite intense efforts, much remains unknown about how to determine potential. Research is needed on how to identify those with potential, how to educate them to acquire knowledge of basic leadership principles, and how to provide training opportunities for learning skills and behaviors for leadership roles at different levels of society, i.e, family, campus, career, community organization, public service.

3.   In considering a paradigm for leadership among nontraditional populations, Young (1986) listed a number of complex needs. On the personal level, there is the question of how to help minority group members develop positive self-awareness, self-growth strategies, and reach self-actualization. Two specific requirements are assistance in learning assertive communication styles and goal setting. At the group level, there is need for development of affiliative group leadership. Specific requirements include special asistance in maintaining group identity and unity, especially when they are held in low esteem or merely tolerated. Language minority students need to develop language skills in the majority language and in their own languages to convey their ideas. A high level of academic language ability is best acquired within the school setting.

It is important to remember that just being members of a group that is not mainstream does not mean that the people are good at working with others of diverse heritage. Members of various culture groups need to acquire the skills to work with diverse groups, which include respect for others and tolerance of differences.

At the same time, they have to master the skills and acquire the technological knowledge that will enable them to compete in mainstream society. They need to be involved in the larger society and interact on many levels. Dedicated instructors who understand the gifted, mentors who have the knowledge and experience in the areas of interest of the students, and persons who can assist them in moving between two cultures can develop leadership in minority language and culture students.

Research and advocacy are needed in every area discussed to bring individualized educational opportunities to our gifted and talented students around the world. Increasingly, we are learning that they are found everywhere. To find them and assist them would incur costs, but we might want to consider that when precious metals and gems were to be found, nations competed at great cost to search for the treasure. Gifted and talented students are the "undiscovered diamonds" of our world. We cannot afford to leave them hidden (Baldwin, 1987).

References

Adderholt-Elliott, M. & Eller, S. (1989). Counseling students who are gifted through bibliotherapy. *Teaching Exceptional Children*, 22(1), 26–31.

Anderson, J.A. (1988). Cognitive styles and multicultural populations. *Journal of Teacher Education*, 29(1), 2–9.

Aramen, J.K. & Berry, G.L. (1987). Self-concept, alienation, and perceived prejudice: Implications for counseling Asian-Americans. *Journal of Multicultural Counseling and Development*, 15(4), 146–160.

Baldwin, A. (1983). Provisions for the gifted child of third world populations: Attitude and adjustments. A report of an explanatory study. Part 1. *Gifted Child International*, 6(1), 38–40.

Baldwin, A. (1987). Undiscovered diamonds: The minority gifted child. *Journal for the Education of the Gifted*, 10(4), 271–285.

Balsamo, K. (1989). An interview with Dr. June Maker. *Challenge*, 7(3), 57–60.

Bernstein, S.D. (1988). Minority gifted children in the middle school. *Challenge*, 7(2), 5–8.

Bothmer, R. (1988). A state of mind: On defining giftedness. *The Gifted Child Today*, 60(1), 36.

Brickman, W. (1988). The multilingual development of the gifted. *Roeper Review*, 10(4), 247–250.

Chan, S. (1986). Parents of exeptional Asian children. In Kitano, M.K. & Chinn, P.C. (Eds.) *Exceptional Asian children and youth*. Reston, VA: Council for Exceptional Children (36–53).

Chávez, J., Burton, L., & López, D. (1986–1987). The needs of rural and urban teachers in bilingual special education. *Rural Educator*, 8 (2), 8–12.

Colangelo, N. (1985). Counseling needs of culturally diverse gifted students. *Roeper Review*, 8(1), 2–3.

Costantino, G., Malgady, R., & Rogler, L. (1985). *Cuento therapy: Folklore as culturally sensitive psychotherapy for Puerto Rican children*. Maplewood, NJ: Waterfront.

Dabney, M. (1988). An alternative model for identification of potentially gifted students: A case study. In Jones, R. (Ed.) *Psychoeducational assessment of minority group children.* Berkeley, CA : Cobb & Henry (273–296).

Daniels, R. (1988). American Indians: Gifted, talented, or forgotten? *Roeper Review, 8*(2), 80–82.

Dodd, J., Nelson, J.R., & Peralez, E. (1988-1989). Understanding the Hispanic student. *The Rural Educator, 10*(2), 8–13.

Dunn, R., Gemake, J., Jalali, F., & Zenhausern, R. with Quinn, R., and Spiridakis, J. (1990). Cross-cultural differences in learning styles of elementary age students from four ethnic backgrounds. *Journal of Multicultural Counseling and Development, 18*, 69–93.

Eby, J. (1989). Risks to children related to school district gifted programs. In Lakebrink, J. (Ed.) *Children at risk.* Springfield, IL: Charles C. Thomas (pp. 277–291).

Feldhusen, J. & Kennedy, D. (1988). Preparing gifted youth for leadership roles in a rapidly changing society. *Roeper Review, 10*(4), 226–229.

Fetterman, D. (1988). *Excellence and equity: A qualitatively different perspective on gifted and talented.* Albany: State University of New York.

Fortner, M.J. (1988). Educational programs and practices for academically able students in the United States, Japan, and Germany. *Roeper Review, 11*(4), 185–188.

Gallagher, J. (1988). Notes from the desk. *Journal for the Education of the Gifted, 12*, 1.

Gardner, H. (1983). *Frames of mind. The theory of multiple intelligences.* New York: Basic Books.

Gardner, H. (1987). Beyond the IQ: Education and human development. *Harvard Educational Review, 57*(2), 187–193.

Gregory, D.A. (1987). Nurture, challenge, caring: A plea for young, gifted children. *Communicator, 17*(1), 9–13.

Gregory, D.A., Starnes, W., & Blaylock, A. (1988). Finding and nurturing potential giftedness among black and Hispanic students. In Ortiz, A. & Ramírez, B. (Eds.) *Schools and the culturally diverse exceptional students: Promising practices and future directions.* Reston, VA: Council for Exceptional Children (pp. 76–84).

Greenlaw, M.J. & McIntosh, M. (1988). *Educating the gifted.* Chicago: The American Library Association Press.

Gross, M. (1989). The pursuit of excellence or the search for intimacy? The forced choice dilemma of gifted youth. *Roeper Review, 11*(4), 189–219.

Guilford, J.P. (1956). The structure of intellect. *Psychological Bulletin, 53*, 267–293.

Hakuta, K. (1986). *Mirror of language: The debate on bilingualism.* New York: Basic Books.

Hanson, M., Lynch, E., & Wayman, K. (1990). Honoring the cultural diversity of families when gathering data. *Topics in Early Childhood Special Education, 10*(1), 112–131.

Imison, I., Endean, L., & Smith, D. (Eds.) (1986). *Gifted and talented children: A national concern.* Second National Conference on Gifted and Talented Children. Toowanda/Queensland, Australia: Darling Downs Institute Press.

Karnes, F.A. & Marquardt, R.G. (1988). The Pennsylvania Supreme Court decision on gifted education. *Roeper Review, 32*(4), 360–361.

Kirschenbaum, R. (1988). Methods for identifying the gifted and talented American Indian student. *Journal for the Education of the Gifted, 9*(3), 53–63.

Keating, D.R. & MacLean, D.J. (1987). Cognitive processing, cognitive ability and development: A consideration. In Vernone, P.A. (Ed.) *Speed of information processing.* Norwood, NJ: Ablex.

Maker, C.J. (1986). *Critical issues in gifted eductation: Defensible programs for the gifted.* (3rd Ed.) Rockville, MD: Aspen.

Marland, S.P. (1972). Report to Congress of the United States by the Commission on Education. Washington, DC: U.S. Printing Office.

Matthews, D. (1988). Gardner's Multiple Intelligence Theory: An evaluation of relevant research: Literature and a consideration of its application to gifted education. *Roeper Review, 11*(2), 100–104.

Mercado, C. (in press). Researching research: A Student-teacher collaborative project. In Ambert, A.N. & Alvarez, M.D. (Eds.). *Puerto Rican children on the mainland: Interdisciplinary perspectives.* New York: Garland.

Ogden, F. & Germinario, V. (1988). *The at-risk student: Answers for educators.* Lancaster, PA: Technomic Publishers.

Ortiz, V. & Volloff, W. (1987). Identificaton of gifted and accelerated Hispanic students. *Journal for the Education of the Gifted, 11*(1), 45–55.

Passow A.H. (1988). Reflections on three decades of education of the gifted. *Gifted Child International, 5*(2), 79–82.

Perlman, R. & Chamberlain, P. (1988). Interpreters and the assessment of language minority students for special education placement: Training implications. *Counterpoint, 9*(1), 18–25.

Ramírez, M. (1988). Cognitive styles and cultural democracy in action. In Wurzel, J. (Ed.) *Toward multiculturalism.* Yarmouth, ME: Intercultural Press.

Ramírez, M. & Castañeda, A. (1974). *Cultural democracy, bicognitive development and education.* New York: Academic Press.

Renzulli, J.S. (1978). What makes giftedness? Re-examining a definition. *Phi Delta Kappan, 60*(3), 180–184.

Renzulli, J.S. (1988). A decade of dialogue on the three-ring conception of giftedness. *Roeper Review, 11*(1), 18-25.

Renzulli, J.S. (1989). The Secondary Triad Model. *Journal for the Education of the Gifted, 13*(1), 55–77.

Renzulli, J.S. & Reis, S. (1987). A non-elitist approach to serving the gifted and talented. *The School Administrator, 41*(11), 15–16.

Richert, E.S. (1985). Identification of gifted students in the United States: The need for pluralistic assessment. *Roeper Review, 8*(2), 68–72.

Roedell, W. (1989). Early development of gifted children. In Olzewski-Kubilius, P. & VanTassel-Baska, J. *Patterns of influence on gifted learners; the home, the self and the school.* New York: Teachers College Press.

Rueda, R.S., Rodríguez, R.F., & Prieto, A.G. (1981). Teachers' perceptions of competencies for instructing bilingual/multicultural children. *Exceptional Children*, *48*(3), 268–270.

Schlesinger, B. (1987). Considerations in the identification of the talented child from non-English speaking backgrounds. *Gifted Education International*, *4*, 160–162.

Shaughnessy, M. (1990). Cognitive structures of the gifted: Theoretical perspectives, factor analysis, triarchic theories of intelligence, and insight issues. *Gifted Education International*, *6*(3), 149–151.

Silverman, L. (in press). *Gifted education: A developmental approach.* Columbus, OH: Charles E. Merrill.

Sisk, D. (1987). *Creative Teaching of the gifted.* New York: McGraw Hill.

Sisk, D. (1988a). Children at risk: The identification of the gifted among the minority. *Gifted Education International*, *5*, 138–141.

Sisk, D. (1988b). Leadership development for cross-cultural understanding. *Gifted Child Today*: Nov-Dec.

Smutny, J.K., Veenker, K., & Veenker, S. (1989). *Your gifted child. How to recognize and develop the special talents in your child from birth to age seven.* New York: Facts on File.

Sternberg, R.J. (1985). *Beyond IQ: A triarchic theory of human intelligence.* New York: Cambridge.

Tapia, M. (in press). Motivational orientation of Puerto Rican children. In Ambert, A.N. & Alvarez, M.D. (Eds.) *Puerto Rican children on the mainland: Interdisciplinary perspectives.* New York: Garland.

Terman, L.M. (1925). *Genetic studies of genius: Vol. 1: Mental and physical traits of a thousand gifted children.* California: Stanford Unversity Press.

Thomas, R.M. (1987). Exceptional abilities and educational rights: Concern for the handicapped and gifted in Britain, China, and Indonesia. In Farrow, D. (Ed.) *Human rights and education.* Oxford: Pergamon Press.

Tonemah, S.A. (1987). Assessing American Indian gifted and talented students' abilities. *Journal for the Education of the Gifted*, *10*, 181–194.

Torrance, E.P. (1969). Creative positives of disadvantaged children and youth. *Gifted Child Quarterly*, *13*, 71–81.

Torrance, E.P. (1977). *Discovery and nurturance of giftedness in the culturally different.* Reston, VA: Council for Exceptional Children.

Young, J.W. (1986). Developing nontraditional leaders. *Journal of Multicultural Counseling and Development*, *14*(3). 108–115.

Annotated Bibliography

Balsamo, K. (1989). An interview with Dr. June Maker. *Challenge, 7*(3), 57–60.

Dr. Maker discusses the differences in learning styles when solving problems between Anglo Americans (analytical) and Hispanics (holistic). She advocates a pluralistic approach to teaching, incorporating both learning styles, thus adding to a child's repertoire. She also advocates additive bilingualism. According to Dr. Maker, what is needed in education is genuine respect for differences.

Borland, J.H. (1989). *Planning and implementing programs for the gifted.* New York: Teachers College Press.

An important theme in this book is the use of a systems approach to program planning based on and responsive to specific locations.

Clark, B. (1988). *Growing up gifted* (3rd Ed.). Columbus, OH: Charles E. Merrill.

Includes a sections on culturally diverse students and the use of the community and mentors in programs for the gifted.

Delisle, J.R. (1987). *Gifted kids speak out.* Minneapolis, MN: Free Spirit.

Interviews with gifted students, ages six to thirteen, in the U.S., Canada, Germany, and Australia, yield insights into this population. Valuable for parents and teachers as well as gifted students themselves.

Feldhusen, J. & Kennedy, D. (1988). Preparing gifted youth for leadership a rapidly changing society. *Roeper Review, 10*(4), 226–230.

The authors discuss the development of leadership and consider topics, such as education in future studies, Bloom's taxonomy as applied to gifted students, and critical thinking.

Feldhusen, J., VanTassel-Baska, J., & Seeley, K. (Eds.) (1989). *Excellence in educating the gifted.* Denver, CO: Love.

A compilation of chapters by well-known authors which includes materials on inclusion of poor, rural, and cultural minority children in programs for the gifted.

Fetterman, D. (1988). *Excellence and equity: A qualitatively different perspective on gifted and talented.* Albany: State University of New York Press.

Contains a valuable description of the California program for the gifted and talented. The issue of minority gifted students is examined within the framework of excellence and equity in education.

Green, M. (1989). *Minorities on campus: A handbook for enhancing diversity.* Washington, DC: American Council on Education.

Discusses diversity, cultural heritage, increasing number of minority students in college, leadership, and support for minority students.

Greenlaw, M.J. & McIntosh, M. (1988). *Educating the gifted.* Chicago: American Library Association.

An overview of issues on the gifted and talented with a useful extensive annotated bibliography arranged by topic.

Hsia, J. (1988). *Asian-Americans in higher education and at work.* Hillsdale, NJ: Lawrence Erlbaum.

Discusses the high achievement of Asians and the overrepresentation of this population in science and technology.

Maker, C.J. & Shiever, S. (Eds.) (1989). *Defensible programs for cultural and ethnic minorities.* Vol. II of the Critical Issues in Gifted Education Series. Austin, TX: Proed.

The book is organized in sections containing articles about specific ethnic minority groups, such as Hispanics, Native Americans, Asian Americans, and African Americans. Includes definition of each population, demographics, cultural and linguistic characteristics, appropriate methods of identification and instruction for the group, and curricular recommendations. A good overview of the education of bilingual gifted students.

McIntosh, M. & Greenlaw, M.J. (1986). Fostering the post secondary aspirations of gifted urban minority students. *Roeper Review, 9,* 104–107.

Discusses the discrepancy between actual potential of gifted urban minority students and their self-perceived potential. Argues for the need for counseling for this population.

Milgram, R.U. (Ed.) (1989). *Teaching gifted and talented learners in regular classrooms.* Springfield, IL: Charles Thomas.

Provides ideas for teachers that can be applied for use with culturally diverse students with high levels of ability in the regular classroom.

Ornstein, A.C. & Levine, D.U. (1989). Class, race, and achievement. *Journal of Teacher Education, 17*(23).

A discussion of several factors related to middle class teachers and the achievement of minority disadvantaged students.

Saunders, J., with Espeland, P. (1986). *Bringing out the best: A resource guide for parents of young gifted children.* Minneapolis, MN: Free Spirit.

Contains discussions of matters related to gifted children, with a good section on advocacy. Resources include addresses of useful magazines published in languages besides English.

Silverman, L. (in press). *Gifted education: A developmental approach.* Columbus, OH: Charles E. Merrill.

Defines giftedness as developmental advancement. The author describes her approach to identification and instruction of the gifted.

Sleeter, C. & Grant, C. (1987). An analysis of multicultural education in the United States. *Harvard Educational Review, 57,* 421–444.

Various instructional models in multicultural education are discussed providing a basis for instructional choices.

Sternberg, R. & Davidson, J. (1986). *Conceptions of giftedness.* New York: Cambridge University Press.

The articles on gifted education included in this book are timely and well written. Offers a general overview of the subject and suggestions for future research.

Valsine, J., (Ed.) (1988). *Child development in culturally structured environments.* Norwood, NJ: Ablex.

Describes comparative approaches to students with special needs, including the gifted.

VanTassel-Baska, J. (1988). *Comprehensive curriculum for gifted learners.* Needham, MA: Allyn & Bacon.

Describes useful paradigms for conceptualizing curriculum for the gifted. The broad range of topics includes affective curriculum and computers.

VanTassel-Baska, J. (1989). The role of the family in the success of disadvantaged gifted learners. *Journal for the Education of the Gifted, 13,* 22–36.

Fifteen case studies are presented on disadvantaged gifted students, nine of the studies concern minority students.

Whitmore, J. (1987). Conceptualizing the issue of underserved populations of gifted students. *Journal for the Education of the Gifted, 10,* 141–153.

A special issue dealing with populations at-risk of not being identified for inclusion in gifted programs.

Young, J.L. (1986). Developing nontraditional leaders. *Journal of Multicultural Counseling and Development, 14*(3), 108–115.

A leadership paradigm for schools. Discusses its application to nontraditional students and its implications.

CHAPTER VIII

Teacher Training in Bilingual Education and English as a Second Language: Recent Research Developments

Liliana Minaya-Rowe

Introduction

Provision of bilingual programs and English as a second language education services to linguistic minority populations continues to be a vital function in many teacher training programs at institutions of higher education (henceforth "university") across the nation. Universities have a role to play in the preparation of personnel who, in some capacity, will be or are meeting the educational and linguistic needs of limited English proficient students.

The major functions of universities are to research, to teach, and to provide services. Some functions cannot be separated from the public needs. It is only to the extent to which it can satisfy a wide spectrum of public needs that a university is worthy of public support. Bilingual bicultural education and English as a second language (ESL) training programs are important to universities in the nation because a good fraction of the workforce—the resource—in the United States consists of approximately 35 million people from diverse ethnic and language backgrounds (Waggoner, 1987). Therefore, the quality of university based bilingual and English as a second language training programs greatly influences the general welfare.

This chapter stresses the institutionalization of teacher training programs of bilingual bicultural education and English as a second language and its relationship to: (a) continuity and permanency of programs; (b) programs' relationship to the mission of universities and to their functions of research and teaching; and (c) provision of services.

The chapter also discusses the relationship of these three functions to staff development partnerships between school districts and universities, as related to institutionalization. Finally, the chapter will discuss action research activities conducted in the bilingual and English as a second language classrooms and the results of research activities that are implemented as instructional activities through teaching and services. Action research is a cooperative and concurrent process which facilitates reflection and action in schooling and which is conducted by researchers (usually university professors, specialists, experts) and practitioners (usually teachers, principals, staff developers). Action research allows practitioners to become co-researchers, to conduct research, and to implement research results in their district, school, or classroom (Lieberman, 1986; Tikunoff, 1985). The discussion will include the case study of a university's efforts to institutionalize its own teacher training program in bilingual education (1980–1990).

Institutionalization

Institutionalization is defined as a socioeducational, political, and economic process of legitimacy that systematically integrates the program of bilingual education or English as a second language teacher training with the academic system of a university. The process makes the program a regular part of the university's academic offerings (Chu & Levy, 1984; Johnson & Binkley, 1987; Mercado, 1985; OBEMLA, 1989).

The institutionalization of graduate and undergraduate bilingual and English as a second language teacher training programs was linked to Dean of the School of Education grant programs as early as 1978 and to Educational Personnel Training Programs (EPTPs) as early as 1974 (R. Muñiz & J. Brown, personal communications, July 18, 1990). Both Dean's and EPTP's grants were initiated with sponsorship and funding from the U.S. Department of Education under Title VII of the Elementary and Secondary Education Act. Dean's grants were aimed at establishing or setting up bilingual education programs at universities that requested such funding and whose grant proposals of program development and implementation were reviewed and approved by the Office of Bilingual Education and Minority Languages Affairs (OBEMLA). Funding included salaries for a Title VII project director, secretarial staff, external evaluator fees, supplies, travel, equipment, etc. It was then expected by OBEMLA and promised by the university that, during the three-year federal funding cycle, the university would design a structural and comprehensive program and that such program would be approved by the institution. Approval of the program includes meeting the university's academic and administrative structure standards and becoming part of its regular program offerings. The university was expected to continue offering the program as external funding was decreased. In 1984, Dean's grants were renamed Training Development and Improvement Programs (J. Gómez, personal communication, July 19, 1990).

EPTPs aimed at funding, for the most part, institutionalized programs and programs to be in the categories indicated above. This funding also included students' tuition and fees, stipends, books, and travel to field experiences.

A cursory review of the literature indicated scattered success reports of program institutionalization at universities (Arciniega, 1980; Baecher, 1983; Baca, 1984; Chu & Levy, 1984; Minaya-Rowe, 1989). Two national surveys report on the success as well as prediction of future success of 79 undergraduate and graduate programs (Johnson & Binkley, 1987; RMC Research Corporation, 1981); and 56 undergraduate programs (NCBE, 1984). These reviews did not include examples of universities that have kept their funding levels and high student enrollments when universities ceased to be federally funded. In other words, the universities surveyed had their bilingual programs in place, but still depended on federal funding for administering them.

Indicators of Institutionalization

Most case and survey studies have used program institutionalization criteria proposed by the RMC study. Based on interviews with 43 Title VII directors and administrators, RMC researchers identified the following eight indicators of institutionalization.

1. *Active support of administrators.* RMC researchers identified many forms of active administrative support. For example, in one university the dean organized and chaired a Bilingual Education Advisory Committee to discuss curricular issues and program policies, an activity which strengthened the status of the program and also resolved some turf issues that had arisen among the faculty. In other universities, administrators were professionally very active in the field of bilingual education. In the one or two universities in which administrators were

not supportive, it was concluded that it was due to lack of regard toward the Title VII Director.

2. *Positive attitudes of non-bilingual education faculty.* According to an RMC finding, most faculty outside the program were supportive of the program or at least did not create obstacles for institutionalization of the program.

3. *Faculty support through institutional funds.* About two-thirds of the bilingual faculty surveyed by RMC were supported entirely by institutional funds.

4. *Faculty tenure status.* The RMC study revealed that 56 percent of the bilingual faculty were on tenure track and 31 percent had tenure. RMC states that both criteria 3 and 4 are strong indicators of university commitment as the program grows older. In its first or second year when the program is newly established, it is not uncommon to have the director and faculty on "soft" or federal money and on nontenure or nonpermanent positions. This is partly due to university policies that do not permit tenure-track or promotion eligibility when the faculty are paid on soft money.

5. *Program continuation without federal Title VII funds.* Administrators and directors reported that the program would continue without federal funds as the university planned to assume program costs when Title VII funding ceased. Their reports carried significant weight in overall RMC judgments of the prospects for program survival and continuation. No mention was made, however, of institutions that had kept student enrollment levels in their bilingual training programs after federal funding had decreased.

6. *Involvement of several professionals in program operations.* RMC reported that in some sites it was clear that the vitality of the program was mainly due to the skill and dedication of one or two key faculty members who were responsible not only for the daily management and administration but for teaching most or all of the required courses. In a few cases, these faculty members were serving in a void of university commitment. It seemed that were these persons to leave, the bilingual program would not continue. The study also considered the number of faculty of language minority background in the university as a whole. Programs in institutions with a large number of faculty who were members of the language and cultural group(s) served by the bilingual education graduates, and/or who were bilingual, seemed to have a better chance of continuation than programs in institutions where the only bilingual bicultural faculty were on the bilingual education program staff.

7. *Compatibility with institutional priorities.* The RMC study reported that the extent of compatibility was related to which of the three traditional purposes of a university a particular university focuses on: research, teaching, or service. Most bilingual programs were housed in research- and theory-oriented institutions. In some of these sites non-bilingual faculty and administrators saw the bilingual program as incompatible with the institution's research focus. In response to this concern, its bilingual faculty attempted to strengthen the research base of the bilingual program. The presence of the state bilingual education legislation and certification were important variables in assessing compatibility, since such certification and legislation legitimizes the existence of the curriculum and courses within the School of Education framework.

8. *Sufficient high enrollment levels to sustain the program.* This last predictor was probably the single most important indicator of program institutionalization, according to the RMC study. Every academic program in general depends upon some minimum number of enrollees to justify faculty and other instructional resources. A number of variables influence whether or not there would be enough students to justify a program. The variables are: (a) whether or not the state has bilingual education certification and/or a law requiring bilingual education programs in schools. Certification guarantees a certain level of demand for bilingual education teachers that can be expected to contribute to a minimum level of enrollment; (b) whether or not the program students are dependent upon Title VII stipends or fellowships for continuing their enrollment in the program. This is influenced by the level of tuition at the university, the proportion of students of ethnic minorities, and the socioeconomic status of the students; and (c) the geographic proximity of competing bilingual education programs and opportunities for financial assistance in those universities.

In 1987 OBEMLA organized the first Colloquium to Strengthen Educational Personnel Training Programs with the participation of Directors of these federally funded programs. The Colloquium also included the participation of selected representatives of State Education Agencies and Multifunctional Resource Centers. They met to discuss three issues that in both OBEMLA Officers' and EPTP Directors' opinions needed to be addressed in order to implement their programs; namely, coordination, evaluation, and institutionalization.

Coordination. EPTP Directors agreed that activities to integrate services and resources across universities, State Education Agencies, Local Education Agencies and the community at large are crucial in successful program functioning. They expressed the need to define and clarify EPTP's roles and responsibilities in initiating and participating in coordination activities. They felt that these activities can contribute to a common understanding of standards for bilingual and English as a second language EPTPs.

Evaluation. EPTP Directors suggested that OBEMLA take the lead in allocating sufficient funds (5 percent to 7 percent of EPTP budget) for evaluation activities. They felt that OBEMLA should include in EPTP requests for proposals specific requirements and standards for evaluation designs, data collection, and evaluation coverage in the preparation of summary reports.

Institutionalization. EPTP Directors agreed that: (a) placement of faculty in tenure-track positions is critical to program continuance; (b) student enrollment levels can seriously affect program institutionalization; (c) coordination with and involvement of faculty members outside the program can facilitate program permanency; and (d) universities must negotiate for adequate funds from federal and home sources to meet program goals initially, and to sustain achievement of program goals over time.

Participants had the opportunity for expanded group discussion on these three issues. The faculty placement group concluded that five steps should be taken to institutionalize bilingual programs by bringing its faculty into the university community: (a) design strategies for recruiting and retaining bilingual faculty in the university community; (b) develop communication support networks by establishing mentoring programs to assist bilingual faculty in achieving permanent faculty status; (c) promote staff development by prodding the university to provide research funds to bilingual faculty, and by ensuring the availability of resources for their participation in professional and academic conferences; (d) review tenure and promotion criteria established to ensure that the requirements are clearly understood by incoming bilingual faculty and that the criteria are relevant to bilingual program needs; and (e) build faculty visibility by acting as sources of language minority education research.

The student enrollment group proposed that the following are to be considered to assist program institutionalization: (a) the linguistic and educational needs of language minority students in the area to be served; (b) the State Education Agency certification and licensure requirements; (c) the characteristics of the trainee populations to be served by the bilingual program; and (d) university capabilities to offer the training program.

The coordination group proposed that to achieve bilingual program institutionalization, the university must: (a) allocate funds for the program; (b) place bilingual program faculty on tenure or tenure track; and (c) convene interdisciplinary and advocacy committees to guide program development and build support for the project.

The budget group formulated the premise that bilingual program budget functions must be intimately tied into program administrative frameworks with responsibilities for budget management clearly delineated, delegated, and coordinated if the program is to be institutionalized. The group also asserted that the bilingual program director has to use his or her management skills to plan for institutionalization. The director needs to (a) tie the program's goals to the university's goals and missions with regard to affirmative action policies, regional needs dictated by demographic realities, and efforts to develop leadership skills in language minority populations; and (b) apprise the university of the benefits available through bilingual program cost sharing, in the areas of student support, faculty publishing, research and travel—bilingual faculty can bring visibility and prestige to the university.

The federal government, through OBEMLA, has had an active role in the institutionalization of bilingual teacher training programs via funding at the request of universities. Figure 1 summarizes the process.

Staff Development

Inservice Training

Staff development can be defined as an inservice system that ensures that bilingual and English as a second language education professionals regularly enhance their academic knowledge and professional performance. It consists of ways to embed professional growth opportunities into the work life of teachers and administrative and supervisory personnel (Calderón & Marsh, 1988; Mercado, 1985).

A review of the literature on staff development for teachers of bilingual and English as a second language programs indicates that for the most part staff development has been treated as inservice efforts within the school districts with little or no involvement of universities. School districts have engaged individual university faculty to deliver

Figure 1. Institutionalization of teacher training programs
in bilingual education and English as a second language

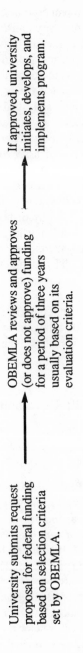

University submits request
proposal for federal funding
based on selection criteria
set by OBEMLA.

OBEMLA reviews and approves
(or does not approve) funding
for a period of three years
usually based on its
evaluation criteria.

If approved, university
initiates, develops, and
implements program.

Program possesses all or some of the eight characteristics for institutionalization.
Program is made part of the University's regular offerings.

workshops without the institution's active involvement. University teacher training programs have been considered separate from staff development where staff development would be an adjunct service training, not linked to the same academic standards as preservice university training.

Dimensions of Inservice Training

The Arawak Report (1986) on staff development models points to four program dimensions to be included in inservice training. They are: (a) readiness—the assessment of the social climate and the governance structure; (b) planning—conducting a needs assessment, identifying available resources, determining objectives, selecting appropriate content, scheduling the training activities, and determining incentives; (c) training—implementing inservice modes; and (d) post-training—conducting follow-up activities and evaluating the effectiveness of the inservice program.

The Report indicates that few staff development programs have all the characteristics listed above and that there is a discrepancy between what the research says should be happening and what really occurs in most training sessions. Few programs recognize, use, or respond to differences in teachers' experiences, insights, and expertise. Programs do not vary on the basis of the different content areas which teachers teach, nor are teachers involved in decision-making processes regarding training goals and content. Very few training activities go on beyond a few months. Furthermore, systematic feedback on post-training practice and implementation of training contact is rare. Staff development for bilingual education and English as a second language teachers often assumes traditional forms, such as a workshop led by a consultant. These are often one-shot experiences with little or no follow-up to determine how much teachers have really learned and how effectively they are implementing newly acquired teaching strategies in their classrooms.

Recent literature on general educational staff development abounds with reports of innovative and effective training, content and processes (Joyce, Showers, & Rolheiser-Bennett, 1987; Joyce & Showers, 1988; Showers, Joyce, & Bennett, 1987). Few staff development programs have been implemented based on innovative practices and on research on effective staff development programs for teachers of limited English proficient students. The following are examples of innovative staff development projects:

1.   The Multi-District Trainer of Trainers Institute (Calderón, 1987). The Institute was developed to provide training to bilingual and English as a second language teachers and to prepare trainers in their local school districts. It is a one- to three-year program that requires intensive summer sessions with six follow-up sessions throughout the year. The total days of training range between 12 and 15 a year. The training is sequenced into day-long sessions conducted by recognized experts, and this is followed by a day of application to particular student needs, teaching techniques, and curriculum and staff development designs. Between sessions, participants observe each other's practice of the new strategies learned and provide peer coaching.

Results of the Institute's evaluations have indicated some success. Ninety percent of former participants have had some impact on curriculum development of program implementation at the school or district level (Calderón & Marsh, 1988; Macías, 1986).

2.   Bilingual Education Training Institute (NCBE, 1988). Training focuses on instructional strategies for preparing sixth- through eighth-grade students for the high school proficiency test in math, reading and writing in English. The training program addresses the following topics: (a) development of oral proficiency; (b) developmental reading instruction; (c) teaching content subjects; and (d) developing reading proficiency in the content areas. Participating teachers have reacted positively to the program. More cooperation and exchange between school administrators and teachers are also reported as a result of program participation.

3.   The Language Development Specialist Academy operated by the Bilingual Education Multifunctional Resource Center at Hunter College in New York City (Ward, 1987) attempts to identify teachers who teach limited English proficient students effectively. Participating teachers are trained to increase their expertise by sharing the instructional strategies they consider to be most linked to successful instruction. External resource persons are brought in to discuss new developments and skills in teaching. The Academy also makes available the expertise and skills of these teachers to other teachers who may want to join the program.

4.   The peer coaching model of the Illinois Resource Center (Kwiat, 1988) focuses on the whole language approach to literacy development and sheltered instruction in the content areas. Mainstream, bilingual, and English as a second language teachers begin training by analyzing

the literature, followed by workshops in which strategies are discussed and demonstrated by consultants and practicing teachers. Coaching and companionship are incorporated into the participants' repertoire of teaching strategies. Results confirm that peer coaching is a viable model for teachers of limited English proficient students.

Staff development has traditionally been considered as separate from the university's functions of teaching, research, and services. Even reports of the most recent innovative forms of staff development, such as the Institute and the Academy which are housed at universities, make little or no mention of how staff development activities such as theirs can impact their own teacher training programs. Figure 2 illustrates such a state of affairs.

Figure 2. Staff development unrelated to
university's functions and teacher training program
in bilingual education and English as a second language

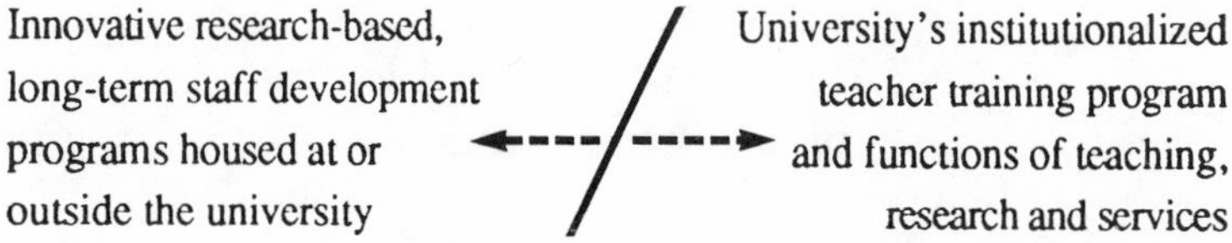

Innovative research-based,   University's institutionalized
long-term staff development   teacher training program
programs housed at or   ◀----/----▶ and functions of teaching,
outside the university   research and services

Staff Development and Institutionalization

The following studies focus on how staff development serves the process of institutionalization of teacher training programs at universities. Mercado (1985) describes a research based approach for staff development provided by the New York Multifunctional Resource Center. She proposes that centers and universities are outsiders looking in because they are separate from the school districts, but they can enter into partnerships to design inservice training activities. She considers the Center as mediator of research to demonstrate how research and theory suggest ways to improve instruction or to determine the content and process of training in an objective and systematic manner.

Mercado describes a process (not content) approach to staff development which includes the following factors: (a) personal/

informal—establishing channels of communication, cultivating relationships based on trust and mutual support; (b) collegiality—providing a forum for teachers to share experiences and techniques that they have found to be successful; (c) reflection and analysis—guidance to analyze, understand, and clarify misconceptions and deal with behaviors and situations that arise in the course of a typical day; (d) accommodating to diversity in learning styles of participants; (e) interactive—recognizing that theory and practice can validate each other. She stresses that staff development benefits both teachers' professional development and the students they serve.

A university perspective to staff development has been described by Collier (1985). She considers teacher training a young and emerging field. Like Mercado, she points to the application of theory to practice and to cooperative research projects between universities and school districts. Collier concludes that there are university faculty members who are highly committed and determined to institutionalize bilingual and English as a second language teacher training programs and who can work to strengthen the link between research and the classroom.

Staff Development as an Element of Institutionalization

A Case Study

This is a case study of a university that has been involved in staff development partnerships with school districts with large language minority populations to implement its graduate teacher training program in bilingual bicultural education. The program was initiated in 1980 with a Title VII Dean of the School of Education Project and has been supported throughout these years with federal funding through Educational Personnel Training Programs or Doctoral Fellowships. The program has for the last nine years offered the master's and doctoral degrees and the post-master sixth-year professional diploma as part of the School of Education regular offerings (Minaya-Rowe, 1981). It meets the following indicators of institutionalization: (a) sufficiently high student enrollment levels to justify faculty and instructional media resources; (b) active support of administrators and faculty to contribute to the status and academic standards of the program; (c) positive attitudes of non-bilingual education faculty or at least faculty who do not create obstacles to program implementation and institutionalization; (d) two permanent faculty positions funded by the university and a third one proposed; (e) both faculty tenured and promoted; (f) commitment that the program will continue without Title VII funds; (g) involvement of several faculty and administrators in program operations, such as conference moderators and presenters, members of program advisory committees; and (h) compatibility with university established priorities to provide training services to school districts via staff development.

Six years ago, in an effort to strengthen its three functions of teaching, research, and services, the University approached School District A and proposed a staff development partnership project. School District A is the largest city in the state. It was chosen because it serves the largest concentration of limited English proficient students in the state, approximately 5,800 students enrolled in bilingual programs, and the second largest language minority student population in the region. Two years ago, five other large school districts were approached by the university for the same reason.

Figure 3 illustrates seven staff development steps taken during the last six years to accomplish such partnerships.

1. *University's initiative.* Linkages are developed between the University's and District A's administrations. Unlike other instances, staff development was not requested of the University. It was the University's initiative to offer its services to District A. A tenured associate professor was assigned one-third of her contract time at the University to conduct the staff development.

The University requested technical assistance on staff development models from two Bilingual Education Multicultural Resource Centers (MRCs). Directors from the New England MRC at Brown University and the California MRC at San Diego State University trained the University faculty and administrators on: (1) staff development models and techniques; and (2) reviews of the literature and ongoing research in teacher training. In 1983, the University had organized a statewide mini-conference on bilingual education research needs in the State which yielded a research agenda for the University. Dr. James Cummins was the conference keynote speaker.

2. *District A receptive of University's offer.* District A conducted a survey of teacher training inservice needs. The survey yielded two important ways for the University to provide technical assistance in the area of teaching English as a second language across all grades of instruction: (1) vocabulary development plan; and (2) curriculum development.

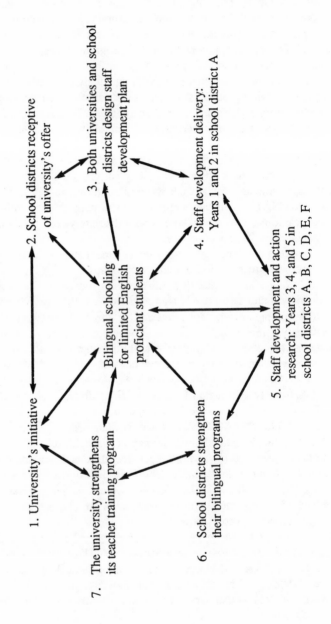

Figure 3. Staff development steps

3. *Both the University and District A design staff development plan.* After the areas of staff development needs were specified, the locations of inservice training were scheduled to be offered in the schools where most of the teachers participating in the training worked and right after the school day ended. The vocabulary development plan was initiated in the 1986 Fall semester with a group of fourteen middle school bilingual and English as a second language teachers and the bilingual assistant director. Although the areas of training needs had been surveyed, the plan allowed for content flexibility throughout the staff development delivery period. For example, during the first meeting the group was asked to write anonymously questions of immediate concern that could be used to start their training. This informal interview, plus the survey findings, allowed the teachers' specific knowledge and methodology needs to be considered. It also gave both trainers and trainees a frank relationship and an atmosphere of open communication. Changes are more likely to occur when those involved in schooling find a common ground and focus on issues of common concern to educators and school administrators rather than be bound to staff development designs imposed on them (Sarason, 1982).

4. *Staff development delivery: Years 1 and 2.* Five groups of teachers and administrators, or a total of 70, have so far completed training. Participants were elementary, middle school, high school, bilingual, and English as a second language teachers and administrators. The course offerings mirrored regular academic semesters, that is, each staff development group received training in an equivalent academic semester, weekly two-hour meetings for fifteen weeks plus an official in-service day. The workshops reflected the same academic standards as those of regular university graduate courses.

Pedagogical and psycholinguistic research information was presented based on the contributions of major researchers in the field (Cummins, 1981, 1989; Krashen, 1981, 1988). The groups read, analyzed, and discussed the research information provided. The University also organized four annual conferences in the form of round tables to strengthen the base of information discussed and provide opportunities for staff development trainees to participate in them as presenters of position papers or as panel discussants. Dr. Krashen was keynote speaker at the Round Table on the Acquisition and Teaching of English as a Second Language in 1986, Dr. Jim Cummins was keynote speaker in a two-day training institute in 1987, Dr. Lily Wong Fillmore was keynote speaker at the Round Table on Learning the Language of School in 1988, and Dr. Ana Celia Zentella was keynote speaker at the Round

Table on Code Switching and its Implications for Bilingual Schooling in 1989.

An example of the groups' positive attitude was the preparation of two co-authored documents aimed at partially trained audiences. The first product was a 108-page co-authored guidebook entitled *Second Language Acquisition Through Vocabulary Development via Concepts* (Axelson et al., 1986). The guide discusses Cummins' and Krashen's theoretical foundations and recent research developments in support of their theories. It also provides ideas for incorporating theories and developments into the content-based or sheltered English classroom of the bilingual program's English as a second language component.

The second co-authored product is a 76-page curriculum guide entitled *Teaching English to Speakers of Other Languages: From First Conversations to Academic Proficiency* (Axelson et al., 1987). *Teaching English* deals with grades 7–12 English as a second language goals, objectives, and lesson components.

The preparation of these documents was intended to develop ownership in the theory and its application to the bilingual classroom and to share with other colleagues in District A. However, the National Clearinghouse for Bilingual Education has selected, adapted, and published *Second Language* as part of the Clearinghouse's Program Information Guide Series for distribution to a nationwide audience with the new title *Facilitating Transition to the Mainstream: Sheltered English Vocabulary Development* (Axelson et al., 1988).

5. *Staff development and action research: Years 3, 4, and 5*. The experiences with District A have led the University to begin the same four-step process mentioned above with other school districts. The University approached five school districts in the state to discuss staff development partnerships to suit their needs. It conducted a survey of technical assistance and training needs for the six districts now participating in the project. Figure 4 summarizes the needs assessed.

In 1988, the University also received a Title VII Educational Personnel Training Program grant to train staff developers via a sixth-year post-masters diploma and an administrative certificate. The program is interdisciplinary and field based. It has a minimum of 30 credits. Six of these credits are for a seminar for trainers of teachers of limited English proficient students and a corresponding practicum. Figure 5 lists the staff devleopment workshops given by program students to three school districts in four areas of training needs.

The staff development activities cited above have provided both the University and school districts with opportunities for action research.

Although the research contributions of scholars are needed, there is an advantage and a necessity to apply theories to practice. That is, bring together the theory driven with the problem driven. Action research involves a close collaboration between the person who can make common sense observations and the person who can turn those observations into research questions (Pelto & Pelto, 1978).

Teachers and student trainers involved in staff development plans, administrators and University faculty have started the development of an action research agenda built into their bilingual programs. A first effort in articulating a research agenda which involves teacher delivery and second language acquisition in transitional bilingual classrooms was reported in *Sheltered English for Language Minority Students* (Agosto et al., 1989). The premise for this and future efforts is that both practitioners and theoreticians are researchers, whether they are university professors, classroom teachers, specialists, administrators, or university students. Teachers involved in the Sheltered English project proved to be researchers in the sense that they were constantly experimenting in their classrooms, trying some methodological variations or alternative ways to implement their teaching. The research orientation emerges as much from theoretical proposals as from the practice.

School districts have a role in setting up their own action research agenda in such a way that the research developments derived from it would have an impact on their bilingual programs and a broader impact on other bilingual programs in the state and in the country. The benefits seem to be mutual for the districts and the University.

6. *School districts strengthen their bilingual program.* The reward of the partnership has been two-fold: (a) selected teachers seem to have strengthened their knowledge of the pedagogical and linguistic research. They have made presentations at the school district's annual conferences and monthly workshops, at the State's Association for Bilingual Bicultural Education conference, and at the National Association for Bilingual Education conference on the process and products of staff development. Some are now involved in curriculum committees and peer coaching activities, and some have been promoted; and (b) selected teachers have continued their studies toward their master's, sixth-year, or Ph.D. degree at the University or at other universities in the state.

7. *The University strengthens its bilingual training program.* The main benefits for the University have been two-fold: (a) the University has responded to the training needs of bilingual program personnel with a staff development plan. Staff development is now seen at the University School of Education as an integral part of the School's mission based

Figure 4. 1989 technical assistance and training needs

Assessed need	A	B	C	D	E	F
Workshops in:						
approaches for motivating student's learning	X					X
assessing and diagnosing students						
computer applications in learning		X			X	
cooperative learning	X					
ESOL in the content areas/sheltered English	X	X	X			
grouping and individualization	X	X	X	X	X	
parent/community involvement				X	X	X
reading						X
reading in the ESOL classroom	X					
reading in the vernacular second language	X	X			X	X
special education for the LEP student						
theory/practice on bilingual education				X		X
transitioning students to mainstream	X	X	X	X	X	X
Classroom demonstrations in:						
grouping and individualization			X	X		
ESOL in the current areas				X		
Acquiring/developing curricula/materials for:						
acquisition/evaluation of materials						X
high school bilingual education program			X			
newly arrived Jamaican students		X				
reading, math, social studies and science in middle and high school					X	

Assessed need	A	B	C	D	E	F
Revising curricula/materials in:						
ESOL	X	X		X	X	
Spanish language arts		X		X	X	
history and culture		X				
multicultural education	X				X	
Evaluation/assessment materials/procedures:						
acquisition/development of assessment procedures						X
develop CRTs for ESOL program, grades 7–12, to measure mastery of levels 1–3,					X	
identify instruments to better assess students entering/exiting program	X					
identify reliable procedures/tests to assess language proficiency	X	X				
General areas of interest/concern of staff:						
developing model for bilingual transitional classroom without mainstreaming		X				
improving communication between staffs of bilingual and all-English programs						X
improving special education for LEP student			X			
increasing parent involvement			X			
information on gifted/talented LEP programs		X				
strengthening district's transitional model	X					
training staff in all-English program	X			X		
training staff in new language enrichment programs				X		

(Colón-LaFontaine, 1989)

Figure 5. Fall 1989 and spring 1990 staff development workshops

	Transition/ Mainstream	Sheltered English/ whole language	L1 reading/ Spanish	Parental involvement
School district B	Feb. 21, 3–5 p.m. Four sixth-year students-trainers and faculty member	March 29, 3–5 p.m. Five sixth-year student-trainers and faculty member	April 25, 3–5 p.m. Three sixth-year student-trainers and faculty member	
School district A	March 31, 9 a.m.–1 p.m., May 3 and 17, 2:30–4:30 p.m. Seven sixth-year student-trainers and faculty member			
School district F			Dec. 4, Feb. 16, and April 5, 3–5 p.m. Two sixth-year student-trainers and faculty member	Nov. 30, 12-2 p.m. Feb. 16 and April 27, 6-8:30 p.m. Five sixth-year student-trainers and faculty member

on this experience; and (b) the implementation of its graduate programs at the master's, sixth-year and Ph.D. levels and its course offerings. The University has also continued to hold its round tables, which have provided forums for discussion between and among practitioners and theoreticians.

At the center of Figure 3 is the heart of this staff development effort: how to better serve LEP students. This is due to the educational partnership and the participatory conditions provided between and among school districts and universities to empower limited English proficient students via properly implemented schooling.

Action Research and Teacher Training in Bilingual Education and English as a Second Language

Cooperative Research

This section proposes that school districts, universities, state departments of education, research centers, multifunctional resource centers, OBEMLA, the National Association for Bilingual Education, and other relevant agencies can participate in joint and cooperative research. Especially important to such an endeavor are the contributions of teachers and administrators in public and private schools who are closest to what is going on. No one group needs to have a monopoly on good ideas and on hard work. Coalitions of practitioners and theoreticians may be particularly effective. However, big, prestigious groups must be restrained from regarding the classroom teacher as a person who is merely carrying out research orders. Probably, a principal and teachers in a school will provide some of the most critical input to the understanding of what is going on in the areas of bilingualism, biculturalism, and bilingual education (Díaz, Moll, & Mehan, 1986; Montero-Sieburth & Pérez, 1987).

Cooperative research of this nature can also mean that both practitioners and theoreticians are researchers, whether they are university professors, classroom teachers, specialists, administrators, or students. A classroom teacher is a researcher in the sense that (s)he is constantly experimenting in the classroom, trying out things that may or may not work, continuing with them or trying some variations or alternative ways. The research orientation needs to come as much from the theoretician as from the practitioner in a coordinated effort between those two (Cazden, 1983; Freeman, 1989; Trueba, 1988).

All bilingual programs—not just the innovative programs—can have a research component built into it. School districts, in close partnership and coordination with above-named research partners, need to have a role in setting up the bilingual education program in such a way that the research developments derived from it have an impact on the program and a broader impact within and across the state, the nation, and abroad (Secada, 1990). This close coordination is needed in order to: (a) articulate the principles on which the districts are operating; (b) determine the needs of the districts; and (c) design research with some degree of confidence. However, the autonomy of individual researchers must also be protected (Schensul, 1985).

Partnerships. The partnership between school districts and universities must be based on a two-way relationship. For example, a school district with a wide commitment to bilingual education for Hispanics has as a goal that students who go through the system will emerge as fluent speakers of Spanish and English. But that district also has periodic evaluation needs for the funding sources. In this instance in which evaluation and research can be thought of as closely related, the universities can (a) help the district achieve its short-term goals by answering the basic questions it has for reporting purposes; and, at the same time, (b) conduct some innovative basic or process-oriented research through the establishment of a long-range research agenda (Ogbu, 1987; Valadez & Patino Gregoire, 1990).

Principles of action research. What basic principles can be followed to delineate research activities? A review of the existing literature reveals the following research needs:

1.   Longitudinal research in addition to cross-sectional research. All individuals and institutions who are in a position to make research contributions can conduct short- and long-range longitudinal research. Cross-sectional studies have a role to play and provide certain kinds of insights. However, in order to collect information and be able to take a retrospective look at the cumulative impact of a child's becoming bilingual, researchers must have a commitment to follow children from the time they enter kindergarten until after they graduate from secondary school. Some of these children may have chosen not to go to a liberal arts college but to vocational education or other form of higher education or none at all. The researcher's main goal must be to go back and look at the cumulative impact of educational and social experiences of students becoming bilingual over long periods of time as they are involved in

different interactions in the community, home, school, and other settings (Jacob & Jordan, 1987).

2. Exploration of the diversity of methodological approaches and the complementary roles to be played between qualitative (e.g., ethnographic) research and quantitative research. Researchers need to bring together both qualitative as well as quantitative studies. Research designs that include observation of general patterns, trends, and tendencies as well as minute details of language behavior usage of children, one-to-one, in various and diverse settings are necessary. The information collected in this type of research does not uniquely apply in an idiosyncratic fashion to the particular children studied but allows higher-order generalizations to be made with the data obtained. Quantification provides one kind of credibility but often remains unconvincing unless supported by adequate, qualitative, descriptive statements (Erickson, 1984; Pelto & Pelto, 1978).

3. Looking at the totality of ongoing needs of bilinguals based on a diversity of disciplinary involvement. Researchers can consider several interdisciplinary angles in order to best use their resources. For example, a research project within the field of developmental psycholinguistics may be related to sociolinguistics or child development to understand the totality and diversity of the development of bilingualism in children (Cummins, 1986, 1989). Psychologists, linguists, anthropologists and sociologists need to talk to each other with respect to the kinds of phenomena they are studying. This will pave the way for the development of interdisciplinary perspectives in the conception of research projects. Effective communication among specialists can be promoted through the prompt publication of research results (Freeman, 1989).

4. Research should contain not only classroom interactions but the broader context of the home and the community. Researchers need to balance micro-oriented studies in terms of types of research and implications of the research with studies that go beyond the classroom. What happens in the classroom, in very specific interactions, is only one aspect. The understanding of that interaction does not explain what happens in the broader context of the school and outside the school. There is an urgent need to conduct research to provide alternative understandings and explanations of the so-called academic failure or failure of adjustment of language minority students in the school system. Research results have sometimes been maximized only because they can be controlled methodologically (Hakuta, 1990; Snow, 1990). In doing so, researchers have penalized themselves by looking only at

some aspects of the phenomenon in question. The alternative must be to look at the classroom interaction, the school, and the community. Research needs to provide answers to questions such as: Why does a child, who operates very competently in English in the community, move into another context—the school—and freeze when (s)he tries to do math in English and has to switch to his or her native language?

Implementation of Action Research Activities

Action researchers need to consider the theoretical principles that have been consistently supported in the literature. They are encouraged to use this information as a basis for generating other studies and for interpreting the data gathered for a specific study. The specification of research activities in bilingual education and English as a second language cannot obscure the fact that there are issues for which there already exist some valid answers. Those issues have already been studied in a variety of different contexts based on theories that predict outcomes of bilingual education programs under a variety of different conditions.

Action research needs to be based on what is known in bilingual education and English as a second language not only from the point of view of planning further studies but also of defending the principles underlying bilingual education (Crawford, 1989). Research outcomes must, then, be stated with authority because they have been validated across a variety of different contexts. Action research needs to be based on the concept that there is nothing as practical as a good theory and must unify facts with it (Lieberman, 1986; Tikunoff, Ward & Griffin, 1979).

There exists a pool of knowledge that accounts for research conducted or being conducted in bilingual bicultural education that needs to be disseminated. Researchers can make full use of the resources that are available from the National Clearinghouse for Bilingual Education, the Center for Applied Linguistics, the Evaluation and Assessment Centers, the Multifunctional Resource Centers, the National Association for Bilingual Education, the Teachers of English to Speakers of Other Languages Association, and other research institutions. Furthermore, with the coordination and partnerships between school districts, state education departments, universities, and other relevant sources, a great amount of information on available research on bilingual education and English as a second language could be collected and disseminated at regional, state, and local levels.

Action research must consider experiences that have been conducted in other settings with other ethnic groups and different languages. A theory can predict certain outcomes; the validity of that theory is precisely how well it can account for the data under different conditions. In bilingual and English as a second language programs in the Americas, Europe, Asia and Africa, theoretical principles are operating across languages. For example, students all over the world gain in the acquisition and transfer of language skills because of bilingual instruction (Chamot, 1988; Skutnabb-Kangas, 1984; Zentella, 1988).

Action research needs to stress the principle that bilingual education is an enriching phenomenon—cognitively, socially, linguistically, culturally (Cummins, 1989; Hakuta, 1986). Research has evidenced that LEP students who are instructed through two languages—for example, Spanish and English, Navajo and English—do at least as well in the acquisition and development of academic skills in English as equivalent students in an all-English program (August & García, 1988; Holm & Holm, 1990; Willig, 1985). Research has also shown that students who are instructed in the second language—for example, English students instructed in Spanish or in French—do not lose out in the acquisition of native language skills. There is a lag in the development of these skills until formal English Language Arts is introduced, usually around grades 2 or 3, but then there is a rapid shift and gain in English skills (Lindholm & Dolson, 1988; Swain & Wong Fillmore, 1984).

Action researchers need to be sensitive to the kinds of changes that are occurring at the broader socio-political level (Cummins, 1989; Hornberger, 1990). They need to conduct research to expand the potential of bilingual education through enrichment programs which include minority and majority students (Rhodes, Crandall, & Christian, 1990; Tucker, 1990). The programs' goal would be bilingualism—that is, full development of first and second language skills. Action researchers need to try out and evaluate some of these concepts and determine what principles are operating within these contexts.

The reader needs to recognize the need for more research on conceptual input into how certain categories of research overlap, how they are related theoretically, and if they can be collapsed into one research category. For example, language assessment relates to language dominance, language proficiency, and language disability. A conceptual clarification is needed into what these issues are. Both practitioners and theoreticians need to work simultaneously to clarify these concepts to determine where the overlap starts and where it ends.

Finally, regional and state educational institutions can create a research incentives program to support and reward research initiatives through the competition of small grant research proposals.

Conclusion

This chapter has focused on institutionalization, staff development, and action research in bilingual and English as a second language teacher training. The first section addressed institutionalization efforts by universities and the federal government to establish programs to train educational personnel to address the needs of language minority students. Also discussed were two national surveys: the RMC study of 79 programs and the NCBE study of 56 programs. Eight indicators of institutionalization of undergraduate and graduate teacher training programs were discussed. They included: active support of administrators, positive attitudes of non-bilingual education faculty, faculty support through institutional funds, faculty tenure status, program continuation without federal funds, involvement of professionals in program operations, compatibility with institutional priorities, and sufficiently high enrollment levels to sustain the program. The section also presented the results of the 1987 EPTP Colloquium to implement the coordination, institutionalization, and evaluation components of each program.

The second section addressed staff development, including staff development partnerships between school districts and universities. It reviewed selected innovative staff development programs, such as (a) the Multi-district Trainer of Trainers Institute which consists of 12 to 15 days of training per year on the theory, its application, and peer coaching; (b) the Bilingual Education Training Institute with emphasis on instructional teaching strategies in math, reading, and writing in English; (c) the Language Development Specialist Academy which focuses on the development of expertise within a school or district through sharing instructional strategies and through external technical support specialists; and (d) the Illinois Resource Center peer coaching model between mainstream, bilingual, and English as a second language teachers on literacy and content-based language instruction.

This section also discussed a staff development case study on efforts by a university's bilingual training program to assist school districts with inservice training and technical assistance. The training was expected to strengthen the institutionalization of the university's teacher training program in bilingual bicultural education and the district's teaching strategies. Seven staff development steps were proposed: university's initiative, districts receptive of university's offer, both district and university plan staff development, staff development delivery during the first two years of the plan, staff development and action research during the following years, districts strengthen their bilingual programs, and university strengthens its bilingual training program.

The third and last section discussed action research principles to delineate research activities; it presented selected samples of research areas, its components and activities; and it suggested ways to implement them. The section proposed four principles to be considered in research in bilingual education and English as a second language: that research is needed to consider a longitudinal nature in addition to a cross-sectional one; complementary roles between qualitative and quantitative research; an interdisciplinary involvement; and a context of the classroom and home.

Action Research Needs in Bilingual Education and English as a Second Language

What kinds of research activities or areas on bilingual education and English as a second language need to be investigated? Despite the fact that most research is interrelated and that there is a great amount of overlapping, it is possible to organize research topics around areas of research. Based on a cursory review of the literature, 16 areas are being presented. These areas have been found in need of research. A sample of research components and examples of research activities are also included.

1. Language-related area, with the following components.

(a) The simultaneous and successive processes of first and second language acquisition. Examples include: the acquisition and development of mother languages other than English; the acquisition and development of English as a second language; and the development or underdevelopment of bilinguals.

(b) The social development of code-switching of bilinguals: the spectrum of speech styles of bilinguals; and adults compared to children.

(c) Language attrition: stages of first and second language shift or loss; and relation to language acquisition processes.

(d) The teaching of languages: comprehensional and communicative competence (listening, speaking, reading, and writing); eclecticism (meaning- and grammar-based methodology; and school and non-school strategies).

(e) Biliteracy and skill transfer: native language literacy installment; the development of writing skills in L1 and L2; independent or related to different languages; transfer of skills beyond the linguistic levels into cognitive levels.

2. Assessment, with the following research components and activities.

(a) Language dominance and proficiency testing: improvement of language dominance and language proficiency instruments; assessment of comprehensional (receptive) and communicative (productive) competence; right or left hemispheric processing with success in L2 acquisition; and relation to levels of instruction.

(b) Achievement testing: more relevance to language minority students; test characteristics in the content areas; and development of measures of achieved cognitive skills.

(c) IQ testing: measurement of accumulated experience of a particular language minority group; and measurement of learning rate of students of similar ethnic origin and different socio-economic status.

(d) Identification criteria: academic and affective indicators considered as exit criteria; and for limited and non-English proficient students who are language disabled.

(e) Language lateralization: utilization of dichotic listening and visual shift techniques; and patterns of hemispheric lateralization in bilinguals and monolinguals.

(f) Test construction: for the limited English proficient student without the knowledge of a specific concept; for non-Western society limited English proficient; culturally relevant as opposed to culturally biased; and language function and language use related to kinds of tasks posed on tests for adults, young adults, and children.

3. Bilingual special education, with the following examples of research activities: incidence of limited and non-English proficient students in special education classes by categories of exceptionality; ratio of exit from special education classes by ethnic category and by category of exceptionality; parents' rights in terms of special education for their children.

4. Curriculum, with the following examples of research activities: material development by levels of instruction, language background, and areas of curriculum; approaches to be used with undereducated

populations; curriculum tied to action research; development of an ethnic arts curriculum; and contributions of limited and non-English proficient students' oral folk culture.

5. Teacher training, with examples of research activities such as: staff development for teachers and administrators; institutionalization processes; sensitivity and awareness training for staff and faculty of bilingual students; participatory conditions of school districts, state departments of education, universities, etc., in the articulation of training programs; emphasis on language and culture the student brings to the classroom; and content and performance as pre-service and inservice training components.

6. Culture, with the following examples of research issues: primary characteristics of personality manifested through a student's culture(s); ways to encourage biculturalism; relationship to language acquisition and development and learning styles; and use of oral folk culture to improve academic abilities and linguistic proficiencies.

7. Slow learners, with the following examples of research activities: impact of bilingual schooling on slow learners; bilingual slow learners compared with monolingual slow learners; factors affecting learning (socioeconomic, sociolinguistic, etc.); and bilingual vocational experiences to improve motivation in disadvantaged young adults and adults.

8. Migration, with the following examples of research activities: migration patterns of specific linguistic minority communities; social class variation of migration; and occupational mobility in relation to family stress and parent-child relationship.

9. Significant Bilingual Instructional Features (SBIF) which include the following research issues: application of SBIF results at the state and local levels; conditions under which specific features of instruction are associated with good outcomes; and impact of SBIF study for staff development and teacher training.

10. Dropouts, with the following examples of research activities: causal factors for dropping out of school; impact of drop-out program in the affective domain; and components of a drop-out program.

11. Mainstreaming, with the following examples of research issues: range of variation of mainstreaming from one school to the other; performance of mainstreamed students after one, two, and three years in a regular program; and performance of students who are never mainstreamed.

12. Microcomputers, with the following examples of research activities: use of the computer in the academic areas as well as language

development; access to computers in bilingual programs; and benefits of computer programming, general computer literacy and computer assisted instruction in the bilingual and English as a second language classroom.

13. Remedial education, with research activities such as: the interplay between bilingual education and remediation; characteristics of an effective remediation component; and construction of remediation materials.

14. Bilingualism and cognitive development, with the following areas of research: relationship between bilingualism and cognitive development from a theoretical and practical point of view; and association of bilingualism with enhancement of cognitive flexibility and creativity.

15. Bilingual education law and amendments, with the following examples of research activities: variations in the implementation of the bilingual education laws in the bilingual classroom; and characteristics of language policies in the country.

16. Program evaluation, with the following examples of research activities: characteristics of a bilingual program evaluation model; and design and development of a model to meet the characteristics of a specific school population.

References

Agosto, V., Collazo, M., Colón, E., Hernández, I., & Minaya-Rowe, L. (1989). *Sheltered English for limited English proficient students. Hartford, CT: Hartford Public Schools.*

Arawak Consulting Corporation. (1986). A study of alternative inservice staff development approaches for local education agencies serving minority language/limited English proficient students. A model of inservice approaches. *Executive Summary*, pp. 1–22.

Arciniega, T. (1980). Institutionalizing bilingual education in colleges of education. ERIC No. ED 198 987.

August, D., & García, E.E. (1988). *Language minority education in the United States: Research, policy and practice.* Springfield, IL: Charles C. Thomas.

Axelson, R., Bush, M., Caro, J., Gaffey, L., Gray, N., Guzmán, R., Hazel, D., Kristofik, P., Medina, P., Minaya-Rowe, L., Patterson, M. E., Pierce, M.W., & Stark, L. K. (1987). *Teaching English to speakers of other languages: From first conversations to academic proficiency. Curriculum guide, grades 7–12.* Hartford, CT: Hartford Public Schools.

Axelson, R.G., George, L., Guzmán, R.P., Hoffman, W., Laureano, F., Minaya-Rowe, L., Piskor, I., Ramos-Ocasio, A., Rivas, R.K., Rivera-Ruiz, D., Sheehan, M., Spudic, L., Woykovsky, V., & Zalatimo, L. (1988). *Facilitating transition to the mainstream: Sheltered English vocabulary development.* Compiled by Valdez Pierce, L. Wheaton, MD: National Clearinghouse for Bilingual Education.

Axelson, R., George, L., Guzmán, R., Hoffman, W., Laureano, F., Minaya-Rowe, L., Piskor, I., Ramos-Ocasio, A., Rivas, R.K., Rivera-Ruiz, D., Sheehan, M., Woykovsky, V. R., & Zalatimo, L. (1986). *Second language acquisition through vocabulary development via concepts. A guidebook.* Hartford, CT: Hartford Public Schools.

Baca, L. (1984). Teacher education programs. ERIC No. ED 256 108.

Baecher, R.E. (1983). Institutionalizing bilingual education within university structures. In Padilla, R.V., (Ed.), *Theory, technology, and public policy on bilingual education* (pp. 377–392). Rosslyn, VA: National Clearinghouse for Bilingual Education.

Calderón, M. (1987). The art of training and coaching: Multicultural teacher training institute/case studies project. Paper presented at the Eastern conference on improving the educational achievement of limited-English proficient students. Baltimore, MD: State Educational Agencies of the Council of Chief State School Officers.

Calderón, M. & Marsh, D. (1988). Applying research on effective bilingual instruction in a multidistrict inservice teacher training program. *NABE Journal, 12*(2), 133–152.

Cazden, C. (1983). Can ethnographic research go beyond the status quo? *Anthropology & Education Quarterly, 14*(1), 33-41.

Chamot, A.U. (1988). Bilingualism in education and bilingual education: The state of the art in the United States. *Journal of Multilingual and Multicultural Development, 9*(1–2), 11–35.

Christian, D., Spanos, G., Crandall, J., Simich-Dudgeon, C., & Willets, K. (1990). Combining language and content for second-language students. In Padilla, A.M., Fairchild, H.H., & Valadez, C.M. (Eds.) *Bilingual education: Issues and strategies* (141–156). Newbury Park, CA: Sage.

Chu, H., & Levy, J. (1984). Institutionalizing a bilingual training program: Case study of George Mason University. *NABE Journal, 8*(3), 43–54.

Collier, V.P. (1985). University models for ESL and bilingual teacher training. In National Clearinghouse for Bilingual Education, *Issues in English language development* (81–90). Rosslyn, VA: InterAmerica Research Associates.

Crawford, J. (1989). *Bilingual education: History, politics, theory, and practice.* Trenton, NJ: Crane.

Cummins, J. (1981). The role of primary language development in promoting educational success for language minority students. *Schooling and language minority students: A theoretical framework* (pp. 3–49). Developed by the

Office of Bilingual Bicultural Education, California State Department of Education. Los Angeles: Evaluation, Dissemination and Assessment Center.

Cummins, J. (1989). _Empowering minority students_. Sacramento, CA: California Association for Bilingual Education.

Díaz, S., Moll, L.C., & Mehan, H. (1986). Sociocultural resources in instruction: A contextspecific approach. In California State Department of Education, _Beyond language: Social and cultural factors in schooling language minority students_. Los Angeles, CA: Evaluation, Dissemination, and Assessment Center, California State University.

Erickson, F. (1984). What makes school ethnography "ethnographic"? _Anthropology & Education Quarterly, 15_(1), 51–66.

Freeman, D. (1989). Teacher training, development, and decision making: A model of teaching and related strategies for language teacher education. _TESOL Quarterly, 23_(1), 27–45.

Hakuta, K. (1986). _Mirror of language: The debate on bilingualism_. New York: Basic Books.

Hakuta, K. (1990). Language and cognition in bilingual children. In Padilla, A.M., Fairchild, H.H. & Valadez, C.M. (Eds.) _Bilingual education: Issues and strategies_ (47–59). Newbury Park, CA: Sage.

Hernández, N. (1980). Institutionalizing bilingual education in schools, colleges, and departments of education. Programmatic concerns at IHEAs. ERIC No. ED 191 643.

Holm, A. & Holm, W. (1990). Rock Point, a Navajo way to go to school: A valediction. In Cazden, C.B. & Snow, C.E. (Eds.) _English plus: Issues in bilingual education_ (pp. 170–184). Newbury Park, CA: Sage.

Hornberger, N.H. (1990). Bilingual education and English-only: A language planning framework. In Cazden, C.B. & Snow, C.E. (Eds.) _English plus: Issues in bilingual education_ (pp. 12–26). Newbury Park, CA: Sage.

Jacob, E., & Jordan, C. (1987). Moving to dialogue. _Anthropology & Education Quarterly, 18_(4), 259–261.

Johnson, D.M., & Binkley, J.L. (1987). Management and organizational structure in university bilingual education programs: A national survey of Title VII. _NABE Journal, 11_(2), 95–115.

Joyce, B., & Showers, B. (1988). _Student achievement through staff development_. White Plains, New York: Longman.

Joyce, B., Showers, B., & Rolheiser-Bennett, C. (1987). Staff development and student learning: A synthesis of research on models of teaching. _Educational Leadership_ (October), 11–23.

Krashen, S. (1981). Bilingual education and second language acquisition. In _Schooling and language minority students: A theoretical framework_ (pp. 51–79). Developed by the Office of Bilingual Bicultural Education, California State Department of Education. Los Angeles: Evaluation, Dissemination and Assessment Center.

Krashen, S., & Biber, D. (1988). _On course_. Sacramento, CA: California Association for Bilingual Education.

Kwiat, J. (1988). A peer coaching model for teachers of limited English proficient students. Paper presented at the meeting of the American Education Research Association.

Lieberman, A. (1986). Collaborative research: Working with, not working on. . . . *Educational Leadership, 43*(5), 28–32.

Lindholm, K.J., & Dolson, D. (1988). *Bilingual immersion education: Promoting language and academic excellence for language minority and majority students in the same program.* Los Angeles: University of California, Center for Language Education and Research.

Macías, R. (1986). Teacher preparation for bilingual education. Compendium of papers on the topic of bilingual education of the Committee on Education and Labor, House of Representatives, 99th Congress, 2nd session. Washington, DC: U.S. Government Printing Office.

Mercado, C.I. (1985). Models of inservice teacher training. In National Clearinghouse for Bilingual Education, *Issues in English language development* (pp. 107–114). Rosslyn, VA: InterAmerica Research Associates.

Minaya-Rowe, L. (1989). Staff development for teachers of language minority students: Case study of the University of Connecticut. *Language, Culture, and Curriculum, 2*(1), 43–53.

Montero-Sieburth, M., & Pérez, M. (1987). Echar pa'lante, moving onward: The dilemmas and strategies of a bilingual teacher. *Anthropology & Education Quarterly, 18*(3), 180–189.

National Clearinghouse for Bilingual Education (1984). *A study of teacher training programs in bilingual education: Executive summaries, volumes I and II. Part C research agenda.* Rosslyn, VA: InterAmerica Research Associates.

National Clearinghouse for Bilingual Education (1988). Innovative staff development approaches. Occasional Papers 4. Wheaton, MD: NCBE.

Office of Bilingual Education and Minority Languages Affairs (1989). *Colloquium to strengthen educational personnel training programs: Training educational personnel to work with language minority populations.* Washington, DC: Georgetown University Press.

Ogbu, J.V. (1987). Variability in minority school performance: A problem in search of an explanation. *Anthropology & Education Quarterly, 18*(4), 312–334.

Pelto, P.J. & Pelto, G.H. (1978). *Anthropological research. The structure of inquiry.* New York: Cambridge University Press.

Rhodes, N., Crandall, J., & Christian, D. (1990). "Key Amigos": A partial immersion program. In Padilla, A.M., Fairchild, H.H., & Valadez, C.M. (Eds.) *Foreign language education: Issues and strategies.* Newbury Park, CA: Sage.

RMC Research Corporation (1981). *A study of teacher training programs in bilingual education. Volume I.* Mountain View, CA: RMC Research Corporation.

Sarason, S. (1982). *The culture of the school and the problem of change.* Boston, MA: Allyn and Bacon.

Schensul, J.J. (1985). Cultural maintenance and cultural transformation: Educational anthropology in the eighties. *Anthropology & Education Quarterly, 16*(1), 63–68.

Secada, W.G. (1990). Research, politics, and bilingual education. In Cazden, C.B. & Snow, C.E. (Eds.) *English plus: Issues in bilingual education* (81–106). Newbury Park, CA: Sage. Publications.

Showers, B., Joyce, B., & Bennett, B. (1987). Synthesis of research on staff development: A framework for future study and a state-of-the-art analysis. *Educational Leadership,* (November), 77–87.

Skutnabb-Kangas, T. (1984). *Bilingualism or not: The education of minorities.* Clevedon, England: Multilingual Matters.

Snow, C.E. (1990). Rationales for native language instruction: Evidence from research. In Padilla, A.M., Fairchild, H.H., & Valadez, C.M. (Eds.), *Bilingual education: Issues and strategies* (pp. 60–74). Newbury Park, CA: Sage.

Swain, M. & Wong Fillmore, L.W. (1984). Child second language development: Views from the field on theory and research. Paper presented at the 18th Annual TESOL Conference, Houston, Texas.

Tikunoff, W.J. (1985). *Applying significant bilingual instructional features in the classroom.* Rosslyn, VA: National Clearinghouse for Bilingual Education.

Tikunoff, W., Ward, B., & Griffin, G. (1979). *Interactive research and development on teaching. Final report.* San Francisco: Far West Laboratory for Educational Research and Development.

Trueba, H.T. (1988). Culturally based explanations of minority students' academic achievement. *Anthropology & Education Quarterly, 19*(3), 270–287.

Tucker, G.R. (1990). Second language education: Issues and perspectives. In Padilla, A.M., Fairchild, H.H., & Valadez, C.M. (Eds.) *Innovations in language education: Vol. 2. Immersion and foreign language education.* Newbury Park, CA: Sage.

Valadez, C.M., & Patino Gregoire, C. (1990). Development of a bilingual education plan. In Padilla, A.M., Fairchild, H.H., & Valadez, C.M. (Eds.) *Bilingual education. Issues and strategies* (pp. 106–125). Newbury Park, CA: Sage.

Waggoner, D. (1987). Foreign born children in the United States in the eighties. *NABE Journal, 12*(1), 23–49.

Ward, B. (1987). Using a clinical approach to teacher development. In Fradd, S. & Tikunoff, W. (Eds.) *Bilingual education and special education: A guide for administrators.* Boston: Little, Brown.

Willig, A.C. (1985). A meta-analysis of selected studies on the effectiveness of bilingual education. *Review of Educational Research, 55,* 269–317.

Zentella, A.C. (1988). The language situation of Puerto Ricans. In McKay, S.L. & Wong, S.C. (Eds.) *Language diversity. Problem or resource?* (pp. 140–165). New York: Newbury House.

Annotated Bibliography

Calderón, M., & Marsh, D. (1988). Applying research on effective bilingual instruction in a multi-district inservice teacher training program. *NABE Journal, 12*(2), 133–152.

Describes and analyzes staff development strategy to help teachers apply existing research on bilingual education in their classrooms. The strategy consists of five components: (1) study of the theoretical basis of teaching methodology, such as the natural approach to second language acquisition; (2) observation of demonstrations by experts in the methods; (3) practice of the methods; (4) feedback in protected conditions; and (5) coaching one another at the school.

Cazden, C. (1983). Can ethnographic research go beyond the status quo? *Anthropology & Education Quarterly, 14*(1), 33–41.

Discusses the role of social science research in program design and school improvement and argues for a broader view of research relevance not only in translating the outcome into improved skills of the practitioner, but also in considering that practitioners possess skills, a view of reality, a vision of the achievable, and a commitment to act.

Chamot, A. U. (1988). Bilingualism in education and bilingual education: The state of the art in the United States. *Journal of Multilingual and Multicultural Development, 9*(1–2), 11–35.

Discusses the current status and future directions of education for limited English proficient students in elementary and secondary schools in the United States. Estimates of numbers of students and qualified teachers, types of school programs and teacher training programs, and future directions are reviewed.

Chu, H., & Levy, J. (1984). Institutionalizing a bilingual training program: Case study of George Mason University. *NABE Journal, 8*(3), 43–54.

Discusses eight characteristics of institutionalization based on the 1981 RMC study of bilingual training programs and relates them to the process of institutionalization of the bilingual training program at George Mason University in Fairfax, Virginia.

Cummins, J. (1989). *Empowering minority students.* Sacramento, CA: California Association of Bilingual Education.

Reviews the psychoeducational concepts of language proficiency, language learning, bilingualism, and academic development among minority students in relation to the social and historical context in which schools operate. The author proposes an intervention model, a framework for considering what types of interventions are required to reverse the pattern of minority students' school failure, and an implementation model in terms of programs and strategies to meet specific needs. The author argues that interventions become possible when educators define their role as empowering minority students; i.e., when students experience a sense of control over their own lives and develop the ability, confidence, and motivation to succeed academically.

Díaz, S., Moll, L.C., & Mehan, H. (1986). Sociocultural resources in instruction: A context-specific approach. In California State Department of Education, *Beyond language: Social and cultural factors in schooling language minority students* (pp. 187–230). Los Angeles, CA: Evaluation, Dissemination, and Assessment Center, California State University.

Discusses school success and failure via ethnographic descriptions of the culture and community as a powerful resource to improve student performance. The authors propose that the student's problems in school can be traced to the social organization of schooling. The research indicates that English-language programs in the schools tend to underestimate the capabilities of the language minority student.

Hakuta, K. (1990). Language and cognition in bilingual education. In Padilla, A.M., Fairchild, H.H., & Valadez, C.M. (Eds.), *Bilingual education: Issues and strategies* (47–59). Newbury Park, CA: Sage.

Discusses the importance of theoretical issues in linguistics, education, and cognition underlying bilingual education and the socio-cultural context of research. Criticizes the racially motivated assumptions that bilingualism is a cognitive handicap and that bilingual individuals are intellectually inferior.

Johnson, D.M., & Binkley, J.L. (1987). Management and organizational structure in university bilingual education programs: A national survey of Title VII. *NABE Journal, 11*(2), 95–115.

Describes characteristics of the management and organizational structure of bilingual education academic degree (doctoral, master's, and bachelor's) programs based on a large-scale study of 95 programs in 56 colleges and universities. Issues examined include the role of the director and faculty in program operations, the allocation of funds, the relationship between funding and student enrollment, and management features.

Krashen, S., & Biber, D. (1988). *On course.* Sacramento, CA: California Association for Bilingual Education.

Discusses principles underlying successful programs for limited English proficient students and examines programs that are consistent with the principles. The authors suggest that students in these programs acquire English rapidly and well, and achieve good scores on academic tests, whether tested in English or their first language.

Lomax, P. (Ed.) 1989. *Increasing school effectiveness and facilitating staff development through action research.* Avon, England: Multilingual Matters.

Argues that research in education should incorporate an examination of the value system of schools. Discusses techniques to improve classroom interaction through an action research approach.

McCarthy, M. (1987). A slice of life: Training teachers through case studies. *Alumni Bulletin, Harvard Graduate School of Education Association Bulletin, 32*(1), 9–11.

Discusses the use of a case method technique in teacher training. The author offers specific examples of the case method approach and argues that this method fosters an active level of participation, thereby producing sharper analytic and problem-solving skills in participants.

Mercado, C.I. (1985). Models of inservice teacher training. In National Clearinghouse for Bilingual Education, *Issues in English language development* (pp. 107–114). Rosslyn, VA: InterAmerica Research Associates.

Discusses a collegial approach to teacher training with trainers who are collaborators and mentors working closely with teachers, sharing, exploring, reflecting, and visiting classrooms to achieve quality instruction.

Padilla, A.M. (1990). Bilingual education: Issues and perspectives. In Padilla, A.M., Fairchild, H.H., & Valadez, C.M. (Eds.) *Bilingual education: Issues and strategies* (pp. 15–26). Newbury Park, CA: Sage.

Reviews the policy, research, and programmatic debates surrounding bilingual education. The author emphasizes the need for bilingual education proponents to develop a paradigm, a coherent tradition, in the development of bilingual education programs, teaching strategies, and research approaches. Calls for the joining together of people, organizations, and institutions to establish the goal of a "language-competent" society.

Rossett, A. & Rodríguez, A.M. (1988). Assuring access to instructional technologies for language minority students: A case study of a teacher training program. *NABE Journal, 13*(1), 43–58.

Describes the federally funded Bilingual Instructional Technologies (BIT) program, designed to train bilingual educators in educational computing and instructional design. A total of 65 bilingual teachers participated in the program. The article describes the BIT program in detail.

Secada, W. G. (1990). Research, politics, and bilingual education. In Cazden, C.B. & Snow, C.E. (Eds.) *English plus: Issues in bilingual education* (pp. 81–106). Newbury Park, CA: Sage.

Explores issues and events in legislation, litigation, and the role of research in policy debates and analyzes how political forces and research findings have played a role in legislation and appropriations for educational programs for language minority students. The author points out that basic research on second language acquisition and on relationships between intellectual development and bilingualism is relevant to policy debates.

Tikunoff, W.J. (1985). *Applying significant bilingual instructional features in the classroom*. Rosslyn, VA: National Clearinghouse for Bilingual Education.

Reflects on findings from the Significant Bilingual Instructional Features descriptive study and puts them into a perspective that will facilitate and encourage their use by teachers and administrators. Explains process of successfully instructing limited English proficient students to achieve English and basic skills acquisition.

Trueba, H.T. (1988). Culturally based explanations of minority students' academic achievement. *Anthropology & Education Quarterly, 19*(3), 270–287.

Examines the learning environments for academic success for all children in terms of theoretical and practical approaches that (1) recognize the significance of culture in specific instructional settings, (2) prevent stereotyping of minorities, (3) help resolve cultural conflicts in school, (4) integrate the home and the school cultures, and (5) stimulate the development of communicative and academic skills. The author proposes that these approaches permit applied ethnographers to turn failure into success.

Watson, K. & Roberts, R. (1988). Multicultural education and teacher training: The picture after Swann. *Journal of Multilingual and Multicultural Development, 9*(4), 339–352.

Describes a survey conducted to determine whether the Swann Report recommendations that teacher training institutions place greater emphasis on multicultural education in their training courses were followed. The survey questionnaires were sent to 105 teacher training institutions and 73 responded. Analysis of the data indicated that, although there are many individuals committed to prepare students for teaching in a pluralistic society, there is still a need for more effective support in teacher training programs.

Willig, A.C. (1985). A meta-analysis of selected studies on the effectiveness of bilingual education. *Review of Educational Research*, 55, 269–317.

Critiques the 1981 U.S. Department of Education report on the effectiveness of bilingual education programs and discusses the purpose of bilingual education and the nature of bilingual education programs. The author examines the methodological weaknesses of the report in terms of the gross oversimplification in the method of tallying the results of primary studies, and the failure to apply equally rigorous research standards to all studies when interpreting their results. Proposes methodology to enable the gleaning of all relevant information from the primary studies included in the report without ignoring the complexities inherent in the evaluation of bilingual education.

CHAPTER IX

Psychoeducational Assessment of Language Minority Children: Current Perspectives and Future Trends

María D. Alvarez

Introduction

This chapter reviews the literature on the psychoeducational assessment of language minority (LM) and limited English proficient (LEP) students, emphasizing 1988 to 1990 publications. It builds upon a previous review (Alvarez, 1988), where publications spanning from 1986 to 1987 were emphasized. As in that previous review, current issues and practices pertinent to psychoeducational assessment in general are discussed as well as issues specifically relevant to LM groups. In addition, this chapter summarizes the major outcomes of the past decade and offers a look into the challenges and themes anticipated for the 1990s. The chapter is written with the recognition that the assessment of LM students is embedded within the larger context of assessment in general: It profits from its advances and is constrained by its limitations.

Psychoeducational Assessment in the 1980s: An Overview

Psychoeducational assessment of LM and LEP students clearly came of age during the 1980s. It became established as a field unto itself with its own literature base and its own intricacies. The 1980s— especially the last five years—were characterized by a geometrical expansion of professional publications and presentations related to the assessment of LM and LEP children. If increased professional dissemination is a valid indicator of the importance a profession places on an issue and the knowledge that is being generated in a field, there is reason to believe that the 1990s will be a promising and hopeful decade for the sensitive and unbiased assessment of LM and LEP children.

Despite this unprecedented productivity, a bird's-eye view of the information generated over the past decade reveals that low-incidence language and ethnic groups continue to be overlooked as are the varying exceptionalities. There is little in the published scientific literature regarding the assessment of blind or partially sighted bilinguals, of deaf and hard-of-hearing bilinguals, of mentally retarded bilinguals, and the assessment of personality and behavior disorders among LM children. The area of bilingual preschool assessment is also a neglected field, though with recent legislation regarding infants and toddlers, this state of affairs is expected to change fast.

Equally scanty are efforts toward development of alternative procedures for identifying gifted and talented bilingual children and adolescents. Likewise, efforts designed to detect and identify potential dropouts among LM and LEP students are still sorely lacking from screening processes.

About 12.5 percent of students nationwide come from LM backgrounds, and this reaches 30.1 percent in the 20 largest school districts (National Advisory and Coordinating Council on Bilingual Education [NACCBE], 1988). In addition, the 1980s highlighted the diversity of LM populations—which now includes about 100 unique language groups—and the constant influx that fuels this diversity. Language minority populations are constantly shifting and linguistic groups emerge unexpectedly. For instance, according to State Department reports (cited in NACCBE, 1988) Southeast Asian immigrants increased from fewer than 10,000 before 1975 to 808,811 in 1987. The Hispanic population grew from 14.6 million in 1980 to 19.4 million in 1988, a shift from 6.4 percent to 8.1 percent of the total U.S. population. The fastest growing Hispanic group were Mexican Americans (U.S. Department of Commerce, 1985; 1988).

In addition, it is important to understand that not all language communities present the same LEP rates. The National Advisory and Coordinating Council on Bilingual Education (1988) estimated that among Vietnamese and Hispanic communities about three out of four persons are LEP, in contrast to the four or five out of ten that characterize other language communities. These data are striking because Hispanics represent the largest segment of the LM population in the United States, and the Vietnamese represent the largest percentage among the group of recent Asian migrants.

Some language minority groups, such as the Spanish speaking, are widely recognized because of their sheer numbers. Other groups are considered to be of low incidence. Yet what may be a low incidence language group in one setting may be a primary language group in another. A Haitian student is a rarity in California yet commonplace in New York City or Boston. Thus, in a field of constantly changing linguistic communities and evolving school populations the term "low incidence" may be a misnomer. The shifts and changes in populations that took place during the 1980s highlighted that professionals working in schools today must be equipped to understand and to be sensitive to cultural and linguistic diversity.

Major Types of Assessment Used with LM Students

Alvarez (1988) distinguishes among four kinds of assessment currently used with LM students: (a) English proficiency testing; (b) language proficiency testing; (c) language assessment for special education; and (d) psychoeducational assessment. These will be summarized below. More detailed descriptions may be found in Alvarez (1988). Standardized tests occupy a prominent role in language testing. Other popular methods are interviewing, checklists, rating scales, observation, and self-report. Close and open-ended techniques have been used, characterized by various degrees of open-endedness such as storytelling, story retelling, and structured interviewing.

English Proficiency Testing

English proficiency testing entails an evaluation of general oral communication ability in English and is a method popular in assessing newly arrived students from low incidence language groups. In this kind of evaluation, a student's language skills are explored only in the second language, English.

Language Proficiency Testing

Language proficiency testing refers to the general screening for
language proficiency that takes place when students are identified for
regular or bilingual education. In pedagogical contexts, proficiency
testing usually entails an assessment, in two languages, of both oral
and written competencies, though in actual practice, surprisingly few
school districts explore native language skills, and the superficiality of
the measures used open the way for misclassification (Baker, 1990).

At the oral level, both comprehension (listening) and production
(speaking) are explored. At the written level, both reading (a receptive
skill) and writing (an expressive activity) are assessed. In exploring oral
skills, reference is usually made to criteria such as phonology (mastery
of the sound system/accent), morphology (vocabulary and word
knowledge), syntax (grammar), fluency (smoothness of communication),
semantics (meaning), and pragmatics (getting one's point across in a
language). In exploring written language, it is customary to evaluate
decoding (word recognition), reading comprehension (both literal and
inferential), and writing ability (spelling, organization, vocabulary,
mechanics, general communication ability). Some linguists consider
phonology, morphology, and syntax to be surface level structures of
language, while semantics and pragmatics are viewed as deeper
dimensions; each one is separate but at the same time interdependent
with the other.

Another important distinction is the context-sensitive nature of
linguistic dominance. Sociolinguists have emphasized the importance
of domains such as home, school, church, and community. These
domains become diagnostically relevant to the degree that a student
may be more proficient in one language for one domain and in another
language for another domain. Cummins (1984) pointed out the difference
between language used in everyday context-embedded conversations
and that required in more rigorous context-reduced academic tasks, a
distinction rather important in educational settings. De León (1990) has
adapted a checklist to help distinguish between both.

The view of language that prevails in school-based language
proficiency assessments emphasizes structural criteria and views
language as a process that can be segmented into its component parts.
Thus, most instruments used in schools follow a paper-and-pencil format
and measure vocabulary, syntax, or the four skills of listening, speaking,
reading, and writing. To be sure, language assessment technology has
improved—judging by comparisons of first and second versions of tests

and of early vs more recent instruments—but the evidence shows it is far from perfect (Baker, 1990). Yet, the field of language itself is rapidly evolving. Language is no longer viewed as the sum of its parts but as a total entity whose subskills need to be viewed holistically (Hamayan, Kwiat, & Perlman, 1985).

The pressure for change in the way schools identify children for regular or bilingual programs responds to at least three factors. First, the emphasis is shifting from structural to pragmatic criteria; from an emphasis on phonology, word knowledge, and syntax to an emphasis on pragmatics and communicative competence (Hakuta & García, 1989; A.G. Ramírez, 1990). Empirical evidence in support of the shift is available. Working with a sample of bilingual children suspected of learning disorders, Damico, Oller, and Storey (1983) found that pragmatic criteria (i.e., nonfluences, revisions, timing of responses, appropriateness of responses, use of nonspecific vocabulary, topic maintenance, and need for repetition) were better predictors of linguistic and academic performance than surface-oriented criteria based on morphological or syntactic structures.

Second, Jax (1988) cites research showing that many children who passed school language proficiency tests were mainstreamed but later referred for special education (SPED) on account of low achievement, poor reading skills, or poor oral skills. The conclusion is that the tests used in language proficiency assessments are only tapping at the more superficial aspects of language and may identify as linguistically competent children who are not yet equipped to handle the kind of language required in context-reduced academic settings. What is in essence sheer lack of mastery of the English language may quickly turn into a SPED problem.

Third, there is pressure building for more spontaneous, free-flowing language elicitation methods (Cazden, 1977; Damico, 1985; Prutting, 1984) that consider the various contexts in which language occurs and the various purposes for which language is used (e.g., interactional, instrumental, informative). Accordingly, current trends in language testing call for holistic, integrative assessment methods. Paper-and-pencil tests narrowly focusing on discrete aspects do not adequately capture the nuances of human communication. Yet, school-based language proficiency assessment remains a highly test-based enterprise —due to expediency and the need to screen hundreds of children.

To be sure, the rather open-ended, naturalistic observations of language interactions required to tap at communicative competence, are time consuming. Ortiz and Polyzoi (1988) reported that the analysis of language using pragmatic criteria may take from 15 to 20 hours, given the need for obtaining conversational samples in two languages, and then transcribing, editing, segmenting, plus identifying and counting errors. The shift from linguistic competence to communicative competence will probably be slow.

Language Assessment in Special Education

The third type of assessment refers to the more thorough and detailed evaluation of children's oral language competencies, as may be needed by speech and language clinicians or by other diagnosticians seeking more differentiated breakdowns of children's oral language; it is usually performed in the context of a SPED referral. There is more openness in this kind of assessment to incorporate both structural and pragmatic criteria, given that more time is allotted to it and that a trained speech and language clinician usually conducts this type of evaluation. Yet in surveying the speech and language assessments of LEP and Anglo children in California, Langdon (1989) concluded that the heaviest diagnostic emphasis continues to be placed on discrete-point tests. Langdon (1988, 1989) advocates comprehensive evaluations in the two languages, more specificity as to the contexts and the languages in which language samples are obtained, and increased emphasis on background information regarding the child, family, health, and school history.

Ideally, a variety of language samples should be obtained from a variety of settings and in interaction with a variety of people. Fradd, Barona, and Santos de Barona (1989) recommend three oral samples each containing 10 to 15 minutes of student language. Furthermore, the evaluation should look at a range of structural and pragmatic criteria. Structural criteria usually include analysis of mean length of utterance, syntactical and semantic errors, subject-verb agreements, use of possessives, plurals, irregular verb forms, past-tense markings, plus analyses of articulation, receptive and expressive vocabulary, listening comprehension, etc. Pragmatic criteria include perlocutionary (e.g., touching, smiling) and illocutionary (e.g., pointing, showing) acts; topic maintenance, selection, and changes; aspects of turn taking, such as initiation, response, pauses, feedback to speakers, conciseness, role playing, etc. Many school districts include at least some pragmatic component, most commonly through checklists.

Psychoeducational Assessment

Given its close connection with special education placement, psychoeducational assessment is the most controversial of all assessments currently used with LM students (Cummins, 1984; Galagan, 1985). Ideally, psychoeducational assessment entails an analysis of a broad gamut of data (e.g., linguistic, cognitive, perceptual, motor, emotional, social, behavioral, and academic) and presupposes a thorough review of a student's past records and of a student's past and current learning history, plus awareness of learning and teaching styles. Data-gathering procedures have largely relied on tests, but interviews and observations by one or more observers in several settings are not only legislated but vehemently advocated (Figueroa, 1990b).

The focus of the psychoeducational diagnostic process has traditionally been limited to the children themselves within the microcosm of the testing situation, often referred to in the literature as the deficit model or the medical model. But there is increasing legislative and professional pressure for substituting this narrow scope for a wider macrosystemic perspective. This wider perspective views children in interaction with the different elements of the environments to which they are exposed at home, in their communities, in their schools, and within their classrooms. In short, psychoeducational assessment should reflect the multiplicity of factors underlying school learning and personal-social adaptation of children in the various environments in which they live and learn.

Assessment of bilinguistic competencies. Among bilingual children, particular attention should be given to language, especially in its interface with reading and writing skills. Language is important in a psychoeducational evaluation because it permeates just about every aspect of the curriculum even at the early elementary level (Danwitz, 1976) and shows consistent correlations with reading (Hammill & McNutt, 1981). In the case of bilingual children, there are added reasons for looking at both first (L1) and second (L2) languages: (a) the degree of mastery a student exhibits in L1 correlates with mastery of L2 at both the oral and the written levels (Cummins, 1984); (b) the degree of intactness in both oral and written language functions in L1 is important in entertaining or ruling out learning disorders in L2; and (c) a bilingual-biliterate evaluation more accurately represents the full range of oral and written linguistic competencies of a bilingual-biliterate learner, which results in better educational planning and more informed decision-making.

A clinician skilled in the nuances and intricacies of language is better equipped to determine whether school difficulties of LEP students relate to temporary problems due to limited command of English, to transient adaptation difficulties, or to more serious underlying language and learning disorders. This is a critical question and the subject of great concern for those interested in the accurate assessment of LM children (Benavides, 1988; Ortiz & Polyzoi, 1988).

To emphasize the importance of the two languages is not to close one's eyes to the existence of different ways of going about the assessment process. According to Alvarez (1988) the levels of diagnostic attention given to language range from systematic exploration of both L1 and L2 by a bilingual/bicultural clinician to minimal or no exploration of L1 by a linguistically untrained monolingual clinician. In between are various levels of attention paid to language (L2 explored with L1 component; L2 explored with sensitivity to L1) and various levels of training by people conducting the evaluation (trained interpreter under supervision of monolingual clinician, inservice trained monolingual clinician). Investigators who have reviewed a large number of student SPED protocols (Cummins, 1984; García & Yates, 1986; Maldonado-Colón, 1986) conclude that little diagnostic attention is paid to language in bilingual evaluations.

Figueroa (1989) has warned about the perils of using interpreters, a practice he believes may be inevitable with low incidence language groups but altogether unwarranted for large groups. Yet the practice is widespread (Nuttall, 1987). In fact, training in work with interpreters is one of the competencies proposed for bilingual SPED assessment personnel in California (Ramage, 1986), and various programs aimed at training people to serve as interpreters have been developed.

Assessment of cognitive functioning. One major component of psychoeducational evaluations is the assessment of cognitive functioning; reviews of the literature reflect this priority (Caterino, 1990; Holtzman & Wilkinson, 1991). The activism of the last two decades has discouraged the use of IQ scores; it is now customary to speak of "ranges of functioning." Another shift entails the move from end-products to processes, from global scores to more differentiated breakdowns of cognitive functions and skills: memory, attention, concentration, organizational abilities. Within each skill, there is an interest to look at even more differentiated functions. Thus, memory is no longer the monolithic entity largely dependent on verbal content that Ebbinghaus studied a century ago, but attempts are made to break it down into visual vs auditory vs kinesthetic recall, short term vs long term, rote vs meaningful, contextual vs isolated. There are instructional techniques and curricular modifications that can be adapted to these more differentiated needs of learners, and the breakdowns can lead to closer match between assessment and curriculum.

Assessment of personal/social functioning. While cognition receives much attention, the assessment of personality functioning is given low-priority as seen in a recent review of projective techniques conducted by Barona and Hernández (1990). In addition to the existence of potentially confounding variables such as ethnicity, language, or acculturation, three problematic factors uncovered by these investigators are: (a) school psychologists—as studied by Vukovich—administer projective tests more frequently to Hispanics than to Anglos or African Americans; (b) most school psychologists surveyed by Prout reported they used projectives in the majority of their evaluations yet felt inadequately trained to use them; and (c) as training programs spend less time teaching projectives, self-study of such techniques is on the increase. Each one of these factors by itself can have serious implications for LM children. There seems to be a disparity between what school psychology trainers perceive as training priorities, where the field is heading, and what practicing school psychologists are actually doing in the field.

Cultural Variables in the Assessment of LM Children

Culture and Learning Styles

Culture continues to be considered of major impact in LM assessment and a source of potential misunderstanding (Miller-Jones, 1989). It is important not only to consider the learning and behavior styles, attitudes, beliefs, and other cultural manifestations but also the examiner's own attitudes toward such. Flexibility, a problem-solving approach, and an advocacy stand toward LM youth are considered key strategies for the school psychologist working with LM children (Vázquez-Nuttall, De León, & Valle, 1990).

Chamberlain and Medeiros-Landurand (1990) describe the major cultural variables impinging on any assessment process: cooperative vs competitive orientations, varied conceptions of time, polychronic vs monochronic interactional patterns, handling of space (proximity), bodily movements, touching, eye contact, gender, verbal and non-verbal

communication patterns, and perceptual and cognitive styles. In each
of these areas, there may be differences between mainstream examiners
and minority children, or vice versa as the case may be.

While cautioning against stereotyping, cultural characteristics of
Hispanics, Asian Americans, Native Americans, and African Americans
are summarized for school psychologists by Vázquez-Nuttall, De León,
and Valle (1990). The authors also summarize various family and social
factors for each group as well as school issues.

Degree of acculturation to U.S. life. One of the aspects that is not
often alluded to is the differential degree of acculturation and the stage
of migration at which children and families find themselves (Alvarez,
1977). For instance, there is a tendency to speak about Hispanics as
though they were a culturally homogenous group. In reality Hispanics
and other language minority communities are composed of individuals
at different degrees of acculturation into continental, urban life.
Acculturation entails aspects such as language proficiency; knowledge
and use of resources; familiarity with the styles of interaction, attires,
foods, and entertainment patterns of the host culture, and the like.
According to the 1980 Census (cited in Huang & Ying, 1989) among
Chinese residing in the United States, 37 percent are native born and
63 percent are foreign born; the migration process is still ongoing and
a fresh experience for some but not for others. Another difference is
the socioeconomic variation presented by certain groups normally clasped
together. For instance, while Asian/Pacific Islanders are often clustered
together, there is much socioeconomic variation among Asian groups.
Except for Southeast Asian refugees, the Chinese have the highest
number of persons living below the poverty level of all Asian groups
in the United States (Huang & Ying, 1989).

Current Trends in Psychoeducational Assessment:
Encouraging Developments

While certain issues appear far from resolution, there is reason for
optimism in current attempts to make psychoeducational assessment a
fairer process. On the positive side the following are identified: (a) the
theme of advocacy and empowerment on behalf of LM students, parents,
and teachers; (b) evolving trends in the psychoeducational diagnostic
process; (c) alternative assessment methods; (d) new approaches for

linking assessment to instruction; (e) commitment to referral prevention and prereferral interventions; and (f) increased dissemination efforts.

Advocacy on Behalf of LM Groups

The major advocacy efforts on behalf of LM children and their families in the last decades were channeled through legislation and litigation (García, 1990). Major legal battles were fought and resulted in successful court rulings, consent decrees, or legislation on behalf of LM students; advocacy organizations were established to make sure the agreed-upon mandates are followed. Yet these changes occur within a large macrosystemic context. Within the microcosm of individual children, families, teachers, and schools, the major theme is that of empowerment (Correa, 1990; Cummins, 1986; Trachtman, 1990). All involved with children become active advocates on their behalf. Cummins (1989) refers to this as a "pedagogy for empowerment" (p. 117).

Vázquez-Nuttall, De León, and Valle (1990) perceive school psychologists with special skills in dealing with minority children as liaisons between school and home and between home and community, as consultants and inservice trainers for other colleagues and school staff, and as interpreters of U.S. mainstream culture and programs for families who may be unfamiliar with them. In addition, the National Advisory and Coordinating Council on Bilingual Education (1988) advocates for the training of administrators and educators not specifically assigned to programs for LEP students "so that all educational personnel will be sensitive and capable of responding appropriately to the needs of individual students" (p. 86).

Empowering parents of LM students. Parents can—and should—be empowered to advocate for their children and appraised of their children's educational needs. Figler (in press), in working with Boston-based Puerto Rican families of special needs children, found that most families in her sample did not fully understand the nature of the programs attended by their children, many of whom were enrolled in substantially separate classes. Practitioners should remember that while it may be legislated that parents be informed of certain issues, that they be given copies of reports and IEPs, that records be open to them, or that they attend staffing sessions on behalf of their children, it does not mean parental participation is a reality. In fact, these were the conclusions reached by Bennett (1988a) in his ethnographic study of hearing impaired

Hispanic children and their families. Likewise, the evidence reviewed
by Jones (1988) indicates there are problems with participation and
barriers often stem from school personnel.

Empowering parents may be difficult especially with groups that
have little tradition of interacting with school systems. But it is certainly
a step that behooves all concerned with the well-being of LM children
and adolescents. Correa (1989) highlights the importance of family
involvement and suggests ways in which parents and schools can go
about facilitating this involvement.

Evolving Trends in Psychoeducational Assessment

Advocacy-oriented assessments. Cummins (1989) recommends an
advocacy approach to the assessment of minority children. This entails
a broadening of the conceptual basis for assessment in such a way that
it goes beyond psychoeducational considerations and that the pathology
is located not within the child, but "within the societal power relations
between dominant and dominated groups, in the reflection of these
power relations between school and communities, and in the mental
and cultural disabling of minority students that takes place in classrooms"
(p. 116).

Elaborating on the advocacy theme, De León (1990) suggests an
advocacy-oriented assessment process (AAP) whereby diagnosticians
play an advocacy role at every step of the process and take into account
all the variables that may impinge on LM learners. The AAP also calls
for analysis of domestic, community, school, classroom, and student
variables and takes careful note of context-embedded vs context-reduced
language proficiency in an effort to ascertain whether learning problems
are genuine or result from lack of linguistic proficiency.

Functional assessments. Another model that may hold potential for
LM students is the functional approach to assessment proposed by Sugai
and Maheady (1988). This type of assessment entails an examination
of students' academic/behavioral performance within the context of
their existing instructional environments. This model avoids placing the
responsibility for learning or performance on the student; evaluation
focuses on the instructional process itself (i.e., teaching behaviors,
instructional organization) and on those teacher and student behaviors
that can be modified. Its major components are: (a) analysis of classroom
and school learning environments; (b) collection of data that are directly
relevant to teaching; (c) attention to the predisposing factors that

characterize learners, teachers, administrators, and other school personnel (e.g., culture, expectations, tolerance levels); (d) focus on student and teacher behaviors and the context and conditions under which they occur; and (e) develop and implement prereferral interventions that force an assessment of students' current learning environment and provide documentation for each attempt.

Sugai and Maheady (1988) also advocate for a series of ongoing interventions and assessments over a period of time in which school psychologists, regular teachers, SPED teachers, and administrators all collaborate.

Alternative Assessment Methods

Review of past history and past records. The importance of past history has been found to be especially relevant with migrant worker children, who may move from year to year and often within the same school year. Salend (1990) and Coballes-Vega and Salend (1988) describe the usefulness of computerized nationwide data systems such as the Migrant Student Record Transfer System (MSRTS) to alleviate some of the problems posed by frequent moving, especially in the case of SPED students, for whom time is likely to be wasted. The MSRTS collects and maintains health and academic records for more than half a million migrant children throughout the United States. Where applicable, SPED data are also recorded including services provided, assessment results, handicapping conditions, individualized educational programs (IEPs), and references for locating key personnel in the child's previous school.

In her own clinical work, the author found that for various reasons many children referred for SPED evaluation had switched from regular to bilingual to regular programs (or vice versa) along their school careers. Often the changes in program resulted from a family move, with the child moving into a district not offering a bilingual option and then moving back again into a district that did. The curricular discontinuity of such moves can be detrimental to skill acquisition. Related to the need to consider curricular exposure is the need to take into account "transition" students, i.e., students who have just been mainstreamed after several years of bilingual instruction; the instructional shift is sometimes abrupt, and students may not be equipped to handle it (NACCBE, 1988), which can be misleading in terms of the disparity created between English academic achievement and potential.

Observation. Observation is highly valued in the assessment of bilingual children (Esquivel, 1985; Fradd, Barona, & Santos de Barona, 1989; Wilen & Sweeting, 1986). It has been found useful in general assessment and in the assessment of language abilities. Referring to language assessment, Figueroa (1990b) calls observation "the most useful and informative" of current approaches. He considers observation more useful than home language surveys or standardized tests. The technique proposed by Figueroa includes dialogues with the child in L1 and L2; interviews with teachers, parents, and peers on the child's formal and informal communicative competence; and observations of the child's involvement in games that entail sociodramatic play.

According to Alvarez (1988), observations may range from the casual to the systematic; from participant observation to direct observation through videotapes and recordings. Observations in different settings (classroom, lunchroom, recess, home, community), and by different observers (parents, teachers, diagnosticians) are useful since people are known to behave differently under different circumstances and under different levels of structure. Observations may have a restricted or an expanded focus, depending on whether the object of study is the individual child, or the whole group, as seen in classroom interaction analyses.

A systematic approach to observation is the practice of using checklists or record forms. De León (1990) proposes such a form for analyzing context-embedded and context-reduced language.

Interviews. Interviews also range from the casual to the systematic and are considered a useful tool with bilingual children (Esquivel, 1985; Wilen & Sweeting, 1986). Interviews may be used in eliciting past history and background information regarding the child (e.g., developmental history, education, health); the family (e.g., household data, language use patterns, coping and support systems); or current classroom performance. They may also be useful in assessing children's self-perceptions, feelings, or coping skills. Relevant interviewees are children, parents, teachers, and other school personnel.

Ecological assessment. Ecological assessment views the individual as part of and embedded in the larger context of an environment. The major tools of ecological assessment are focused observations and interviewing. A variant of ecological assessment is the analysis of learning environments. Psychoeducational assessment is often isolated from the learning environment where it occurs. For instance, even among persons charged with assessment, there is often a lack of familiarity with the curricular options subsumed under bilingual programs: bilingual-biliterate instruction (where both L1 and L2 are used in teaching, in communication) and bilingual-monoliterate programs (where literacy is taught only in L2, but both L1 and L2 are used for communication), despite the fact that such programs result in different instructional implications for learners.

A harder-to-detect difficulty is that not all bilingual programs are similar in the amount of instruction allocated to one or the other language. There seems to be disparity between what is written "on paper" and what is observed in practice (NACCBE, 1988). In one school in which the author worked, the first grade was truly bilingual, and both teacher and aide exhibited native, or near native, speaker competencies in the two languages. The second grade, taught by a Spanish-dominant teacher, emphasized Spanish to the neglect of English. The third grade, taught by another truly bilingual teacher, emphasized English due to philosophical—not linguistic—views of the teacher. The fourth grade was bilingual, and the fifth grade, taught by an English dominant "bilingual" teacher, again emphasized English. Thus, the teaching that goes on in a "bilingual" classroom often results from the linguistic competencies and/or philosophical convictions of the teachers involved, quite apart from district or school policy and regardless of the official label applied to the service delivery model. As bilingual programs are often housed under administrators who cannot evaluate these differences in instructional emphases, they often go undetected. Thus, what is important is curriculum rather than assumptions about "equal time" allotted to instruction of one language or the other. While the instructional implications may be major, it is difficult to detect such curricular subtleties.

Test-teach-test paradigms. Test-teach-test paradigms are considered an attractive alternative to standardized tests in that they can be used in promoting learning, not just in measuring (Duran, 1989). Major exponents of this paradigm are Feuerstein and colleagues (Feuerstein, Rand, & Hoffman, 1979). Their diagnostic system, the Learning Potential Assessment Device (LPAD), attempts to assess children's learning capacity rather than provide a measure of what children know. The LPAD aims at tapping the very act of learning and the manners and modalities through which learning is best achieved. Tasks follow a structured progression, but the emphasis is on flexibility rather than on a rigid adherence to test instructions and procedures as is required in standardized testing. Since processes—rather than products—are key, examiners assume the active role of teachers rather than the passive role of test administrators. The educational complement of the LPAD is Instrumental Enrichment (IE) (Feuerstein, Rand, Hoffman, & Miller, 1980), a system of cognitive redevelopment addressed to the process of learning itself and to developing the strategies for learning how to learn.

Because they stemmed from work with migrant, low SES children and adolescents in Israel, LPAD and IE appear relevant to LM children in the United States, yet their strengths and weaknesses in this setting have not yet been fully established (Figueroa, 1990b; Holtzman & Wilkinson, 1991). Given the approach to assessment in most U.S. settings—where cognitive explorations serve decision making purposes, where psychological work is reimbursed on a "per head" basis, and where evaluations are conducted under time constraints—incorporation and adoption of such techniques will probably move slowly. The potential utility of the approach for bilingual SPED has been highlighted in a case study of a Hispanic boy (Haywood, 1988).

Working with Budoff's test-teach-test approach, Hausman (1988) also found the approach useful in tapping at cognitive resources masked by more conventional approaches in the case of a Mexican American special needs youth.

Linking Assessment to Instruction

Several techniques link assessment to instruction. Among these are curriculum based assessment, criterion referenced testing, and the portfolio approach.

Curriculum-based assessment (CBA). The importance of a close connection between assessment and the situations in which teaching and learning normally take place continues to be emphasized (Au, Scheu, Kawakami, & Herman, 1990), and CBA is currently being tried out on a large scale for bilingual exceptional students as part of the Innovative Approaches Research Project (*Forum*, 1990). The aim of CBA is to design assessment systems that are as close to ongoing classroom activities as possible.

Criterion referenced testing (CRT). Data based assessment processes such as CRT continue to be advocated for offering direct feedback to teachers, allowing comparisons over time, and flowing directly from instruction. A system for informally assessing written work which holds potential for LM students has been recently proposed (Minner, Prater, Su:lavan, & Gwaltney, 1989). It entails eliciting a writing sample in response to a picture or questions about an experience a student has had. Teachers can then analyze it with regard to fluency, sentence types, vocabulary, structure, and ideation.

The portfolio approach. The portfolio approach to assessment of reading and literacy is one more effort in the movement toward linking assessment to the situations in which teaching and learning normally take place. Almost no reference could be located regarding the use of portfolios with LM students. However, the approach appears to have great potential (for use of this approach as a screening procedure with LM young children, see Harris Stefanakis' chapter in this volume). Portfolios document students' reading and writing growth over a period of time. As Farr (cited in Jongsma, 1989) indicates, portfolios are traditionally used by professionals such as artists and models as a way of accumulating work samples showing the scope of their work, their evolving interests, and their abilities.

While there is a great deal of variation, as currently used in schools, portfolios are a growing, evolving description of students' reading and writing experiences and of other indicators of learning. Students (alone or with teachers and parents) select essays, poems, or stories they have written or tests they have taken. They keep track of books, articles, or newspaper clippings they have read and meet regularly with their teachers to discuss the contents or share reactions about reading and writing. Teacher's running notes or reading development checklists and student's self-evaluations may also be included in a portfolio. Matthews (1990) also reports of teachers who collect audiotapes of their student's reading. It is precisely students who do poorly on standardized tests who may benefit the most from keeping track of samples of work performed under more natural conditions and from this periodic sampling and close monitoring of their class work.

Valencia (1990) highlights several aspects of the portfolio approach: (a) it deals with authentic texts representing actual classroom and life reading tasks; (b) it captures the process of learning over a period of time; (c) it is multidimensional; and (d) it is based on active collaboration between teacher and student. In addition to academic data, portfolios may include information on motivational and affective dimensions (Au, Scheu, Kawakami, & Herman, 1990).

Referral Prevention and Prereferral Interventions

Minority overrepresentation in special education continues to be a problem. Once a referral is made, the likelihood of testing is high;

and once testing occurs, strong gravitational forces toward SPED placement are set into motion. Reynolds (cited in García & Ortiz, 1988) calculated that the referral-to-assessment-to-placement rates oscillate between 75 percent and 90 percent.

One way of alleviating the problem is through preventing premature referrals by providing various supports to mainstream teachers and by identifying alternative practices and curricular modifications that can be implemented prior to referral (García & Ortiz, 1988; Maheady, Towne, Algozzine, Mercer, & Ysseldyke, 1983). The process has taken the form of teacher assistance teams, teacher support groups, various consultation models with differing degrees of collaboration, prereferral screening instruments or checklists, etc. Some models pair mainstream teachers with SPED teachers or with pupil support personnel such as school psychologists or LD specialists; other models pair up administrators and teachers; still others include only mainstream teachers. Teams may be made up of two people or more. They may consist of a core group, or membership may be determined according to need. Prereferral activities are praised on many grounds: for their cost effectiveness by reducing inappropriate referrals; for their potential to reduce misplacement; for strengthening teacher capabilities; for making it possible to keep students within least restrictive environments; for enhancing collaboration between school personnel and reducing some of the isolation of teaching; and for helping to pinpoint what the diagnostic nuances of a case may be.

Prereferral screening instruments. Benavides (1988) describes the Prereferral Screening Instrument (PSI), developed for prereferral screening of LM students. The PSI records four kinds of data: background information, educational history, achievement/behavioral information, and previous tests and other screening.

Teacher Assistance Teams. Ortiz and García (1988a) and García and Ortiz (1988) propose a comprehensive prereferral model for LM students. The model is based on the use of Teacher Assistance Teams—comprised of regular classroom teachers—to assist individual teachers in prereferral problem solving. The process entails analyzing teacher characteristics (e.g., teaching style, language proficiency, culture, expectations, perceptions); instructional variables (past learning history, basic skill acquisition, mastery levels); student characteristics (e.g., language, culture, SES, experiential background); and using all resources available during all stages of the process. A major goal of the prereferral process is to distinguish between real handicapping conditions and transient difficulties students might be having due to language, adaptation, or curricular mismatches. An important secondary goal is to ameliorate the quality of regular education for LM students by inviting reflection, enlisting collaboration, maximizing resources, and enabling teachers to better deal with LM students.

Collaborative decision making models. While not specifically suggested for LM students, the collaborative model proposed by Donaldson and Christiansen (1990) brings together all educators responsible for a student's daily instruction and provides a framework for determining the least intrusive forms of assistance needed to maintain special needs students in the regular classroom. The model consists of five basic options: (a) behavior management (self-monitored, teacher-mediated, peer-mediated); (b) part-time assistance (team teaching, peer tutoring, buddy systems); (c) instructional options (adapted regular curriculum, modified instructional delivery, modifications in required student responses); (d) instructional options combined with part-time assistance; and (e) full-time assistance (team teaching, paraprofessional, volunteer). Depending on the case, the team might consider one or several of these options and will proceed to determine how they will be implemented and evaluated. Only after these possibilities are exhausted does the team consider pull-out alternatives.

Mainstream assistance teams (MATs). MATs, like other systems of prereferral support to classroom teachers, are also aimed at finding ways of assisting teachers with the classroom and instructional modifications necessary to maintain difficult to teach students in the regular classroom (Fuchs, Fuchs, & Bahr, 1990). How MATs differ from other systems is in their experimental focus: A strong effort is made at systematizing the process, at finding the best possible combinations of consultant/consultee, to test out issues of efficiency, and the most streamlined way of providing teachers the support they need.

Emphasis on high school students. Referral prevention and prereferral interventions are particularly needed at the high school level, where the association between SPED and dropping out of school is strong, especially among those classified as learning disabled (LD) or emotionally handicapped (EH) (Wyche, 1989). Language minority/LEP students enrolled in SPED who are not receiving bilingual services run the highest risk of dropping out. Current dropout rates are reported to fall between 60 percent and 70 percent for Hispanic SPED students (Larson, 1989; Wolman, Bruininks, & Thurlow, 1989). It is thus necessary to exercise extreme caution with high school and overage middle school students. A concerted effort by both parents and educators is essential in dropout prevention to ensure that special education does not precipitate student dropout.

Teacher empowerment. With student diversity increasing at an unprecedented pace, teachers need to be equipped to handle diversity in their classrooms: linguistic, cultural, socioeconomic, or family based diversity. Increased and more efficient support systems should increase teachers' ability to handle this diversity, which, in turn, would decrease referrals. The themes of teacher empowerment and collaboration are gaining popularity.

Correa (1990) asserts that empowerment allows teachers to decide what kind of inservice training is helpful to them and to seek out the supports and help they need in the classroom. Johnson, Pugach, and Devlin (1990) suggest a supportive system in which teachers freely use one another's expertise and in which collaborative bonds are established between teachers and administrators, between regular and special educators, between teachers across disciplines, and between schools and communities.

Increased Dissemination Efforts

The 1980s were a decade of great productivity in building up the knowledge base on LM children. Dissemination reached an all-time high. Pre-convention institutes, conferences, symposia, training programs, workshops, and presentations focusing on LM children abounded. Just within the course of the last three years, two training manuals (Minnesota Department of Education, 1987; Prewitt-Díaz, 1990) and several edited volumes (Ambert, 1988; Fradd & Tikunoff, 1987; Fradd & Weismantel, 1989; Gibbs & Huang, 1989; Hamayan & Damico, 1991; Jones, 1988a; Ortiz & Ramírez, 1988; Samuda, Kong, Cummins, Lewis, & Pascual-Leone, 1989) were published. There were also book chapters in several important publications (Duran, 1988; Figueroa, 1990a; Moran, 1990; Puente, 1990; Vázquez-Nuttall, De León, & Valle, 1990) and an unprecedented number of journal articles.

Professional organizations gave much attention to LM children: The Joint Committee on Testing Practices published the *Code of Fair Testing Practices in Education* (1988), a set of recommendations for test developers and test users—geared to the general public— that aims at advancing the quality of testing practices and that addresses concerns of different ethnic, racial, and linguistic groups. At this writing, the American Psychological Association's publication *Guidelines for Providers of Psychological Services to Ethnic and Culturally Diverse Populations* is in press. The National Association of Schools Psychologists sponsored a major publication (Barona & García, 1990); the Council for Exceptional Children devoted a special issue of *Exceptional Children* to Hispanic SPED students (Figueroa, Fradd, & Correa, 1989); a special issue of *American Psychologist* on children and their development included several relevant articles (Hakuta & García, 1989; Miller-Jones, 1989). In addition, a journal exclusively devoted to LM concerns was funded under a special grant, *The Journal of Educational Issues of Language Minority Children*. There is barely a volume on the disciplines related to the human services professions that does not include an article on LM children, be it education, psychology, counseling, reading, learning disabilities. Knowledge is being generated at a fast pace. The times are indeed auspicious.

Lingering Barriers

Despite advances in psychoeducational testing, several maladaptive practices continue to linger. They bring into question the viability of test based assessment and the very nature of the psychoeducational process. This section focuses on the following barriers: (a) biases in the assessment process; (b) duplication of services; (c) lack of change in assessment practices; (d) use of "standard" batteries; and (e) questionable technical adequacy of tests.

Biases in the Assessment Process

Being essentially a social situation, the assessment process is vulnerable to various effects from initial referral to the last stages of decision making. Variables such as sex, physical appearance, behavior differences, parental power, SES, minority status, language proficiency, ethnicity, and special learning needs have all been found to impinge on teachers' and diagnosticians' impressions about learners. The more of these characteristics children exhibit, the more vulnerable will be their position in the school system. Thus, language minority, low-income youngsters who also have a learning handicap are in an extremely sensitive situation.

Cervantes (1988) summarizes the various points in the assessment and decision making process where biases can creep in: (a) referral; (b) instrument selection; (c) instrument administration; (d) instrument interpretation; and (e) actual decision making following assessment. The first four stages have received much attention in the literature over the last two decades and will not be emphasized here. At the same time the scope of the process has been expanded in such a way that it rarely relies exclusively on instruments but rather on a variety of data that includes observations by various observers plus parental input. The fifth stage, that of biases following assessment, however, deserves special mention given its insidiousness, the difficulties in detection, and its importance for actual service delivery.

Over a decade ago, the report Double Jeopardy (Massachusetts Advocacy Center, 1978) highlighted the biases that can follow assessment. It found that students in Massachusetts were being placed into substantially separate programs in the following order: blacks, black Hispanics, white Hispanics, and whites. By contrast, they were being recommended for the more desirable private placements in the following order: whites, white Hispanics, black Hispanics, and blacks. Similar— though less dramatic—contrasts were found in the different program prototypes, suggesting strong biases creeping into the assessment and/ or decision making process. Unfortunately, this situation is still all too common.

Other irregularities that come to the attention of practitioners include: Children waiting for services not yet available with subsequent loss of instructional time; children integrated into programs in which they do not fully belong, pending availability of more appropriate programs specified in their IEPs. In addition, Willig and Ortiz (1991) caution against biased IEPs that do not take into account the preferred language of instruction, the type of language intervention required (whether language enrichment, language development, or language remediation), the use of curricula and materials appropriate for culturally and linguistically diverse populations, the learning styles and other learner characteristics. In addition, they underscore the importance of selecting optimal instructional approaches. Willig and Ortiz (1991) also point at what may be considered a Pandora's Box: How effective are special education teachers' instructional strategies and how much are teachers able to attain the goal of "individualizing" instruction? Though they fall outside the scope of this review, these are legitimate concerns for anyone working in bilingual or regular special education.

Duplication of Services

LM and LEP children served by public school systems, especially in inner city settings, tend to come from low income homes and from homes where there is little parental power vis-à-vis the mainstream society. Families may be involved with several agencies at the same time for several needs: health, housing, legal cases of another sibling. As a result there may be multiple referrals of the same child, often resulting in multiple assessments. It is not uncommon for a child to be tested within a span of two/three months by two different agencies. Agencies familiar with the difficulties school systems often have in complying with the 30-day limit of the referral/assessment process may seek other referral sources, in addition to the school, in the hopes that one of them will expedite services. This may lead to duplication of services, a practice from which children should be protected. Besides the problems duplication poses for test validity, the already overtested SPED bilingual population is further subject to unnecessary overtesting.

Lack of Change in Assessment Practices

Current assessment practices still hinge largely around the referral-classification-placement model based on one diagnostic session. The "medical model" approach whereby the blame for academic failure is placed on the learner, entails that the "causes" of failure be sought primarily within the learners. While alternative test- and non-test based techniques have achieved much dissemination; and the value of observation, learning environments, and curriculum has been emphasized; most SPED assessments are test-based and rely on analyses of strengths and needs of learners as identified in norm referenced tests.

The lack of change in assessment and the limited expansion of criteria are felt to be responsible for the continued underrepresentation of language minority children, especially Hispanics, in programs for the gifted and talented (Cohen, 1988).

The lack of change in the process is also felt to be responsible for the overrepresentation of LM and LEP students in speech/language handicapped and in LD categories, though problems with LD assessment appear to be a "state of the art" malady, since LD overrepresentation affects Anglo students as well (Merrell & Shinn, 1990). Overrepresentation also has to do with the limited services available to students who for other reasons (e.g., limited English language mastery, limited previous schooling prior to migration) may need additional inputs; lacking the tools and resources to help these children, teachers proceed on to refer them for special education (Cosden, 1990).

Use of "Standard" Batteries

The use of "standard" batteries, often referred to as the "cattle-dip" approach (what is good for one cow must be good for all others), is widely criticized (Batsche, 1984; Ysseldyke, Regan, Thurlow, & Schwartz, 1981). This approach refers to the practice of applying the same battery of tests or the same assessment procedures for all students regardless of referral concerns or questions. Investigators who have studied large numbers of SPED protocols of Hispanic children (Cummins, 1984; García & Yates, 1986; Maldonado-Colón, 1986) found no difference in the procedures used for assessing Anglo or Hispanic children, even in cases where children's English proficiency was at stake.

Batsche (1984) believes "standard" batteries lead to "placement" rather than to intervention strategies; to a one-method as opposed to a multi-method format; and it may only be fit to address general rather than specific concerns. As an alternative, he proposes a team-based, referral-oriented, consultative approach to assessment and decision making.

Questionable Technical Adequacy of Tests

Test development for bilingual students has progressed slowly and is plagued with difficulties. While there is much proliferation of information regarding cultural variables, an increasing number of guidelines and fair testing practices plus professional productivity have been invested in instrument development or in identifying the approaches more compatible with LM children. Most instruments available in non-English languages are in Spanish. This is not surprising, since Hispanics represent 8.1 percent of the total U.S. population, some 19.4 million persons (U.S. Department of Commerce, 1988).

Over half the tests developed for bilingual populations measure language proficiency, and follow a linguistic competence rather than a communicative competence approach. Despite the well documented dangers of translations (Figueroa, 1989, 1990b; Ford, 1980; Kim, 1980), several instruments currently used in the assessment of personality, depression, anxiety, and other psychological constructs are translations which in most instances have not even been renormed on a non-English population. Other measures boast inclusion of Hispanics or African Americans in their standardization samples but lump both groups in a "non-white" category. With the exception of TEMAS, a well researched and field tested projective test for use with Hispanic children and youth, most of the recently developed measures are Spanish reading achievement tests, the most recent one probably being La Prueba de Logros en Español (Psychological Corporation, 1989) and the Instrumento para Diagnosticar Lecturas (Blanchard, García, & Carter, 1989). The Ambert Reading Test (Ambert, 1990) is a criterion referenced test developed to identify reading difficulties in Spanish speakers, grades K through 6. A Spanish-language version of the Slingerland Screening Tests, used in identifying specific language disability in reading, writing, and spelling, was recently published after many years of field testing in Puerto Rico by Dr. Lillian Strong (Educators Publishing Service, 1989).

Even more troublesome are evaluations of technical adequacy in tests specifically developed for use with bilingual populations. Martin and Sikorsky (1986) reviewed 26 such instruments (14 language dominance or proficiency; 4 cognitive; 3 achievement; 4 social/emotional; and 1 other). They found that 38 percent of the manuals did not report any validity or reliability studies; 46 percent did not report sample size, and among those that did, 35 percent used fewer than 100 participants as their norm group. Based on their analysis of technical quality, the investigators felt they could only recommend four or five instruments out of the 26 reviewed. Thus, the current state of the art in testing technology for LM populations is weak.

Evolving Knowledge Base on Low Incidence Groups

Low incidence language/culture groups and low incidence exceptionalities have been traditionally underserved. Judging by the rate at which information is accumulating, however, there is reason for hope. This section reviews publications of the last three years regarding the following groups: (a) Asian Americans; (b) Native Americans; (c) migrant special needs children; (d) gifted and talented bilinguals; and (e) hearing impaired Hispanics. One hopes that in future reviews there will be substantial information on other currently underrepresented groups so as to warrant separate sections.

Asian Americans

The overrepresentation of Asian students in classes for the gifted and talented—2.5 percent general enrollment but 5.0 percent enrollment in gifted programs (Cohen, 1988), their generally high levels of educational achievement (Sue & Okazaki, 1990), and the low rates of severe psychopathology implied by the low use of inpatient mental health services relative to other ethnic groups (Snowden & Cheung, 1990) have contributed to create an image of a "model" minority, which, in turn, obscures the difficulties and complexities faced by the general population of Asians (Huang & Ying, 1989). Several investigations (reported in Snowden & Cheung, 1990) suggest that part of the low use of mental health services among Asians may be explained not in terms of excellent coping abilities but in terms of the level of tolerance families exhibit toward disruptive members and the sense of shame associated with use of such services. Once admitted, lengths of stay are longer for Asians than for any other ethnic group at least in county and state mental hospitals. The picture is currently incomplete due to lack of reliable knowledge about prevalence of disorder among Asian/ Pacific Islanders and lack of information on help seeking patterns, family health culture, perceived effectiveness of services, etc.

The complexities of this population are often overlooked. There are currently some 30 distinct ethnic and cultural groups under the rubric of Asian Americans, and, with the exception of the Japanese, the group is composed largely of immigrants (Huang & Gibbs, 1989). Huang and Ying (1989) present the dilemmas faced by Chinese American youth and review some of the major sociocultural issues pertinent to their sensitive assessment. A training manual to help educators achieve greater understanding of Chinese American children, their families, and issues surrounding their psychological and linguistic assessment is offered by Tinlos, Tan, and Leung (1988).

Nagata (1989) summarizes the major family, social, and migration issues pertaining to the assessment and understanding of Japanese

American children, including attitudes toward mental health services. A major aspect emphasized by Nagata is that the current pattern of service underutilization seen among Japanese Americans does not diminish the need for providing culturally sensitive interventions. Huang (1989) focuses on Southeast Asian refugees from Vietnam and Cambodia and offers insights into the challenges confronting these youth.

Sue and Okazaki (1990) interpret the educational success of Asian Americans not in terms of values that emphasize hard work, family solidarity, patience, or thrift but in terms of the opportunities denied to this group in noneducational avenues such as leadership, entertainment, sports, or politics. They express the opinion that "to the extent that mobility is limited in noneducational avenues, education becomes increasingly functional as a means for mobility when other avenues are blocked" (p. 917).

Lupi and Woo (1989) address the question of cultural and linguistic distortions in current psychoeducational instruments for East Asian students. They also discuss cultural and linguistic patterns characteristic of East Asians that will help evaluators limit bias in assessment. A more in-depth account of these and other issues can be found in Leung (1988, 1990) and in Woo (1988).

Native Americans

An extremely heterogeneous group, there are an estimated 517 federally recognized native entities between Alaska and the lower 48 states, 36 state-recognized American Indian tribes, and some 200 distinct tribal languages (cited in LaFromboise & Low, 1989). While aspects such as poverty, underachievement, increasing urbanization, the straddling between two cultures, and the pressure for acculturation into mainstream U.S. society put a common thread among Native American groups, distinct traditions, beliefs, practices, and social organization may vary from tribe to tribe and render the situation more complex.

The literature of the last three years (LaFromboise & Low, 1989; Vázquez-Nuttall, De León, & Valle, 1990) offers some perspectives regarding the personal and sociocultural factors that impinge on the accurate assessment of Native American children. Ramírez and Johnson (1988) give an overview of current practices and policies regarding American Indian children and youth with special needs and identify areas of further study and research. Henry and Pepper (1990) deal with the cognitive, affective, and cultural dimensions of learning style among

Native American children and its implications for teaching and schooling.

Technical efforts are reported by Tempest and Skipper (1988) who developed WISC-R norms for Navajo Indians. Using a sample of Native American and white adults, investigators (Davis, Hoffman, & Nelson, 1990) compared results of the California Psychological Inventory and found significant differences between women in the two groups, which they explained in terms of cultural factors and role expectations. Of concern to the investigators were the differences found on several scales used in personnel selection where—if the cultural element is not considered—Native Americans may be at a disadvantage. Studies with American Indian adolescents using the Center for Epidemiologic Studies Depression Scale (Manson, Ackerson, Dick, Baron, & Fleming, 1990) also caution about the use and interpretation of such scale with this population. The above studies underscore the potential for misinterpretation when instruments normed on one population are used for another.

Migrant Special Needs Children

Salend and associates (Coballes-Vega & Salend, 1988; Reynolds & Salend, 1990; Salend, 1990) have called attention to migrant worker special needs children. For migrant worker children—most of whom are of Hispanic origin—assessment is viewed as a key element in providing appropriate educational services. As suggested by Coballes-Vega and Salend (1988), guidelines for assessing migrant students include: identifying cultural and language background, examining adaptive behavior, checking past school history through the Migrant Student Record Transfer System (MSRTS), determining medical needs, parental involvement, interviews with past teachers, choosing appropriate assessment instruments, curriculum-based assessments, and establishing a network of community resources. Reynolds and Salend (1990) further point out the high risk of dropping out for migrant students with disabilities; such students are in a particularly vulnerable position.

Gifted and Talented Bilinguals

As is the case with mainstream children, more emphasis is given in bilingual SPED to disabilities than to strengths. Though strongly advocated by the professional community (Gallagher, 1988), the education of gifted and talented children has been a stepchild of the varying exceptionalities field. In addition, with the exception of Asians— who are actually overrepresented—language minority children are underrepresented in programs for the gifted. Hispanics, for instance, make up 9.1 percent of the school population but only 4.7 percent of those attending gifted programs (Cohen, 1988). An expansion and redefinition of the concept of giftedness and a search for the variables that indicate giftedness among minority groups are in order. Pearson and DeMers (1990) summarize efforts to that effect.

One of the difficulties in identifying gifted LM children is that most attend regular classrooms and mainstream teachers are not equipped to understand bilingualism and to spot giftedness among such groups. Bermúdez and Rakow (1990) studied teachers' degree of awareness of the cultural and linguistic variables that affect student behavior to determine how equipped mainstream teachers were to identify giftedness among Hispanic LEP students. They found such teachers lacked monitoring skills such as observation, interviewing, or informal and formal assessment measures that would help them identify giftedness.

Deaf and Hard-of-Hearing Children

Though a rather comprehensive review of psychoeducational assessment for the hearing impaired was recently conducted (Allen, Abraham, & Stoker, 1988), literature on children caught in the double predicament of being LM plus hearing impaired has been slow in building up. Bennett (1987, 1988a) explores the challenges of incorporating Hispanic deaf children and their families into formal schooling and into special education . Using participant observation over a two-year period, Bennett (1988b) conducted detailed ethnographic studies of 12 young deaf and hearing impaired Hispanic children attending private and public schools. Issues of assessment and parental-school interface are highlighted. Of particular interest are the observations that school personnel tended to be rather rigid in their perspectives, attributing difficulties to either home or child, a far cry from the "ecological" model that genuinely takes into account learning environment, parents, home, and community.

It is hoped that in the decade ahead more attention will be focused on low incidence groups such as the ones described here and that a wider literature base will begin to emerge on behalf of these groups. Other challenges expected of the 1990s are described below.

Future Trends and Evolving Research Needs

Several challenges lie in the next decade, and new developments are expected to take place. This section summarizes some of the expected changes based on current trends: (a) build up of the knowledge base on traditionally underserved and low incidence groups; (b) increased reliance on computerized psychological testing for both testing and interpretation; (c) innovations and changes in testing practices; and (d) changes in the training of educators and psychologists with collaborative efforts increasingly emphasized.

Servicing of Traditionally Underserved Groups

For a variety of reasons, certain ethnic minority groups and children with low incidence exceptionalities have been traditionally underserved. Documentation regarding best practices toward working with these groups is scant. As described above, for Asian Americans, the situation is rapidly changing, likely as a result of increasing numbers. For other groups, such as young preschool children, the major push has been legislative, and information is expected to develop at a fast pace during the 1990s. The knowledge base for other low incidence populations is expected to build at a slower but steady pace.

Computerized Psychological Testing

Computers are swiftly making their way into clinical practice and the American Psychological Association recently issued guidelines regarding computer-based testing (APA, 1986). Mainstream professionals are already experimenting with computer-based assessments and reading diagnosis via microcomputers. Special educators working with LD children (Watkins & Kush, 1988) found computerized assessments to be superior to traditional paper-and-pencil formats in terms of efficiency, student preference, and accuracy. No such efforts are yet reported for bilingual students, though sophisticated bilingual teacher-training programs in computer-assisted instruction and interactive video instruction are already operating in several universities and a body of literature is piling up regarding the feasibility of computer-assisted instruction (CAI) and interactive video instruction with LEP and LM children (cf. Faltis & DeVillar, 1990). At the same time, since microcomputers are now solidly established in special education as an instructional tool, it is only a matter of time when the two advances will merge into a bilingual/special education formula.

Research and practice with computer-based test interpretations (CBTI) and computer-assisted test interpretations (CATI) are also becoming increasingly common among mainstream populations (Gutkin & Wise, 1990; Wainer, et al., 1990) and increasingly more accessible with the options of 24-hour mail-in services or the even faster telephone/modem connections between testing services and clinicians' offices. In addition, computer-generated psychological reports are gaining popularity and proliferating at a fast rate as can be seen in the ad sections of professional newspapers and in the catalogs of test publishers. Special caution is needed in using these computerized interpretations with LM children, as they normally do not take into account issues of language, culture, or work styles so important for such students.

What seems more promising—from the perspective of clients—is the use of computer technology in test development and in testing itself not just in test correction and interpretation. As Haney and Madaus (1989) expressed it: "This vision suggests that testing might take place at a video terminal that would present the student with a simulation requiring open-ended decision making of the sort that might be encountered in real life" (p. 685). Such expanded methods would in addition make traditional formats like the multiple-choice or the "one-correct answer" obsolete. Another interesting development is using computer-generated voice prints in the diagnosis of oral reading, which allows examiners to make diagnostic observations not readily apparent from listening only (Casteel & Strange, 1990).

Test Innovations and Alternative Assessments

The 1990s will undoubtedly bring about innovations in testing formats and alternative ways of assessing student learning and abilities.

Test innovations. Multiple-choice measures relying on the single right answer may well be substituted by more open-ended performance-based assessments and by instruments that offer teachers and students feedback as to how instruction and learning can be improved. Educators and researchers in Connecticut are currently working toward designing and field testing performance based assessments with a $1 million grant from the National Science Foundation and similar attempts are also reported in California (Moses, 1990).

Pikulski (1990) notes several innovations in his review of two standardized reading tests from Australia and Great Britain. The Australian test, for instance, assesses comprehension by written (or dictated) retelling in such a way that more than one correct response is possible. There is flexibility as to what passages teachers choose for students. They are instructed to choose passages that students are able to read and respond to. The British test uses an innovative format which does not look at all like a test but rather like a short, colorful, illustrated paperback. In addition, the Teacher's Manual is relaxed in its instructions, encourages help where needed, and instructs teachers to remind students to refer back to the test for answers or to consider that not all the answers are directly stated in the text.

Current trends also reflect increasing interest in informal assessments for LM students (De León, 1990). It is in addition expected that more interest will be reflected for bilingual populations in such teaching/ learning strategies as portfolios. As Pikulski (1989) expressed it, referring to reading, "assessment of reading must shift from being test-centered to being teacher- and pupil-centered" (p. 80).

Training and Professional Practice Needs

School psychology and bilingual special education are fields in transition. Demographic shifts in LM populations, changing perceptions of professional roles, evolving family structures, are bringing about new roles and requiring expertise in areas not currently emphasized in training. There is a need to match field-based needs with professional training.

Demographic shifts underscore the need for increased training in working with language and culturally different populations. This requires both the training of personnel who themselves are members of LM groups as well as expanding the knowledge base regarding such groups for all students currently in training.

There is currently a need to meet evolving trends in assessment. The repertoire of practices and techniques used in psychoeducational assessment needs to be expanded. Training in techniques such as observation, interviewing, test-teach-test paradigms, and in the practices that seek to link assessment with instruction (e.g., CBA, CRT, portfolios) should complement training in standardized techniques. Another important curricular addition deals with language, bilingualism, language assessment theories, assessment, etc. Another neglected area is reading, both theory and diagnosis. In their survey of practicing school psychologists, Fish and Margolis (1988) found major discrepancies between training and actual job responsibilities. Psychologists in their sample acknowledged limited training and a need for more expertise in reading yet reported that 77 percent of their referrals entailed reading problems for which they felt ill-equipped. Thus, training has to come closer to actual field needs.

The 1980s highlighted the need for collaboration among school personnel. Professionals working in schools today need to be equipped for collaborative roles and for consultative roles as the demands build up for indirect rather than direct services in schools. Prereferral consultations, teacher assistance teams, and mainstream assistance teams will all necessitate consultative skills on the part of school people, and this should be reflected in the training of teachers and support personnel.

Summary and Conclusions

This chapter reviewed the literature on psychoeducational assessment of language minority children, emphasizing 1988 through 1990 publications. The chapter provided an overview of the issues prominent in the 1980s and of emerging trends for the 1990s. Major types of assessment used with LM students were presented, including English proficiency testing, language proficiency testing, language assessment in special education, and psychoeducational assessment. Current trends and lingering barriers were summarized. Current trends included: advocacy on behalf of LM groups, new trends in psychoeducational assessment, alternative assessment methods, linking assessment to instruction, and referral prevention and prereferral interventions. Lingering barriers included: biases in the assessment process, duplication of services, lack of change in the assessment process, use of "standard" batteries, and questionable technical adequacy of tests.

A section was dedicated to reviewing recent publications on several low incidence language/culture groups and exceptionalities. Given the constant flux in linguistic communities and the constantly evolving school populations, people working in today's schools need to understand diversity.

While the literature and scientific basis for working with LM children continues to grow, what professionals concerned with the non-biased assessment of LM and LEP students currently need is an armamentarium of flexibility, cultural and linguistic sensitivity, improved collaboration with other professionals, and a commitment to constantly search for updated knowledge and best practices.

References

Allen, W., Abraham, S., & Stoker, R. (1988). Providers and practices in psychoeducational assessment of the hearing impaired in educational settings. *Diagnostique, 14*, 26–48

Alvarez, M.D. (1977). Practical considerations in the psychoeducational assessment of minority students: The case of bilingual Hispanics. *Proceedings of a Multi-Cultural Colloquium on Non-Biased Pupil Assessment* (pp. 79–116). Albany: State Education Department.

Alvarez, M.D. (1988). Psychoeducational assessment of bilingual students: Current trends and major issues. In Ambert, A.N. (Ed.) *Bilingual education and English as a second language: A research handbook, 1986–1987* (pp. 297–332). New York: Garland.

Ambert, A.N. (Ed.). (1988). *Bilingual education and English as a second language: A research handbook (1986–1987)*. New York: Garland.

Ambert, A.N. (1990) Ambert Reading Test (ART). New York: Arcadia.

American Psychological Association (1986). *Guidelines for computer-based tests and interpretations*. Washington, DC: Author.

American Psychological Association (in press). *Guidelines for providers of psychological services to ethnic and culturally diverse populations*. Washington, DC: Author.

Au, K.H., Scheu, J.A., Kawakami, A.J., & Herman, P.A. (1990). Assessment and accountability in a whole literacy curriculum. *The Reading Teacher, 43*, 574–578.

Baker, K. (1990). Bilingual education's 20-year failure to provide civil rights protection for language-minority students. In Barona, A. & Garcia, E.E. (Eds.) *Children at risk: Poverty, minority status, and other issues in educational equity* (pp. 29–51). Washington, DC: National Association of School Psychologists.

Barona, A., & Hernandez, A.E. (1990). Use of projective techniques in the assessment of Hispanic school children. In Barona, A. & Garcia, E.E. (Eds.) *Children at risk: Poverty, minority status, and other issues in educational equity* (pp. 297–304). Washington, DC: National Association of School Psychologists.

Barona, A., Santos de Barona, M., Flores, A.A., & Gutierrez, M.H. (1990). Critical issues in training school psychologists to serve minority school children. In Barona, A. & Garcia, E.E. (Eds.) *Children at risk: Poverty, minority status, and other issues in educational equity* (pp. 187–200). Washington, DC: National Association of School Psychologists.

Batsche, G.M. (1984) Referral-oriented, consultative approach to assessment/ decision making. Kent, OH: National Association of School Psychologists.

Benavides, A. (1988). High risk predictors and prereferral screening for language minority students. In Ortiz, A.A. & Ramirez, B.A. (Eds.) *Schools and the culturally diverse exceptional student: Promising practices and future directions* (pp. 19–31). Reston, VA: The Council for Exceptional Children.

Bennett, A.T. (1987). *Schooling the different: Case studies of Hispanic deaf children's initiation into formal schooling.* Jackson Heights, NY: The Lexington Center.

Bennett, A.T. (1988a). Gateways to powerlessness: Incorporating Hispanic deaf children and families into formal schooling. *Disability, Handicap, and Society, 3,* 119–151.

Bennett, A.T. (1988b). *Schooling the different: Incorporating deaf Hispanic children and families into special education.* London: Taylor & Francis.

Bermúdez, A.B. & Rakow, S.J. (1990). Analyzing teacher's perceptions of identification procedures for gifted and talented Hispanic limited English proficient students at risk. *The Journal of Educational Issues of Language Minority Students, 7,* Special Issue, 21–33.

Blanchard, J.S., Garcia, H.S. & Carter, R.M. (1989). *Instrumento para diagnosticar lecturas (IDL).* Dubuque, IA: Kendall/Hunt.

Bourg, E.F., Bent, R.J., McHolland, J., & Stricker, G. (1989). Standards and evaluation in the education and training of professional psychologists: The National Council of Schools of Professional Psychology Mission Bay Conference. *American Psychologist, 44,* 66–72.

Casteel, C.P. & Strange, J.H. (1990). Using computer-generated voice prints to diagnose oral reading processing. *The Reading Teacher, 44,* 68–70.

Caterino, L.C. (1990). Step-by-step procedure for the assessment of language-minority children. In Barona, A. & Garcia, E.E. (Eds.) *Children at risk: Poverty, minority status, and other issues in educational equity* (pp. 269–282). Washington, DC: National Association of School Psychologists.

Cazden, C. (1977). Language assessment: Where, what, and how. *Anthropology and Education, 8,* 83–90.

Cervantes, H.T. (1988). Nondiscriminatory assessment and informal data gathering: The case of Gonzaldo L. In Jones, R.L. (Ed.) *Psychoeducational assessment of minority group children: A casebook* (pp. 239–256). Berkeley, CA: Cobb & Henry.

Chamberlain, P. & Medeiros-Landurand, P. (1991). Practical considerations for the assessment of LEP students with special needs. In Hamayan, E.V. & Damico, J.S. (Eds.) *Limiting bias in the assessment of bilingual students* (pp. 111–156). Austin, TX: Pro-Ed.

Coballes-Vega, C. & Salend, S.J. (1988). Guidelines for assessing migrant handicapped students. *Diagnostique, 13,* 64–75.

Code of Fair Testing Practices in Education (1988). Washington, DC: Joint Committee on Testing Practices. (Information about the Joint Committee is available from the Joint Committee on Testing Practices, American Psychological Association, 1200 17th St., NW, Washington, DC 20036).

Cohen, L.M. (1988). Meeting the needs of gifted and talented minority language students: Issues and practices. *New Focus,* National Clearinghouse for Bilingual Education, Occasional Papers in Bilingual Education (8).

Correa, V. (1989). Involving culturally diverse families in the educational process. In Fradd, S.H. & Weismantel, M.J. (Eds.) *Meeting the needs of culturally and linguistically different students: A handbook for educators* (pp. 130–144). Boston: Little, Brown.

Correa, V. (1990). Advocacy for teachers. *Teaching Exceptional Children,* 22(2), 7–9.

Cosden, M.A. (1990). Expanding the role of special education. *Teaching Exceptional Children,* 22(2), 4–7.

Cummins, J. (1984). *Bilingualism and special education: Issues in assessment and pedagogy.* San Diego, CA: College Hill.

Cummins, J. (1986). Empowering minority students: A framework for intervention. *Harvard Educational Review, 56,* 18–36.

Cummins, J. (1989). A theoretical framework for bilingual special education. *Exceptional Children, 56,* 111–119.

Damico, J.S. (1985). Clinical discourse analysis: A functional approach to language assessment. In Simon, C. (Ed.) *Communication skills and classroom success: Assessment of language learning-disabled students* (pp. 164–204). San Diego: College Hill.

Damico, J.S. (1991). Descriptive assessment of communicative ability in limited English proficient children. In Hamayan, E.V. & Damico, J.S. (Eds.) *Limiting bias in the assessment of bilingual students* (pp. 157–218). Austin, TX: Pro-Ed.

Damico, J.S., Oller, J.W., & Storey, M.E. (1983). The diagnosis of language disorders in bilingual children: Surface-oriented and pragmatic criteria. *Journal of Speech and Hearing Disorders, 48,* 385–394.

Danwitz, M.W. (1976). Identification and treatment of language disorders in young children. Paper presented at the meeting of the Orton Society, New York, NY.

Davis, G.L., Hoffman, R.G., & Nelson, K.S. (1990). Differences between Native Americans and Whites on the California Psychological Inventory. *Psychological Assessment, 2,* 238–242.

De León, J. (1990). A model for an advocacy-oriented assessment process in the psychoeducational evaluation of culturally and linguistically different students. *The Journal of Educational Issues of Language Minority Students, 7,* Special Issue, 53–67.

Donaldson, R. & Christiansen, J. (1990). Consultation and collaboration: A decision-making model. *Teaching Exceptional Children, 22*(2), 22–25.

Duran, R.P. (1988). Testing of linguistic minorities, In Linn, R. (Ed.) *Educational measurement* (3rd ed., pp. 573–587). New York: Macmillan.

Duran, R.P. (1989). Assessment and instruction of at-risk Hispanic students. *Exceptional Children, 56,* 154–158.

Educators Publishing Service. *Spanish Adaptation of the Slingerland Screening Tests.* Cambridge, MA: Author.

Esquivel, G. (1985). Best practices in the assessment of limited English proficient and bilingual children. In Thomas, A. & Grimes, J. (Eds.) *Best practices in school psychology.* Kent, OH: National Association of School Psychologists.

Faltis, C.J. & DeVillar, R.A. (Eds.). (1990). *Language minority students and computers.* Binghamton, NY: Haworth.

Feuerstein, R., Rand, Y., & Hoffman, M. (1979). *The dynamic assessment of retarded performers. The Learning Potential Assessment Device: Theory, instruments, and techniques.* Baltimore: University Park Press.

Feuerstein, R., Rand, Y., Hoffman, M. & Miller, R. (1980). *Instrumental enrichment: An intervention program for cognitive modifiability.* Baltimore: University Park Press.

Figler, C.S. (in press). Puerto Rican families on the U.S. mainland: Stresses and support systems. In Ambert, A.N. & Alvarez, M.D. (Eds.) *Puerto Rican children on the mainland: Interdisciplinary perspectives.* New York: Garland.

Figueroa, R. (1989). Psychological testing of linguistic-minority students: Knowledge gaps and regulations. *Exceptional Children, 56,* 145–152.

Figueroa, R. (1990a). Assessment of linguistic minority group children. In Reynolds. C.R. & Kamphaus, R.W. (Eds.) *Handbook of psychological and educational assessment of children: Intelligence and achievement.* New York: Guilford.

Figueroa, R. (1990b). Best practices in the assessment of bilingual children. In Thomas, A. & Grimes, J. (Eds.) *Best practices in school psychology-II* (pp. 93–106). Washington, DC: The National Association of School Psychologists.

Figueroa, R.A., Fradd, S.H., & Correa, V. (1989). Meeting the multicultural needs of the Hispanic students in special education (special issue). *Exceptional Children, 56*(2).

Fish, M.C. & Margolis, H. (1988). Training and practice of school psychologists in reading assessment and intervention. *Journal of School Psychology, 26,* 399–404.

Ford, B. (1980). Some considerations in construction and administering language proficiency tests. In Rodriguez, V. (Ed.). *Language proficiency assessment: What does that mean. A report of the NABE Pre-Conference Workshop.* Los Alamitos, CA: National Center for Bilingual Research.

Forum (1990). An assessment and intervention model for the bilingual exceptional child. *13*(3), 6–7.

Fradd, S.H., Barona, A., & Santos de Barona, M. (1989). Implementing change and monitoring progress. In Fradd, S.H. & Weismantel, M.J. (Eds.) *Meeting the needs of culturally and linguistically different students: A handbook for educators* (pp. 63–105). San Diego, CA: College Hill.

Fradd, S.H., & Tikunoff, W.J. (Eds.). (1987). *Bilingual education and bilingual special education: A guide for administrators*. Boston: Little, Brown.

Fradd, S.H., & Weismantel, J. (Eds.). (1989). *Meeting the needs of culturally and linguistically different students: A handbook for educators*. Boston: Little, Brown.

Fuchs, D., Fuchs, L.S., & Bahr, M.W. (1990). Mainstream assistance teams: A scientific basis for the art of consultation. *Exceptional Children, 57*, 128–139.

Galagan, J.E. (1985). Psychoeducational testing: Turn out the lights, the party's over. *Exceptional Children, 52*, 288–299.

Gallagher, J.J. (1988). National agenda for educating gifted students: Statements of priorities. *Exceptional Children, 55*, 107–114.

Garcia, E.E. (1990). Language-minority education litigation policy: "The law of the land." In Barona, A. & Garcia, E.E. (Eds.) *Children at risk: Poverty, minority status, and other issues in educational equity* (pp. 53–63). Washington, DC: National Association of School Psychologists.

Garcia, S.B. & Ortiz, A.A. (1988). Preventing inappropriate referrals of language minority students to special education. *New Focus*, National Clearinghouse for Bilingual Education, Occasional Papers in Bilingual Education (5).

Garcia, S.B. & Yates, J.R. (1986). Policy issues associated with serving bilingual exceptional children. In Willig, A.C. & Greenberg, H.F. (Eds.) *Bilingualism and learning disabilities: Policy and practice for teachers and administrators* (pp. 113–134). New York: American Library.

Gerber, M.M. & Levine-Donnerstein, D. (1989). Educating all children: Ten years later. *Exceptional Children, 56*, 17–27.

Gibbs, J.T. & Huang, L.N. (1989). A conceptual framework for assessing and treating minority youth. In Gibbs, J.T. & Huang, L.N. (Eds.) *Children of color: Psychological interventions with minority youth* (pp. 1–29). San Francisco: Jossey-Bass.

Gutkin, T.B. & Wise, S. (1990). *The computer and the decision-making process*. Hillsdale, NJ: Erlbaum.

Hakuta, K. & Garcia, E.E. (1989). Bilingualism and education. *American Psychologist, 44*, 374–379.

Hamayan, E. & Damico, J.S. (Eds.). (1990). *Limiting bias in the assessment of bilingual students*. Austin, TX: Pro-Ed.

Hamayan, E.V., Kwiat, J.A., & Perlman, R. (1985). *The identification and assessment of language-minority students: A handbook for educators*. Arlington Heights, IL: Illinois Resource Center.

Hammill, D. & McNutt, G. (1981). *The correlates of reading: The consensus of thirty years of correlational research.* Austin, TX: Pro-Ed.

Haney, W. & Madaus, G. (1989). Searching for alternatives to standardized tests: Whys, whats, and whithers. *Phi Delta Kappan, 70,* 683–687.

Hausman, R.M. (1988). The use of Budoff's learning potential assessment techniques with a Mexican-American, moderately handicapped student. In Jones, R.L. (Eds.) *Psychoeducational assessment of minority group children: A casebook* (pp. 65–75). Berkeley, CA: Cobb & Henry.

Haywood, C. (1988). Dynamic assessment: The Learning Potential Assessment Device. In Jones, R.L. (Ed.). *Psychoeducational assessment of minority group children: A casebook* (pp. 39–63). Berkeley, CA: Cobb & Henry.

Henry, S.L. & Pepper, F.C. (1990). Cognitive, social, and cultural effects on Indian learning style: Classroom implications. *The Journal of Educational Issues of Language Minority Students, 7,* Special Issue, 85–97.

Hilliard, A.G. (1989). Back to Binet: The case against the use of IQ tests in the schools. *Diagnostique, 14,* 125–135.

Holtzman, W.H. & Wilkinson, C.Y. (1991). Assessment of cognitive ability. In Hamayan, E.V. & Damico, J.S. (Eds.) *Limiting bias in the assessment of bilingual students.* (pp. 247–280). Austin, TX: Pro-Ed.

Huang, L.N. (1989). Southeast Asian refugee children and adolescents. In Gibbs, J.T. & Huang, L.N. (Eds.). *Children of color: Psychological interventions with minority youth* (pp. 278–321). San Francisco: Jossey-Bass.

Huang, L.N. & Gibbs, J.T. (1989). Future directions: Implications for research, training, and practice. In Gibbs, J.T. & Huang, L.N. (Eds.) *Children of color: Psychological interventions with minority youth* (pp. 30–66). San Francisco: Jossey-Bass.

Huan, L.N. & Ying, Y. (1989). Chinese American children and adolescents. In Gibbs, J.T. & L.N. Huang (Eds.) *Children of color: Psychological interventions with minority youth* (pp. 30–66). San Francisco: Jossey-Bass.

Jax, V.A. (1988). Understanding school language proficiency through the assessment of story construction. In Ortiz, A.A. & Ramirez, B.A. (Eds.). *Schools and the culturally diverse exceptional student: Promising practices and future directions* (pp. 45–50). Reston, VA: The Council for Exceptional Children.

Johnson, L.J., Pugach, M.C., & Devlin, S. (1990). Professional collaboration. *Teaching Exceptional Children, 22*(2), 9–11.

Jones, R.L. (1988a). *Psychoeducational assessment of minority group children: A casebook.* Berkeley, CA: Cobb & Henry.

Jones, R.L. (1988b). Psychoeducational assessment of minority group children: Issues and perspectives. In Jones, R.L. (Ed.) *Psychoeducational assessment of minority group children: A casebook* (pp. 13–35). Berkeley, CA: Cobb & Henry.

Jongsma, K.S. (1989). Portfolio assessment. *The Reading Teacher, 43,* 264–265.

Kim, K.K. (1980). Adaptation of English proficiency instruments for Korean. In Rodriguez, V. (Ed.) *Language proficiency assessment: What does that mean. A report of the NABE pre-conference workshop.* Los Alamitos, CA: National Center for Bilingual Research.

LaFromboise, T.D. & Low, K.G. (1989). American Indian children and adolescents. In Gibbs, J.T. & Huang, L.N. (Eds.) *Children of color: Psychological interventions with minority youth* (pp. 114–147). San Francisco: Jossey-Bass.

Langdon, H.W. (1988). Gloria: A bilingual language/learning disabled student. In Jones, R.L. (Ed.) *Psychoeducational assessment of minority group children: A casebook* (pp. 257–269). Berkeley, CA: Cobb & Henry.

Langdon, H.W. (1989). Language disorder or difference: Assessing the language skills of Hispanic students. *Exceptional Children, 56,* 160–167.

Larson, K.A. (1989). Task-related and interpersonal problem-solving training for increasing school success in high-risk young adolescents. *Remedial and Special Education, 10*(6), 32–52.

Leung, E.K. (1988). Cultural and acculturational commonalities and diversities among Asian Americans: Identification and programming considerations. In Ortiz, A.A. & Ramirez, B.A. (Eds.) *Schools and the culturally diverse exceptional student: Promising practices and future directions* (pp. 86–95). Reston, VA: The Council for Exceptional Children.

Leung, E.K. (1990). Early risks: Transition from culturally/linguistically diverse homes to formal schooling. *The Journal of Educational Issues of Language Minority Students, 7,* 35–52.

Lupi, M.H. & Woo, J.Y.T. (1989). Issues in the assessment of East Asian handicapped students. *Diagnostique, 14,* 147–158.

Maheady, L., Towne, R., Algozzine, B., Mercer, J., & Ysseldyke, J. (1983). Minority overrepresentation: A case for alternative practices prior to referral. *Learning Disability Quarterly, 6,* 448–456.

Maldonado-Colón, E. (1986). Assessment: Considerations upon interpreting data of linguistically/culturally different students referred for disabilities or disorders. In Willig, A.C. & Greenberg, H.F. (Eds.) *Bilingualism and learning disabilities: Policy and practice for teachers and administrators* (pp. 69–77). New York: American Library.

Manson, S.M., Ackerson, L.M., Dick, R.W., Baron, A.E., & Flemming, C.M. (1990). Depressive symptoms among American Indian adolescents: Psychometric characteristics of the Center for Epidemiologic Studies Depression Scale (CES-D). *Psychological Assessment, 2,* 231–237.

Martin, M. & Sikorsky, S. (1986). Technical adequacy of tests for bilingual students. Paper presented at the meeting of the National Association of School Psychologists, Hollywood, FL.

Massachusetts Advocacy Center (1978). *Double Jeopardy.* Boston: Author.

Matthews, J.K. (1990). From computer management to portfolio assessment. *The Reading Teacher, 43,* 421–421.

Merrell, K.W. & Shinn, M.R. (1990). Critical variables in the learning disabilities identification process. *School Psychology Review, 19,* 74–82.

Miller-Jones, D. (1989). Culture and testing. *American Psychologist, 44,* 360–366.

Minner, S., Prater, G., Sullavan, C., & Gwaltney, W. (1989). Informal assessment of written expression. *Teaching Exceptional Children, 21*(2), 76–79.

Minnesota Department of Education, (1987). *A resource handbook for the assessment and identification of LEP students with special education needs.* White Bear Lake, MN: Minnesota Curriculum Services Center.

Moran, R. (1990). The problem of cultural bias in personality assessment. In C.B. Reynolds & R.W. Kamphaus (Eds.) *Handbook of psychological and educational assessment of children: Personality, behavior, and context.* New York: Guilford.

Moses, S. (1990). Assessors seek test that teaches. *APA Monitor, 21*(11), 1–37.

Nagata, D.K. (1989). Japanese American children and adolescents. In Gibbs, J.T. & Huang, L.N. (Eds.) *Children of color: Psychological interventions with minority youth* (pp. 67–113). San Francisco: Jossey-Bass.

National Advisory and Coordinating Council on Bilingual Education (1988). *Twelfth Annual Report.* Washington, DC: Author.

Nichols, C.E., & Nichols, R.S. (1990). *Dropout prediction and prevention (DPP).* Brandon, VT: Clinical Psychology Publishing Company.

Nuttall, E.V. (1987). Survey of current practices in the psychological assessment of LEP children. *Journal of School Psychology, 25,* 53–61.

Ortiz, A.A. & García, S.B. (1988). A prereferral process for preventing inappropriate referrals of Hispanic students to special education. In Ortiz, A.A. & Ramirez, B.A. (Eds.) *Schools and the culturally diverse exceptional student: Promising practices and future directions* (pp. 6–18). Reston, VA: The Council for Exceptional Children.

Ortiz, A.A. & Polyzoi, E. (1988). Language assessment of Hispanic learning disabled and speech and language handicapped students: Research in progress. In Ortiz, A.A. & Ramirez, B.A. (Eds.) *Schools and the culturally diverse exceptional student: Promising practices and future directions* (pp. 32–44). Reston, VA: The Council for Exceptional Children.

Ortiz, A.A. & Ramírez, B.A. (Eds.) (1988). *Schools and the culturally diverse exceptional student: Promising practices and future directions.* Reston, VA: The Council for Exceptional Children.

Pearson, C.A. & DeMers, S.T. (1990). Identifying the culturally diverse gifted child. In Barona, A. & Garcia, E.E. (Eds.) *Children at risk: Poverty, minority status, and other issues in educational equity* (pp. 283–296). Washington, DC: National Association of School Psychologists.

Pianta, R.C. & Reeve, R.E. (1990). Preschool screening of ethnic minoirty children and children of poverty: Issues for practice and research. In A. Barona & E.E. Garcia (Eds.). *Children at risk: Poverty, minority status,* and other issues in educational equity (pp. 259–268). Washington, DC: National Association of School Psychologists.

Pikulski, J.J. (1989). The assessment of reading: A time for change? *The Reading Teacher, 1*, 80–81.

Pikulski, J.J. (1990). The role of tests in a literacy assessment program. *The Reading Teacher, 43*, 686–688.

Prewitt-Díaz, J.O. (1990). *The process and procedures for identifying exceptional language minority students*. College Park, PA: Division of Curriculum and Instruction, The Pennsylvania State University.

Prout, T.H. (1983). School psychologists and social-emotional assessment techniques: patterns in training and use. *School Psychology Review, 12*, 377–384.

Prutting, C. (1984). Assessing communicative behavior using a language sample. In Omark, D.R. & Erickson, J.G.(Eds.). *The bilingual exceptional child* (pp. 89–102). San Diego: College Hill.

Psychological Corporation. *Aprenda: La Prueba de Logros en Español*. New York: Author.

Puente, A.E. (1990). Psychological assessment of minority group members. In Goldstein, G. & Hersen, M. (Eds.) *Handbook of psychological assessment* (second edition). New York: Pergamon.

Pugach, M.C. & Johnson, L.J. (1989). Prereferral interventions: Progress, problems, and challenges. *Exceptional Children, 56*, 217–226.

Ramage, J.C. (1986). Legal influences on the assessment process. Paper presented at the meeting of the National Association of School Psychologists, Hollywood, FL.

Ramirez, A.G. (1990). Perspectives on language proficiency assessment. In Barona, A. & Garcia, E.E. (Eds.) *Children at risk: Poverty, minority status, and other issues in educational equity* (pp. 305–324). Washington, DC: National Association of School Psychologists.

Ramirez, B.A. & Johnson, M.J. (1988). American Indian exceptional children: Improved practices and policy. In Ortiz, A.A. & Ramirez, B.A. (Eds.). *Schools and the culturally diverse exceptional student: Promising practices and future directions* (pp. 128–140). Reston, VA: The Council for Exceptional Children.

Reynolds, C.J. & Salend, S.J. (1990). Issues and programs in the delivery of special education services to migrant students with disabilities. *The Journal of Educational Issues of Language Minority Students, 7*, Special Issue, 69–83.

Salend, S.J. (1990). A migrant education guide for special educators. *Teaching Exceptional Children, 22*(2), 18–21.

Salvia, J. & Ysseldyke, J.E. (1988). *Assessment in special and remedial education* (4th ed.). Boston: Houghton Mifflin.

Samuda, R.J., Kong, S.L., Cummins, J., Lewis, J., & Pascual-Leone, J. (Eds.) (1989). *Assessment and placement of minority students*. Toronto: Hogrefe.

Snowden, L.R. & Cheung, F.K. (1990). Use of inpatient mental health services by members of ethnic minority groups. *American Psychologist, 45,* 347–355.

Sue, S. & Okazaki, S. (1990). Asian-American educational achievements: A phenomenon in search of an explanation. *American Psychologist, 45,* 913–920.

Sugai, G. (1988). Educational assessment of the culturally diverse and behavior disordered student: An examination of critical effect. In Ortiz, A.A. & Ramirez, B.A. (Eds.) *Schools and the culturally diverse exceptional student: Promising practices and future directions* (pp. 63–75). Reston, VA: The Council for Exceptional Children.

Sugai, G. & Maheady, L. (1988). Cultural diversity and individual assessment for behavior disorders. *Teaching Exceptional Children, 21*(1), 28–31.

Tempest, P. & Skipper, B. (1988). Norms for the Wechsler Intelligence Scale for Children-Revised for Navajo Indians. *Diagnostique, 13,* 123–129.

Tinlos, M., Tan, A., & Leung, B. (1988). *Assessment of Chinese-speaking limited English proficient students with special needs.* Sacramento, CA: Resources in Special Education.

Trachtman, G.M. (1990). Best practices in political activism. In Thomas, A. & Grimes, J. (Eds.) *Best practices in school psychology-II* (pp. 563–574). Washington, DC: National Association of School Psychologists.

U.S. Department of Commerce (1985). *We . . . the Mexican Americans, the Puerto Ricans, the Cubans, and the Hispanics from other countries in the Caribbean, Central and South America, and from Spain.* Washington, DC: Author.

U.S. Department of Commerce (1988). The Hispanic population in the United States (Advance report). March 1988. Washington, DC: Author.

U.S. Department of Education (1989). Tenth Annual Report to Congress on the Implementation of the Education of the Handicapped Act (Executive Summary). *Exceptional Children, 56,* 7–9.

Valencia, S. (1990). A portfolio approach to classroom reading assessment: The whys, whats, and hows. *The Reading Teacher, 43,* 338–340.

Vázquez-Nuttall, E., De León, B. & Valle, M. (1990). Best practices in considering cultural factors. In Thomas, A. & Grimes, J. (Eds.). *Best practices in school psychology-II* (pp. 219–233). Washington, DC: National Association of School Psychologists.

Voukovich, D.H. (1983). The use of projective assessment by school psychologists. *School Psychology Review, 12,* 358–364.

Wainer, H., Dorans, N.J., Flaugher, R., Green, B.F., Mislevy, R.J., Steinberg, L., Thissen, D. (1990). *Computerized adaptive testing: A primer.* Hillsdale, NJ: Erlbaum.

Wiggins, G. (1989). A true test: Toward more authentic and equitable assessment. *Phi Delta Kappan, 70,* 703–713.

Wilen, D.K. & Sweeting, C.M. (1986). Assessment of limited English proficient Hispanic students. *School Psychology Review, 15,* 59–75.

Willig, A.C. & Ortiz, A.A. (1991). The nonbiased individualized educational program: Linking assessment to instruction. In Hamayan, E.V. & Damico, J.S. (Eds.) *Limiting bias in the assessment of bilingual students* (pp. 281–302). Austin, TX: Pro-Ed.

Wolman, C., Bruininks, R.H. & Thurlow, M.L. (1989). Dropouts and dropout programs: Implications for special education. *Remedial and Special Education, 10*(5), 6–20,50.

Woo, J.Y.T. (1988). *Handbook on the assessment of East Asian students.* New York: Hunter College of CUNY, Bilingual Education Programs.

Wyche, L.G. (1989). The Tenth Annual Report to Congress: Taking a significant step in the right direction. *Exceptional Children, 56,* 14–16.

Ysseldyke, J., Regan, R., Thurlow, M., & Schwartz, S. (1981). Current assessment practices: The "cattle-dip" approach. *Diagnostique, 6*(2), 16–27.

Annotated Bibliography

Alvarez, M.D. (1988). Psychoeducational assessment of bilingual students: Current trends and major issues. In Ambert, A.N. (Ed.) *Bilingual education and English as a second language: A research handbook, 1986–1987* (pp. 297–332). New York: Garland.

Reviews the literature on bilingual educational assessment for 1986 and 1987. Gives an overview of three types of assessment (English proficiency testing, bilingual language proficiency testing, and language assessment in special education) but concentrates on a fourth type: psychoeducational assessment of bilingual students. Discusses positive steps toward non-biased assessment: legislation/litigation, use of alternative test and non-test based techniques, referral prevention and prereferral interventions, shift from placement to instructional planning, and increased dissemination efforts regarding the assessment of language minorities. Barriers cited are: continued biases in assessment, lack of change in the assessment process, use of "standard" batteries, and questionable technical adequacy of tests.

Barona, A. & Garcia, E.E. (Eds.) (1990). *Children at risk: Poverty, minority status, and other issues in educational equity.* Washington, DC: National Association of School Psychologists.

This edited volume is an essential resource for school-based and other professionals who interact with minority children in various capacities. The book addresses major issues surrounding minority children's current status from an educational and psychological perspective. It is organized along four major sections: (a) issues in educational equity; (b) delivery of educational services and interventions with low SES and minority children; (c) educational support practices; and (d) assessment of ethnic minority children. This last section includes state of the art articles on preschool screening, identification of culturally diverse gifted children, use of projective techniques in assessing Hispanic children, language proficiency assessment, and use of achievement tests with LEP students. A step-by-step procedure for assessing LM children is also included.

Coballes-Vega, C. & Salend, S.J. (1988). Guidelines for assessing migrant handicapped students. *Diagnostique, 13,* 64–75.

Migrant handicapped students are underserved and underidentified. Assessment is viewed as a key element in providing appropriate educational services to migrant children. Suggested guidelines for assessing migrant students include: identifying cultural and language background, examining adaptive behavior, checking past school history through the Migrant Student Record Transfer System (MSRTS), determining medical needs, parental involvement, interviews with past teachers, choosing appropriate assessment instruments, curriculum-based assessments, and establishing a network of community resources.

Figueroa, R., Fradd, S. & Correa, V. (Eds.) (1989). Meeting the multicultural needs of the Hispanic students in special education (Special Issue). *Exceptional Children, 56*(2).

State-of-the-art papers dealing with bilingual special education. Articles address a variety of issues, including theory, definition, instruction, and current training needs. Of particular interest are the three articles that focus on the psychological and/or linguistic assessment of Hispanics and LM students.

Gibbs, J.T. & Huang, L.N. (Eds.) (1989). *Children of color: Psychological interventions with minority youth.* San Francisco: Jossey-Bass.

Discusses issues involved in clinical assessment and treatment of minority group children and adolescents from six major ethnic groups (African American, Chinese American, Japanese American, American Indian, Mexican American, mainland Puerto Ricans) and two emerging groups (South East Asian refugees and biracial youth). Written from an ecological perspective that recognizes the impact of social and environmental factors, chapters are organized to facilitate across-group comparisons. Most chapters follow a similar format and include sections on demography, epidemiology of psychological and behavioral disorders, cultural and family characteristics, sociocultural issues in assessment, and intervention and treatment strategies appropriate for each minority group.

Hamayan, E. & Damico, J.S. (Eds.) (1991). *Limiting bias in the assessment of bilingual students.* Austin, TX: Pro-Ed.

Collection of articles addressing both theoretical and practical issues regarding the assessment of LEP students. Chapters deal with second language acquisition, assessment of communicative ability, educational assessment, assessment of cognitive ability, cultural and linguistic issues in assessing LEP students with special needs, and linking assessment to instruction. Two appendices offer annotated bibliographies of tests of communicative ability and of tests of academic ability.

Jones, R.L. (Ed.) (1988). *Psychoeducational assessment of minority group children: A casebook.* Berkeley, CA: Cobb & Henry.

A collection of case studies reflecting different approaches to the identification-assessment-placement process for minority children. Of particular relevance for LM Hispanic children are the two case studies that follow a dynamic assessment perspective (one with Feuerstein's LPAD/IE model, a more dated one follows Budoff's learning potential assessment); the two case studies dealing with adaptive behavior assessment (one uses SOMPA, the other the Texas Environmental Adaptation Measure); and the two case studies on bilingual assessment where linguistic issues are emphasized. Three other case studies bear relevance for other LM groups: the case study of an Eskimo emotionally disturbed boy, and that of two Southeast Asian students.

The Journal of Educational Issues of Language Minority Students. 1910 University Drive, Education Building 215, Boise State University, Boise, ID 83725.

Published by the Bilingual Education Teacher Preparation Program at Boise State University, the Journal is published three times a year under a special Title VII grant from the U.S. Department of Education, Office of Bilingual Education and Minority Language Affairs (OBEMLA). A peer-review publication, the Journal is distributed free of charge to interested parties and "serves as a vehicle of information dissemination regarding issues important in the education of LM students." In addition, it "serves to disseminate the results of educational research and innovative approaches to deal with educational problems encountered by language minority children or other related topics." It is the first professional publication exclusively dedicated to LM concerns.

Lupi, M.H. & Woo, J.Y.T. (1989). Issues in the assessment of East Asian handicapped students. *Diagnostique, 14,* 147–158.

Explores cultural and linguistic caveats in evaluating East Asian students. Offers explanations and suggestions for modifying and/or eliminating biases and distortions when working with such students. Describes how East Asian cultural philosophies may influence school behavior and considers cultural and linguistic pitfalls in assessment materials. Key cultural and linguistic differences are described to assist evaluators in assessing East Asian students.

Minnesota Department of Education (1987). *A resource handbook for the assessment and identification of LEP students with special education needs.* White Bear Lake, MN: Minnesota Curriculum Services Center.

This school-based practitioner-oriented handbook covers a variety of topics relevant to LEP special needs students: steps involved in process; gives an assessment and identification model for LEP students; use of interpreters and translations; prereferral procedures; steps in special education referrals; general issues and concerns in assessment and eligibility; IEP development; and program evaluation. The manual also includes information regarding the assessment of learning aptitude, academics, adaptive behavior, social-emotional functioning, language and communication, and perceptual-motor skills. There is a section on resources in LEP special education. Another section provides sample home language questionnaires in different languages, teacher checklists, social/medical/developmental history forms, etc.

Ortiz, A.A. & Garcia, S.B. (Eds.) (1988). *Schools and the culturally diverse exceptional student: Promising practices and future directions.* Reston, VA: Council for Exceptional Children.

A selection of papers presented at CEC's 1986 Ethnic and Multicultural Symposia, the book focuses on the education of culturally and linguistically diverse exceptional students. Several chapters are devoted to the assessment of LM students and to referral prevention. Other chapters deal with demography, community-based education, parental involvement, and model programs in bilingual SPED. Several exceptionalities are discussed, including giftedness, speech and language handicaps, behavior disorders, and learning disabilities. Ethnic groups emphasized are Hispanics, African Americans, Native Americans, and Asian Americans.

Prewitt-Diaz, J.O. (1989). *The process and procedures for identifying exceptional language minority children.* University Park, PA: College of Education, Pennsylvania State University.

Written for school personnel, the book gives an overview of language minority persons and provides specific guidelines for prereferral, referral, assessment, identification, and placement of LM children. Its specific focus is residents of the mid-Atlantic region of the United States. In very didactic fashion, 31 major points are summarized throughout the book and highlighted as "Educational Tips."

CHAPTER X

The Education of Language Minorities: An Overview of Findings and a Research Agenda

Alba N. Ambert

Introduction

The predominant theme in the recent research in bilingual education and ESL appears to be the varied, complex, and often external factors which affect the academic performance of language minority students. In the past, the research emphasis with this population was on language development. Although language development in general and English language acquisition, specifically, are still of utmost concern to researchers and educators in the field of bilingual education and ESL, a growing recognition of the factors that affect the language acquisition process and overall academic performance is in evidence. These factors, less obvious than linguistic characteristics, are often overlooked in the schools. Furthermore, the schools are charged with bearing great responsibility for the academic failure of many language minorities. Researchers and educators are no longer looking at individual, familial, and cultural factors to explain school performance. They are addressing issues such as racism, teachers' motivational orientations, and the inevitable conflicts between the values of the home and those of the schools. These important issues are prominent in the direction of current educational research.

An Overview

Social Contexts

The preceding research review indicates that past conceptualizations of the education of language minority students which concentrated on linguistic and cognitive factors are no longer useful in explaining the academic difficulties children from diverse backgrounds face. The education of language minority children must be framed within a social, political, and economic framework that takes into consideration racism, cultural discontinuities between the home and the school, the attitudes of the majority towards minorities, social status, lowered teacher expectations, curricular tracking, social isolation, educational segregation which is related to segregation in society and discriminatory educational treatment. The continued high placement of language minority children in special education classes is a good example of the latter. The stress and anxiety these factors create in the language minority student have a definite negative impact on cognitive functioning. Considering the psycho-emotional burden language minority children carry, a great deal of it created by the schools themselves, it is not surprising that their academic performance lags behind language majority children's and they drop out of school at an alarming rate.

Acculturation

Acculturation of language minority students in U.S. society is an important component of the issues that affect them in school. Research results indicate that acculturation affects language proficiency, academic achievement, social and emotional adjustment, self-concept, and identity. Acculturation is not always positive. Surprising results have emerged from research studies that show that the more acculturated some language minority adolescents are, the less well-adjusted they are emotionally. Acculturation in itself is a complex phenomenon which is affected by gender, age, level of education, social distance between home and host country, personality, and socioeconomic status. In addition, not all groups face the same acculturation problems and effects. For example, refugees are a distinct group which differ from other immigrants in substantial ways and will react to acculturation differently.

Academic Contexts

The academic contexts of bilingualism and second language acquisition have been explored extensively in the research reviewed. What is clearly emerging is a multifaceted phenomenon which looks at the student's linguistic development from cognitive, social, communicative, and psychological perspectives. Perhaps as a result of this, combined with the changing political agenda in the United States, there are myriad program options for students of limited English proficiency, from native language maintenance while English is acquired to submersion in an all-English program with language majority students. How much native language and how much English is used in the classroom is a major source of controversy in schools. The misconception that native language instruction deters English language development is still strong. The research, however, indicates that skills transfer from one language to another and native language instruction may in fact facilitate learning English. Furthermore, bilingualism may enhance children's cognitive skills.

Early Childhood

The young language minority child deserves special attention. Often identified as at-risk because of linguistic and cultural factors, the research has explored successful programs, which include validating the children's native language and culture by incorporating the linguistic and cultural elements of the home in the curriculum and encouraging parents to participate in the children's learning process. These efforts have proven successful in assuring the academic success of young language minority children at a critical stage when they are introduced to formal learning.

Literacy and Children's Literature

In concert with current research directions, literacy development in language minority children has explored the social context of written language and the home and community influences on literacy development. Literacy is perceived as an activity which must engage and be meaningful to the learner. Therefore, to be successful, reading instruction should be modified to capitalize children's cognitive, linguistic, and cultural resources and utilize the cognitive resources of the children's households. Collaborative approaches among teachers have proved successful in the literacy development of language minority children in both the native language and English. In encouraging the pleasure of reading, it is important to select children's books carefully. Books for language minority children should be well written, have multicultural themes, and preferably consist of original literature. The watered-down, basal-type books children are exposed to are often boring and of little interest.

The Gifted

The underrepresentation of language minority children in programs for the gifted is a major concern to researchers. The identification of children who come from linguistic and culturally diverse backgrounds as gifted is fraught with difficulties. However, several model programs exist which have been successful in identifying and providing an appropriate education for gifted language minority students.

Teacher Training

Teacher training in bilingual education and English as a second language continues to be the focus of much research effort. The emphasis of teacher training today is directed toward action research wherein universities and schools form partnerships and conduct research in areas of need. The results of this research will not only assist in the development of appropriate teacher training programs but will also inform educators and assist them in making appropriate educational decisions for language minority children.

Assessment

Information on the assessment of language minority students has proliferated in the last few years. Researchers are recommending use of alternative assessment methods, linking assessment to instruction, and there appears to be an emphasis on the prevention of referrals and prereferral interventions. However, there continue to be difficulties in the assessment of language minorities. These include biases in the assessment process, service duplication, an unchanging assessment process which continues to depend on "standard" batteries and the questionable technical adequacy of tests. In addition, very little has emerged in the assessment of low incident language groups and low incidence disabilities.

A Research Agenda

Although a large body of research has emerged in bilingual education and English as a second language, the preceding chapters emphasize the areas that are still unresearched or underresearched. The more we know about the phenomenon known as bilingualism, the more in touch we are with the realities of language minority students, the more we realize how much needs to be done, both in research and in the development of effective academic programs. The following are the research needs found in the specific areas addressed in this volume.

Social Contexts

Racism. More ethnographic research is needed to explore the effects of racism on the academic performance of language minority students. It has been found that some language minority groups and some individuals within groups respond differently to racism. Why is this so?

As we learn more about the damaging effects of racism and discrimination, we require more information about interventions that are most successful in reducing racism. We need more information on training programs to prepare language majority teachers and administrators to respond with sensitivity to linguistic and cultural diversity. Is it possible to develop program models and instructional techniques which will effectively raise the social status of language minority students?

Isolation. Researchers need to address the issue of the social isolation of students in bilingual education programs. An exploration of the quantity and quality of contact bilingual program students have with language majority students is needed as well as the kind of contact which would enhance the academic development of language minority students placed in bilingual programs. Further research is needed on the benefits of two-way bilingual program model in reducing the isolation of language minority children in more traditional bilingual programs.

Relationships with language majority groups. More information is needed on the relationships between language minority students and their language majority peers and how these relationships influence the learning process.

Social variables. Since cultural and linguistic differences do not fully account for the academic difficulties of some language minority students, it is important to explore further societal factors which seem to have alienating effects on language minorities. Discontinuities between the values of the home and the school, the lower expectations of teachers toward members of certain minority groups, and the negative attitudes of the mainstream society toward specific minorities (very often validated by the media), need to be studied within the context of the realities of the schools and society. Intervention models to decrease the stresses imposed on language minority students caused by a society's lack of acceptance and hostility need to be developed.

Acculturation

Interactive nature of the process. Further research is needed on the interactive nature of the acculturation process. What are the effects of acculturation on subordinate groups? What are the effects on the dominant group?

Gender. Research is needed to compare acculturation according to gender, especially in language minorities who come from societies where traditional roles of males and females are rigid. How do these populations deal with the changing roles of men and women, girls and boys, in U.S. society as a whole and in schools in particular? What are the stresses and interpersonal and intergenerational difficulties they encounter as a result of gender conflicts?

Intercultural experiences. The study of foster families described in this volume underscores the need to understand the effects of intercultural experiences on groups that come in contact with one another.

Contextual variables. Research is needed to identify the contextual variables that interact in the acculturation process. An understanding of how the language policies of the host country and the attitudes of refugee sponsors affect the acculturation process is necessary.

Behavior. More information is needed on the behaviors of acculturating individuals (use of computers, dietary practices, dating, use of health and social services). This will help us understand how levels of acculturation affect behavior in daily life.

School populations. Research emphasis on the acculturation of school-aged populations is needed, especially those language minority groups underrepresented in current research efforts. We need more information on native peoples, Haitians, Dominicans, Central Americans, Middle Easterners, among others.

Acculturation and reacculturation. Large numbers of Puerto Rican students experience circular migration, that is, they move back and forth between the U.S. mainland and Puerto Rico. Research is needed on the acculturation and reacculturation processes of these students, including an examination of the family unit as a whole to understand the Puerto Rican migrant, reverse migrant, and circulatory migrant families and the stresses inherent in these experiences. What are the effects of acculturation and reacculturation on students' emotional, psychological, and academic realms? What can be done in the schools to counteract the negative effects?

Acculturation and emotional adjustment. More research is necessary on the emotional costs of acculturation. What are the effects of acculturation on identity and self-concept? How well adjusted are language minorities who have acculturated well? Are there differences in the emotional costs of acculturation among different linguistic minority groups?

Academic Contexts

Language development. Research is needed on the simultaneous and successive processes of first and second language acquisition. The acquisition and development of native languages other than English, the acquisition of English as a second language, and the development or underdevelopment of bilinguals are topics that need to be explored. Research is also needed on the social development of code-switching of bilingual students, the spectrum of speech styles of bilinguals, and how adult bilinguals compare to children. Language shift or loss and its relation to language acquisition processes need to be explored.

English language development. Considering the duration of transitional bilingual education programs, future research should explore alternative programs to assist language minority children to acquire English effectively in preparation for mainstream classes.

Native language instruction. Although it is clear that children can maintain their native language without retarding development of English, there is no clear understanding of the mechanisms that facilitate transfer of skills from one language to another. Future research is needed to understand how transfer of skills occurs and use this knowledge in facilitating transfer in the classroom.

Cognitive gains of bilingualism. It appears that there is no cognitive cost to the development of bilingualism. On the contrary, it is possible that bilingualism enhances children's cognitive skills. Research which explores the specific cognitive and academic functioning of bilingual children is necessary to confirm the cognitive gains of bilingualism.

Speed of English language acquisition. Further research is needed on the time needed to acquire English as a second language. More information is warranted on the varied factors that affect the time it takes for non-English speaking students to learn English. Factors which affect speed of acquisition, such as age, motivation, societal attitudes toward language minority groups, specific instructional approaches, native language proficiency, use of native language, and others need to be analyzed.

Effective ESL programs. Researchers need to compare different ESL methods as applied to different language minority populations to determine what method or combination of methods is most effective for specific groups.

Reading. Research results indicate that reading skills acquired in the native language transfer to English and result in higher reading achievement in English. Future research needs to explore the link between overall literacy in the native language and overall literacy in the second language.

Curriculum. More research is needed on appropriate curriculum development for children at different levels of language proficiency. Action research for curriculum development would assist teachers and other educators in developing curricula for traditional areas as well as nontraditional areas such as ethnic arts curriculum and oral folk culture. More work needs to be done with teachers who work with language minority students on cooperative learning methods which seem to be more compatible with the cultural backgrounds of language minority children.

Early Childhood Education

Language and cognition. The relationship between language and thinking needs to be explored and how both language and thinking affect attitudes, self-awareness, and identity formation in young language minority children. Studies should focus on the intricate interrelationships of cognition and emotional adjustment on native language development and second language acquisition.

Individual and societal roles in bilingualism. Researchers need to explore how the native language can be maintained in some language minority groups. Lower levels of language vitality at the community level may affect the language proficiency of individuals. Comparative social groups should be examined to help clarify how the community or the environment affects the maintenance of a native language and learning a second language. More research on the relationship between the social milieu of the young bilingual child and learning is needed.

Research, practice, and policy interface. Research needs to be generated on the processes of bilingualism in young children and the nature and effectiveness of early childhood education programs for language minority populations. A merging of researchers, practitioners, and policymakers is necessary to maintain an ongoing dialogue in the formation of policy and practice in bilingual early childhood education. Continued collaborative research efforts will help bridge the gap which still exists between research and practice.

Linguistic minorities and linguistic majorities. Further research needs to explore the effectiveness of language immersion programs for young English-speaking children learning a second language in conjunction with native speakers of the language. Research on two-way bilingual education programs for young children from both language majority and language minority backgrounds can provide useful information on how to achieve continuity between diverse cultural groups.

Literacy

Forms and functions. Research is needed on the forms and functions of literacy in the home and the community and the application of that knowledge to classroom literacy programs.

Cognitive resources. More information needs to be generated within ethnolinguistic communities to identify household cognitive resources which can be used to promote the development of biliteracy in school settings.

Teachers and peers. Researchers need to explore how teachers and peers can best assist and guide students to accomplish tasks beyond the students' independent level and encourage the learner's cognitive development.

Native language. The role of the student's native language in the development and assessment of English literacy needs to be examined.

English reading. More information is needed on how reading in English influences growth in and knowledge of the spoken language.

Use of technology. The uses of technology to promote biliteracy development (use of word processing programs for composing or writing, for example) need to be explored.

Children's Literature

Quality literature. More original quality literature is needed to encourage language minority children to read for pleasure. The literature should contain multiethnic themes and treat minority and ethnic group characters with more universal characteristics.

Literature and basal readers. A comparison of the effects on reading achievement between use of original literature and basals or worksheets is needed to confirm the limited research that has been done which suggests that original literature is more effective in promoting reading achievement than basals, worksheets, or scripted reading curricula.

Reading responses. Qualitative studies are needed to identify the responses of language minority children to a variety of themes, to stories written bilingually and monolingually, to a variety of illustrated texts, and to children's original work. These studies would assist teachers in the selection of books to be used in the classroom.

The Gifted and Talented

Identification. Further research efforts are needed to develop procedures to identify language minority children with high intellectual potential. What are the abilities and talents language minority children have that, though differing from the mainstream child, reveal potential? Research is needed on the role of teachers in identifying language minority children as gifted and the factors that influence their decisions.

Assessment. Non-discriminatory instruments are needed to properly assess gifted language minority children taking into account linguistic, cultural, and socioeconomic factors. Instruments need to be developed for and normed on specific language minority populations. The instruments should consider the multiple intelligences children bring into academic tasks, such as creativity, spatial abilities, linguistic competence (in the dominant language), and interpersonal and intrapersonal abilities.

Programs. Researchers need to explore appropriate academic programs to promote the academic achievement and development of leadership skills of gifted language minority students. Comparisons among different program models need to be made in order to decide which models work effectively for specific language minority groups. Research is warranted on the training needs of bilingual teachers of the gifted to assist them in developing appropriate programs.

Teacher Training

Longitudinal research. Teacher training would benefit greatly from the results of longitudinal studies which collect data over long periods of time and take a retrospective look at the cumulative impact of students' bilingualism. Following children from kindergarten to high school graduation may help teachers discover the educational and social impact of bilingualism.

Methodological approaches. Researchers need to gather both qualitative as well as quantitative studies and explore the complementary roles played between them. Research is needed designed to include observation of general patterns, trends and tendencies, and details of language behavior usage of children in groups and on a one-to-one basis as well as in diverse settings. This type of information allows for higher-order generalizations that would be most useful in the training of bilingual and ESL teachers.

Involvement of diverse disciplines. Research projects are needed which consider various interdisciplinary aspects in order to understand the complex phenomenon of the development of bilingualism in children. Research projects in which psychologists, linguists, anthropologists, educators, and sociologists, for example, are involved would be extremely helpful in developing theories on bilingualism and second language acquisition and the application of these theories to teacher training and classroom practice.

Home and community. Teacher training programs would benefit from research which balances micro-oriented studies with studies that go beyond the classroom. The understanding of the interaction between what happens in the school and what happens outside the school is extremely important for educational practice. There is a need for research which offers alternative understandings and explanations for what seems to be language minority children's academic failure and failure to adjust to the school environment. Research needs to answer questions such as why a child who functions competently in English in the community has to switch to his or her native language when moved into the context of the school and cannot perform in English.

Staff development. Research on the best ways to train teachers and administrators to work with language minority students, including sensitivity and awareness training is necessary. School districts, state departments of education and universities need to articulate training programs for school personnel serving language minorities; therefore, research is needed to assist in the articulation of training goals.

Assessment

Research is needed on the best assessment practices to be applied to language minority children with low incidence exceptionalities, such as the visual and hearing impaired. Research is also needed on the proper assessment of low incidence language groups and young preschool language minorities.

Test innovations need to be explored for application with language minority groups. Computer-based assessments and reading diagnosis, more open-ended assessments based on performance in different settings, and the development of instruments that give teachers and students feedback on the teaching and learning process need to be explored. More research is also needed on the informal assessment of language minority students, including the portfolio approach to assessment.

The growing diversity in U.S. schools requires that school psychologists and other bilingual special education practitioners obtain more training in working with linguistically and culturally diverse populations. This training should also be incorporated in preservice training programs. Teachers and school psychologists need to be trained in techniques that will provide alternatives to traditional testing, such as observation, interviewing, and in linking assessment with instruction.

APPENDIX I

Multifunctional Resource Centers (MRC)

Service Area 1:

New England MRC
Brown University
345 Blackstone Blvd.
Providence, RI 02906
(401) 274-9548

Specialty Area:

English literacy for LEP students

Service Area 2:

New York MRC
Hunter College
645 Park Avenue
New York, NY 10021
(212) 772-4764

Specialty Area:

Bilingual adult education

Service Area: 3:

Mid-Atlantic MRC
8737 Colesville Rd., Suite 900
Silver Spring, MD 20910
(301) 588-5947

Specialty Area:

Bilingual program administration

Service Area 4:

Florida Atlantic University MRC
College of Education
20th Street
Boca Raton, FL 33431
(407) 367-2301

Specialty Area:

Bilingual special education

Service Area 5:

Midwest Bilingual Education MRC
2360 East Devon Avenue, Suite
3011
Des Plaines, IL 60018
(312) 296-6070

Specialty Area: English literacy for non-literate
                                             secondary LEP students

Service Area 6:   Upper Great Lakes MRC
                                             University of Wisconsin
                                             Center for Education Research
                                             1025 West Johnson Street
                                             Madison, WI 53706
                                             (608) 263-4216

Service Area 7:   Southwest Education Development
                                                 Laboratory
                                             211 East Seventh Street
                                             Austin, TX 78701
                                             (512) 476-6861
Specialty Area: ESL and other alternatives

Service Area 8:   University of Oklahoma MRC
                                             Division of Continuing Education
                                                 and Public Affairs
                                             555 Constitution Avenue
                                             Norman, OK 73037
                                             (405) 325-1731
Specialty Area: Counseling for LEP students

Service Area 9:   Interface Network, Inc.
                                             4800 SW Griffith Drive, Suite 202
                                             Beaverton, OR 97005
                                             (503) 644-5741
Specialty Area: Parent involvement

Service Area 10:   Arizona State University MRC
                                             College of Education, Tempe, AZ
                                                 85287
                                             (602) 965-2012
Specialty Area: Issues in LEP student attrition

Service Area 11:   Southern California MRC
                                             San Diego State University
                                             6363 Alvarado Court, Suite 226
                                             San Diego, CA 92120
                                             (619) 594-5193
Specialty Area: Bilingual education for gifted and
                                                 talented students

Service Area 12:	ARC Associates, Inc. 310 Eighth Street, Suite 220 Oakland, CA 94607 (415) 763-1490
Specialty Area:	Bilingual education for new immigrant/refugee students
Service Area 13:	Metropolitan University MRC Apartado 21150 Rio Piedras, Puerto Rico 00928 (809) 766-1717
Specialty Area:	Career education programs for LEP students
Service Area 14:	ARC Associates, Inc. 1314 South King St., Suite 1456 Honolulu, HI 96814 (808) 531-7802
Specialty Area:	Educational technology in bilingual programs
Service Area 15:	University of Guam Project BEAM College of Education, UDG Station Mangilao, GU 96913 (671) 734-4113
Specialty Area:	Relationship between L1 orthographics and English literacy

APPENDIX II

Organizations

ASPIRA of New York
Office of Research and Advocacy
332 E. 149 Street
Bronx, NY 10452
Center for Applied Linguistics
1118 22nd Street, N.W.
Washington, DC 20037

Center for Prevention and Recovery of Dropouts
Intercultural Development Research Association
5835 Callaghan, Suite 350
San Antonio, TX 78228

English Plus Information Clearinghouse (EPIC)
Joint National Committee for Languages
20 F Street, N.W., Fourth Floor
Washington, DC 20036

ERIC Clearinghouse on Adult, Career and Vocational Education
Ohio State University
National Center for Research in Vocational Education
1960 Kenney Road
Columbus, OH 43210

ERIC Clearinghouse on Urban Education
Teachers College, Columbia University
Institute for Urban and Minority Education
525 W. 120th Street
New York, NY 10027

National Association for Bilingual Education
1201 16th Street, N.W., Room 407
Washington, DC 20036

National Clearinghouse for Bilingual Education
11501 Georgia Avenue, Suite 102
Wheaton, MD 20902

National Council of La Raza
Los Angeles Program Office
548 S. Spring Street, Suite 802
Los Angeles, CA 90013

Teachers of English to Speakers of Other Languages (TESOL)
1118 22nd Street, N.W., Suite 205
Washington, DC 20037

APPENDIX III

Journals and Newsletters

The Bilingual Family Newsletter
Multilingual Matters, Inc.
Bank House, 8a Hill Road
Clevedon, Avon 8521 7HH
England

Bilingual Review/La Revista Bilingue
Office of the Graduate School, SUNY
Binghamton, NY 13901

Bilingual Special Education Newsletter
University of Texas
Department of Special Education
Education Building, 306
Austin, TX 78712-1290

English Language Teaching Journal
Oxford University Press
Walton Street, Oxford OX2 6DP
England

Findlay College Newsletter
Center for Bilingual Multicultural Studies
1000 North Main Street
Findlay, OH 45840

Intercultural Development Research Association Newsletter
5835 Callaghan Street, Suite 350
San Antonio, TX 78228

Journal of Asian Pacific Communication
Multilingual Matters, Inc.
Bank House, 8a Hill Road
Clevedon, Avon 8521 7HH
England

The Journal of Educational Issues of Language Minority Students
1910 University Drive
Education Building 215
Boise State University
Boise, ID 83725

Journal of Language and Social Psychology
Multilingual Matters, Inc.
Bank House, 8a Hill Road
Clevedon, Avon 8521 7HH
England

Journal of Multilingual and Multicultural Development
Multilingual Matters, Inc.
Bank House, 8a Hill Road
Clevedon, Avon 8521 7HH
England

Language, Culture and Curriculum
Multilingual Matters, Inc.
Bank House, 8a Hill Road
Clevedon, Avon 8521 7HH
England

Language and Education
Multilingual Matters, Inc.
Bank House, 8a Hill Road
Clevedon, Avon 8521 7HH
England

The Language Teacher
Multilingual Matters, Inc.
Bank House, 8a Hill Road
Clevedon, Avon 8521 7HH
England

Language Teaching
Cambridge University Press
Edinburgh Building
Shaftesbury Road, Cambridge CB2 2RU
England

NABE Journal
National Association for Bilingual Education
1201 16th Street, N.W., Room 407
Washington, DC 20036

TESOL Quarterly
Teachers of English to Speakers of Other Languages
1118 22nd Street, N.W., Suite 205
Washington, DC 20037

AUTHOR INDEX

Aasby, S. 145
Abraham, S. 327, 332
Abi-Nader, J. 7, 8, 17, 38, 45
Achondo, M. 213
Ackerson, L.M. 326
Ada, A.F. 204, 205, 206, 210
Adderholt-Elliott, M. 246, 250
Agard, J. 210
Agosto, V. 275, 288
Allen, W. 327, 332
Allport, G. 27, 38
Alvarez, M.D. 299, 301, 306,
  308, 312, 332, 342
Alvarez, R.R. 21, 38, 45
Ambert, A.N. xvi, xviii, 77, 101,
  102, 124, 164, 318, 323, 332
Anderson, J.A. 224, 250
Appel, R. 130
Aramen, J.K. 245, 250
Arciniega, T. 261, 288
Arias, B. 20, 23, 38, 45
Ariza, M. 152, 161, 164
Atkinson, P.A. 137
Au, K.H. 10, 39, 314, 315, 332
August, D. 97, 99, 109, 114, 122,
  123, 124, 130, 283, 288
Axelson, R.G. 274, 288, 289

Baca, L. 26, 42, 50, 261, 289
Baetens Beardsmore, H. 100, 124,
  130
Bahr, M.W. 317
Baker, C. 130
Baker, K.A. 114, 124, 302, 303,
  332
Baldwin, A. 225, 239, 250

Balsamo, K. 233, 250, 254
Bassano, S. 28, 38
Baron, A.E. 326
Barona, A. 304, 307, 312, 319,
  332, 333, 342
Bates, E. 104, 124
Batsch, G.M. 322, 333
Beal, G. 202
Benavides, A. 306, 333
Bennett, A.T. 207, 292, 309, 327,
  333
Ben-Zeev, S. 103, 124
Bermudez, A.B. 327, 333
Bernstein, S.D. 221, 234, 250
Berry, G.L. 245
Berry, J.W. 55, 56, 58, 61, 87,
  90
Biber, D. 290
Bild, E.R. 130
Binkley, J.L. 260, 261, 294
Birba, L. 75, 88
Blanc, M. 132
Blanchard, J.S. 323, 333
Blosser, B. 189
Boggs, S.T. 5, 7, 10, 38, 44
Borland, J.H. 254
Bothmer, R. 220, 250
Bowerman, M. 97, 125
Bowman, B.T. 198, 205
Bracken, B. 144, 161
Bradley, J. xvi, xviii
Braine, M.D.S. 97, 125
Brauer, J.Z. 199, 205
Brice-Heath, S. 182, 187
Brickman, W. 235, 250
Britton, J. 151

Brown, R.A.   97, 100, 125
Bullivant, B.M.   67, 68, 87, 90
Bunting, E.   210
Buriel, R.   189
Burt, M.   107, 110, 126
Burton, L.   240, 241, 250

Calderón, M.   293
Callies, A.   77, 89
Canales, M.   104, 125, 207
Cardoza, D.   189
Carell, P.L.   190
Carey, J.C.   66, 89
Carrasco, R.   105
Carrera, J.W.   69, 87, 91
Carringer, D.C.   125
Carrow, E.   145, 162
Carter, T.P.   117, 125
Cashion, M.   191
Castañeda, A.   9, 43, 223, 252
Casteel, C.P.   320, 333
Caterino, L.C.   306, 333
Cazden, C.   4, 38, 280, 289, 293, 333
Cerny, M.   167
Cervantes, H.T.   320, 333
Chamberlain, P.   243, 245, 252, 307, 333
Chamot, A.U.   119, 125, 283, 289, 293
Chan, S.   244, 250
Chang, A.S.C.   142, 152, 162, 164
Chang, G.L.   173, 175, 187
Chang, M.   144, 163
Chang, Y.L.   157, 162, 187, 190
Chatfield, M.L.   117, 125
Chávez, J.   240, 241, 250
Chen, G.   59, 87
Cheung, F.K.   324
Chomsky, N.   97, 125
Christian, D.   283, 289, 291
Christiansen, J.   317, 335
Christison, M.E.   28, 38
Clark, B.   254
Clark, C.   68, 87

Clemant, R.   27, 38, 45
Cloud, N.   60, 87, 90
Coballes-Vega, C.   311, 326, 334, 343
Coelho, E.   28, 38
Cohen, E.   24, 28, 38
Cohen, L.M.   321, 324, 327, 334
Colangelo, N.   245, 246, 250
Cole, M.   9, 38, 104, 125
Collier, V.   9, 30, 31, 33, 34, 38, 46, 119, 128, 270, 289
Collins, L.M.   75, 88
Colón, N.   17, 38
Comer, J.   xvi, xviii
Commins, N.L.   72, 87, 91
Conant, F.R.   173
Correa, V.   309, 310, 318, 334
Cosden, M.A.   322, 334
Costantino, G.   246, 250
Crandall, J.   283, 291
Crawford, J.   xvi, xviii, 30, 33, 38, 282, 289
Cuellar, I.   57, 87
Cullinan, B.E.   203, 205, 207
Cummins, J.   3, 11, 14, 15, 16, 27, 35, 39, 46, 98, 103, 114, 125, 135, 190, 198, 205, 273, 281, 283, 289, 290, 293, 302, 304, 306, 309, 310, 322, 224

Dabney, M.   228, 251
Damico, J.S.   303, 318, 334
Danesi, M.   131
Daniels, R.   228, 229, 234, 251
Danwitz, M.W.   305, 334
Darcy, N.T.   102, 125
Davidson, D.H.   168
Davis, G.L.   326, 334
de Kanter, A.A.   114, 124
Delacre, L.   211
de la Garza, J.   194
De León, J.   302, 307, 308, 309, 310, 312, 330, 334
Delgado-Gaitan, C.   7, 39, 46
Delisle, J.R.   254

DeMers, S.T. 327
De Paola, T. 211
Díaz, R.M. 102, 103, 126
Díaz, S. 17, 39, 179, 188, 279, 290, 294
Dick, R.W. 326
Dodd, J. 235, 251
Dodson, C.J. 142, 143, 154, 162, 165
Dolson, D. 6, 39, 283, 291
Donaldson, R. 317, 335
Dore, J. 104, 125
Dornbusch, S. 68, 87
Dowley, G. 104, 125
Dulay, H. 107, 110, 126
Dunn, R. 224, 251
Duran, R. 126, 313, 318, 335

Eagen, R. 191
Eby, J. 221, 227, 237, 251
Edelsky, C. 177, 187, 192, 201, 206
Egan, M.G. 76, 77, 88, 94
Eisenbruch, M. 76, 87, 91
Eller, S. 246, 250
Endean, L. 212, 252
Erickson, F. 4, 39, 42, 13, 14, 18, 19, 20, 35, 46, 281, 290
Ervin-Tripp, S.M. 104, 108, 126
Esquivel, G. 312, 335

Fagan, W.T. 131
Falodun, S. 175
Faltis, C.J. 131, 329, 335
Feldhusen, J. 234, 251, 254
Feldman, C. 102, 126
Ferdman, B. 177, 187, 191
Ferhadi, A. 150, 162
Fetterman, D. 216, 238, 251, 254
Feuerstein, R. 313, 314, 335
Figler, C. 309, 335
Figueroa, R. 305, 306, 312, 314, 318, 323, 335, 343
First, J.M. 69, 87, 91
Fish, M.C. 331, 335

Fishman, J.A. 47
Flemming, C.M. 326
Ford, B. 323, 335
Fortner, M.J. 238, 251
Foster, L. 151, 163
Fouyad, N. 144,161
Fradd, S.H. 304, 312, 318, 336
Franco, J.N. 56, 87
Franklin, E.A. 154, 162, 165
Franson, C. 133
Freeman, Y. 154, 155, 157, 162, 164, 175, 187, 191, 200, 202, 205, 280, 290
Freire, P. 15, 39
Fuchs, D. 317, 336
Fuchs, L.S. 317, 336

Galagan, J.E. 305, 336
Galambos, S.J. 103, 126
Gallagher, J. 238, 251, 326, 336
Gallerano, B.H. 143, 152, 163
Gallimore, R. 10, 41
Garaway, M.K. 211
Garcia, E.E. xv, xviii, 97, 98, 99, 100, 101, 102, 104, 105, 109, 114, 117, 122, 123, 126, 130, 132, 139, 144, 158, 160, 162, 165, 283, 288, 303, 309, 336
Garcia, H.S.
Garcia, J. 202, 205
Garcia, M. 85, 87
Garcia, R.L. 200, 206
Garcia, S.B. 306, 316, 322, 336
Gardner, H. 217, 251
Gardner, R.C. 26, 27, 32, 33, 39, 47, 111, 126
Gass, S. 132
Gemake, J. 224, 251
Genesee, F. 3, 15, 17, 24, 27, 31, 32, 34, 39, 47
Genishi, C. 199
Germinario, V. 246, 252
Gibbs, J.T. 318, 324, 336, 343
Gibson, M.A. 12, 25, 40
Ginishi, C. 211

Giroux, H.A.   178, 187, 191
Glenn, C.L.   162, 165
Goble, P.   211
Goldenberg, C.N.   178, 187, 191
Goldman, S.   162, 165
Gonzalez, G.   97, 98, 101, 126, 133
Goodman, K.   199, 200, 206
Gordon, M.M.   55, 87
Gougis, R.A.   25, 40, 45, 47
Gould, L.J.   114, 117, 127, 132
Green, M.   255
Greenlaw, M.J.   216, 219, 225, 280, 240, 248, 251, 255
Gregory, D.A.   226, 251
Gross, M.   245, 245, 251
Guerreo Rea, J.   213
Guilford, J.P.   217, 251
Gulatson, M.   125
Gutkin, T.B.   329, 336

Hadaway, N.   202, 205
Hakuta, K.   xv, xviii, 22, 40, 97, 100, 102, 103, 108, 110, 114, 117, 123, 126, 127, 132, 139, 160, 162, 175, 176, 187, 235, 251, 281, 283, 290, 294, 303, 336
Hall, C.   175, 187, 192
Hall, W.   104, 125
Halliday, M.   104, 127
Halstead, J.W.   166, 303, 318, 336, 343
Hamayan, E.   166, 303, 318, 336, 343
Hamers, J.F.   132
Hammerly, H.   113
Hammill, D.   305, 337
Haney, W.   329, 337
Hansen, D.   123
Hanson, M.   243, 244, 251
Harmon, S.   177, 187, 192, 201, 206
Harris, L.C.   56, 87
Harris, L.J.   81, 89

Harris Stefanakis, E.   148, 162, 315
Hatch, E.   110, 127
Hausman, R.M.   314, 337
Havill, J.   211
Hayden, H.R.   131
Hayes, E.B.   192
Hayes, S.   212
Haywood, C.   314, 337
Heath, S.B.   5, 6, 8, 40, 48
Henry, S.L.   325, 337
Hernández, A.E.   290, 307
Herskovits, M.T.   55, 89
Heymsfeld, C.   201, 206
Hickman, J.   207
Hiller, R.J.   21, 22, 44, 53
Hilliard, A.G.   337
Hisserich, J.C.   75, 88
Hoffman, D.M.   12, 25, 40
Hoffman, M.   313, 314
Hoffman, R.G.   326
Holm, A.   283, 290
Holm, W.   27, 39, 47
Holobow, N.   27, 39, 47
Holtzman, W.H.   146, 146, 163, 168, 306, 314, 337
Holubec, E.J.   28, 40
Hornberger, N.   31, 33, 40, 48, 175, 176, 178, 179, 187, 188, 193, 283, 290
Hsia, J.   255
Huang, L.N.   308, 318, 324, 325, 337,
Hudelson, S.   117, 127, 133, 174, 175, 177, 188, 193
Huerta, A.   101, 127
Hurtado, A.   48
Hurwitz, J.   212
Hymes, D.   4, 38, 104, 127

Ianco-Worral, A.   102, 127
Ima, K.   76, 79, 87, 92
Imber, M.   22, 40, 23
Imison, I.   215, 252
Irujo, S.   7, 40

Jacob, E. 281, 290
Jacobs, J.S. 201, 206
Jacobs, L. 19, 40, 48
Jacobs, W.J. 212
Jacobson, L. 16, 43
Jalali, F. 224, 251
Jarvis, C. 153, 162, 166
Jasso, R. 56, 87
Jax, V.A. 303, 337
John, V. 4, 38
Johnson, B. 145, 163
Johnson, D. 28, 40, 260, 261, 290, 294
Johnson, L.J. 337
Johnson, M.J. 335
Johnson, N.A. 63, 89
Johnson, P.J. 63, 87
Johnson, R.T. 28, 40
Jones, R.L. 310, 318, 337, 344
Jongsma, K.S. 315, 337
Jordan, C. 281, 290
Jordan, K. 7, 10, 39, 11, 40, 44, 53
Joyce, B. 267, 290, 292

Kagan, S. 28, 29, 30, 41, 49
Kanazawa, H. 49
Kaplan, R. 9, 41, 49
Karnes, F.A. 247, 252
Keating, D.R. 217, 252
Kennan, E. 110, 127
Kennedy, D. 234, 251, 254
Kessler, C. 103, 127, 133
Kiang, P. 21, 41, 49
Kim, B.W. 158, 162
Kim, K.K. 322, 338
Kim, U. 55, 58, 61, 87, 90
Kirschenbaum, R. 22, 230, 252
Koopmans, M. 146, 162, 166
Krashen, S.D. 97, 107, 110, 119, 128, 273, 290, 294
Kreeft, J.P. 188, 194
Kurtines, W. 56, 89
Kurusa, B. 212
Kwiat, J. 268, 291, 303

LaFramboise, T.D. 325, 338
Landsman, M. 68, 87
Lambert, W.E. 26, 26, 27, 32, 33, 39, 41, 47, 102, 111, 126, 128
Langdon, H.W. 304, 338
Langer, J.A. 172, 174, 188
Lapkin, S. 24, 44
Larsen-Freeman, D. 110, 128
Larson, K.A. 338
Lasisi, M.J. 175, 188, 194
Lauver, P.J. 64, 66, 89
Leaf, M. 212
Lee, E. 76, 77, 88, 92, 133
Lega, L.I. 55, 87
Leopold, W.F. 100, 102, 128
Lesley, T. 55, 64, 88
Leung, B. 133, 324, 338
Leung, E.K. 56, 88, 93, 338
Levin, P.F. 10, 41
Levine, D.U. 255
Levine, H. 213
Liberto, J.C. 190
Lieberman, A. 100, 101, 128, 260, 282, 291
Liebkind, K. 49
Liederman, H. 68, 87
Lincoln, C. 140, 163
Lindholm, K.J. 33, 41, 50, 155, 156, 162, 167, 283, 291
Linton, R. 55, 89
Lomax, P. 295
López, D. 240, 241, 250
Loveday, L. 45
Low, K.G. 325
Luce, E.F. 80, 88, 93
Lukmani, Y. 26, 41
Lupi, M.H. 325, 338, 344
Lynch, E. 243, 244, 251

Macias, J. 8, 41, 50
Macias, R. 268, 291
MacLean, D.J. 217, 252
MacNab, G. 128
Madaus, G. 329

Madden, C. 132
Maez, L. 101
Maheady, L. 310, 311, 338
Mainous III, A.G. 60, 88
Malgady, R. 246, 250
Malik, A.M. 15, 41, 50
Maker, C.J. 216, 220, 230, 233,
     239, 244, 246, 252, 255
Maldonado-Colon, E. 306, 322,
     338
Manson, S.M. 326, 338
Margolis, H. 331
Marin, B. 74, 88
Marin, G. 74, 88
Marks, G. 75, 88
Marland, S.P. 218, 252
Marquardt, R.G. 247, 252
Martin, M. 338
Matthews, D. 217, 251, 252
Matthews, J.K. 315, 338
Matute-Bianchi, M.E. 11,12, 13,
     25, 42
McCarthy, M. 295
McGroarty, M. 134
McIntosh, M. 216, 219, 225, 230,
     240, 248, 255
McKissack, P. 213
McLaughlin, B. 97, 106, 109, 129
McNutt, G. 305
Medeiros-Landurand, P. 307
Medina, Jr., M. 194
Mehan, H. 17, 39, 279, 290, 294
Mercado, C.I. 173, 182, 183, 188,
     232, 252, 260, 265, 269, 291,
     295
Merrell, K.W. 322m 339
Milgram, R.U. 255
Miller, R. 314, 339
Miller-Jones, D. 307, 319, 339
Minaya-Rowe, L. 261, 270, 291
Minde, T. 55, 58, 61, 87, 90
Minderman, L. 202, 206
Minner, S. 314, 339
Miramontes, O. 134
Mitchell-Kernan, C. 104, 126

Mohatt, G. 4, 42
Mok, D. 55, 58, 61, 87, 90
Moll, L.C. 17, 39, 98, 128, 134,
     173, 179, 180, 181, 183, 188,
     279, 290, 294
Mollica, A. 131
Montero-Sieburth, M. 8, 42, 50,
     279, 292
Morren, R.C. 134
Mortland, C.A. 76, 77, 88, 94
Moses, S. 339

Nadeau, A. 134
Nathenson-Mejia, S. 199, 206
Negata, D.K. 324, 339
Neider, J. 77, 89
Nelde, P.H. 50
Nelson, J.R. 235, 251
Nelson, K.S. 326
Nguyen, T. 7, 42
Nieto, S. 203, 206
Nine Curt, C.J. 6, 42, 50
Norton, R. 9, 42
Nuttall, E.V. 306, 339

Oakes, J. 17, 23, 42
Ogbu, J. 11, 12, 13, 14, 18, 25,
     35, 42, 50, 280, 291
Ogden, F. 246, 252
Ohanian, S. 207
Okazaki, S. 324, 325
Oksaar, E. 135
Oller, J. 26, 42, 50, 303
Olmedo, E.L. 55, 57, 88
Olsen J. W-B. 28, 38
Olsen, L. 70, 88, 94
Onyehalu, A.S. 175
Opperman, P. 153, 162, 166
O'Maley, J.M. 21, 42, 50
O'Malley, M.J. 116, 117, 119, 128
Orfield, G. 21, 42, 50
Ornstein, A.C. 255
Ortiz, A.A. 147, 162, 303, 306,
     316, 318, 339, 345
Ortiz, F.I. 8, 16, 17, 24, 42, 52

Ortiz, V. 222, 223, 252
Ovando, C. 9, 38, 119, 128

Padilla, A.M. 100, 101, 128, 144, 163, 295
Passow, A.H. 242, 252
Patchen, M. 24,43
Peal, E. 102, 128
Pearson, C.A. 327, 339
Pelto, G.H. 275, 281, 291
Pelto, P.J. 275, 281, 291
Peppas, G.W. 84, 88, 95
Peralez, E. 235, 251
Pérez, M. 8, 26, 42, 50, 279
Perlman, R. 243, 245, 252, 303
Peterson, A.V. 84, 88, 95
Pfeger, M. 166
Pharis, B.G. 190
Philips, S. 104, 128
Phillips, S.U. 4, 43, 52
Pickering. C.T. 201, 206
Pikulski, J.J. 330, 340
Polyzoi, E. 147, 162, 303, 306, 339
Porter, R. 22, 43
Preston, D. 132
Prewitt-Díaz, J.O. 83, 88, 95, 318, 340, 345
Prieto, A.G. 240, 253
Prutting, C. 303, 340
Pugh, S.L. 200, 206
Purkey, S.C. 117, 128

Quezada, S. 208
Quinn, M.E. 103, 127, 133
Quintana, D. 58, 59, 89

Rado, M. 151, 163
Rakow, S.J. 327
Ramage, J.C. 306, 340
Ramírez, A.G. 104, 112, 128, 223, 303, 340
Ramírez, B.A. 325, 340
Ramírez, M. 9, 43, 52, 223, 252
Rand, R. 313, 314

Raschio, R.A. 63, 88
Redfield, R. 55, 89
Reetz, L. 167
Reis, S. 227, 228
Renzulli, J.S. 218, 227, 228, 232, 233, 252
Reyhner, J. 200, 206
Reynolds, C.J. 326, 340
Rhodes, N. 283, 291
Rice, E. 213
Richards, J. 106, 129
Richardson, J.L. 75, 88
Richert, E.S. 218, 225, 252
Ritter, P. 68, 87
Roberts, R. 296
Roden, G. 163
Rodgers, T.S. 106, 129
Rodríguez, A. xvi, xviii
Rodríguez, A.M. 140, 163, 295
Rodríguez, R. 48, 151, 163, 167, 240, 253
Roedell, W. 242, 243, 253
Rogers, P. 27, 39, 47
Rogler, L. 246, 250
Rohmer, H. 213
Rolheiser-Bennett, C. 267, 290
Rosebery, A. 173
Rosenthal, R. 16, 43
Ross, J.M. 114, 129
Rossell, C. 114, 129
Rossett, A. 295
Rueda, R. 162, 165, 240, 253
Rumbaut, R.G. 76, 79, 87, 92
Ryan, R. 14, 43

St. John, N. 24, 43
San Miguel, Jr., G. 135
Santos de Barona, M. 304, 312
Sale, L. 208
Salend, S.J. 311, 326, 340
Sarason, S. 273, 292
Saunders, G. 135, 256
Schensul, J.J. 280, 292
Schlesinger, B. 236, 237, 253
Schneider, S.G. 129

Schon, I. 208, 2089
Schumann, J.H. 665
Schram, J.L. 64, 66, 89
Scribner, S. 9, 38, 172, 173, 188
Secada, W. 186, 188, 280, 292, 296
Seeley, K. 254
Seilhamer, E.S. 83, 88, 95
Seliger, H.W. 113, 129
Selinker, L. 132
Serow, R.C. 24, 43
Shafer, R.E. 131
Shafer, S.M. 152, 156, 163
Shantz, C. 104, 129
Shaughnessy, M. 217, 253
Shen, M. 102, 124
Showers, B. 267, 290, 292
Sikorsky, S. 323
Silverman, L. 219, 253, 256
Simich-Dudgeon, C. 175, 188
Sindell, P. 7, 8, 43, 52
Singleton, D. 135
Sisk, D. 215, 221, 223, 248, 253
Skinner, B.F. 97, 129
Skipper, B. 326
Skrabanek, R.L. 100, 129
Skutnabb-Kangas, T. 12, 100, 129, 135, 283, 292
Slavin, R.E. 28, 29, 30, 43
Sleeter, C.E. 16, 43, 256
Smith, D. 215
Smith, N. xvi, xviii
Smith, R.C. 117, 128, 140, 163, 252
Smutny, J.K. 242, 245, 253
Snipper, G.C. 172, 173
Snow, C. 123, 127, 281, 292
Snowden, L.R. 324, 341
Sodowsky, G.R. 66, 89
Solis, J. 75, 87
Sorenson, A.P. 99, 129
Spener, D. 136
Spindler, G.D. 16, 43
Spolsky, B. 26, 43
Sternberg, R.J. 217, 253, 256

Storey, M.E. 393
Story, M. 81, 89
Strouse, J. 136
Suárez-Orozco, M.M. 7, 25, 43, 52
Sue, S. 324, 325, 341
Sugai, G. 311, 341
Sutton, C. 200, 201, 206
Swaffar, J.K. 175, 188, 194
Swain, M. 34, 44, 130, 283, 292
Swan, J. 137
Szapocznik, J. 56, 89

Taleporos, B. 153, 162, 166
Tan, A. 324
Tapia, M.R. 10, 44, 53, 223, 243, 244, 253
Taylor, D.M. 26, 44
Taylor, M. 209
Teitelbaum, H. 21, 22, 44, 53
Tempest, P. 326, 341
Terman, L.M. 216, 253
Tharp, R. 11, 44, 53
Thomas, J. 136
Thomas, R.M. 236, 238, 253
Thomas, S.J. 142, 143, 154, 162, 165
Thompson, R.M. 71, 89, 95
Throne, J. 201, 206
Tiedt, I.M. 203, 206, 209
Tiedt, P.L. 203, 206, 209
Tikunoff, W.J. 117, 129, 158, 163, 260, 282, 292, 296, 318
Tinlos, M. 3, 24, 341
Tobin, J.J. 168
Tonemah, S.A. 220, 223, 229, 253
Torrance, E.P. 216, 224, 253
Torres, M. 136
Trachtman, G.M. 309, 341
Tran, T.V. 82, 89
Travers, J.P. 203, 206, 209
Troike, R.D. 30, 44, 114, 129
Trueba, H. xv, xviii, 3, 12, 13, 14, 15, 18, 35, 39, 53, 89, 182, 188, 280, 292, 296
Tucker, G.R. 283, 292

Tunnell, M.O. 201, 202, 206

Uehara, A. 63, 89

Valadez, C. 112, 118, 144, 163, 280, 292
Valencia, S. 315, 341
Valle, M. 307, 308, 309
Valsine, J. 256
VanPatten, B. 137
VanTassel-Baska, J. 254, 256
Vargas, A. 151, 163, 168
Vásquez, J. 137
Vázquez-Nuttall, E. 307, 308, 309, 341
Veenker, K. 242, 245, 253
Veenker, S. 242, 245, 253
Veltman, C. 27, 44
Verhoeven, L.T. 175, 188, 195
Vigil, F. 26, 42, 50
Vilke, M. 141, 142, 163, 168
Vogt, L. 11, 44, 53
Volloff, W. 222, 223, 252
Vygotsky, L.S. 18, 44, 174, 188

Waggoner, D. 100, 116, 129, 259, 292
Wainer, H. 329, 341
Wald, B. 177, 189
Wallace, C. 206
Walsh, C. 25, 44
Ward, B. 268, 282, 292
Warren, B. 173, 180, 181, 189
Watson, D. 157, 162, 175, 187, 190
Watson, K. 131, 296
Watson-Gegeo, K.A. 10, 44
Wayman, K. 243, 244, 251
Weber, R.M. 176, 189, 195
Wells, G. 173, 174, 178, 187, 189
Westermeyer, J. 77, 89
Whitmore, J. 257
Wilcox, K.A. 145, 163
Wilen, D.K. 312, 341

Wilkinson, C.Y. 146, 163, 168, 306, 314
William, J.D. 172, 173, 189
Willig, A. 114, 129, 283, 292, 297, 320, 342
Winer, L. 28, 38
Wise, S. 329
Witkin, H.A. 9, 44
Wolfram, W. 317
Wong Fillmore, L. 4, 15, 44, 109, 112, 118, 129, 283, 292
Wong-Rieger, D. 58, 49, 89
Woo, J.Y.T. 325, 342
Woodcock, R. 145, 163
Wu, D.Y.H. 168
Wu, S.T. 73, 89, 95
Wyche, L.G. 317, 342

Yamamoto, M. 137
Yates, J.R. 306
Young, J.W. 248, 249, 253, 257
Ysseldyke, J. 322, 342
Yu, V.W.S. 137

Zanger, V.V. xv, xviii, 12, 24, 25, 44, 45, 54
Zelmer, A.E. 64, 89
Zenhausern, R. 224, 251
Zentella, A.C. 105, 129, 283, 292
Zohoori, A.R. 73, 89, 95

SUBJECT INDEX

academic achievement and acculturation 67–68
academic achievement of migrants 83
academic achievement of refugees 79–81
academic underachievement 67–68
academic contexts of language minority education 97–138, 349
acculturation of language minorities 55–96, 308, 348
acculturation and behavior 72, 352
acculturation and cultural changes 81
acculturation and health issues 74–75
acculturation and language use 58–61
acculturation measurement constructs 64–65
acculturation models 55–57
acculturative stress 62
action research and teacher training 279–284
adjustment 66–67, 83, 353
advocacy 309–310
alienation 8, 64
Asians 9, 12, 21, 62, 66, 324–325
assessment 15–16, 144–147, 222, 350–351, 358
assessment, alternative methods 311–314
assessment, biases in 319–323
assessment of bilingual competencies 305–306

assessment of cognitive functioning 306–307
assessment of giftedness 356
assessment of language proficiency 147–148
assessment of personal/social functioning 307

behavior and acculturation 72
biased assessment techniques 319–323
biculturality 68–69
bilingual acquisition 98–106
Bilingual Education Act 120–121
biliteracy 172–174, 175–179
Buraku 12

Cambodians 81
castelike minorities 13
Central Americans 68
children's literature 202–203, 349, 356
Chinese 11, 21, 62, 68, 73, 79
cognition and bilingualism 3, 102–104, 141–144, 354
collaborative research 182–183
computerized psychology testing 328–329
cooperative learning 28–30
criterion referenced testing 314–315
cultural contexts of language minority education 7–9
cultural discontinuities 11–14
cultural hegemony 19
cultural mismatch paradigm 4–13

curriculum-based assessment 314
desegregated schools 24–25
desegregation 20–27
desegregation and bilingual
    education 21–22
discrimination 22–23

early childhood 139–170, 349,
    354–355
early childhood program models
    152–159
ecological assessment 312–313
empowerment framework 14–16
English as a Second Language
    (ESL) programs 110–111
English proficiency testing 301–
    302

Federal and State policies on
    bilingual education 119–122
Filipinos 11
foster care 77–79

gifted students, characteristics of
    219
gifted students, advocacy for 246–
    248
gifted students, counseling of 245–
    246
gifted students, definitions of 216–
    219
gifted students, non-biased
    identification of 221, 356
gifted students, parents of 242–245
gifted students, program models for
    226–233, 357
gifted students, teachers of 239–
    242
gifted and talented bilingual
    students 215–258, 326–327,
    350, 356

handicapped children 327
Hawaiians 10–11

health issues and acculturation 74–
    75
hearing impaired 327
Hmong 19
home/community influences on
    literacy development 184
home experiences 150–152, 184

immersion programs 31–33
immigrants and ethnic minorities
    66–75
instructional programs for language
    minorities 117–119
intelligence and bilingualism 102–
    104
intergroup relations and cognitive
    processes 25–26
intervention programs to facilitate
    acculturation 84–85
interviews 312

Japanese 11, 21

Koreans 9, 62

language assessment in special
    education 304
language proficiency assessment
    302–304
language use and acculturation 4–
    6, 71–72
learning styles 9–10
legal cases 121–122
linguistic development 99–102, 353
literacy 157–158, 171–196, 199–
    202, 349–350, 354, 355
literacy development programs
    179–184
literature for language minority
    children 197–214, 349
low incidence groups 323–328

Mexican Americans 7, 9, 11, 13,
    20–21, 68, 72, 74, 100–101
migrants 83–84, 326

Native Americans 11, 13, 21, 62, 228–230, 325–326

native language acquisition 353

natural order hypothesis second language acquisition 107–108

non-verbal communication 6–7

observation 312

Papago 8

parental involvement 150–152

portfolio approach 148–150, 315

poverty xv–xvi

Project KEEP 10–11

psychoeducational assessment 299–346

psychosocial adjustment of refugees 76–79

psychosocial paradigms 11–20

Puerto Ricans 8, 10, 13, 20, 60–61, 73, 83–84, 101

racism 14, 17, 351

referral prevention 315–316

refugees 75–83

research recommendations 36–37, 86, 122–124, 160–161, 186–187, 204–205, 248–250, 285–288, 330–331, 351–358

resistance 19–20

schooling and immigrant children 69–71

second language acquisition 106–114, 353, 354

second language acquisition, social factors affecting 26–27

secondary cultural discontinuity approach 13–14

segregation of language minorities 20–21, 30–31

sex differences in language use 82–83

social/communicative aspects of bilingualism 104–105

social contexts of language minority education 3–54, 348

social factors and second language acquisition 26–27, 111–113

social integration 20–27

social isolation 27–28, 351

sojourners 63–66

Southeast Asians 58, 76–77, 79, 82–83

special education 18, 300

special education screening 148–150

staff development 265–279

state legislated programs for language minorities 122

target language input 110–111

teacher attitudes and expectations 16–18

teacher-student relationship 8–9

teacher training in bilingual education and ESL 259–298, 357

teacher training in bilingual education and ESL, institutionalization of 260–265, 350

television viewing 73–74

test-teach-test paradigms 313–314

transitional bilingual education programs 117–119

two-way immersion programs 33–34

Vietnamese 7–8, 24, 68, 77–79, 80, 81

young bilingual children 139–170

zones of proximal development 18–20